KT-369-141

Edited by Paul Jennings

THE BOOK OF NONSENSE

An anthology

Futura Publications Limited

A Futura Book

First published in Great Britain by
Raven Books in association with
Macdonald & Jane's Publishers in 1977

First Futura Publications edition 1979

ISBN : 0 7088 1417 4

Printed in Great Britain by
William Collins Sons & Co Ltd, Glasgow

Futura Publications Limited,
110 Warner Road,
Camberwell, London SE5.

CONTENTS

CONTENTS

CONTENTS

CONTENTS

INTRODUCTION

Anybody compiling a serious anthology (and there is no more serious work than compiling an anthology of Nonsense, however airy the end-product) has sooner or later to ferret about in that elegant, thought-inducing, noble-domed, efficiently-serviced intellectual cyclotron, the Eighth Wonder of the World, 'the British Library', formerly the Reading Room of the British Museum.

When I was queuing to get my reader's ticket, the man in front was asked, as everyone is, what subject he was researching. 'The relations between Ferdinand II and Wallenstein,' he replied. When it came to my turn all I could say was 'Well, Nonsense actually.' Of course the staff took it in their stride. The man behind me was an American post-graduate student. 'Boy, I wish I was you,' he said, 'I'm doing a master's on the accounting systems of the Hudson Bay Company.'

This anthology will suffer the fate of all anthologies; many will find their favourite nonsense writer omitted. In the nature of things, he will probably be a fairly modern one. What, no Nat Gubbins, I think guiltily as I write this (he had a marvellous column in the Sunday Express), what about The Gangrel (J. Stewart, a kind of Scottish Beachcomber), what about W. S. Gilbert – that's three G's, already.

I know, I know. All I can say is (a) look at the size of the thing already and (b) it is an attempt to show that although the output of nonsense writing is increasing almost geometrically (as the world itself gets madder?), the thing, as conceived here, springs from a human impulse that has *always* been there. It is a happy historical as well as alphabetical accident that Aristophanes comes so near the beginning.

All right, how *is* it conceived?

Many books and articles, elegant or obscure, profound or slight, have been written about Laughter, The Absurd, Nonsense and the rest of it. Who shall rush in where Bergson has said 'the attitudes, gestures and movements of the human body are laughable in exact proportion as that body reminds us of a mere machine', when Dr Martin Grotjahn has made suggestions about Tenniel's drawing of Alice growing that would have got him jailed a hundred years ago? And when Freud – ah, the hell with it.

Oh, come on, you will say, there must have been *some* principle of selection, no one can make an anthology of Nonsense without having some theory about it.

Well yes. For myself – and it is only a kind of framework that I personally find useful, I don't claim it's objectively true, anyone who tells you *this* is what Humour, or Nonsense, or Laughter *is* has got about as close to it as a dead butterfly pinned out on a museum board is to the surrealist blob of colour fluttering about the summer garden – Nonsense, proper *creative* Nonsense, not accidental Nonsense like, say, the VAT regulations, involves seeing reality from the other side.

It's no accident that the chessboard figures so largely in Lewis Carroll. I'm sure there are two important reasons for this. To deal with the minor one first, chess is mathematics and logic turned into a game, and games have *rules*. The chess grandmaster may be faced with a formless mass of infinite possibilities but the choices he and his opponent make are extremely precise and definite. I don't play chess myself, in fact little girls of ten can beat me at draughts,* but I am sure the chess writers are speaking exactly when they speak of 'an elegant end-game'. It's elegant because it has a shape. Nonsense isn't any old shape. It is *exact*. 'For the snark was a boojum, you see.'

---

* U.S. = checkers.

Of course it was; not a quelje, or a drockle, or a ching-lomp, but a boojum. This is why nursery rhymes, for all their surrealism, are so definite — often giving you the actual number of things; the cow may have jumped over the moon, but there were *three* blind mice, not four or two, there were *seven* maids with *seven* mops, *four-and-twenty* blackbirds baked in the pie, not five and twenty, which would have scanned just as well. And the Quangle-wangle's Hat was 'a hundred and two feet wide, with rib-bons and bibbons on every side' ...

But the second, and major significance of the chessboard is of course that you have to keep changing from seeing it as black squares on a white background to seeing it as white squares on a black one.

Well, this is what Nonsense does. It involves the essential ability to ask *what if*? What if everything was the other way round, or even what if just this little detail were changed? What if it were in another language, what if there were an opera with the plot I am now going to outline (Robert Benchley), what if one thought of A, B and C in the arithmetic books as real people (Stephen Leacock).

Also, what if one produced so-and-so's style, but height-ened it to absurd lengths? That is why some parodies have got into this book, from Max Beerbohm's once-and-for-all distillation of all Elizabethan tragedy in *Savonarola Brown* to Benchley's opera synopses.

I hope most of the pieces in this book are funny *as well*. But Humour, whether in the theatre or in a-funny-thing-happened-to-me-on-the-way-to-the-typewriter pieces (often sneered at by people of the kind that say, with a kind of glum pride, 'I can never remember jokes'; usually they can't even see them, let alone tell them) is a larger, more diffuse idea. It enters the territory, for instance, of human psychology, behaviour and character.

To that extent, Nonsense is more precise and definable. What unites all the pieces in this book, from the almost algebraic lunacy, the marvellous idiot's logic of Lewis Car-

roll or N. F. Simpson, the word-drunkenness of Gelett
Burgess or S. J. Perelman or John Lennon, the grave
fantasies of Cyrano de Bergerac or Denis Norden, to the
parodies, is their ability to make the wrong kind of reader
exclaim 'but it couldn't possibly be like that!'

Not *you*, dear reader, who are now, I hope, holding this
new, inky-smelling, shop-fresh volume and somewhat impatiently skimming through all this before devouring the
real stuff inside (I hope you haven't merely got it out of
the library). But you'd be surprised, unless you've been
in the trade yourself, how many people there *are* like
that. Excellent people, loving parents, responsible citizens
(indeed sometimes they even get jobs as reviewers), sup-
porters of flag days – but destined to go to an honoured
tomb without a smile ever having creased their faces.

Once I used to write a humour column, and indeed only
ceased it when such readers began to preponderate in the
readership of the quality papers, as they used to be called;
and I used to get perplexed, anxious letters from them
every week.

I should have known. Even before I started the column
I had written a piece in a magazine (now under different
management) about trams. I spoke of a certain municipality which bought a new tram, with *windscreen-wipers*,
in 1903, when this was a very new-fangled idea. All the
men in the transport department wanted to drive it, so the
manager said to the two best men 'well, you can start off
this week.' The temptation for the conductor was too
much, and when they got to the first stop he, too, started
doing those inexplicable handle-twiddlings that used to
make trams go. I said there were ominous creakings and
groanings as both drivers recklessly increased the current,
and suddenly 'the only passenger, Mr Ted Fooby, 63, a
retired bender and clicker-on, was amazed to find himself
sprawling in the tramlines with two half-trams speeding
away from him in opposite directions.'

The municipality got fed up with their tram constantly
coming in half, and experimented with a rubber tram,

hoping the men would relent when they saw the tram stretching, but in the end, frightened by the prospect of rubber trams 'stretched tightly through the streets, like chewing-gum, in some Freudian nightmare' they abandoned the idea.

Among the mail there was a great wad of stuff from 'The British Light Transport League'; in with the pamphlet entitled '100 Questions and Answers About Trams' there was a rather angry letter saying that trams couldn't possibly come in half like that, because there was 'a master switch'.

The Nonsense-writer's ability to see things 'from the other side' is nothing new, as I hope this book will show, since it starts with Aristophanes and ends with Monty Python and other exponents very living indeed. It is true there is a bit of a gap after Aristophanes, the next one being Shakespeare. But of course it went on all the time. As everyone knows, or at least everyone knows who has read *A History of English Literature*, by Emile Legouis and Louis Cazamian, 'the scops used to put riddles, to test the sagacity of the guests at banquets' (you knew, of course, that a scop was an old English poet or minstrel). But somehow or other many riotous pieces such as the *Riddles of Cynewulf* got crowded out.

The fact is that a new concentration and refinement of Nonsense took place in 19th-century England, with Lear and Carroll; and again it is not an accident that this was after England had changed the world for ever with the Industrial Revolution. The world of machinery and science – predictable, *damnably* predictable, full of humming wheels and machines that do what they are told to do and yet remorselessly condition men's lives – took over from the world of nature and life-as-it-comes. Lear and Carroll, just as much as the Romantic poets, offered escapes into a surprise country where all this mechanical determinism simply doesn't operate.

England was the first, and America became the most industrialized country. Of course, the Anglo-Saxons have not got a lien on Nonsense; you have only to think of the Surrealists, of the great European circus-clown tradition, of French writers like Raymond Queneau or Alphonse Allais ... but there must be a limit somewhere, and in spite of the fact that neither England nor America can boast anything like the House of Humour and Satire, in Gabrovo, Bulgaria, where there is a National Festival of Humour and Satire held every two years in the second half of May, most of this book is, in fact, from the deep Anglo-American mainstream.

Quite by accident, when the final selection was made I noticed that there was a piece about Understanding Music by America's Benchley, another by England's Boothroyd. There is one piece about pigeons by Thurber, another by Benchley (in fact, Thurber once said he felt that *any* piece on which he had been working 'for two long days was done much better and probably more quickly by Robert Benchley in 1924'). There is a chance to compare the Nonsense plays of America's Ring Lardner and of England's D. B. Wyndham Lewis, that great man, the *first* Beachcomber.

Probably Lardner and Lewis hadn't heard of each other. But here we find ah, you'll *see* what we find; meanwhile let us end our Foreword with the words of J. B. Morton, the inexhaustible, life-giving, follow-*that* Beachcomber.

BEACHCOMBER

Folly

Since this is All Fool's Day, who, I pray you, has a better right to play the fool than he whose delicate white hand pens these words? To-day I summon Folly, to do her honour. Call her Stultitia, call her Anoia, call her anything you please, she is a potent and a delightful goddess. It is she who perches ape-like on the shoulders of great dusty pedants, and reminds them that their weighty discoveries don't matter twopence. It is she who plays the jolly jig to which the old world dances. It is she who opens that little window on to the sane side of things. By the transposition of one word she can turn a thesis into a jest. By one caper she can make a solemn and pompous occasion into an absurd revel. And I am her courtier. I am Prince and Captain of Fools.

Folly will show you the world upside down, albeit with enough gusto and enough shrewdness to make you say, 'I'll be hanged if I don't think this is the right way up, after all!' Folly will make you stand on your head in order to shake up your philosophies a bit, and readjust your ideas. And Folly, sweet Folly, will prevent you from taking your own absurd selves too seriously. You are a comic, pathetic crowd, but she loves you – which is more than any of you deserve. And therefore I, at her bidding, will tell a tale that has never been told before.

There was once a man who lived at Rickmansworth. One day he went into Chorley Wood, which is close at hand, to buy some stamps. While on his way he happened to meet a Belgian whom he knew slightly. He raised his hat and told him that he was on his way to buy stamps.

'How many do you want?' asked the Belgian.

'A dozen or more,' answered the Rickmansworth man.

'I can let you have them,' replied the Belgian.

'Thank you,' said the Rickmansworth man, adding, 'Oh, but they are Belgian stamps. . . .'

Well, I could go on with this story for ages, but I think you've read far enough for me to say 'Ah! April Fools!'

ANON

The common cormorant or shag
Lays eggs inside a paper bag
The reason you will see no doubt
Is to keep the lightning out.
But what these unobservant birds
Have never noticed is that herds
Of wandering bears may come with buns
And steal the bags to hold the crumbs.

ANON

The Man of Thessaly

There was a Man of Thessaly,
And he was wondrous wise:
He jumped into a briar hedge
And scratched out both his eyes.
But when he saw his eyes were out,
With all his might and main
He jumped into another hedge
And scratched them in again.

ANON

Modernist Ballade

I'm going to write a Ballade in irregular metre,
   Having been asked to write one suddenly as we go to
                                press;

To put it into ordinary rhythm might have been neater,
　　But would have had two disadvantages which I will
　　　　　　　　　　　　　　　　　　now express;
　　The first is that Thought loses freedom under the stress
Of rules, dogmas, and everything of that sort of race,
　　And the second is one that you can very easily guess:
Whatever else this Ballade is, it is not commonplace.

One of the oldest titles in the English Peerage is the title
　　　　　　　　　　　　　　　　　　of Lord Petre:
　　One of those who held it in the reign of Queen Bess
(An honest man in his way, but a bit of a bleater,
　　And always hedging on the religious question, more
　　　　　　　　　　　　　　　　　　or less)
　　Wrote in regard to poets: 'They have hardiesse
To putte our old English tongue quite out of face.'
　　It is obvious that this nobleman was blind to his
　　　　　　　　　　　　　　　contemporaries' inventiveness.
Whatever else this Ballade is, it is not commonplace.

Even as it is, however, I have difficulty in finding more
　　　　　　　　　　　　　　　　rhymes in – etre,
　　And still more difficulty in finding any really suitable
　　　　　　　　　　　　　　　　rhymes in – ess;
It would be irrelevant to say that I should like a little
　　　　　　　　　　　　　　　　12h.p. two-seater,
　　And equally irrelevant to remark that I doubt whether
　　　　　　　　　　　　　　　　human societies progress.
　　Simple as my scheme is it is already getting into a sort
　　　　　　　　　　　　　　　　of mess
From which I can hardly extricate it with any tolerable
　　　　　　　　　　　　　　　　grace.
　　My misadventure should be a lesson to all against
　　　　　　　　　　　　　　　　irregularity and excess.
Whatever else this Ballade is, it is not commonplace.

Envoi

Prince, if – with your usual crudity and lack of tact and
address –
You blurt out the plain question whether I have written
in this extraordinary fashion solely in order to fill up
space,
I answer with that brutal cynicism which has come
upon me with advancing years : 'Yes !'
Whatever else this Ballade is, it is not commonplace.

MAX ADELER

The Step-ladder

A step-ladder is an almost indispensable article to persons
who are moving into a new house. Not only do the domes-
tics find it extremely convenient when they undertake to
wash the windows, to remove the dust from the door and
window-frames, and to perform sundry other household duties, but the lord of the castle will require it when
he hangs his pictures, when he fixes the curtains and
when he yields to his wife's entreaty for a hanging shelf
or two in the cellar. I would, however, warn my fellow-
countrymen against the contrivance which is offered to
them under the name of the 'Patent Combination Stepladder'. I purchased one in the city just before we moved,
because the dealer showed me how, by the simple operation of a set of springs, the ladder could be transformed
into an ironing-table, and from that into a comfortable
settee for the kitchen, and finally back again into a stepladder, just as the owner desired. It seemed like getting
the full worth of the money expended to obtain a trio of
such useful articles for a single price, and the temptation
to purchase was simply irresistible. But the knowledge
gained by a practical experience of the operation of the
machine enables me to affirm that there is no genuine
economical advantage in the use of this ingenious article.

Upon the day of its arrival, the servant-girl mounted the ladder for the purpose of removing the globes from the chandelier in the parlour, and while she was engaged in the work the weight of her body unexpectedly put the springs in motion, and the machine was suddenly converted into an ironing-table, while the maid-servant was prostrated upon the floor with a sprained ankle and amid the fragments of two shattered globes.

Then we decided that the apparatus should be used exclusively as an ironing-table, and to this purpose it would probably have been devoted permanently if it had suited. On the following Tuesday, however, while half a dozen shirts were lying upon it ready to be ironed, some one knocked against it accidentally. It gave two or three ominous preliminary jerks, ground two shirts into rags, hurled the flat-iron out into the yard, and after a few convulsive movements of the springs, settled into repose in the shape of a step-ladder.

It became evident then that it could be used with greatest safety as a settee, and it was placed in the kitchen in that shape. For a few days it gave much satisfaction. But one night when the servant had company the bench was perhaps overloaded, for it had another and most alarming paroxysm; there was a trembling of the legs, a violent agitation of the back, then a tremendous jump, and one of the visitors was hurled against the range, while the machine turned several somersaults, jammed itself halfway through the window-sash, and appeared once more in the similitude of an ironing-table.

It has now attained to such a degree of sensitiveness that it goes through the entire drill promptly and with celerity if any one comes near it or coughs or sneezes close at hand. We have it stored away in the garret, and sometimes in the middle of the night a rat will jar it, or a current of air will pass through the room, and we can hear it dancing over the floor and getting into service as a ladder, a bench and a table fifteen or twenty times in quick succession.

Professor Quackenboss

After a while there was a lull in the conversation, and the Professor, who had hitherto remained silent, cleared his throat, and said, quietly,

'I see that they talk of putting up a monument to Christopher Columbus. It's too bad the way people've been fooled about him. He never discovered America, and I've made up my mind to let the people see what kind of an old humbug he is.'

'You say that Columbus didn't discover America?' said Mr Partridge.

'Certainly he didn't. He was a mean, lubberly rascal, who went paddling around in a scow, letting on he was doing big things, when he hadn't courage enough to get out of sight of land.'

'Who did discover it then?'

'Well, I'll tell you fellows in advance of publication, but mind you keep quiet about it. It was Potiphar!'

'What was his first name?'

'First name? Why, he hadn't any. It was only Potiphar – old Pharaoh's Potiphar, you know.'

'How did you find out about it?'

'Why, you know old Gridley, up in the city? Well, last year he was in Egypt, and he brought home a mummy, all wrapped up in bedclothes, and soldered around with sealing-wax. Gridley asked me to come over and help to undress him, and so we went at that mummy, and after rolling off a couple of hundred yards of calico, we reached him. Looked exactly like dried beef. Black as your hat, and just about tender enough to chip down for tea. Gridley said he'd like to know who the old chap was, and I looked him over to find out. You know how they put up a mummy, don't you? Take out all his machinery inside, and fill him up with nutmegs and cinnamon. Then they set a brass door-plate in his stomach, and make some little memoranda, with obituary poetry, and all that kind of thing. Anyhow, after polishing him up with a flesh-brush for a minute or two, I found the door-plate, and with some care I managed to read the inscription on it. It was this: "I am Potiphar, servant of Pharaoh. I was buried three thousand years before the Christian era. I discovered America. C. Columbus was an impostor." That's what the inscription said, and, in my opinion, that settles it. Now, I'll tell you what I'm going to do. I've had a cast made of that dried beef, and I intend to have it swelled all out and made into a statue, and I'm going to set it up at my own expense, alongside the statue of Columbus, and have a sign put on it to the effect that Columbus is a fraud. Then I intend to get up a memorial to Congress, asking it to change the name of the country to Potipharia, and make Potiphar's sacred animal, the cat, the emblematical bird of the nation, instead of the eagle.'

'You say you read the inscription on the plate,' said Partridge. 'I didn't know you understood the language.'

'Can read it as easy as A B C.'

' "Buried three thousand years before the Christian era," I think you said it read. How did old Pot know anything about the Christian era, if he died that long before?'

'Blamed if I know. Cast his prophetic eyes over the future, I s'pose.'

'Well, how could he tell that Columbus was going to claim to discover America?'

'That's so. I dunno. It's kind of queer.'

'Do you know what I think of you?' asked Partridge.

'What?'

'I think that if there was a statue of a humbug to be erected, the nation would choose you for the honour, instead of Columbus, or any other man, ancient or modern.'

'Maybe it would! maybe it would!' said the Professor; and then he refilled his pipe from Partridge's tobacco-pouch, which was lying in a box by his side, and relapsed into silence.

ARISTOPHANES

The Birds

(translation by William Arrowsmith)

Enter Prometheus*, so muffled in blankets as to be completely unrecognizable. His every motion is furtive, but his furtiveness is hampered by an immense umbrella which he carries underneath his blankets. He speaks in a whisper.

PROMETHEUS   Easy does it. I hope old Zeus can't see me. *To a Bird.* Psst. Where's Pisthetairos?

PISTHETAIROS   What in the world is *this*? – Who are you, blanket?

PROMETHEUS   Ssh. Are there any gods on my trail?

PISTHETAIROS   Gods? No, not a god in sight. Who *are* you?

PROMETHEUS   What's the time? Is it dark yet?

PISTHETAIROS   You want the time? It's still early afternoon. Look, who the hell *are* you?

PROMETHEUS   Is it milking-time, or later?

PISTHETAIROS   Look, you stinking bore –

PROMETHEUS   What's the weather doing? How's the visibility? Clear skies? Low ceiling?

PISTHETAIROS   By god, *Raising his stick* if you won't talk –

PROMETHEUS   Dark, eh? Good. I'm coming out. *Uncovers*

PISTHETAIROS   Hullo; it's Prometheus!

PROMETHEUS   Shh. Don't make a sound.

PISTHETAIROS   What's the matter?

---

* *Enter Prometheus:* Mankind's greatest champion and arch foe of Zeus makes his ridiculously furtive entrance on still another philanthropic mission; to warn Pisthetairos of Zeus' plans and secrets. Needless to say, he is extremely anxious to avoid observation by the gods.

PROMETHEUS   Shh. Don't even whisper my name.
              If Zeus spots me here, he'll cook my goose
              but good. Now then, if you want to learn
              the lay of the land in heaven, kindly open
              up this umbrella here and hold it over my
              head while I'm talking.
              Then the gods won't see me.

*Pisthetairos takes the umbrella, opens it up, and holds it
over Prometheus.*

PISTHETAIROS Say, that's clever. Prometheus all over.*
              – All right. Pop underneath and give us
              your news.
PROMETHEUS   Brace yourself.
PISTHETAIROS Shoot.
PROMETHEUS   Zeus has had it.
PISTHETAIROS Since when?
PROMETHEUS   Since the moment you founded the city of
              Cloud-Cuckooland. Since that day not a
              single sacrifice, not even a whiff of smoke,
              no savories, no roast, nothing at all has
              floated up to heaven. In consequence, my
              friend, Olympos is starving to death. And
              that's not the worst of it. All the Stone
              Age gods† from the hill country have gone
              wild with hunger, screaming and gibber-
              ing away like a lot of savages. And what's
              more, they've threatened war unless Zeus
              succeeds in getting your Bird-embargo
              lifted and the tidbit shipments back on the
              move once more.
PISTHETAIROS You mean to say there are *other* gods in

---

* *Say, that's clever. Prometheus all over:* Pisthetairos is impressed
by the ingenuity of Prometheus' umbrella, and compliments him
as deserving of his name (Prometheus meant 'Foresight').

† *All the Stone Age gods:* A free – but I thought plausible – render-
ing of the 'barbarian gods' of the text. If Triballos is a representative of the barbarian gods, then the divinities meant are not merely
uncivilized but Neolithic.

	Heaven? Stone Age Gods?
PROMETHEUS	Stone Age gods for Stone Age people. Exekestides must have something to worship.
PISTHETAIROS	Heavens, they *must* be savages. But what do you call them?
PROMETHEUS	We call them Triballoi.
PISTHETAIROS	Triballoi? From the same root as our word 'trouble', I suppose.
PROMETHEUS	Very probably, I think. But give me your attention. At present these Triballoi gods have joined with Zeus to send an official embassy to sue for peace. Now here's the policy you must follow: flatly reject any offers of peace they make you until Zeus agrees to restore his sceptre to the Birds and consents to give you Miss Universe* as your wife.
PISTHETAIROS	But who's Miss Universe?
PROMETHEUS	A sort of Beauty Queen, the sign of Empire and the symbol of divine supremacy. It's she who keeps the keys to Zeus' thunderbolts and all his other treasures – Divine Wisdom, Good Government, Common Sense, Naval Bases, Slander, Libel, Political Graft, Sops to the Voters –
PISTHETAIROS	And *she* keeps the keys?
PROMETHEUS	Take it from me, friend.

---

* *Miss Universe:* The Greek gives βασιλεία, which means 'sovereignty', 'empire', 'supreme power'. Because she is an unfamiliar abstraction and not a genuine Olympian at all, I have felt free to turn her into a sort of 'Beauty Queen' and to gloss her in the text as 'the symbol of divine supremacy'. In this play she symbolizes the logical conclusion of the Athenian (or the Birds') struggle for domination and universal supremacy. She is what Thoukydides called ἀρχψ' ('empire', 'domination') and what I believe Euripides everywhere in his tragedies meant by the figure of Helen: the prize for which the (Peloponnesian) War was fought.

Marry Miss Universe and the world is yours.
You understand
why I had to tell you this? As Prometheus, after all, my philanthropy is proverbial.

PISTHETAIROS   Yes, we worship you
as the inventor of the barbecue.*

PROMETHEUS   Besides, I loathe the gods.

PISTHETAIROS   The loathing's mutual, I know.

PROMETHEUS   Just call me Timon:
I'm a misanthrope of gods.
But I must be running along.
Give me my parasol. If Zeus spots me now, he'll think I'm an ordinary one-god procession. I'll pretend to be the girl behind the boy behind the basket.

PISTHETAIROS   Here – take this stool and watch yourself march by.

Exit Phometheus in solemn procession, draped in his blanket, the umbrella in one hand, the stool in the other. Pisthetairos and the Attendants retire.

CHORUS†   There lies a marsh in Webfoot Land,

---

* *the inventor of the barbecue:* Because Prometheus gave fire to man.

† *Chorus:* The second installment of the Birds' Travelogue. The subject is Sokrates as psychagogue or psychopomp, the guide of the soul, engaged in calling up spirits from the dead in a little sacrifice which resembles that of Odysseus in Book XI of the *Odyssey.* Sokrates' Stygian assistant is his cadaverous colleague of Athenian life, Chairephon. The scene takes place in the land of Shadowfeet (according to Ktesias, a curious webfooted tribe which lived in Libya; when they lay down for a nap, they held up their huge webfeet as awnings against the sun. To this the Scholiast adds that they had four legs, three of which were used for walking, and the fourth as a tentpole for their tentlike feet). Here, beside a Stygian swamp, haunted by terror, Sokrates summons the soul of Peisandros, an Athenian coward in search of his *psyche* (i.e., courage), by means of sacrifice; but so faint-hearted is Sokrates that he runs away in terror, leaving the bloody victim to the spectral vampire Chairephon.

the Swamp of Dismal Dread,
and there we saw foul SOKRATES
come calling up the dead.

And there that cur PEISANDROS came
to see if he could see
the soul he'd lost while still alive
by dying cowardly.

He brought a special sacrifice,
a little camel lamb;
then, like Odysseus, slit its throat —
he slit its throat and ran!

And then a phantom shape flew down,
a specter cold and wan,
and on the camel's blood he pounced —
the vampire CHAIREPHON!

Enter the Peace Delegation from Olympos; first, Poseidon, a god of immense and avuncular dignity, carrying a trident; then Herakles with a lion skin and club, a god with the character and build of a wrestler and an appetite to match; and finally Triballos, hopelessly tangled up in the unfamiliar robes of Olympian civilization.

POSEIDON   Here we are. And there before us, ambassadors, lies Cloudcuckooland.

Triballos, by now hopelessly snarled up in his robes, trips and falls flat on his face.

              — Damn you! Back on your feet,
              you hulking oaf. Look, you've got your
              robes all twisted up.
              No. Screw them around to the right.
              This way. Where's your dignity, you
              heavenly hick? O Democracy, I fear your
              days are numbered if Heaven's diplomatic
              corps is recruited like this! Dammit, stop
              twitching! Gods, I've never seen a gawkier

	god than you!
	— Look here, Herakles,
	how should we proceed in your opinion?
HERAKLES	You hoid me,
	Poseidon. If I had my way, I'd throttle the guy, *any* guy, what dared blockade the gods.
POSEIDON	My dear nephew,
	have you forgotten that the purpose of our mission here is to treat for peace?
HERAKLES	I'd throttle him all the more.

Enter Pisthetairos, followed by Attendants with cooking utensils. He pointedly ignores the presence of the Divine Delegation.

PISTHETAIROS	To *Attendants*
	Hand me the cheese grater. Vinegar, please. All right, now the cheese. Poke up that fire, somebody.
POSEIDON	Mortal, three immortal gods give you greeting.
	Dead Silence
	Mortal, three immortal —
PISTHETAIROS	Shush: I'm slicing pickles.
HERAKLES	Hey, what kind of meat is dat?
PISTHETAIROS	Those are jailbirds
	sentenced to death on the charge of High Treason against the Sovereign Birds.
HERAKLES	And dat luscious gravy gets poured on foist?
PISTHETAIROS	*Looking up for the first time:*
	Why hullo there: it's Herakles! What do you want?
POSEIDON	Mortal, as the official spokesman
	for the Divine Delegation, I venture to suggest that —
PISTHETAIROS	*Holding up an empty bottle.* Drat it. We're out of oil?
HERAKLES	Out of oil?

Say, dat's a shame. Boids should be basted good.

POSEIDON — As I was on the point of saying, official Olympos regards the present hostilities as utterly pointless. Further, I venture to observe that you Birds have a great deal to gain from a kindlier Olympus. I might mention, for instance, a supply of clean rainwater for your Birdbaths and a perpetual run, say, of halycon days. On some such terms as these we are formally empowered by Zeus to sign the articles of peace

PISTHETAIROS Poseidon, you forget: it was not the Birds who began this war. Moreover, peace is our desire as much as yours. And if you gods stand prepared to treat in good faith, I see no obstacle to peace. None whatsoever. Our sole demand is this:
Zeus must restore his royal sceptre to the Birds. If this one trifling concession seems agreeable to you, I invite you all to dinner.

HERAKLES Youse has said enough. I vote Yes.

POSEIDON You contemptible, idiotic glutton! Would you dethrone your own Father?

PISTHETAIROS I object, Poseidon.
Look at it in this light.
Can you gods be unaware
that you actually stand to increase, not diminish your power, by yielding your present supremacy to the Birds? Why, as things stand now, men go skulking around under cover of the clouds, with impunity committing perjury and in your name too. But conclude alliance with the Birds, gentlemen, and your problems are over forever. How? Suppose, for instance, some man swears a solemn oath by Zeus and the

	Raven and then breaks his word. Suddenly down swoops a Raven when he's least suspecting it and pecks out his eyes!
POSEIDON	Holy Poseidon! You know, I think you've got something there.
HERAKLES	Youse is so right.
POSEIDON	*To Triballos.* What do you say?
TRIBALLOS	*Fapple gleep*
HERAKLES	Dat's Stone Age for Yeah.
PISTHETAIROS	And that's not all. Suppose some fellow vows to make a sacrifice to the gods and then later changes his mind or tries to procrastinate, thinking, *The mills of the gods grind slow; well, so do mine.* We Birds, I can promise you, will put a stop to sophistry like that.
POSEIDON	Stop it? But how?
PISTHETAIROS	Someday our man will be busily counting up his cash or lolling around in the tub, singing away, and a Kite will dive down like a bolt from the blue, snatch up two of his sheep or a wad of cash and whizz back up to the gods with the loot.
HERAKLES	Friend, youse is right. Zeus should give dat sceptre back to the Boids.
POSEIDON	What do *you* think, Triballos?
HERAKLES	*Threatening him with his club.* Vote Yes, bub, or I'll drub youse.
TRIBALLOS	*Schporckl nu?* *Momp gapa birdschmoz kluk.*
HERAKLES	See? He votes wid me.
POSEIDON	If you both see eye to eye, I'll have to go along.
HERAKLES	Dat does it. Hey, youse. The sceptre's yours.
PISTHETAIROS	Dear me, I nearly forgot one trifling condition. We Birds willingly waive any claim we

	might have to Hera: Zeus can have her. We don't object in the slightest. But I must have Miss Universe as my wife. On that demand I stand absolutely firm.
POSEIDON	Then you won't have peace. Good afternoon.

The Delegation prepares to leave, Herakles with great reluctance.

PISTHETAIROS	It's all the same to me. – Oh chef: make the gravy thick.
HERAKLES	God alive, Poseidon, where in the world is youse going? Are we going to war for the sake of a dame?
POSEIDON	What alternative would you suggest?
HERAKLES	Peace, peace!
POSEIDON	You poor fool, don't you realize that you're being tricked? What's more, you're only hurting yourself. Listen here: if Zeus should abdicate his throne in favour of the Birds and then die, you'd be left a pauper. Whereas now you're the legal heir of Zeus. Heir, in fact, to everything he owns.
PISTHETAIROS	Watch your step, Herakles. You're being hoodwinked.

Taking Herakles by the arm and withdrawing a little.

	– Now, just step aside with me. I have something to tell you. Look, you poor chump, your uncle's pulling a fast one. Not one cent of Zeus' enormous estate will ever come to you. You see, my friend, you're a bastard.
HERAKLES	What's dat, fella? *I'm a bastard?*
PISTHETAIROS	Of course you're a bastard – by Zeus. Your mother, you see, was an ordinary mortal woman, not a goddess. In other words, she comes of foreign stock. Which

makes you legally a bastard,* pure and simple.

Moreover, Pallas Athene†.

is normally referred to as The Heiress. That's her title. But how in the name of Zeus could Athene be an heiress if Zeus had any legitimate sons?

HERAKLES   Maybe.

Youse could be right. But what if the Old Man swears I'm his son?

PISTHETAIROS The law still says No.

In any case, Poseidon here, who's been egging you on, would be the first person to challenge the will in court. As your father's brother, he's the next-of-kin, and hence the legal heir.

Let me read you the provisions of the law.

He draws a law book from his robes.

In the words of Solon himself:

SO LONG AS LEGITIMATE ISSUE SHALL SURVIVE THE DECEASED, NO BASTARD SHALL INHERIT. IN THE CASE THAT NO LEGITIMATE ISSUE SURVIVES, THE ESTATE SHALL PASS TO THE NEXT OF KIN.

HERAKLES   Youse mean to say I won't inherit a damn thing from the Old Man?

PISTHETAIROS Not a smitch. By the way,

has your Father ever had your birth legally

---

* *Which makes you legally a bastard:* According to Athenian laws on citizenship, citizens must be born of Athenian fathers and mothers. Herakles, as the son of Zeus (a *bona fide* Olympian) and Alkmene (an ordinary woman, i.e., a foreigner) would be both illegitimate and ineligible for citizenship – according to Athenian law.

† *Pallas Athene is normally referred to as The Heiress:* Because Athens was Athena's 'portion', she was officially called The Heiress.

recorded or had you registered in court as his official heir?

HERAKLES No, never. I always thought there was something fishy.

PISTHETAIROS Come, my boy, chin up. Don't pout at heaven with that sullen glare. Join us. Come in with the Birds. We'll set you on a throne and you can guzzle pigeon's milk the rest of your endless days.

HERAKLES You know, fella,
I been thinking about that dame you want so bad. Well, I vote youse can have her.

PISTHETAIROS Splendid. What do you say, Poseidon?

POSEIDON No. A resounding No.

PISTHETAIROS Then it rests with Triballos.
What's your verdict, my friend?

TRIBALLOS *Gleep? Schnoozer skirt wotta twatch snock!*
Birdniks pockle. Ugh.

HERAKLES He said she's for the Boids. I hoid him.

POSEIDON And I distinctly heard him say the opposite: A firm No – with a few choice obscenities added.

HERAKLES The poor dumb sap never said a doity word.
All he said was: *Give 'er to the Boids.*

POSEIDON I yield.
You two can come to terms together as you please.
Since you seem to be agreed on everything, I'll just abstain.

HERAKLES *To Pisthetairos*
Man, youse is getting everything youse wants.
Fly up to Heaven wid us, and get your missus and anything else your little heart desires.

PISTHETAIROS And we're in luck. This feast of poultry

	I've prepared will grace our wedding supper.
HERAKLES	Youse guys push along. I'll stay here and watch the barbecue.
POSEIDON	Not on your life. You'd guzzle grill and all. You'd better come along with us, my boy.
HERAKLES	Aw, Unc, but it woulda tasted so good.
PISTHETAIROS	*To Attendants* – You there, servants. Bring my wedding clothes along.

B

BEACHCOMBER (J. B. MORTON)

It Depends on Your Name

'If when you enter a drawing-room your name has been wrongly announced, or has passed unheard in the buzz of conversation, make your way at once to the mistress of the house, if you are a stranger, and introduce yourself by name. This should be done with the greatest simplicity and your rank made as little as possible.'
('A Manual of Etiquette')

Butler: (amid buzz of conversation): Brthathathawawa-bthawa! (Nobody flinches.)

Guest: (Approaching hostess, and speaking with the greatest simplicity):
His Highness the Maharajah of Chandernagera-pore and Bhopawal.

Hostess: (turning pettishly): What?

Guest: Chandernagerapore and Bhopawal.

Hostess: (interrupted once more): Eh?

Guest: Chandernagerapore and Bhopawal.

Hostess: All right, show them in.

Guest: (patiently, but with less simplicity): I am his Highness –

Hostess: I know, I know. And I'm the Queen of Iceland. It's the gin, old boy. Now keep quiet, there's a lamb.

I shall never forget that early April morning long ago when Mr. Williamson and I went quietly down the swiftly-flowing Doodle in a duck-punt. The stars were still out, and on our left the badgers were croaking in the selvedge-bosses. An old heron went caumbling down to Widdenham Furlong. We could see the spindrift of dawn on his rosetted biceps.

Suddenly a peregrine, four foot by one, and seven by three, skoomed out of a gazzle-bush. We stood up in the punt and cast our nets at it. They caught in a wild hornbeam which grew by the bank, and the bird whopped on its way to Drivelham Bridge.

That night we had fermitty-pudden in the Cat and Daffodil.

Dr. Strabismus (Whom God Preserve) of Utrecht

Dr. Strabismus (Whom God Preserve) of Utrecht has been asked by leading industrialists to carry out some experiments to discover the effect of music on efficiency. There has long been a theory that people would be happier if they sang or played at their work.

The Doctor visited a large factory yesterday where goloshes are made and packed. He distributed violins to all the workers and told them to play something. Those who were able to master the instrument, owing to previous knowledge of it, quickly became engrossed in their own playing. Three sisters, who rendered Raff's 'Cavatina', failed to turn out a single golosh. On the other hand, those who, after producing a few squeaks, abandoned the instrument, were distracted by the din made by their neighbours, and turned out goloshes so large or so small or so shapeless that their time was wasted. The Doctor carried out his second experiment yesterday before the Board of Industrial Psychology and Psychological Industry.

A number of pianofortes were installed in a jam-making factory, and the workers were encouraged to play certain pieces as they worked. It was found that the instruments quickly became smeared with jam, and that, in consequence of this, the playing was not of a high class.

After the luncheon interval a pip-inserter and a jar-lid-screwer essayed a duet. The black notes were clogged, and the attempt had to be postponed, while the instrument was swilled down with warm water. The doctor came to the conclusion that jam can be made just as well without musical accompaniment. He next tried the effect of the oratorio 'Hiawatha' on door-hinge makers.

The Doctor visited a large door-hinge factory in the Midlands. In the presence of experts from the Board of Industrial Psychology he carried out an experiment to ascertain the effect of singing on the efficiency of the workmen. The piece chosen was the oratorio 'Hiawatha'.

The noise of the machines drowned the opening lines, but gradually the employees warmed to the work, and set up such a bawling that the machines were inaudible. In the excitement of the moment half-completed hinges were passed as completed, and the overseers began to jest and even to throw the hinges out of the windows.

The representative of a firm which had ordered 100,000 hinges expressed the opinion that singing interfered with the work, and when the experts examined the hinges they were compelled to admit that they were a pretty poor lot. Some were large enough for a castle door. Others wouldn't have fitted the doors of a dwarf's potting-shed. The work was careless, unfinished, and slovenly. But all the workers were happy.

Dr. Strabismus (Whom God Preserve) of Utrecht was forced to abandon his fourth experiment in industrial psychology. He visited a glass-blowing establishment, in company with experts. The employees were asked to play the trombone every now and then, to cheer themselves up.

Some complained that they had no breath left after blowing glass. Others complained that, after playing the trombone, they found themselves blowing enormous and meaningless bulbs.

One lady glass-blower became confused in her blowing,

and put such power into the making of a rather delicate
rose-bowl that she blew a perfect rhomboid of a conser-
vatory, went home with hiccoughs, was arrested by the
police for 'advanced alcoholism', and cried herself to sleep
in the local gaol. He next conducted an experiment to
determine the effect of full orchestral performances of
Wagner's music on shipbreaking.

He established the fact that under the stimulus of the
noisier passages enormous ships were smashed to smither-
eens in a surprisingly short time. The inspiration of the
music, lingering in excited brains, even led large numbers
of workmen to visit other parts of the yards, and to
destroy half-built liners, offices, publichouses, workshops,
sheds, timber-yards, and coal-dumps. When the music
ended some lay down in the mud and screamed, others
threw themselves into the water. Doctors were called,
and recommended a month's holiday in the mountains,
without music.

Per contra, under the effect of Offenbach's 'Barcarolle',
an experienced gang engaged on the new battle-cruiser,
H.M.S. Intolerable, turned out a tomfool gondola. Many
were weeping softly as they finished their work.

The Doctor conducted a freak experiment to ascertain
the effect of piccolo-playing in a brewery. Within an hour
forty-three employees were caught in the act of filling
their piccolos with beer. They pleaded lack of musical
ability, but it was found that the sight of these unmusical
men drinking from their piccolos demoralised all the
others, so that they neglected their playing. The experiment was abandoned when the manager himself was discovered in a corner shaking cocktails in the largest piccolo
in Europe.

Labour-Saving

The recent International Exhibition of Inventions had
among its exhibits 'a collapsible clothes-airer in which a

lamp can be put – the invention of a Somerset clergyman'.

Dr. Strabismus (Whom God Preserve), of Utrecht, allowed several of his own recent inventions to be shown. Among these interesting exhibits were to be found:

1. A large marmalade-dish which folds up into the shape of a candle-stick.
2. A wooden sausage which, when reversed, pours out a stream of salad-oil into a bowl, in readiness for mixing the salad.
3. An iron cocktail-shaker which, when hit with great strength, rings the front-door bell and returns the cherry.
4. A thick cut-glass walking-stick filled with very small flannel shirts.
5. A large bucket, open at one end to admit bearer.
6. A rubber wheelbarrow for wiping out illuminated addresses.
7. A dummy filter which can be used as a hat-rack or birdcage.
8. A long-distance bacon-pan, in which bacon can be cooked slowly in a greenhouse.
9. A canvas tomato to balance on a trouser-press (for jugglers, principally).
10. A concrete combined sieve and potato-masher.
11. A receptacle for collecting lamp-iron after earthquakes.
12. A musical ballot-box for wet elections, which, simultaneously, fills bottles with mulberries.

In a Nutshell

Apparently there is some difficulty in understanding the exact position in China. As nearly as possible this is the situation. Ping-Pong, with Un-Hung and Flung-Hi, is moving down through Yo-Ho against Wong-Hu, while Boo-Hu, the Hoo-Hoo's general, is concentrating in front of Sa-Go. Meanwhile Flu, with 400,000,000,000 men is massing his Greens in front of Gong-Gong. On the Wow-Wow front the Baptist General Sing-Song is holding in check the Ultra-Marines, who are menacing Poo-Poo from the direction of Hi. On the west bank of the river Wo, Marshal Rin-Tin-Tin is opposed to the Wang-Ling army, commanded by O-No. The man of the hour is Na-Poo, whose headquarters are at Tatchow, on the Bow-Wow. Sa-Wen is hurrying down from Kiang-Fan with twelve men to reinforce the Moo-Kow front.

So that's that.

Alone With Nature

What is this nurbling sound under the eaves? It is the tiny quagfinch, lured from his nest in the old juniper by this burst of sunshine. By hedge and ditch nature is leading forth the buds that will later burgeon, as burgeon they must.

Already the stream side is dotted with clusters of up-adiddle and old man's foot, and the curious may find in crannies of old walls the lovely bedsoxia, with its trailing stamen and its inverted corolla.

This is the time to pot out your teazle. As the days lengthen and the sun gathers force winged songsters return to the garden — early among them the greater huffle, whose red legs terrify the heron so much.

Raspberries should be mulched a little now.

'Stick it, Nobbler!' (J. A. Froude)

Excuse me-e-e-e wri-wri-ting in-rhythm, but but but thereisa gra-a-a-amophone perlaying as as I write-e.

I will pause a moment until it subsides.

Here we go again. They call me Mimi, but my name is Beachcomber, and I have to turn this stuff out however loudly the music swells. My tiny hand is frozen, but the pen must do its work.

My senses are going ... I begin to see mice in straw hats and starfish in tartans playing piccolos. Puccini, Puccini, tekel, upharsin. Postume, Postume labuntur anni Laurie ... After you, Miss Stein ...

Bang! And then then and silence silence silence silence silence silence silence once for every day in the day in the week week week.

A Cricket Play

'Cricket is not taken seriously enough by the players.' (Evening paper.)

(Scene: The Oval).

UMPIRE:	Out!
BATSMAN:	Oh, please! Not that!
UMPIRE:	Out, I said.
BATSMAN:	Have you thought what this means?
	(*A long pause.*)
	Have you visualised the aftermath; the lonely walk to the pavilion, the jeers of one's mates, the comments in the Press?
UMPIRE:	I see no other course.
BATSMAN:	You yourself, umpire, have fans. You know what it is to run the gauntlet of hostile eyes, to be held up to ridicule. Little children, years hence, will tell the story of how I was given out, l.b.w., in this match, and will say, 'He was given out l.b.w. by Soames.'*
UMPIRE:	You only make it harder for me.
BATSMAN:	(*quickly*): But supposing I were not really out –
UMPIRE:	It would not matter. I have said you are out, and that is all that matters. After all, a man must be either in or out. Life is like that.

* No relation to the wooden-headed old humbug in Mr. Galworthy's Saga (sic).

Some are in, others are not.

BATSMAN: (*with lowered head*): Very well. You are but the victim of a system, and I bear you no ill-will. Your training leads you to believe that I am out. You act according to your lights. Nevertheless (*with raised voice*), I dream of a day when no batsman will ever be out, and when umpire and batsman will work hand in hand to build a better cricket field. Goodbye, umpire, good-bye!

(Exit to pavilion.)

Among the New Religions

A correspondent has asked me to give some details of the new religions I mentioned the other day. I will do so as briefly as I can.

Oblong Movement: Belief in Goodness as a Vital Urge.

Gaga, Ltd. (see also Neo-Cretinism): Rejects belief in Sin or Hope. All things exist only in so far as they are self-conscious.

Mrs. Barlington's Top-Notchers: Rejects belief in death. Nothing is what it really is. Object of Life is Self-Expression.

Sadie's Ethical Boys: Belief in love as a be-all. Men wear no waistcoats. Women bishops.

Juggo: Transrhenanism under another name. Rejects belief in everything.

Upandup: Has been called transcendental rotarianism. One thing is as good as another. Doesn't matter what you do, so long as you don't do it.

The Cœruleans: Rejects belief in Life as an entity. Members call each other 'Pard'. The Big Chief Pard elected for life. No laughing.

Dr. Grant Armitage's Sky-Fans: Sometimes called the 'Songbirds'. Firm belief in hymns. Eat nothing. Drink nothing. Wear no clothes. Simplification-urge is a major tenet.

Bonnie Jeanie

(Air: 'The Eighty-three Men of Moidart')

O ken ye Wullie Broon, Jeanie,
O ken ye Brulzie Glen,
Wi, the haslock on the brig, Jeanie,
A' bu' ca' fu' big ben?

Whaur's the loof noo, Jeanie,
Whaur's the bannock, jo?
My luv's a bleerit caulsie, Jeanie,
An' the gutcher's doit sae low.

Snaw-white was her hairt, Jeanie,
Waulkin' doon the warl,
The midden-creel's a' bracht, Jeanie,
The loof's anint the sparl.

Sair rins the Tees noo, Jeanie,
Deevin' through the glaes,
But a mon's mon's a mon, Jeanie,
Wi'oot a guidman's claes.

Sair rins the Tweed hoocht, Jeanie,
Blithe towmond, bonnie skirl,
The Snowther's blate the criffe, Jeanie,
Wi' birkie frae the sirl.

O ken ye Wullie Broon, Jeanie
Whaur's the limmer noo,
Flicht stricht the bricht licht fa's, Jeanie,
An' mony mair tae you.

Glossary: Bannock: a small ban, white in colour.
           Jo: short for O.
           Gutcher: a ramrod used in curing whitebait.
           Warl: decayed treacle.
           Loof: a cabman's collar in a teapot.

Sparl: a method of boiling glue in Lanark.
Deevin': a goyling sound, like the hoofle
of a fracht.
Towmond: the edge of an egg in midwinter.
Snowther: a frozen handcuff.
Sirl: a glimpse of red flannel on a bridge.

Strange Headgear

On her waved hair she wore a jaunty sailor.
(Description of committee-woman.)
After sitting there cross-legged, trying to look like a hat,
the mariner grows bored and self-conscious. Finally, in a
most unhatlike manner, he lights his pipe, scratches his leg
and begins to whistle
Prodnose: Surely it means sailor-hat.
Myself: If people always said what they meant there
would be less nonsense in the world. No. Half a minute.
No. No. That's all wrong. There would be more nonsense
in the world.

Courageous Woman Thwarts Fools

An attempt to balance a large wooden camel on posts
between the main entrance of a model gasworks and the
side entrance, in which crates were piled, was narrowly
frustrated yesterday by Mrs. Mamsey, of Horsecroft-road,
S. E. 7. 'I saw them trying to do this,' said Mrs. Mamsey, 'so
I said, "You can't do that," and they took no notice, so I
called my husband who works in the laundry there, and
he said to them to stop. But they said they wanted to
balance the wooden camel, and when the police came a
neighbour, Mrs. Cave, had lent them a cart to take the
gasworks away on, and they left the camel.' Mrs. Mamsey,
grey-eyed and forthright, has a son who works in a dis-
tillery near Abergavenny, and a daughter married to a

market-gardener outside Ipswich. She told me how the gasworks was brought in sections a week ago, and put together on the spot. 'It was like one o' them prefabricated 'ouses,' she said. When I asked about the camel, she said the whole neighbourhood had noticed it, but, of course, they knew it wasn't a real camel when the men tried to lift it on to the posts. She thought the crates at the side entrance were empty.

And Again

'Flaps, including dogfish flaps, are lugs or belly walls.'
(Mr. W. Mabane, M.P.)
This answer to a question in the House will not satisfy the trade. It would be truer (and fairer) to say that flaps including lug-walls, are bellyfish flaps with scraps of dog-flap. The flap-wall of lug-belly is not a dog-flap strip except in so far as the after-strap flips of the wallbelly are dogbelly flops, with strips of strop on the flapbelly flop. Or, as we say in basic English, fish-flaps to you, Mrs. Runcorn.

Nothing To Do With Me

A man who applied for an extra cheese ration for a singing mouse which he had trained, received a form and filled it up thus:
1. Where was your last concert engagement? In the larder.
2. Father's name: Whiskers.
3. Father's profession: Captain of the Wainscote Rovers.
4. Mother's maiden name: Squeaker.
5. Present address: Hole-in-the-Floor, 1, Cranberry-crescent.
6. Religion: Cheese-worshipper.
7. Dependent relatives: Grandfather, disabled in trap.

8. Professional name: Pitta-patta.
9. Height: 1¼ ins. Age: 2.

Song of a Pleasure Cruiser

I shall always remember Venice ...
For wasn't that the place
Where Mrs. Mason hurt her foot,
And mother bought the lace?

Do It Now

Influenza can be transferred to healthy ferrets.
(Dr Roberts)
What on earth are we waiting for?

The Stamp

There is no mistaking an Ealing face the whole world over.
(The Rev J. J. Summerhayes)
There was a murmur among the Venetian gondoliers as
the tall and splendid figure, guide-book in strong, brown
hand strolled along the Riva dei Schiavoni. And the oldest
gondolier, contemplating the broad, intelligent face of the
traveller, the eyes full of humour and wisdom, the brow
god-like, the chin firm, whispered in awe: 'That, Giu-
seppe, is an Ealing face! I have heard my mother speak of
the men of Ealing.'

A group of Greek peasants ceased their talk as the
goddess – for such she seemed – glided rather than walked
towards the hill of the acropolis.

There was in her bearing such dignity and poise, in her
face such beauty, behind her spectacles such fire, that a
woman from the fields of Marathon said, 'Surely the gods
return. This is Juno Boopis, the Samian, come again. Or is

it Pallas Athene, returned to restore the world?'

Whereupon an old peasant woman spoke: 'That is an Ealing face,' she said. 'But I do not blame you young ones for mistaking it. So must the goddesses have borne themselves in the times of our fathers.'

The schoolmistress sailed on.

Above the glinting Pacific the sky burned deep blue. The sea rose and fell along the sandy shore, with the easy movement of a sleeping child's breathing. A marooned Finn, in a sailor's jersey, driven nearly mad by two months' loneliness, rose with a sudden cry and dashed to the water's edge. The sea had washed up a body. The Finn saw that the man was dead; but he saw something else in that frank, fearless face.

'He was an Ealing man, poor fellow,' said the Finn.

A man went into a pub with a live lobster sticking out of his pocket. The man next to him at the bar said 'Why don't you take that thing home to dinner?'

'It's had its dinner,' said the man with the lobster, 'I'm just taking it to the cinema.'

The Case of the Twelve Red-Bearded Dwarfs

Another ludicrous scene occurred while Mr. Tinklebury Snapdriver, for the prosecution, was cross-examining Mrs. Tasker.

MR. SNAPDRIVER:	Your name is Rhoda Tasker?
MRS. TASKER:	Obviously, or I wouldn't be here.
MR. SNAPDRIVER:	I put it to you that you were once known as Rough-House Rhoda?
MR. HERMITAGE:	No, m'lud, Rough-House Rhoda is another lady, who I propose to call — a Mrs. Rhoda Mortiboy.
COCKLECARROT:	What a queer name.
A DWARF:	You are speaking of my mother. (*sensation*)
COCKLECARROT:	Is your name Mortiboy?

THE DWARF:	No. Towler's my name.
COCKLECARROT:	(*burying his head in his hands*): I suppose she married again.
THE DWARF:	What do you mean – again? Her name has always been Towler.
COCKLECARROT:	(*groaning*): Mr. Hermitage, what is all this about?
MR. HERMITAGE:	M'lud, there is a third Rhoda, a Mrs. Rhoda Clandon.
COCKLECARROT:	(*to the dwarf, sarcastically*): Is she your mother, too?
THE DWARF:	Yes. My name's Clandon.
COCKLECARROT:	I think, Mr. Snapdriver, we had better proceed without this Rhoda business. My nerves won't stand it.
MR. SNAPDRIVER:	My next witness is the artiste known as Lucinda – a Mrs. Whiting (*Everybody looks at the dwarf*)
COCKLECARROT:	(*with heavy sarcasm*): And, of course –
THE DWARF:	Yes, she is my mother.
COCKLECARROT:	(*roaring*): Then what is your name, you oaf?
THE DWARF:	Charlie Bread. (*Laughter and jeers.*)
COCKLECARROT:	Clear the court! This foolery is intolerable. It will ruin my political career.
MR. SNAPDRIVER:	Now, Mrs. Tasker, you do not deny that on several occasions you drove these dwarfs, a dozen of them, into Mrs. Renton's hall.
MRS. TASKER:	That is so.
MR. SNAPDRIVER:	What was your motive?
MRS. TASKER:	I wanted to drive the dwarfs into her hall.
MR. SNAPDRIVER:	But why? Can you give me any reason? You will admit it is an unusual occupation.

MRS. TASKER:	Not for me. I've done it all my life.
MR. SNAPDRIVER:	You have driven dwarfs into other ladies' houses?
MRS. TASKER:	Certainly.
COCKLECARROT:	Where do you get your supply of dwarfs.
MRS. TASKER:	From an agency. Fudlow and Trivett.
COCKLECARROT:	Extraordinary. Most extraordinary.
MR. HERMITAGE:	Now, Dr. Spunton, is there, to your knowledge, any disease which could account for Mrs. Tasker's strange habits?
DR. SPUNTON:	There is. It is called rufo-nanitis. The spymptoms –
MR. HERMITAGE:	Symptoms.
DR. SPUNTON:	Yes, spymptoms, but I always put a 'p' before a 'y'.
COCKLECARROT:	With what object, might we ask?
DR. SPUNTON:	I can't help it, m'lud.
COCKLECARROT:	Do you say pyesterday?
DR. SPUNTON:	Pyes, unfortunatelpy. It's hereditarpy. Mpy familpy all do it.
COCKLECARROT:	But why 'p'?
DR. SPUNTON:	No, py, m'lud.
COCKLECARROT:	This case is the most preposterous I ever heard. We get nowhere. The evidence is drivel, the whole thing is a travesty of justice. In two weeks we have done nothing but listen to a lot of nonsense. The case will be adjourned until we can clear things up a bit.
DR. SPUNTON:	But I was brought all the wapy from Pyelverton.
COCKLECARROT:	Well, go pyack to Pyelverton. Goodpye, and a phappy pjournepy. Pshaw!

The hearing was held up for a long time today, when the Deputy Puisne Serjeant-at-Arraigns discovered that, owing to an error of the Chief Usher of the Wardrobe, Mr. Justice Cocklecarrot had emerged from the Robing Room with his wig on back to front. According to an old statute of Canute (Op. II.C. in dom: reg: circ: 37. Cap. 9pp:gh: od: ba: ha: 26, per Hohum 46:98 (e). Tan: 64 by 36: zh: vos: H.Mid: sub rosa 49) the wig must be changed round by the Bailiff of the Wards. So they sent a messenger to bring him from Gregson's Dive. When he arrived he had forgotten the words of the prescribed ritual, and instead of taking Cocklecarrot's left foot in his right hand, he took his right foot in his left hand, thus invalidating the whole tomfoolery.

Meanwhile, a brawl was taking place outside the court. A lady bearing a banner which said, 'Litigate, Don't Arbitrate', was accidentally pushed off the pavement by the dwarfs, who had come in a large motor-car.

When Mrs. Tasker arrived, she held a newspaper in front of her face, thus enabling the unwary Press photographers to advertise the *Hunstanton Daily Courier*.

The dwarfs were cross-examined today. At least, one of them was cross-examined.

MR. HERMITAGE:	Your name is Howard Brassington?
THE DWARF:	(*in a deep, loud voice*): It is no such thing.
MR. HERMITAGE:	(*consulting his notes*): What is your name, then?
THE DWARF:	Stanislas George Romney Barlow Barlow Orchmeynders.
MR. HERMITAGE:	Two Barlows?
THE DWARF:	Why not?
MR. HERMITAGE:	You are a night watchman.
THE DWARF:	Why not?
COCKLECARROT:	Mr. Porchminder, you will please answer yes or no.
THE DWARF:	No.
MR. HERMITAGE:	Where were you on the night of 10th April?
THE DWARF:	No.

COCKLECARROT :	(*to counsel*): Apart from retaining fees, would it not be better to speed up this case a bit?
THE DWARF :	Yes.
COCKLECARROT :	Send him away. Call Mrs. Renton.
MR. HERMITAGE :	Speak your mind, Mrs. Renton, speak your mind.
MRS. RENTON :	I will. I accused Mrs. Tasker of driving a dozen red-bearded dwarfs into my hall. She admits she did it. The dwarfs say she did it. Well, what more is there to be said? What are we waiting for?
COCKLECARROT :	Mrs. Renton, you do not understand that certain formalities – er – the Law has its own way of doing things.
MRS. RENTON :	And that is why I have to come here day after day to listen to all this irrelevant foolery – speeches about the Navy, arguments about a dwarf's mother, fuss about dates, and so on.
COCKLECARROT :	I am the first to admit that there have been irregularities and delays in this case, but – (*A dwarf shouts loudly, 'M'lud! M'lud!' Cocklecarrot and Mrs. Renton exchange glances.*)
MR. HERMITAGE :	Well?
THE DWARF :	I think I'm going to be sick.
MRS. RENTON :	That is about the only thing that hasn't happened in this case so far.
COCKLECARROT :	Usher! Remove that dwarf. The time has, I think, come for you, ladies and gentlemen of the jury, to consider this case on its merits.
FOREMAN OF JURY :	And what, sir, would you say were its merits?
COCKLECARROT :	What would you?

FOREMAN: We have not so far understood one
                word of the proceedings.

COCKLECARROT: I must say there have been moments
                when I myself seemed to have lost
                touch with the real world. Neverthe-
                less, certain facts stand out.

FOREMAN: For instance?

COCKLECARROT: I will not be cross-examined by my
                own jury. You are here to deliver a
                verdict, not to question me. You have
                heard the evidence.

FOREMAN: Was that the evidence? All that horse-
                play?

COCKLECARROT: If this continues I shall discharge the
                jury, and the case will be heard all
                over again with a new jury. Stop those
                dwarfs singing! This is not a music
                hall.

MAX BEERBOHM

SAVONAROLA BROWN

ACT III

SCENE: The Piazza

TIME: *A few minutes anterior to close of preceding Act.*
*The Piazza is filled from end to end with a vast seething
crowd that is drawn entirely from the lower orders. There
is a sprinkling of wild-eyed and dishevelled women in it.
The men are lantern-jawed, with several days' growth of
beard. Most of them carry rude weapons — staves, bill-
hooks, crow-bars and the like — and are in as excited a
condition as the women. Some of them are bare-headed,
others affect a kind of Phrygian cap. Cobblers predomi-
nate.*

    Enter LORENZO DE MEDICI *and* COSIMO DE MEDICI. *They*

*wear cloaks of scarlet brocade, and, to avoid notice, hold
masks to their faces.*

COS.
What purpose doth the foul and greasy plebs
Ensure today here?
LOR.   I neither know nor care.
COS.
How enthralled thou art to the philosophy
Of Epicurus! Naught that's human I
Deem alien from myself. (*To a* COBBLER) Make answer,
fellow!
What empty hope hath drawn thee by a thread
Forth from the *obscene hovel where thou starvest?
COB.
No empty hope, your Honour, but the full
Assurance that today, as yesterday,
Savonarola will let loose his thunder
Against the vices of the idle rich
And from the brimming cornucopia
Of his immense vocabulary pour
Scorn on the lamentable heresies
Of the new learning and on all the art
Later than Giotto.
COS.   Mark
             how absolute
The knave is
LOR.

          Then are parrots rational
When they regurgitate the thing they hear!
This fool is but an unit of the crowd,
And crowds are senseless as the vasty deep
That sinks or surges as the moon dictates.
I know these crowds, and know that any man
That hath a glib tongue and a rolling eye
Can as he willeth with them.
     (*Removes his mask and mounts steps of Loggia.*)
             Citizens!

(Prolonged yells and groans from the crowd.)
Yes, I am he, I am that same Lorenzo
Whom you have nicknamed the Magnificent.

*(Further terrific yells, shakings of fists, brandishings
of bill-hooks, insistent cries of 'Death to Lorenzo!',
'Down with the Magnificent!' Cobblers on fringe of
crowd, down c., exhibit especially all the symptoms
of epilepsy, whooping cough and other ailments.)*
You love not me

(The crowd makes an ugly rush. LOR. *appears likely
to be dragged down and torn limb from limb, but
raises one hand in nick of time, and continues:)*
Yet I deserve your love.

*(The yells are now variegated with dubious mur-
murs. A cobbler down c. thrusts his face feverishly
in the face of another and repeats, in a hoarse inter-
rogative whisper, 'Deserves our love?')*
Not for the sundry boons I have bestow'd
And benefaction I have lavished
Upon Firenze, City of the Flowers,
But for the love that in this rugged breast
I bear you.

*(The yells have now died away, and there is a sharp
fall in dubious murmurs. The cobbler down c. says,
in an ear-piercing whisper, 'The love he bears us,'
drops his lower jaw, nods his head repeatedly, and
awaits in an intolerable state of suspense the orator's
next words.)*
I am not a blameless man,
(Some dubious murmurs.)
Yet for that I have lov'd you passing much,
Shall some things be forgiven me.
(Noises of cordial assent.)
There dwells
In this our city, known unto you all,
A man more virtuous than I am, and
A thousand times more intellectual;
Yet envy I not him, for shall I name him? —

He loves not you. His name? I will not cut
Your hearts by speaking it. Here let it stay
On tip o' tongue.

(*Insistent clamour.*)
Then steel you to the shock! —
Savonarola.
(*For a moment or so the crowd reels silently under the shock. Cobbler down* C. *is the first to recover himself and cry 'Death to Savonarola!' The cry instantly becomes general.* LOR. *holds up his hand and gradually imposes silence.*)
His twin bug-bears are
Yourselves and that New Learning which I hold
Less dear than only you.
(*Profound sensation. Everybody whispers 'Than only you' to everybody else. A woman near steps of Loggia attempts to kiss hem of* LOR'S *garment.*)
Would you but con
With me the old philosophers of Hellas,
Her fervent bards and calm historians,
You would arise and say 'We will not hear
Another word against them!'
(*The crowd already says this, repeatedly, with great emphasis.*)
Take the Dialogues
Of Plato, for example. You will find
A spirit far more truly Christian
In them than in the ravings of the sour-soul'd
Savonarola.
(*Prolonged cries of 'Death to the Sour-Souled Savonarola!' Several cobblers detach themselves from the crowd and rush away to read the Platonic Dialogues. Enter* SAVONAROLA. *The crowd, as he makes his way through it, gives up all further control of its feelings, and makes a noise for which even the best zoologists might not find a good comparison. The staves and billhooks wave like twigs in a storm. One would say, that* SAV. *must have died a thousand deaths already.*)

*He is, however, unharmed and unruffled as he reaches
the steps of the Loggia.* LOR. *meanwhile has rejoined*
COS. *in the Piazza.*)

SAV.

Pax vobiscum, brothers!

(*This does but exacerbate the crowd's frenzy.*)

VOICE OF A COBBLER

Hear his false lips cry Peace when there is no
Peace!

SAV.

Are you not ashamed, O Florentines,

(*Renewed yells, but also some symptoms of manly
shame.*)

That hearken'd to Lorenzo and now reel
Inebriate with the exuberance
Of his verbosity?

(*The crowd makes an obvious effort to pull itself together.*)

A man can fool

Some of the people all the time, and can
Fool all the people sometimes, but he cannot
Fool *all* the people *all* the time.

(*Loud cheers. Several cobblers clap one another on
the back. Cries of 'Death to Lorenzo!' The meeting is
now well in hand.*)

Today

I must adopt a somewhat novel course
In dealing with the awful wickedness
At present noticeable in this city.
I do so with reluctance. Hitherto
I have avoided personalities.
But now my sense of duty forces me
To a departure from my custom of
Naming no names. One name I must and shall
Name.

(*All eyes are turned on* LOR., *who smiles uncomfort-
ably.*)

No, I do not mean Lorenzo. He

Is 'neath contempt.

> (*Loud and prolonged laughter, accompanied with hideous grimaces at* LOR. *Exeunt* LOR. *and* COS.)

>> I name a woman's name,

> (*The women in the crowd eye one another suspiciously.*)

A name known to you all — four-syllabled
Beginning with an L.

> (*Pause. Enter hurriedly* LUC., *carrying the ring. She stands, unobserved by anyone, on outskirt of crowd.* SAV. *utters the name:*)

>> Lucrezia!

LUC. (*With equal intensity.*)
Savonarola!

> (SAV. *starts violently and stares in direction of her voice.*)

> Yes, I come, I come!

> (*Forces her way up steps of Loggia. The crowd is much bewildered, and the cries of 'Death to Lucrezia Borgia!' are few and sporadic.*)

Why didst thou call me?

> (SAV. *looks somewhat embarrassed.*)

>> What is thy distress?

I see it all! The sanguinary mob
Clusters round thee! As the antler'd stag
With fine eyes glazed from the too-long chase,
Turns to defy the foam-fleck'd pack, and thinks,
In his last moment, of some graceful hind
Seen once afar upon a mountain-top,
E'en so, Savonarola, didst thou think,
In thy most dire extremity, of me.
And here I am! Courage! The horrid hounds
Droop tail at sight of me and fawn away
Innocuous.

> (*The crowd does indeed seem to have fallen completely under the sway of* LUC.'s *magnetism, and is evidently convinced that it had been about to make an end of the monk.*)

Take thou, and wear henceforth,
As a sure talisman 'gainst future perils,
This little, little ring.

> (SAV. *makes awkward gesture of refusal. Angry mur-
> murs from the crowd. Cries of 'Take thou the ring!'
> 'Churl!' 'Put it on!' etc.*
>
> *Enter the Borgias'* FOOL *and stands unnoticed on
> fringe of crowd.*)

I hoped you'd like it –
Neat but not gaudy. Is my taste at fault?
I'd so look'd forward to – (*Sob*) No, I'm not crying,
But just a little hurt.

> (*Hardly a dry eye in the crowd. Also swayings and
> snarlings indicative that* SAV's *life is again not worth
> a moment's purchase.* SAV. *makes awkward gesture
> of acceptance, but just as he is about to put ring on
> finger, the* FOOL *touches his lute and sings:*)

Wear not the ring,
It hath an unkind sting,
    Ding, dong, ding.
Bide a minute,
There's poison in it,
    Poison in it,
        Ding-a-dong, dong, ding.

LUC.   The fellow lies.

> (*The crowd is torn with conflicting opinions.
> Mingled cries of 'Wear not the ring!' 'The fellow lies!'
> 'Bide a minute!' 'Death to the Fool!' 'Silence for the
> Fool!' 'Ding-a-dong, dong, ding!' etc.*)

FOOL

(*sings*)
Wear not the ring,
For Death's a robber-king,
    Ding, (*etc.*)
There's no trinket
Is what you think it,
    What you think it,
        Ding-a-dong, (*etc.*)

18

(SAV. *throws ring in* LUC.'s *face. Enter* POPE JULIUS
II, *with Papal army.*)

POPE

Arrest that man and woman!

(*Re-enter Guelfs and Ghibellines fighting.* SAV. *and*
LUC. *are arrested by Papal officers. Enter* MICHAEL
ANGELO. ANDREA DEL SARTO *appears for a moment at
a window.* PIPPA *passes.*

*Brothers of the Misercordia go by, singing a Requiem
for Francesca da Rimini. Enter* BOCCACCIO, BEN VEN-
UTO CELLINI, *and many others, making remarks highly
characteristic of themselves but scarcely audible
through the terrific thunderstorm which now bursts
over Florence and is at its loudest and darkest crisis
as the Curtain falls.*)

ACT IV

TIME: *Three hours later.*

SCENE: *A Dungeon on the ground-floor of the Pal-
azzo Civico.*

*The stage is bisected from top to bottom by a wall, on
one side of which is seen the interior of* LUCREZIA's *cell,
on the other that of* SAVONAROLA's.

*Neither he nor she knows that the other is in the next
cell. The audience, however, knows this.*

*Each cell (because of the width and height of the pro-
scenium) is of more than the average Florentine size, but
is bare even to the point of severity, its sole amenities
being some straw, a hunk of bread, and a stone pitcher.
The door of each is facing the audience. Dim-ish light.*

LUCREZIA *wears long and clanking chains on her wrists,
as also does* SAVONAROLA. *Imprisonment has left its mark
on both of them.* SAVONAROLA's *hair has turned white. His
whole aspect is that of a very old, old man.* LUCREZIA *looks
no older than before, but has gone mad.*

SAV.

Alas, how long ago this morning seems
This evening! A thousand thousand aeons

Are scarce the measure of the gulf betwixt
My then and now. Methinks I must have been
Here since the dim creation of the world
And never in that interval have seen
The tremendous hawthorn burgeon in the brake,
Nor heard the hum o' bees, nor woven chains
Of buttercups on Mount Fiesole
What time the sap leapt in the cypresses,
Imbuing with the friskfulness of Spring
Those melancholy trees. I do forget
The aspect of the sun. Yet I was born
A freeman, and the Saints of Heaven smiled
Down on my crib. What would my sire have said,
And what my dam, had anybody told them
The time would come when I should occupy
A felon's cell? O the disgrace of it!
The scandal, the incredible come-down!
It masters me. I see i' my mind's eye
The public prints – 'Sharp Sentence on a Monk.'
What then? I thought I was of sterner stuff
Than is affrighted by what people think.
Yet thought I so because 'twas thought of me,
And so 'twas thought of me because I had
A hawk-like profile and a baleful eye.
Lo! My soul's chin recedes, soft to the touch
As half-churn'd butter. Seeming hawk is dove,
And dove's a gaol-bird now. Fie out upon 't!
LUC.
How comes it? I am Empress Dowager
Of China – yet was never crown'd. This must
Be seen to.

> (Quickly gathers some straw and weaves a crown
> which she puts on.)

SAV.

       Oh, what a degringolade!
The great career. I had mapp'd out for me –
Nipp'd i' the bud. What life, when I come out,
Awaits me? Why, the very Novices

And callow Postulants will draw aside
As I pass by, and say 'That man hath done
Time!' And yet shall I wince? The worst of Time
Is not in having done it, but in doing't.

LUC.

Ha, ha, ha, ha! Eleven billion pig-tails
Do tremble at my nod imperial,
The which is as it should be.

SAV.

              I have heard
That gaolers oft are willing to carouse
With them they watch o'er, and do sink at last
Into a drunken sleep, and then's the time
To snatch the keys and make a bid for freedom.
Gaoler! Ho, Gaoler!

> (*Sound of lock being turned and bolts withdrawn.*
> *Enter the Borgias'* FOOL, *in plain clothes, carrying*
> *bunch of keys.*)

                    I have seen thy face
Before.

FOOL

            I saved thy life this afternoon, Sir.

SAV.

Thou are the Borgias' Fool?

FOOL

              Say rather, was.
Unfortunately I have been discharg'd
For my betrayal of Lucrezia,
So that I have to speak like other men —
Decasyllabically, and with sense.
An hour ago the gaoler of this dungeon
Died of an apoplexy. Hearing which,
I ask'd and obtain'd his billet.

SAV.

                   Fetch
A stoup o' liquor for thyself and me.

              (*Exit* GAOLER.)

Freedom! There's nothing that thy votaries

Grudge in the cause of thee. That decent man
Is doom'd by me to lose his place again
To-morrow morning when he wakes from out
His hoggish slumber. Yet I care not.

> (*Re-enter* GAOLER *with a leathern bottle and two glasses.*)

Ho!
This is the stuff to warm our vitals, this
The panacea for all mortal ills
And sure elixir of eternal youth.
Drink, bonniman!

> (GAOLER *drains a glass and shows signs of instant intoxication.* SAV. *claps him on shoulder and replenishes glass.* GAOLER *drinks again, lies down on floor, and snores.* SAV. *snatches the bunch of keys, laughs long but silently, and creeps out on tip-toe, leaving door ajar.*
>
> LUC. *meanwhile has lain down on the straw in her cell, and fallen asleep. Noise of bolts being shot back, jangling of keys, grating of lock, and the door of* LUC.'*s cell flies open.* SAV. *takes two steps across the threshold, his arms outstretched and his upturned face transfigured with a great joy.*)

How sweet the open air
Leaps to my nostrils! O the good brown earth
That yields once more to my elastic tread
And laves these feet with its remember'd dew!

> (*Takes a few more steps, still looking upwards.*)

Free! — I am free! O naked arc of heaven,
Enspangled with innumerable — no,
Stars are not there. Yet neither are there clouds!
The thing looks like a ceiling! (*Gazes downward.*) And this thing
Looks like a floor. (*Gazes around.*) And that white bundle yonder
Looks curiously like Lucrezia.

> (LUC. *awakes at sound of her name, and sits up sane.*)

There must be some mistake.
LUC. (*Rises to her feet.*)
                There is indeed!
A pretty sort of prison I have come to,
In which a self-respecting lady's cell
Is treated as a lounge!

H. BELLOC

Jim

Who ran away from his Nurse, and was eaten by a Lion.

There was a Boy whose name was Jim;
His Friends were very good to him.
They gave him Tea, and Cakes, and Jam,
And slices of delicious Ham,
And Chocolate with pink inside,
And little Tricycles to ride,
And read him Stories through and through,
And even took him to the Zoo –
But there it was the dreadful Fate
Befell him, which I now relate.

You know – at least you *ought* to know,
For I have often told you so –
That Children never are allowed
To leave their Nurses in a Crowd;
Now this was Jim's especial Foible,
He ran away when he was able,
And on this inauspicious day
He slipped his hand and ran away!
He hadn't gone a yard when – Bang!
With open Jaws, a Lion sprang,
And hungrily began to eat
The Boy: beginning at his feet.

Now, just imagine how it feels
When first your toes and then your heels,
And then by gradual degrees,
Your shins and ankles, calves and knees,
Are slowly eaten, bit by bit.
No wonder Jim detested it!
No wonder that he shouted 'Hi!'
The Honest Keeper heard his cry,
Though very fat he almost ran
To help the little gentleman.
'Ponto!' he ordered as he came
(For Ponto was the Lion's name),
'Ponto!' he cried, with angry Frown.
'Let go, Sir! Down, Sir! Put it down!'

The Lion made a sudden Stop,
He let the Dainty Morsel drop,
And slunk reluctant to his Cage,
Snarling with Disappointed Rage.
But when he bent him over Jim,
The Honest Keeper's Eyes were dim.
The Lion having reached his Head,
The Miserable Boy was dead!

When Nurse informed his Parents, they
Were more Concerned than I can say:
His Mother, as she dried her eyes,
Said, 'Well – it gives me no surprise,
He would not do as he was told!'
His Father, who was self-controlled,
Bade all the children round attend
To James' miserable end,
And always keep a-hold of Nurse
For fear of finding something worse.

The Dromedary

The Dromedary is a cheerful bird:
I cannot say the same about the Kurd.

The Hippopotamus

I shoot the Hippopotamus
With bullets made of platinum,
Because if I use leaden ones
His hide is sure to flatten 'em.

Lord Finchley

Lord Finchley tried to mend the Electric Light
Himself. It struck him dead : And serve him right !
It is the business of the wealthy man
To give employment to the artisan.

Lord Lucky

Lord Lucky, by a curious fluke,
Became a most important duke.
From living in a vile Hotel
A long way east of Camberwell
He rose in less than half an hour,
To riches, dignity and power.
It happened in the following way :
The Real Duke went out one day
To shoot with several people, one
Of whom had never used a gun.
This gentleman (a Mr. Meyer
Of Rabley Abbey, Rutlandshire),
As he was scrambling through the brake,
Discharged his weapon by mistake,
And plugged about an ounce of lead
Piff-bang into his Grace's Head —
Who naturally fell down dead.
His Heir, Lord Ugly, roared, 'You Brute !

Take that to teach you how to shoot!'
Whereat he volleyed, left and right;
But being somewhat short of sight,
His right-hand Barrel only got
The second heir, Lord Poddlepot;
The while the left-hand charge (or choke)
Accounted for another bloke,
Who stood with an astounded air
Bewildered by the whole affair
– And was the third remaining heir.
After the Execution (which
Is something rare among the Rich)
Lord Lucky, while of course he needed
Some help to prove his claim, succeeded.
– But after his succession, though
All this was over years ago,
He only once indulged the whim
Of asking Meyer to lunch with him.

From A Moral Alphabet

E stands for Egg.

MORAL
The Moral of this verse
Is applicable to the Young. Be terse.

F for a Family taking a walk
    In Arcadia Terrace, no doubt;
The parents indulge in intelligent talk,
    While the children they gambol about.

At a quarter-past six they return to their tea,
Of a kind that would hardly be tempting to me,
  Though my appetite passes belief.
There is Jam, Ginger Beer, Buttered Toast,
    Marmalade,
With a Cold Leg of Mutton and Warm Lemonade,

And a large Pigeon Pie very skilfully made
    To consist almost wholly of Beef.

MORAL

A Respectable Family taking the air
    Is a subject on which I could dwell;
It contains all the morals that ever there were,
    And it sets an example as well.

G stands for Gnu, whose weapons of Defence
Are long, sharp, curling Horns, and Common-sense.
To these he adds a Name so short and strong
That even Hardy Boers pronounce it wrong.

How often on a bright Autumnal day
The Pious people of Pretoria say,
'Come, let us hunt the —' Then no more is heard
But Sounds of Strong Men struggling with a word.
Meanwhile, the distant Gnu with grateful eyes
Observes his opportunity, and flies.

MORAL

Child, if you have a rummy kind of name,
Remember to be thankful for the same.

From The Path To Rome

Do you know those books and stories in which parts of
the dialogues often have no words at all? Only dots and
dashes and asterisks and interrogations? I wonder what
the people are paid for it? If I knew I would earn a mint
of money, for I believe I have a talent for it. Look at this —

    THE DUCHESS. ? ? ? ? ?
    CHARLES. ——!
    THE DUCHESS. ! ! ! ! !

    CLARA (*sobs*) ♪ ♪ ♪ ♪ ♪ ♪ ♪

    THE DUCHESS (*To Major Charles*). ☞

CHARLES ~~~~~~~~~~~~ *(exit)*.
THE DUCHESS (*To Clara, sharply*). % % % % % % ?
% ? $!
CLARA.
THE DUCHESS (*In great anger*). ? # * ‖ § ‡ ¶ † ✕ !
CLARA. ███ ███ ███ ███

There. That seems to me worth a good deal deal more
money than all the modern 'delineation of character',
and 'folk' nonsense ever written. What verve! What
terseness! And yet how clear!

ROBERT BENCHLEY

Opera Synopses

*Some Sample Outlines of Grand Opera Plots for
Home Study.*

DIE MEISTER-GENOSSENCHAFT

Scene: *The Forests of Germany*   Time: *Antiquity*
Cast:

STRUDEL *God of Rain*	Basso
SCHMALZ *God of Slight Drizzle*	Tenor
IMMERGLÜCK, *Goddess of the Six Primary Colours*	Soprano
LUDWIG DAS ERWEISS, *The Knight of the Iron Duck*	Baritone
THE WOODPECKER	Soprano

ARGUMENT

The basis of 'Die Meister-Genossenschaft' is an old legend
of Germany which tells how the Whale got his Stomach.

ACT I

The Rhine at Low Tide Just Below Weldschnoffen –
Immergluck has grown weary of always sitting on the

same rock with the same fishes swimming by every day, and sends for Schwul to suggest something to do. Schwul asks her how she would like to have pass before her all the wonders of the world fashioned by the hand of man. She says, rotten. He then suggests that Ringblattz, son of Pflucht, be made to appear before her and fight a mortal combat with the Iron Duck. This pleases Immergluck and she summons to her the four dwarfs: Hot Water, Cold Water, Cool, and Cloudy. She bids them bring Ringblattz to her. They refuse, because Pflucht has at one time rescued them from being buried alive by acorns, and, in a rage, Immergluck strikes them all dead with a thunderbolt.

ACT 2

A Mountain Pass – Repenting of her deed, Immergluck has sought advice of the giants, Offen and Besitz, and they tell her that she must procure the magic zither which confers upon its owner the power to go to sleep while apparently carrying on a conversation. This magic zither has been hidden for three hundred centuries in an old bureau drawer, guarded by the Iron Duck, and, although many have attempted to rescue it, all have died of a strange ailment just as success was within their grasp.

But Immergluck calls to her side Dampfboot, the tinsmith of the gods, and bids him make for her a tarnhelm or invisible cap which will enable her to talk to people without their understanding a word she says. For a dollar and a half extra Dampfboot throws in a magic ring which renders its wearer insensible. Thus armed, Immerglück starts out for Walhalla, humming to herself.

ACT 3

The Forest Before the Iron Duck's Bureau Drawer – Merglitz, who has up till this time held his peace, now descends from a balloon and demands the release of Betty. It has been the will of Wotan that Merglitz and Betty should meet on earth and hate each other like poison, but

Zweiback, the druggist of the gods, has disobeyed and concocted a love-potion which has rendered the young couple very unpleasant company. Wotan, enraged, destroys them with a protracted heat spell.

Encouraged by this sudden turn of affairs, Immerglück comes to earth in a boat drawn by four white Holsteins, and, seated alone on a rock, remembers aloud to herself the days when she was a girl. Pilgrims from Augenblick, on their way to worship at the shrine of Schmürr, hear the sound of reminiscence coming from the rock and stop in their march to sing a hymn of praise for the drying-up of the crops. They do not recognize Immerglück, as she has her hair done differently, and think that she is a beggar girl selling pencils.

In the meantime, Ragel, the paper-cutter of the gods, has fashioned himself a sword on the forge of Schmalz, and has called the weapon 'Assistance-in-Emergency'. Armed with 'Assistance-in-Emergency' he comes to earth, determined to slay the Iron Duck and carry off the beautiful Irma.

But Frimsel overhears the plan and has a drink brewed which is given to Ragel in a golden goblet and which, when drunk, makes him forget his past and causes him to believe that he is Schnorr, the God of Fun. While labouring under this spell, Ragel has a funeral pyre built on the summit of a high mountain and, after lighting it, climbs on top of it with a mandolin which he plays until he is consumed.

Immerglück never marries.

II
IL MINNESTRONE
(Peasant Love)

Scene: *Venice and Old Point Comfort.*

Time: *Early 16th century*

Cast:

ALFONSO, *Duke of Minnestrone*		Baritone
PARTOLA, *a Peasant Girl*		Soprano
CLEANSO		Tenor
TURINO	*Young Noblemen of Venice*	Tenor
BOMBO		Basso
LUDOVICO	*Assassins in the Service of*	Basso
ASTOLFO	*Cafeteria Rusticana*	Methodist

Townspeople, Cabbies and Sparrows

ARGUMENT

'Il Minnestrone' is an allegory of the two sides of a man's nature (good and bad), ending at last in an awfully comical mess with everyone dead.

ACT I

A Public Square, Ferrara — During a peasant festival held to celebrate the sixth consecutive day of rain, Rudolpho, a young nobleman, sees Lilliano, daughter of the village bell-ringer, dancing along throwing artificial roses at herself. He asks of his secretary who the young woman is, and his secretary, in order to confuse Rudolpho and thereby win the hand of his ward, tells him that it is his (Ruldolpho's) own mother, disguised for the festival. Rudolpho is astounded. He orders her arrest.

ACT 2

Banquet Hall in Gorgio's Palace — Lilliano has not forgotten Breda, her old nurse, in spite of her troubles, and determines to avenge herself for the many insults she received in her youth by poisoning her (Breda). She therefore invites the old nurse to a banquet and poisons her. Presently a knock is heard. It is Ugolfo. He has come to carry away the body of Michelo and to leave an extra quart of pasteurized. Lilliano tells him that she no longer loves him, at which he goes away, dragging his feet sulkily.

ACT 3

In Front of Emilo's House – Still thinking of the old man's curse, Borsa has an interview with Cleanso, believing him to be the Duke's wife. He tell him things can't go on as they are, and Cleanso stabs him. Just at this moment Betty comes rushing in from school and falls in a faint. Her worst fears have been realized. She has been insulted by Sigmundo, and presently dies of old age. In a fury, Ugolfo rushes out to kill Sigmundo and, as he does so, the dying Rosenblatt rises on one elbow and curses his mother.

III
LUCY DE LIMA

Scene: *Wales*   Time: 1700 *(Greenwich)*
Cast:
WILLIAM WONT, *Lord of Glenn*   Basso
LUCY WAGSTAFF, *his daughter*   Soprano
BERTRAM, *her lover*   Tenor
LORD ROGER, *friend of Bertram*   Soprano
IRMA, *attendant to Lucy*   Basso
  Friends, Retainers, and Members of the local Lodge
of Elks

ARGUMENT

'Lucy de Lima' is founded on the well-known story by Boccaccio of the same name and address.

ACT I

Gypsy Camp near Waterbury – The gypsies, led by Edith, go singing through the camp on the way to the fair. Following them comes Despard, the gypsy leader, carrying Ethel, whom he has just kidnapped from her father, who had previously just kidnapped her from her mother. Despard places Ethel on the ground and tells Mona, the old hag, to watch over her. Mona nurses a secret grudge against Despard for having once cut off her leg, and decides to change Ethel for Nettie, another kidnapped child. Ethel pleads with Mona to let her stay with Despard, for she has fallen in love with him on the ride over. But Mona is obdurate.

ACT 2

The Fair – A crowd of sightseers and villagers is present. Roger appears, looking for Laura. He can not find her. Laura appears, looking for Roger. She can not find him. The gypsy queen approaches Roger and thrusts into his hand the locket stolen from Lord Brym. Roger looks at it and is frozen with astonishment, for it contains the portrait of his mother when she was in high school. He then realizes that Laura must be his sister, and starts out to find her.

ACT 3

Hall in the Castle – Lucy is seen surrounded by every luxury, but her heart is sad. She has just been shown a forged letter from Stewart saying that he no longer loves her, and she remembers her old free life in the mountains and longs for another romp with Ravensbane and Wolfshead, her old pair of rompers. The guests begin to assemble for the wedding, each bringing a roasted ox. They chide Lucy for not having her dress changed. Just at this moment the gypsy band bursts in and Cleon tells the wedding party that Elsie and not Edith is the child who was stolen from the summer-house, showing the blood-stained bowler as proof. At this, Lord Brym repents and gives his blessing on the pair, while the fishermen and their wives celebrate in the courtyard.

What – No Budapest?

A few weeks ago, in this space, I wrote a little treatise on 'Movie Boners', in which I tried to follow the popular custom of picking technical flaws in motion pictures, detecting, for example, that when a character enters a room he has on a bow tie and when he leaves it is a four-in-hand.

In the course of this fascinating article I wrote: 'In the picture called *Dr. Tanner Can't Eat* there is a scene laid in Budapest. There is no such place as Budapest.'

In answer to this I have received the following communication from M. Schwartzer, of New York City:

'Ask for your money back from your geography teacher. There is such a place as Budapest, and it is not a small village, either. Budapest is the capital of Hungary. In case you never heard of Hungary, it is in Europe. Do you know where Europe is? Respectfully yours,' etc.

I am standing by my guns, Mr. Schwartzer. There is no such place as Budapest. Perhaps you are thinking of Bucharest, and there is no such place as Bucharest, either.

I gather that *your* geography teacher didn't tell you about the Treaty of Ulm in 1802, in which Budapest was eliminated. By the terms of this treaty (I quote from memory):

'Be it hereby enacted that there shall be no more Budapest. This city has been getting altogether too large lately, and the coffee hasn't been any too good, either. So, no more Budapest is the decree of this conference, and if the residents don't like it they can move to some other place.'

This treaty was made at the close of the war of 1805, which was unique in that it began in 1805 and ended in 1802, thereby confusing the contestants so that both sides gave in at once. Budapest was the focal point of the war, as the Slovenes were trying to get rid of it to the Bulgks, and the Bulgks were trying to make the Slovenes keep it. This will explain, Mr. Schwartzer, why there is no such place as Budapest.

If any word other than mine were needed to convince you that you have made a rather ludicrous mistake in this matter, I will quote from a noted authority on non-existent cities, Dr. Almer Doctor, Pinsk Professor of Obduracy in the university of that name. In his *Vanished Cities of Central Europe* he writes:

'Since 1802 there has been no such place as Budapest. It is too bad, but let's face it!'

Or, again, from *Nerdlinger's Atlas* (revised for the Carnation Show in London in 1921):

'A great many uninformed people look in their atlases for the city of Budapest and complain to us when they cannot find it. Let us take this opportunity to make it clear that there is no such place as Budapest and has not been since 1802. The spot which was once known as Budapest is now known as the Danube River, by Strauss.'

I would not rebuke you so publicly, Mr. Schwartzer, had it not been for that crack of yours about my geography teacher. My geography teacher was a very fine woman and later became the mother of four bouncing boys, two of whom are still bouncing. She knew about what happened to Budapest, and she made no bones about it.

In future communications with me I will thank you to keep her name out of this brawl.

How To Understand Music

... We first have the introduction by the wood-winds, in which you will detect the approach of summer, the bassoons indicating the bursting buds (summer and spring came together this year, almost before we were aware of it) and the brasses carrying the idea of winter disappearing, defeated and ashamed, around the corner. Summer approaches (in those sections where you hear the 'tum-tiddy-ump-ump-tiddy-ump-ump.' Remember?) and then, taking one look around, decides that the whole thing is hardly worth while, and goes back into its hole – a new and not entirely satisfactory union of the groundhog tradition with that of the equinox. This, however, ends the first movement, much to the relief of everyone.

You will have noticed that during this depicting of the solstice, the wind section has been forming dark colours right and left, all typical of Tschaikovski in his more wood-wind moods. These dark colours, such as purple, green, and sometimes W and Y, are very lovely once they are recognized. The difficulty comes in recognizing them, especially with beards on. The call of the clarinet, occurring at intervals during this first movement, is clearly the voice of summer, saying, 'Co-boss! Co-boss! Co-boss!' to which the timpani reply, 'Rumble-rumble-rumble!' And a very good reply it is, too.

The second movement begins with Strephon (the eternal shepherd, and something of a bore) dancing up to the hut in which Phyllis is weaving honey, and, by means of a series of descending six-four chords (as in Debussy's *Reflets dans l'eau* which, you will remember, also makes no sense), indicating that he is ready for a romp. Here we hear the dripping coolness of the mountain stream and the jump-jump-jump of the mountain goat, neither of which figures in the story. He is very eager (tar-ra-ty-tar-ra-ty-tar-ra-ty) and says that there is no sense in her being difficult about the thing, for he has everything arranged. At this the oboes go crazy.

I like to think that the two most obvious modulations, the dominant and the subdominant respectively, convey the idea that, whatever it is that Strephon is saying to Phyllis, nobody cares. This would make the whole thing much clearer. The transition from the dominant to the subdominant (or, if you prefer, you may stop over at Chicago for a day and see the bullfights) gives a feeling of adventure, a sort of Old Man River note, which, to me, is most exciting. But then, I am easily excited.

We now come to the third movement, if there is anybody left in the hall. The third movement is the most difficult to understand, as it involves a complete reversal of musical form in which the wood-winds play the brasses, the brasses play the timpani, and the timpani play 'drop-the-handkerchief'. This makes for confusion, as you may very well guess. But, as confusion is the idea, the composer is sitting pretty and the orchestra has had its exercise. The chief difficulty in this movement lies in keeping the A strings so tuned that they sound like B-flat strings. To this end, small boys are employed to keep turning the pegs down and the room is kept as damp as possible.

It is here that Arthur, a character who has, up until now, taken no part in the composition, appears and, just as at the rise of the sixth in Chopin's *Nocturne in E Flat* one feels a certain elation, tells Strephon that he has already made plans for Phyllis for that evening and will he please get the hell out of here. We feel, in the descent of the fourth, that Strephon is saying 'so what?' Any movement in which occurs a rise to the major third suggests conflict (that is, a rise from the key-note to the major third. Get me right on that, please) and similar rise to the minor third, or if you happen to own a bit of U.S. Steel, a rise to 56, suggests a possibility of future comfort. All this, however, is beside the point. (Dorothy Angus, of 1455 Granger Drive, Salt Lake City, has just telephoned in to ask 'what point?' Any point, Dorothy, any point. When you are older you will understand.)

This brings us to the fourth movement, which we will omit, owing to one of the oboes having clamped his teeth down so hard on his mouth-piece as to make further playing a mockery. I am very sorry about this, as the fourth movement has in it one of my favourite passages – that where Strephon unbuttons his coat.

From now on it is anybody's game. The A minor prelude, with its persistent chromatic descent, conflicts with the *andante sostenuto*, where the strings take the melody in bars 7 and 8, and the undeniably witty theme is carried on to its logical conclusion in bars 28 and 30, where the pay-off comes when the man tells his wife that he was in the pantry all the time. I nearly die at this every time that I hear it. Unfortunately, I don't hear it often enough, or long enough at a time.

This, in a way, brings to a close our little analysis of whatever it was we were analysing. If I have made music a little more difficult for you to like, if I have brought confusion into your ear and complication into your taste, I shall be happy in the thought. The next time you hear a symphony, I trust that you will stop all this silly sitting back and taking it for what it is worth to your ear-drums to your emotions, and will put on your thinking caps and try to figure out just what the composer meant when he wrote it. Then perhaps you will write and tell the composer.

Contributors To This Issue

Unfortunately the current issue of our magazine has had to be abandoned because of low visibility and an epidemic of printers' nausea, but we felt that our readers would still want to know a little something of the private lives of our contributors. At any rate, here we go:

ELMWOOD M. CRINGE, who contributed the article *Is Europe?* is a graduate of Moffard College and, since graduation, has specialized in high tension rope. He is thirty-two years old, wears a collar, and his hobbies are golf, bobbing for apples, and junket.

HAL GARMISCH, author of *How It Feels to be Underslung*, writes: 'I am young, good-looking, and would like to meet a girl about my own age who likes to run. I have no hobbies, but I am crazy about kitties.'

MEDFORD LAZENBY probably knows more about people, as such, than anyone in the country, unless it is people themselves. He has been all over the world in a balloon-rigged ketch and has a fascinating story to tell. *China Through a Strainer*, in this issue, is not it.

ELIZABETH FEDELLER, after graduation from Ruby College for Near Sighted Girls, had a good time for herself among the deserted towns of Montana and writes of her experiences in a style which has been compared unfavourably with that of Ernest Hemingway. She is rather unattractive looking.

On our request for information, GIRLIE TENNAFLY wrote

us that he is unable to furnish any, owing to a short memory. He contributed the articles on *Flanges: Open and Shut*, which is not appearing in this issue.

We will let ESTHER RUBRIC tell about herself: 'Strange as it may seem,' writes Miss Rubric, 'I am not a "highbrow", although I write on what are known as "highbrow" subjects. I am really quite a good sport, and love to play tennis (or "play at" tennis, as I call it), and am always ready for a good romp. My mother and father were missionaries in Boston, and I was brought up in a strictly family way. We children used to be thought strange by all the other "kids" in Boston because my brothers had beards and I fell down a lot. But, as far as I can see, we all grew up to be respectable citizens, in a pig's eye. When your magazine accepted by article on *How to Decorate a Mergenthaler Linotype Machine*, I was in the "seventh heaven". I copied it, word for word, from Kipling.'

DARG GAMM is too well-known to our readers to call for an introduction. He is now at work on his next-but-one novel and is in hiding with the Class of 1915 of Zanzer College, who are preparing for their twentieth reunion in June.

We couldn't get IRVIN S. COBB or CLARENCE BUDINGTON KELLAND to answer our request for manuscripts.

Down With Pigeons

St. Francis of Assisi (unless I am getting him mixed up with St. Simeon Stylites, which might be very easy to do as both their names begin with 'St.') was very fond of birds, and often had his picture taken with them sitting on his shoulders and pecking at his wrists. That was all right, if St. Francis liked it. We all have our likes and dislikes, and I have more of a feeling for dogs. However, I am not *against* birds as a class. I am just against pigeons.

I do not consider pigeons birds, in the first place. They

are more in the nature of people; people who mooch. Probably my feeling about pigeons arises from the fact that all my life I have lived in rooms where pigeons came rumbling in and out of my window. I myself must have a certain morbid fascination for pigeons, because they follow me about so much – and with evident ill-will. I am firmly convinced that they are trying to haunt me.

Although I live in the middle of a very large city (well, to show you how large it is – it is the largest in the world) I am awakened every morning by a low gargling sound which turns out to be the result of one, two, or three pigeons walking in at my window and sneering at me. Granted that I am a fit subject for sneering as I lie there, possibly with one shoe on or an unattractive expression on my face, but there is something more than just a passing criticism in these birds making remarks about me. They have some ugly scheme on foot against me, and I know it. Sooner or later it will come out and then I can sue.

This thing has been going on ever since I was in college. In our college everybody was very proud of the pigeons. Anyone walking across the Yard (Campus to you, please) was beset by large birds who insisted on climbing up his waistcoat and looking about in his wallet for nuts or raisins or whatever it is you feed pigeons (bichloride would be my suggestion, but let it pass).

Gods knows that I was decent enough to them in my undergraduate days. I let them walk up and down my back and I tried to be as nice as I could without actually letting them see that I was not so crazy about it. I even gave them chestnuts, chestnuts which I wanted myself. I now regret my generosity, for good chestnuts are hard to get these days.

But somehow the word got around in pigeon circles that Benchley was anti-pigeon. They began pestering me. I would go to bed at night, tired from overstudy, and at six-thirty in the morning the Big Parade would begin. The line of march was as follows: Light on Benchley's win-

dow sill, march once in through the open window, going
'Grumble-grumble-grumble' in a sinister tone. Then out
and stand on the sill, urging other pigeons to come in and
take a crack at it.

There is very little fun in waking up with a headache
and hearing an ominous murmuring noise, with just the
suggestion of a passing shadow moving across your window sill. No man should be asked to submit to this *all*
his life.

I once went to Venice (Italy), and there, with the rest
of the tourists, stood in awe in the centre of St. Mark's
Piazza, gazing at the stately portals of the church and
at the lovely green drinks served at Florian's for those
who don't want to look at the church all of the time.

It is an age-old custom for tourists to feed corn to the
pigeons and then for the pigeons to crawl all over the
tourists. This has been going on without interruptions ever
since Americans discovered Venice. So far as the records
show, no pigeon has ever failed a tourist – and no tourist
has ever failed a pigeon. It is a very pretty relationship.

In my case, however, it was different. In the first place,
the St. Mark's pigeons, having received word from the
American chapter of their lodge, began flying at me in
such numbers and with such force as actually to endanger
my life. They came in great droves, all flying low and
hard, just barely skimming my hat and whirring in an
ugly fashion with some idea of intimidating me. But by
that time I was not to be intimidated, and, although I
ducked very low and lost my hat several times, I did not
give in. I even bought some corn from one of the vendors
and held it out in my hand, albeit with bad grace. But, for
the first time in centuries, no pigeon fell for the corn
gag. I stood alone in the middle of St. Mark's Square, holding out my hand dripping with kernels of golden corn, and
was openly and deliberately snubbed. One or two of the
creatures walked up to within about ten feet of me and
gave me a nasty look, but not one gave my corn a tumble.
So I decided the hell with them and ate the corn myself.

Now this sort of thing must be the result of a very definite boycott, or, in its more aggressive stage, an anti-Benchley campaign. Left to myself, I would have only the very friendliest feelings for pigeons (it is too late now, but I might once have been won over). But having been put on my mettle, there is nothing that I can do now but fight back. Whatever I may be, I am not yellow.

Here is my plan. I know that I am alone in this fight, for most people like pigeons, or, at any rate, are not antagonized by them. But single-handed I will take up the cudgels, and I hope that, when they grow up, my boys will carry on the battle on every cornice and every campus in the land.

Whenever I meet a pigeon, whether it be on my own window sill or walking across a public park, I will stop still and place my hands on my hips and wait. If the pigeon wants to make the first move and attack me, I will definitely strike back, even to the extent of hitting it with my open palm and knocking it senseless (not a very difficult feat, I should think, as they seem to have very little sense).

If they prefer to fight it out by innuendo and sneering, I will fight it out by innuendo and sneering. I have worked up a noise which I can make in my throat which is just as unpleasant sounding as theirs. I will even take advantage of my God-given power of speech and will say, 'Well, what do you want to make of it, you waddling, cooing so-and-sos?' I will glare at them just as they glare at me, and if they come within reach of my foot, so help me, St. Francis, I will kick at them. *And* the next pigeon that strolls in across my window ledge when I am just awakening, I will catch with an especially prepared trap and will drag into my room, there to punch the living daylights out of him.

I know that this sounds very cruel and very much as if I were an animal hater. As a matter of fact, I am such a friend of animals in general that I am practically penniless, I have been known to take in dogs who were obviously impostors and put them through college. I am a sucker for kittens, even though I know that one day they will grow into cats who will betray and traduce me. I have even been known to pat a tiger cub, which accounts for my writing this article with my left hand.

But as far as pigeons go, I am through. It is a war to the death, and I have a horrible feeling that the pigeons are going to win.

EDMUND CLERIHEW BENTLEY

The Art of Biography
Is different from Geography.
Geography is about maps,
But Biography is about chaps.

Sir Christopher Wren
Said, 'I am going to dine with some men.
'If anyone calls
'Say I am designing St. Paul's.'

Sir Humphry Davy
Detested gravy.
He lived in the odium
Of having discovered sodium.

John Stuart Mill,
By a mighty effort of will,
Overcame his natural *bonhomie*
And wrote *Principles of Political Economy*.

What I like about Clive
Is that he is no longer alive.
There is a great deal to be said
For being dead.

Edward the Confessor
Slept under the dresser.
When that began to pall,
He slept in the hall.

I do not extenuate Bunyan's
Intemperate use of onions,
But if I knew a wicked ogress
I would lend her *The Pilgrim's Progress*.

'Susaddah!' exclaimed Ibsen,
'By dose is turdig cribson!
'I'd better dot kiss you.
'Atishoo! Atishoo!'

'Dear me!' exclaimed Homer,
'What a delicious aroma!
'It smells as if a town
'Was being burnt down.'

It was rather disconcerting for Hannibal
To be introduced to a cannibal
Who expressed the very highest opinion
Of cold pickled Carthaginian.

I count Zinghis Khan
As rather an over-rated man.
After all, what could be easier
Than conquering from the Pacific to Silesia?

Sir James Jeans
Always says what he means:
He is really perfectly serious
About the universe being mysterious.

The meaning of the poet Gay
Was always as clear as day,
While that of the poet Blake
Was often practically opaque.

Lewis Carroll
Bought sumptuous apparel
And built an enormous palace
Out of the profits of *Alice*.

'Dinner time?' said Gilbert White,
'Yes, yes – certainly – all right.
'Just let me finish this note
'About the Lesser White-bellied Stoat.'

Professor Dewar
Is a better man than you are.
None of you asses
Can condense gases.

When they told Cimabue
He didn't know how to cooeee
He replied, 'Perhaps I mayn't,
'But I do know how to paint.'

George the Third
Ought never to have occurred.
One can only wonder
At so grotesque a blunder.

The digestion of Milton
Was unequal to Stilton.
He was only feeling so-so
When he wrote *Il Penseroso*.

Dante Alighieri
Seldom troubled a dairy.
He wrote the *Inferno*
On a bottle of Pernod.

Henry the Eighth
Took a thucththethion of mateth.
He inthithted that the monkth
Were a lathy lot of thkunkth.

Edgar Allan Poe
Was passionately fond of roe.
He always liked to chew some
When writing anything gruesome.

It is curious that Handel
Should always have used a candle.
Men of his stamp
Generally use a lamp.

CYRANO DE BERGERAC

Voyage To The Moon

'Now I must tell you the manner in which I came here myself. You have not forgotten, I suppose, that my name is Elijah, for I told you so just now. You must know then that I was in your world and that I dwelt with Elisha, a Hebrew like myself, on the banks of the Jordan where I spent among books a life pleasant enough not to make me regret that it was continually passing away. However, as the enlightenment of my spirit increased, the knowledge of the enlightenment I did not possess increased also. Whenever our priests reminded me of Adam I could not forbear sighing at the recollection of that perfect Philosophy he had possessed. I despaired of being able to acquire it, when one day, after I had sacrificed to expiate the sins of my mortal Being, I fell asleep and the Angel of the Lord appeared to me in a dream. As soon as I awoke I failed not to labour at those things he had commanded me; I took of loadstone two square feet and cast it into a furnace, and when it was purged, precipitated and dissolved, I drew out the attractive principle, calcined the whole elixir and reduced it to the bulk of a medium-sized ball.

'Following upon these preparations I had made a very light chariot of iron and some months later, all my engines being completed, I entered my ingenious cart. Perhaps you will ask what was the use of this appliance? Know then that the Angel told me in my dream that if I desired to acquire the perfect knowledge I wished for I should rise from the world to the Moon, where I should find the Tree of Knowledge in Adam's Paradise and as soon as I had tasted its fruit my soul would perceive all the truths a created mind can perceive. For this voyage I had built my chariot. I got into it and when I was well and firmly seated in it I cast the loadstone ball high into the air. Now I had expressly made my iron machine thicker in the middle than at the ends and so it was lifted immediately in perfect equilibrium because it moved always more eagerly in that part. Thus, directly I arrived where the loadstone had drawn me I threw up the ball again in the air above me.'

'But,' I interrupted, 'how did you throw the ball so straight above your chariot that it never went sideways?'

'I see nothing astounding in this adventure,' said he, 'for when the loadstone was cast into the air it attracted the iron straight to it and consequently it was impossible that I should rise sideways. I must tell you that I held the ball in my hand and continued to rise because the chariot rushed always towards the loadstone which I held above it; but the movement of the iron to join with the ball was so vigorous that it bent my body double and I dared not attempt the new experiment more than once. In truth it was a very surprising spectacle to behold, for I had polished the steel of this flying house carefully and it reflected on all sides the light of the Sun so keenly and sharply that I myself thought I was being carried away in a chariot of fire. At length after I had many times thrown the ball upwards and had flown after it, I arrived (as you did) at a place where I began to fall towards this world; and because at the moment I happened to be holding the loadstone ball tightly in my hands my chariot pressed against me to approach the body which attracted it and therefore did not leave me. All I had to fear now was breaking my neck, but to preserve myself from that I threw the ball from time to time so that my machine, feeling itself attracted back, would rest and so break the force of my fall. Finally, when I was about two or three hundred toises above the ground I threw the ball out on either side level with the chariot, sometimes in the one direction and sometimes in the other, until my eyes discovered the Earthly Paradise. Immediately I failed not to throw my loadstone above it and, when the machine followed, I let myself fall until I saw I was about to be hurled against the ground; then I threw the ball upwards a foot only above my head and this little cast diminished altogether the speed I had acquired in falling so that my descent was no more violent than if I had jumped down my own height. I will not describe to you my amazement at the sight of the marvels which are here, because it was very similar to that which I perceive has just perturbed you.

'You must know, however, that the next day I came upon the Tree of Life, by whose means I prevented myself from growing old. Age very soon disappeared and the serpent went up in smoke.'

At these words I said, 'Venerable and holy Patriarch, I should be happy to know what you mean by this serpent which disappeared.'

With a laughing face he replied thus: 'I forgot, O my son, to reveal to you a secret which could not hitherto have been imparted to you. You must know then that after Eve and her husband had eaten the forbidden apple, God punished the serpent that had tempted them by confining it in man's body. Since then in punishment for the crime of the first father every human being who is born nourishes in his belly, a serpent, the issue of the first one. You call this the bowels and think them necessary for the functions of life, but learn that they are nothing else than a serpent coiled upon itself in several folds. When you hear your guts rumble, it is the serpent that hisses and, according to that gluttonous nature with which he formerly incited the first man to eat too much, asks for food himself. God, to punish you, desired to make you mortal like other animals, and caused you to be possessed by this insatiable beast, to the intent that if you feed him too much you choke yourself or, if you refuse him his pittance when the starveling gnaws your stomach with his invisible teeth, then he rumbles, he rages, he pours out that venom which doctors call bile and so hests you with the poison he pours into your arteries that you are soon destroyed by it' ...

... My conductor led me into a magnificently furnished room but I saw nothing prepared to eat. Such a lack of meat when I was perishing of hunger forced me to ask him where the table was laid. I did not hear what he replied, for three or four young boys, the host's children, came up to me at that instant and with great civility undressed me to the shirt. This new ceremonial vastly astonished me, but I dared not ask its reason of my handsome attendants; and when my guide asked how I should like to begin I know not how I was able to reply with these two words: 'A soup'. Immediately I smelt the odour of the most succulent simmering that ever hit the nose of a rich sinner. I tried to get up from my place to track down with my nose the source of this agreeable vapour, but my guide prevented me: 'Where are you going?' said he, 'we will take a walk soon, but this is the time to eat; finish your soup and then we will have something else.'

'But where the devil is the soup?' cried I in a rage. 'Have you made a wager to banter me all day?'

'I thought,' he replied, 'that you had seen at the town whence we came either your master or someone else taking his meals; that is why I did not tell you of their methods of eating in this country. But since you are still ignorant of it, let me tell you that here they live on nothing but vapour. The art of cookery here is to enclose in large, specially moulded vessels the fumes which rise from meats, and, having collected several kinds and several tastes, according to the appetite of those they entertain, they open the vessel which holds this odour and then another and then another until the company is quite satisfied. Unless you have already lived in this manner you will never believe that the nose unassisted by the teeth and throat can perform the office of the mouth in feeding a man; but I will make you see it by experience.'

He had scarcely finished his promise when I smelled successively as they entered the room so many agreeable and nourishing vapours that I felt myself completely satisfied in less than a half-quarter of an hour. When we had risen he said, 'This should not cause you a great deal of surprise, since you cannot have lived so long without having noticed that in your world cooks and pastry-cooks, who eat less than people of other occupations, are nevertheless fatter than they are. Whence is their fatness derived, unless it be from the smell of the food that perpetually surrounds them, penetrates their bodies and nourishes them? People in this world enjoy a more vigorous and less interrupted health, because their food causes hardly any excrements, which are the origin of almost all diseases. You were surprised perhaps when they undressed you before the meal, because the custom is never employed in your country, but here it is, and it is done in order that the animal may imbibe the vapour more easily' ...

... They asked me why I came so late.

'It is not my fault,' I replied to the cook, who was complaining of it, 'several times in the street I asked what time it was, but they only answered by opening the mouth, clenching the teeth and writhing the face askew.'

' "What!" cried everybody, "you did not know they were telling you the time that way?" '

'Faith,' I replied, 'they might show their great noses to the Sun all they would before I should have learnt it.'

' "Tis a convenience", said they, which permits them to dispense with a watch. With their teeth they make so exact a dial that when they wish to tell someone the time they simply open their lips and the shadow of their nose falling upon them marks the hour as if upon a dial. Now, in order that you may know why every one in this land has a large nose, learn that as soon as a woman is delivered the midwife carries the child to the Prior of the Seminary.

18

And, at the end of a year his nose is measured before the assembly of experts by the Syndic, and if by this measure it is found too short, the child is reputed a Snub-nose and handed over to the priests, who castrate him. You will perhaps ask the reason of this barbarity and how it happens that we, among whom virginity is a crime, establish continence by force? Learn then that we act in this way from thirty centuries of observation showing that a large nose is a sign over our door that says, "Here lodges a witty, prudent, courteous, affable, generous and liberal man", and that a small nose is the sign-post of the opposite vices. That is why we make eunuchs of our snub-nosed children, for the Republic prefers to have no children from them than children like them' ...

... ' "And I," said he, "will prove to you the contrary. To begin with, suppose that you ate a Mohammedan; you convert him consequently into your own substance! Is it not true that when you have digested this Mohammedan he is changed partly into flesh, partly into blood, partly into seed? You embrace your wife and with the seed drawn entirely from this Mohammedan's body you cast the mould of a pretty little Christian. I ask: will the Mohammedan have his body at the resurrection? If the earth yields it up to him, the little Christian will not have his body, since it is only a part of the Mohammedan's. If you tell me that the Christian will have his, God will have to take from the Mohammedan's body. And so inevitably one or the other will be without a body! You will reply perhaps that God will reproduce from matter a body to furnish the one who is without a body? Yes, but another difficulty stops us. Suppose the damned Mohammedan is resurrected and God gives him a new body, because the Christian has stolen his old one, since the body alone does not make the man, any more than the soul alone, but the two joined together in one person, and since the soul and the body each departed from the man whole, if God then makes the Mohammedan another body, it is no longer the same individual. So God damns a man who is not the man who has merited Hell. One body has whored, it has criminally abused all the senses and, to punish this body, God casts into the fire another, which is virgin and pure, and has never lent its organs to the performance of the slightest crime. And what is even more ridiculous is that this body will have deserved both Hell and Paradise; for, in so far as it is Mohammedan, it must be damned, and in so far as it is Christian, it must be saved. Thus God cannot put it in paradise without being unjust and rewarding with glory instead of with the damnation it deserved as Mohammedan; and He cannot cast it into Hell without being unjust and rewarding with eternal death instead of the blessedness it deserved as Christian. Then, if He wishes to be just, He must both save and damn this man eternally" ' ...

BASIL BOOTHROYD

Can You Read Music?

Rachmaninov, as everyone knows, used to get mad with people who thought his C sharp minor Prelude described a man nailed into his coffin on insufficient medical evidence who kept banging on the lid to attract passers-by. Rachmaninov said that this was rubbish. He simply had the idea of writing a prelude, selected a key, and wrote it. Why he couldn't have selected an easier key is neither here nor there, and only opens up that old mystery for halting executants, viz. what have all the other keys got that the key of C hasn't? But I realize that this is the lower criticism, and a subordinate theme at that.

What I'm concerned with at the moment is the man who announced the Egmont Overture on the radio the other day, and told me I was in for 'a thrilling expression of the composer's belief in human rights'. Now, I haven't thought very highly of Beethoven in the past. His

work has seemed a bit thick and straining to me, not unlike a dull but efficient exhibition of weight-lifting; nor do
I care for his endings, with enough repetitions of the
common chord to make me yell 'All right, all *right*'. But
this new light on the man sends my respect shooting up.
A composer who can juggle the reed, brass and catgut to
convey his belief in human rights is fully entitled to have
his scaled-down bust on the top of school pianos. The
theme isn't an easy one to get over in an orchestral score.
You can't even fall back on onomatopeia, really. Tchaikovsky with his bells of Moscow leaves us in no doubt what's
going on. Delius with his cuckoos is instantly interpret-
able. But getting eighty musicians to sound like the Magna
Carta is another kettle of drums.

As a matter of fact, the whole business of getting the
musical message worries me. What are the composers saying to us, as we close our eyes and concentrate, trying to
forget that the contra-bassoonist looks exactly like Roy
Welensky? Works with evocative titles are simple. The
Skaters' Waltz leaves us in no doubt of Waldteufel's intention, apart from a passing speculation whether the
skating is ice or roller. No one mutters 'What the hell is
this?' when their programme clearly advertises Night on
the Bare Mountain. But there you are, of course. The programme blows the gaff. Can we honestly say that if we
didn't know the title in advance we shouldn't sit through
Night on the B.M. thinking that Moussorgsky was rhap-
sodizing about collective farms or men's-wear trends?
Even The Skaters' Waltz, if rashly loosed on a non-French-
speaking public as *Les Patineurs*, could have them tapping
their feet dreamily to private visions of pastry-cooks at
work in sun-drenched Provence.

When we come, therefore, to works coldly and aca-
demically titled Etude, or Suite for Oboe and Strings, or
Concerto No. 47, the whole field of interpretation lies
open. They could be telling us about ethics; the Zuyder
Zee; the lack of moral fibre among deck-hands on a lentil
ship. It's just a matter of taking our pick. What is the

Alban Berg violin concerto all about, to take a somewhat challenging example? This is the work, as you will recall wryly, in which the soloist appears to select notes at random for a long time and then stop. What is Herr Berg saying to *you*, as you sit there looking rapt and thinking how well a few bars of 'Bam-Bam-Bammy Shore' would drop in at this point? It's all very well to be told by the programme about the chromatic major ninth suggesting a 'joyous upsurge of the spirit'; as far as I'm concerned, this particular passage has a sharp melancholy, and suggests men trying to drag a tree up a rocky slope, its branches constantly getting snagged up with tough little shrubs (chord of the major thirteenth, very likely) and immense irregular boulders (supertonic seventh to B flat). On the other hand, the lady sitting next to us, who was trying to beat time but has now given up, wears a faint reminiscent smile. To her, perhaps, the music speaks of happy Sheffield tram rides of long ago; or of the feeling you get when you hear birds running about in the false roof and wonder if you ought to go up there and get them out.

By what authority – this is what I want to know – by what authority does the programme note on the Tchaikovsky Sixth tell me that in the fourth movement I'm being treated to 'a grim dance between Death and the Neurotic, with a last hysterical protest against the inevitable? Who spread this story in the first place? Tchaikovsky? I see that the Dvorak No. 8 ('known as No. 4' but what the heck) gives me a picture of the composer 'at first in church, later in his garden'; while his No. 9 ('known as No. 5', if you like documentation) shows him 'filled with sympathy for the oppressed coloured peoples.' All right. If you say so. And thanks for all your help.

But do I need it? Granted, if I'm told about the church and the garden and the coloured folk, I can probably make myself hear tombs and outhouses and Uncle Tom's Cabin. But if I'm not told – and I didn't ask to be – what's to prevent me hearing greyhounds being exercised, or heavily photogenic waves crashing on the esplanade at Hove?

I don't mind accepting a tip or two on the technical side. I might easily miss 'the drone-bass on the cellos suggesting bagpipes' (and glad to, actually). In the same way, 'the inverted secondary theme returning a semitone higher' could well elude me, and I welcome these simple aids to added enjoyment. But when it comes to what the composer is *saying*, could I make a few personal decisions? For instance:

Haydn's No. 102 in B flat expresses his lifelong fear of falling through the bottom of a sedan chair.

The greater part of the works of Liszt reflect his advocacy of cheap boots for agricultural workers.

In his variations on the Paganini theme, Brahms is commenting subtly on physics and dynamics, including light-hearted references to Boyle's Law and Fletcher's Trolley.

I'm quite prepared to have these views challenged by people who think they know better. Perhaps they do know better. But if I'm not as free as the next man to express an opinion, then it looks to me as if Beethoven, standing up for me as he did in the Egmont, was more or less wasting his time.

Why Dogs Bite Gardeners

You mustn't think I'm not sorry for Lady Astor of Hever, because I am. It's no joke to break your foot and have to crawl about the estate, accompanied by three barking French whippets, until gardeners come to the rescue and wheel you to safety in a barrow. On the other hand, if you're a gardener loading a lady into a barrow, it's no joke to be bitten by three French whippets 'apparently thinking the gardeners were abducting their mistress'. Lord Astor, even, was moved to comment: 'It was hard luck to be bitten ... but the men seemed to understand. We hadn't the heart to scold the dogs.'

My source of information is one of the more nobility-fancying Press gossips, and as this particular piece carried news not only of the Astors but of the Queen, Prince Philip, Princess Birgitta of Sweden, Prince Johan of Hohenzollern, Sir Guy and Lady Shaw-Stewart, Sir Timothy Eden, Lord Downe, Lord Combermere and the Earl of Leicester, it was obviously impossible to introduce any sort of statement from mere gardeners. As Lord Astor said – avoiding any degrading suggestion of direct spokesmanship – they seemed to understand. The point I want to make is that the dogs didn't. They barked for help, and when help came they attacked it. It now gives me great pleasure to attack the dogs. The Astors may not have had the heart to scold them. I have.

These dogs, like all dogs, were fools. Admirers of the canine intelligence, so-called, tweedy folk of the 'he-understands-every-word-we-say' school, will be shocked to read this. And not before time. 'How lucky', they have been saying to each other, 'that the dogs were there to bark for help. And of *course* when those great rough gardener men came stamping round in their horrid gaiters they bit them. Why, poor little things, they must have been in an awful state.' I don't take this view. I take one or two others.

(a) The dogs weren't barking for help at all. They were just barking. This is the average dog's contribution to any already exasperating situation, and is one of many pointers to the essential dimness of the species. If the dog had any whit of the intelligence ascribed to him he would know that, for instance, any domestic crisis involving, say, dropped crockery or a bird catching fire on removal from the oven, would be a good time to get out of sight under the table and stay there. How many dogs have the intelligence to see this? Instead, they go into fits of yelping hysterics, showing the whites of their eyes and plunging into the storm-centre, where they trip people up and get their feet wedged in the vegetable-rack. Lady Astor's dogs were instinctively making a confounded nuisance of themselves. Either they resented her being on all fours, trying to get into their act, or they felt intuitively that she was in trouble, and that a concerted bout of shrill barking would stand a good chance of making things more difficult than they were already. Intelligence didn't come into it.

(b) Supposing, just for the sake of argument, that it did. Supposing they worked this thing out rationally.

1st FRENCH WHIPPET: (*in French, but never mind*) Look chaps, Mistress has fallen down.

2nd F.W.: How come? I wasn't watching.

3rd F.W.: Tripped, I think. What's she saying?

1st F.W.: Sounds like, 'oo, my foot.' She's starting to crawl. Ought we to get help?

2nd F.W.: Pardon? Sorry, interesting smell here. Well, she won't get far at that rate. What about a good bark? Might fetch the gardeners.

3rd F.W.: Not a bad idea. All set then?

All: Row-row! Row-row-row! Row-row-row-row! Row-row-row (Etc)

How's that for a reconstruction, dog-lovers? Chime in with your theories all right, does it? Good. Then let's move forward in time about ten minutes. Dimly, above the canine SOS, feet are heard approaching through the under-growth.

All F.W.'s: (*as before*) Row-row! Row-row-row-row! (Etc.)

1st F.W.: Here come the gardeners, chaps.

2nd F.W.: They've spotted her.

3rd F.W.: They're lifting her up. Row-row-row!

1st F.W.: Row-row!

2nd F.W.: They've fetched a barrow. Row-row-row!

3rd F.W.: Ready boys? They're putting her into it. Stand by to bite gardeners.

1st F.W.: Bags I first. Grrr-rr-rr!

All: Grrr!

They sink teeth into gardeners' calves, ankles, wrists, etc.

Of course, I realize I haven't a chance of swaying dog-lovers. They'll soon find a way to explain and defend this sudden lapse from rational Good Samaritan into berserk fangster. One of the gardeners, no doubt, was wearing a jumble-sale hat, formerly the property of a Russian agent. Or the dogs had been following the Lady Chatterley case, and feared the worst as soon as they saw a coarse hand laid on their stricken mistress.

Well, I'm sorry. I've nothing against dogs, any more than I've anything against the Astors. I just want to explode the intelligence myth, that's all. I've even got a dog of my own. His name's Spot, and you only have to mention a word that rhymes with it, such as clot or guillemot, and he's up from the hearthrug trying to get an imaginary biscuit out of the hand you're holding your glass in. Other indications of his having no sense whatsoever include seeing off the goldfish, thinking it's bedtime and cringing into his kennel in mid-afternoon when all you've suggested is a strategic walk around the garden, trying to go upstairs when two men are coming down with a wardrobe, jumping up for twenty minutes at a tennis-ball on a string plainly two feet out of range, not being able to find a bit of cheese-rind he's standing with his foot on, and barking his head off every night at six when I come home, still not knowing my footsteps from a Broadmoor fugitive's after seven years of hearing them every night at six.

Dogs are fools, but at least I know it. When mine finds me crawling home on all fours with a broken foot it won't surprise me at all if he sinks his teeth in the rescue party. The real surprise will be if he doesn't sink them in me.

ERNEST BRAMAH

Kai Lung Unrolls His Mat

The Story of Wan and the Remarkable Shrub

... At a period so remote that it would be impious to doubt whatever happened then, a venerable and prosperous philosopher, Ah-shoo by name, dwelt at the foot of a

mountain in a distant province. His outward life was
simple but reserved, and although he spent large sums of
money on fireworks and other forms of charity he often
professed his indifference to wealth and position. Yet it
must not be supposed that Ah-shoo was unmindful of the
essentials, for upon it being courteously pointed out to
him, by a well-disposed neighbour who had many
daughters of his own, that in failing to provide a reliable
posterity he was incurring a grave risk of starvation in
the Upper World, he expressed a seemly regret for the
oversight and at once arranged to marry an elderly person
who chanced at the time to be returning his purified wearing apparel. It was to this incident that the one with whom
this related story is chiefly concerned owed his existence,
and when the philosopher's attention was diverted to the
occurrence he bestowed on him the name of Wan, thereby
indicating that he was born towards the evening of his
begetter's life, and also conveying the implication that
the achievement was one that could scarcely be expected
to be repeated. On this point he was undoubtedly inspired.

When Wan reached the age of manhood the philosopher
abruptly Passed Above without any interval of prepara-
tion. It had been his custom to engage Wan in philosophical discussion at the close of each day, and on this occasion
he was contrasting the system of Ka-ping, who maintained
that the world was suspended from a powerful fibrous
rope, with that of Tai-u, who contended that it was sup-
ported upon a substantial bamboo pole. With the clear
insight of an original and discerning mind, Ah-shoo had
already detected the fundamental weakness of both
theories.

'If the earth was indeed dependent on the flexible re-
tention of an unstable cord, it is inevitable that during
the season of Much Wind it must from time to time have
been blown into a reversed position, with the distressing
result that what was the East when we composed ourselves to sleep would be the West when we awoke from
our slumber, to the confusion of all ordinary process of

observation and the well-grounded annoyance of those who, being engaged upon a journey, found themselves compelled to return and set out again in the opposite direction. As there exists no tradition of this having ever happened it is certain that the ingenious Ka-ping did not walk in step with the verities.'

'Then the system of the profound Tai-u is the one to be regarded?' inquired Wan respectfully.

' "Because Hi is in the wrong it does not automatically follow that Ho is necessarily right",' quoted Ah-shoo, referring to the example of two celebrated astrologers who were equally involved in error. 'The ill-conceived delusion of the obsolete Tai-u is no less open to logical disapproval than the grotesque fallacy of the badly informed Ka-ping. If a rigid and unyielding staff of wood upheld the world it is obvious that when the ground became dry and crumbling, the upper end of the pole would enlarge the socket in which it was embedded, and the earth, thus deprived of a firm and stable basis, would oscillate with every considerable movement upon its upper side. Even more disturbing would be the outcome of a season of continuous flood, such as our agreeable land frequently enjoys, for then, owing to the soft and pliant nature of the soil, and the ever-increasing weight of the impending structure, the pole would continue to sink deeper and deeper into the mass, until at length it would protrude upon the upper side, when the earth, deprived of all support, would slide down the pole until it plunged into the impenetrable gloom of the Beneath Parts.'

'Yes,' suggested Wan with becoming deference, 'if the point of the staff concerned should have been resourcefully embedded in a formidable block of stone —'

'The system of the self-opinionated Tai-u contains no reference to any such block of stone,' replied Ah-shoo coldly, for it was not wholly agreeable to his sense of the harmonies that the one who was his son should seek to supply Tai-u's deficiency. 'Furthermore, the difficulty of hewing out the necessary incision for the head of the pole to fit into, in view of the hardness of the rock and the inverted position in which the workers must necessarily toil, would be insuperable. Consider well another time, O Wan, before you intervene. "None but a nightingale should part his lips merely to emit sound".'

'Your indulgent censure will henceforth stimulate my powers of silence,' declared the dutiful Wan in a straightforward voice. 'Otherwise it would have been my inopportune purpose to learn of your undoubted omniscience what actually does support the earth.'

'The inquiry is a natural one,' replied Ah-shoo more genially, for it was a desire to set forth his own opinion on the subject that had led him to approach the problem, 'and your instinct in referring it to me is judicious. The world is kept in its strict and inflexible position by —'

Who having found a jewel lifts his voice to proclaim the fact, thereby inviting one and all to claim a share? Rather does he put an unassuming foot upon the spot and direct attention to the auspicious movements of a distant flock of birds or the like until he can prudently stoop to secure what he has seen. Certainly the analogy may not be exact at all its angles, but in any case Ah-shoo would have been well advised to speak with lowered voice. It is to be inferred that the philosopher did not make a paper boast when he spoke of possessing the fundamental secret of the earth's stability but that the High Powers were unwilling at that early stage of our civilization for the device to become generally understood. Ah-shoo was therefore fated to suffer for his indiscretion, and this took the form of a general stagnation of the attributes, so that although he lingered for a further period before he Passed Above he was unable to express himself in a coherent form. Being deprived of the power of speech he remembered, when too late, that he had neglected to initiate Wan into any way of applying his philosophical system to a remunerative end; while it so happened that his store of wealth was unusually low owing to an imprudently generous contribution to a scheme for permanently driving evil beings out of the neighbourhood, by a series of continuous explosions.

It is no longer necessary to conceal the fact that throughout his life Ah-shoo had in reality played a somewhat two-faced part. In addition to being a profound philosopher and a polite observer of the forms he was, in secret, an experienced magician and in that capacity he was able to transmute base matter into gold. For this purpose he kept a variety of coloured fluids in a shuttered recess of the wall, under a strict injunction. Having now a natural craving to assure Wan's future comfort he endeavoured by a gesture to indicate this source of affluence, confident that the one in question would not fail to grasp the significance of anything brought to his notice at so precise a moment, and thus be led to test the properties of the liquids and in the end to discover their potency. Unfortunately, Ah-shoo's vigour was by this time unequal to the required strain and his inefficient hand could not raise itself higher than to point towards an inscribed tablet suspended at a lower level upon the wall. This chancing to be a delineation of The Virtues, warning the young against the pursuit of wealth, against trafficking with doubtful Forces, and so forth, Wan readily accepted the gesture as a final encouragement towards integrity on the part of an affectionate and pure-minded father and dutifully prostrating himself he specifically undertook to avoid the enticements described. It was in vain that the distracted Ah-shoo endeavoured to remove this impression and to indicate his meaning more exactly. His feeble limb was incapable of a more highly sustained effort, and the more desperately he strove to point the more persistently Wan kowtowed acquiescently and bound himself by an ever-increasing array of oaths and penalties to shun the snare of riches and to avoid all connection with the forbidden. Finally, this inability to make himself understood engendered a fatal acridity within the magician's throat, so that, with an expression of scarcely veiled contempt on his usually benevolent features, he rolled from side to side several times in despair and then passed out into the Upper Region.

It was not long before Wan began to experience an uncomfortable deficiency of taels. The more ordinary places of concealment were already familiar to his investigating thumb, but even the most detailed search failed to disclose Ah-shoo's expected hoard. When at length very little of the structural portion of the house remained intact, Wan was reluctantly compelled to admit that no such store existed.

'It is certainly somewhat inconsiderate of the one to whom my very presence here is due, to have inculcated in me a contempt for riches and a fixed regard for The Virtues, and then to have Passed Away without making any adequate provision for maintaining the position,' remarked Wan to the sharer of his inner chamber, as he abandoned his search as hopeless. 'Tastes such as these are by no means easy to support.'

'Perchance,' suggested Lan-yen, the one referred to, helpfully, 'it was part of an ordered scheme, thereby to inspire a confidence in your own exertions.'

'The confidence inspired by the possession of a well filled vault of silver will last an ordinary person a lifetime,' replied Wan, with an entire absence of enthusiasm. 'Further, the philosophical outfit, which so capably enables one to despise riches in the midst of affluence, seems to have overlooked any system of procuring them when destitution threatens.'

ROBERT JONES BURDETTE

The Legend of Mimir

It is a beautiful legend of the Norse land. Amilias was the village blacksmith, and under the spreading chestnut treekjn, his village smithophjken stood. He the hot iron gehammered and sjhod horses for fifty cents all round please.

He made tin hjelmets for the gjodds, and stove pjipe trousers for the hjeroes.

Mimir was a rival blacksmith. He didn't go in very much for defensive armour, but he was lightning on two-edged Bjswords and cut and slash svjcutlasssses. He made cheese knives for the gjodds, and he made the great Bjsvsstnsen, an Arkansaw toothpick that would take a free incision clear into the transverse semi-colon of a cast-iron Ichthyosaurus, and never turn its edge. That was the kind of a Bhjairpin Mimir said he was.

One day Amilias made an impenetrable suit of armour for a second-class gjodd, and put it on himself to test it, and boastfully inserted a card in the *Svensska Norder-bjravisk jkanaheldesplvtden-skgorodovusaken*, saying that he was wearing a suit of home-made chilled Norway merino underwear that would knick the unnumbered saw teeth in the pot metal cutlery of the ironmongery over the way. That, Amilias remarked to his friend Bjohnn Bjrobinsson, was the kind of a Bdjueckk he was.

When Mimir spelled out the card next morning, he said, 'Bjjj!' and went to work with a charcoal furnace, a cold anvil, and the new isomorphic process, and in a little while he came down-street with a sjword that glittered like a dollar-store diamond, and met Amilias down by the new opera-house. Amilias buttoned on his new Bjarmor and said :

'If you have no hereafter use for your chyjeese kjnife, strike.'

Mimir spat on his hands, whirled his skjword above his head, and fetched Amilias a swipe that seemed to miss everything except the empty air, through which it softly whistled. Amilias smiled, and said 'Go on,' adding that 'it seemed to him he felt a general sense of cold iron some-where in the neighbourhood, but he hadn't been hit.'

'Shake yourself,' said Mimir.

Amilias shook himself and immediately fell into halves, the most neatly divided man that ever went beside himself.

'That's where the boiler-maker was away off in his diagnosis,' said Mimir, as he went back to his shop to put up the price of cutlery 65 per cent, in all lines, with an unlimited advance on special orders.

Thus do we learn that a good action is never thrown away, and that kind words and patient love will overcome the harshest natures.

The Type-writer

CARDINAL — 'Beneath the sliding rule of men entirely great
　　　　　The type-writer is greater than the sword.'

OLDGOLD — 'Who swored, my lord?'

CARDINAL — 'The man who received the type-writer letter;
　　　　　The printers who set up the copy;
　　　　　Whole worlds spelled in the space of one
　　　　　　　　　　small m,
　　　　　With all the letters piled on top of one
　　　　　　　　　　another.
　　　　　Like to a Chinese sentence standing on its
　　　　　　　　　　head.
　　　　　What sense is there in this — "Rgw? GHops
　　　　　　　　　　fll dww d ¶"
　　　　　And yet I know it means "the horse fell
　　　　　　　　　　dead."
　　　　　In all the lexicons we use there's no such
　　　　　　　　　　word
　　　　　As "kbftMa)$n ¶ ;" yet full well I know
　　　　　It stands in this man's note for "information;"
　　　　　I have so learned the tangled language of the
　　　　　　　　　　thing
　　　　　That all its jargon is writ plain for me;
　　　　　But solely do I fear that, learning it,
　　　　　I have made a hopeless wreck of temperate
　　　　　　　　　　speech,
　　　　　And lost my front-pew standing in the syna-
　　　　　　　　　　gogue.

See, all around this line of consonants
Scarred with lost capitals, the proof-reader
                                    has drawn
His awful circle with the pencil blue;
Stand off : while on this correspondent's head
I launch the cuss of our Composing Room.
                            (The cuss.)
Dog gone the billy be dog goned man of
                                    thumbs,
The diddledy dag goned chalky fingered loon
Y gum;' gaul; od rabbit; jeeminy pelt!
Gad zooks; odd beddikins; by Venus' glove;
By Mars his gauntlet; by the river side;
Sweet by and by, and bo oh, baby by —
(At this point the caitiff slowly withers
                                    away).

GELETT BURGESS

From Burgess Unabridged

Samoa has an ideal language, and there it was I got my
inspiration. Can't we make English as subtle as Samoan?
I wondered. There they have a single word, meaning, 'A
– party – is – approaching – which – contains – neither
– a – clever – man – nor – a – pretty – woman.' Another
beautiful word describes 'A – man – who – climbs – out –
on – the – limbs – of – his – own – breadfruit – tree – to
– steal – the – breadfruit – of – his – neighbour.' *Suiia*
means 'Change – the – subject – you – are – on dangerous
– ground.' Another is : 'To – look – on – owl – eyed –
while – others – are – getting – gifts.' Have we anything in
English as charmingly tactful as this? No, our tongue is
almost as crude as pidjin-English itself, where piano is
'Box-you-fight-him-cry.'

But the time has come for a more scientific attempt to
enlarge the language. The needs of the hour are multi-

farious and all unfilled. There are a thousand sensations that we can describe only by laborious phrases or metaphors, a thousand characters and circumstances, familiar to all, which shriek for description.

It has, of course, been tried before. Think what a success the scheme was when it was so long ago attempted. The first Nonsense Book containing really new words was published in 1846 by Edward Lear, but he failed to appreciate his opportunity. Of all his names, the 'Jumblies' alone survive. Lewis Carroll later went about it more deliberately. His immortal poem, 'Jabberwocky,' has become a classic; but even in that masterpiece, how many words are adapted to modern use? 'Slithy' perhaps and 'Chortle' – though no one has ever been able to pronounce it properly to this day. Oh yes, 'Galumph,' I forgot that. Not even 'The Hunting of the Snark' has made the title role popular amongst bromides. Why? His fatal rule was, 'Take care of the sounds and the sense will take care of itself.'

A dozen years ago a little girl tried it with fair success. In her 'Animal Land, where there are no People,' however, I can find no word I have ever heard used outside its covers, no word like 'Hoodlum' or 'Flunk' or 'Primp', 'Quiz', 'Cabal' or 'Fad' or 'Fake.'

The thing must be done, and so I did it. Slang is sporadic; its invention is crude and loose. It is a hit-or-miss method, without direction or philosophy. Our task is serious; we must make one word blossom where a dozen grew before. A myriad necessities urge us. I found myself often confronted with an idea which baffled me and forced me to talk gibberish. How, for instance, can one describe the appearance of an elderly female in plush dancing a too conscientious tango? How do *you*, gentle reader, portray your emotion when, on a stormy night, as you stand on the corner the trolley-car whizzes by and fails to stop for you? Where is the word that paints the mild, faint enjoyment of a family dinner with your wife's relations?

You see how inarticulate you are, now, don't you, when

a social emergency arises? – when you want to give swift tongue to your emotions? What can you say when you're jilted? – how mention the feeling of a broken finger-nail on satin – your esthetic delight in green-trading-stamp furniture? How do you feel with a person whose name you cannot quite remember? Why, we need at least a gross of assorted nouns this very day! What is the name of a business enterprise that was born dead? What do you call the woman who telephones to you during business hours? What is a female who wears dirty white gloves? What is a man who gives you advice 'for your own good'? Well, behold a guide to help you – read 'Burgess Unabridged.' It is the dictionary of the Futurist language!

Yes, my modest 'Unabridged' will 'fill a long-felt want.' It will solidify the chinks of conversation, express the inexpressible, make our English language ornamental, elegant, distinguished, accurate. Other dictionaries have recorded the words of yesterday, my lexicon will give the words of tomorrow. What matter if none of them is 'derived from two Greek words'? My words will be imaginotions, penandinkumpoops, whimpusles, mere boojums rather than classic snarks, for I shall not construct 'Portmanteau' words, like Lewis Carroll. I shall create them from instinctive, inarticulate emotions, hot from the depths of necessity. No 'Onomatopoeia,' either, for I do not hold with those who say that the origin of language is in the mere mimicry of natural sounds. No, like the intense poetic pre-Raphaelite female, who says and feels that her soul is violet, when I see a hand-embroidered necktie, I dive deep in my inner consciousness and bring up, writhing in my hand, the glad word, 'Gorgule,' or 'Golobrification' or 'Diabob.'

100 Choice Selections

1. AGOWILT	Sickening terror, unnecessary fear, sudden shock

2. ALIBOSH — A glaringly obvious falsehood or exaggeration

3. BIMP — A disappointment, a futile rage, a jilt

4. BLEESH — An unpleasant picture; vulgar or obscene

5. BLURB — Praise from one's self, inspired laudation

6. BRIPKIN — One who half does things; second-hand, imitation

7. COWCAT — An unimportant guest, an insignificant personality

8. CRITCH — To array one's self in uncomfortable splendour

9. CULP — A fond delusion, an imaginary attribute

10. DIABOB — An object of amateur art, adorned without taste

11. DIGMIX — An unpleasant, uncomfortable or dirty occupation

12. DRILLIG — A tiresome lingerer, one who talks too long

13. EDICLE — One who is educated beyond his intellect, a pedant

14. EEGOT — A selfishly interested friend, a lover of success

15. ELP — A tricky, sly or elusive person, a promiser

16. FIDGELTICK — Food that it is a bore to eat; a taciturn person

17. FLOOIJAB — An apparent compliment with a concealed sting

18. FRIME — An educated heart, one who does the right thing

19. FUD — A state of disorder or deshabille, a mess

20. FROWK — A spicy topic, a halfwrong act, a sly suggestion

21. GEEFOOJET   An unnecessary thing, an article seldom used

22. GIXLET   One who has more heart than brains, an entertainer

23. GLOOGO   Foolishly faithful without reward; loyal, fond

24. GOIG   One whom one distrusts intuitively, suspicious

25. GOLLOHIX   An untimely noise, a disturbance, especially at night

26. GOLOBRIFY   To adorn with unmeaning and extravagant ornament

27. GORGULE   A splendiferous, over-ornate object or gift

28. GORM   A human hog; to take more than one's share

29. GOWYOP   A perplexity wherein familiar things seem strange

30. GUBBLE   Society talk, the hum of foolish conversation

31. HUZZLECOO   An intimate talk, a confidential colloquy

32. HYGOG   An unsatisfied desire, something out of one's reach

33. HYPRIJIMP   A man who does woman's work; one alone amid women

34. IGMOIL   A sordid quarrel over money matters

35. IMPKIN   A superhuman pet, a baby in beast form

36. IOBINK   An unplaceable resemblance, an inaccessible memory

37. JIP   A *faux pas*, a dangerous subject of conversation

38. JIRRIWIG   A traveller who does not see the country

39. JUJASM   An expansion of sudden joy after suspense

40.	JULLIX	A mental affinity, one with similar tastes or memory
41.	JURP	An impudent servant or underling, a saucy clerk
42.	KIDLOID	A precocious or self-assertive child. *Enfant terrible*
43.	KIPE	To inspect appraisingly, as women do one another
44.	KRIPSLE	An annoying physical sensation or defect
45.	LALLIFY	To prolong a story tiresomely, or repeat a joke
46.	LEOLUMP	An interrupter of conversations, an egoistic bore
47.	LOOBLUM	Palatable but indigestible food; flattery
48.	MACHIZZLE	To attempt unsuccessfully to please, to try to like
49.	MEEM	An artificial half-light that women love; gloom
50.	MOOBLE	A mildly amusing affair, a semi-interesting person
51.	MOOSOO	Sulky, out of sorts or out of order; delayed
52.	NINK	An 'antique' resurrected for decorative effect
53.	NODGE	The only one of its kind, or having no mate
54.	NULKIN	The secret explanation, the inside history
55.	OOFLE	A person whose name one cannot remember; to forget
56.	OROBALDITY	Modern mysticism, a short cut to success
57.	OVOTCH	A thing in style, the current fad
58.	PALOODLE	To give unnecessary advice; one who thus bores

59. PAWDLE	One vicariously famous, or with undeserved prominence
60. PERSOTUDE	Social warmth or magnetism, amount of popular favour
61. POOJE	To embarrass; a regrettable discovery
62. QUINK	An expression or mood of anxious expectancy
63. QUISTY	Useful and reliable without being ornamental
64. QUOOB	A person or thing obviously out of place, a misfit
65. RAWP	A reliably unreliable person, one always late
66. RIZGIDGET	An inability to make up one's mind, an indecision
67. ROWTCH	To eat in extraordinary fashion, to gormandize
68. SKINJE	To feel shudderingly, to shrink from instinctively
69. SKYSCRIMBLE	To go off at a tangent, mentally; to escape logic
70. SLUB	A mild indisposition which does not incapacitate
71. SNOSH	Vain talk; a project that is born dead
72. SPIGG	A decoration of overt vanity; to attract notice, paint
73. SPILLIX	Accidental good luck, uncharacteristically skilful
74. SPLOOCH	One who doesn't know his own business; a failure
75. SPUZZ	Mental force, aggressive intellectuality, stamina
76. SQUINCH	To watch and wait anxiously, hoping for a lucky turn
77. TASHIVATION	The art of answering without listening to questions
78. THUSK	Something that has quickly passed from one's life

80. UDNEY   A beloved bore; one who loves but does not understand

81. UGLET   An unpleasant duty too long postponed

82. UNK   An unwelcome, inappropriate or duplicate present

83. VARM   The quintessence of sex; sex hatred or antipathy

84. VILP   An unsportsmanlike player, a bad loser, a braggart

85. VOIP   Food that gives no pleasure to the palate

86. VORGE   Voluntary suffering, unnecessary effort or exercise

87. VORIANDER   A woman who pursues men or demands attentions

88. WHINKLE   Hypocritical graciousness; to glow with vanity

89. WIJJICLE   A perverse household article, always out of order

90. WOG   Food on the face; unconscious adornment of the person

91. WOWZE   A female fool, an unconsciously ridiculous woman

92. WOX   A state of placid, satisfied contentment

93. WUMGUSH   Women's insincere flattery of each other

94. XENOGORE   An interloper who keeps one from interesting things

95. YAB   A monomaniac or fanatic, enthusiasm over one thing

96. YAMNOY   A bulky, unmanageable object to be carried

97. YOD   A ban or restriction on pleasant things

98. YOWF   One whose importance exceeds his merit, a rich fool

| 99. ZEECH | A monologuist; one who is lively, but exhausting |
| 100. ZOBSIB | An amiable blunderer, one displaying misguided zeal |

Thus no. 27:

| GORGULE, *n.* | 1. An unwished-for gift; an unnecessary, splendiferous object. 2. Elaborate bad taste. |
| GOR'GU-LOUS, *a.* | Ornamental, but not useful. |

A gorgule is the imitation malachite clock, the fancy brass lamp, the green plush sofa, gorgulous with curves, writhing spirals, tassels, gimp and fring. (See *Diabob*.)

A hand-embroidered necktie is a gorgule. So are lacy, frilled, bedribboned boudoir-caps, without any boudoir; and fancy smoking jackets; and corset-covers with chiffon roses, theatrical act drops and scenic interiors – anything too royal for humble use (See *Golobrifaction*).

Most wedding presents are gorgules. 'Heavens, I wish someone would break that!' Need one describe the gorgule? A brass-and-onyx prodigy. A celluloid toilet set, in a plush casket, a chandelier of the epoch of 1880, a silverplated ice-pitcher or a set of lemonade-tumblers in coloured glass. (See *Gefoojet*).

Ever received a loving cup, grand and gorgulous? Once you were proud of it; now you're willing to have the children lug it to the seashore and shovel it full of sand. Why did you subscribe for that large folio *edition de luxe* 'Masterpieces of Foreign Art,' a gorgule in nine monstrous volumes – price $85.75?

Don't forget that eiderdown fan. It's a gorgule. Give it to the cook.

> *Behold this gorgulated chair –*
> *A weird, upholsterrific blunder!*
> *It doesn't wonder why it's there,*
> *So don't encourage it to wonder;*

For Gorgules such as this don't know
That they're impossible, and therefore
They go right on existing, so
This is the whyness of their wherefore.

———

If the Streets were filled the Glue,
What d'you S'pose that you would do?
If you should Go to Walk at Night,
In the Morning you'd be Stuck in Tight!

———

If People's Heads were Not so Dense —
If We could Look Inside,
How clear would Show each Mood and Tense —
How Often have I Tried!

———

The Proper Way to Leave a Room
Is not to Plunge it into Gloom;
Just Make a Joke before you Go
And then Escape before They Know.

———

I never saw a Purple Cow,
I never hope to see one;
But I can tell you, anyhow,
I'd rather see than be one.

———

Ah Yes! I Wrote the 'Purple Cow'
I'm Sorry, now, I Wrote it!
But I can Tell you, Anyhow,
I'll Kill you if you Quote it!

The Purpil Cowe

A Mayde there was, femely and meke enow
She fate a-milken of a purpil Cowe:
Rofy hire Cheke as in the Month of Maye,
And fikerly her merry Songe was gay
As of the Larke uprift, wafhen in Dewe;
Like Shene of Sterres, Sperkled hire Eyen two.
Now came ther by that Way a hardy Knight
The Mayde efpien in morwening Light.
A faire Person he was – of Corage trewe
With lufty Berd and Chekes of rody Hewe:
Dere Ladye (quod he) far and wide I've ftraied
Vncouthe Aventure in Strange Contrie made
Fro Berwicke unto Ware. Parde I vowe
Erewhiles I never faw a purpil Cowe!
Fayn wold I knowe how Catel this can be?
Tel me I pray you, of yore Courtefie!
The Mayde hire Milken ftent – Goode Sir she saide,
The Master's Mandement on vs ylaid
Decrees that in thefe yclept gilden Houres
Hys kyne shall ete of nought but Vylet Floures!

C

PATRICK CAMPBELL

Noulded Into The Shake Of A Goat

When I was a tall sensitive boy at school I once sent up for a booklet about how to be a ventriloquist.

I was always 'sending up' for things – variable focus lamps, propelling pencils with choice of six differently coloured leads, air-pistols discharging wooden bullets, scale-model tanks with genuine caterpillar action, tricks in glass-topped boxes, and so on – anything, I suppose, to vary the monotony of straight games and education.

The booklet arrived at breakfast time one morning in a large square envelope. I told the other boys it was a new stamp album, and got on with my shredded liver poached in water. I wanted the voice-throwing to come as a real surprise.

We had twenty minutes after breakfast in which to get our things ready for first school. I had a quick run through the new book.

It was called *Ventriloquism in Three Weeks*. On the first page it explained that ventriloquism came from the Latin *ventriloquus* – 'a speaking from the belly.' There was also a drawing of a school-boy smiling pleasantly at a railway porter carrying a trunk. From the trunk came hysterical cries of 'Help! Help! Murder! Police!'

It was just the sort of thing I was aiming at. I slipped the book in with my other ones, and hurried off to first school

In the next fortnight I put in a good deal of practice,

sitting right at the back of the class, watching my lips in a small piece of mirror, and murmuring, 'Dah, dee, day, di, doy, doo.'

It was necessary, however, to be rather careful. Dr Farvox, the author of the book, suggested that it might be as well to perform the earlier exercises 'in the privacy of one's bedroom or den.' Dr Farvox was afraid that 'chums or relatives' might laugh, particularly when one was practising the 'muffled voice in the box.'

The best way to get this going, Dr Farvox said, was to experiment 'with a continuous grunting sound in a high key, straining from the chest as if in pain.'

He was right in thinking that this exercise ought to be performed in the privacy of the bedroom. It was inclined to be noisy – so noisy, indeed, that I was twice caught straining in a high key during practical chemistry, and had to pretend that I'd been overcome by the fumes of nitric acid.

But in the end, it was the easy, pleasant smile that terminated my study of what Dr Farvox described as 'this amusing art.'

It happened one Saturday morning, in the hour before lunch, ordinarily a pleasant enough period devoted to constitutional history. Bill the Bull, who took the class, was usually fairly mellow with the prospect of the weekend before him, and there was not much need to do any work.

As was by now my invariable custom I was seated at the back of the room with a large pile of books in front of me. I was working on the Whisper Voice, which had been giving me a considerable amount of difficulty.

'Lie down, Neddy, lie down,' I whispered, watching my lips closely in the glass.

'It's due in dock at nine o'clock.'

Not bad.

'Take Ted's Kodak down to Roy.'

There it was again – the old familiar twitch on 'Kodak.'

I sat back, relaxing a little. Dr Farvox was strongly in

favour of the Smile. 'What the young student,' he said, 'should aim at from the first is an easy and natural expression. He should Smile.'

I smiled. Smiling, I whispered, 'Take Ted's Kodak down to Roy.'

To my absolute horror I found myself smiling straight into the face of Bill the Bull.

He stopped dead. He was in the middle of something about the growth of common law, but my smile stopped him dead in his tracks.

'Well, well,' said Bill, after a moment. 'How charming. And good morning to you, too.'

I at once buried my face in my books, and tried to shove the mirror and *Ventriloquism in Three Weeks* on one side.

Bill rolled slowly down the passageway between the desks. He was an enormous Welshman with a bullet head, and very greasy, straight black hair. He took a subtle and delicate pleasure in driving the more impressionable amongst us half mad with fear at least five days a week.

'Such pretty teeth,' said Bill. 'How nice of you to smile at me. I have always wanted to win your admiration.'

The other boys sat back. They knew they were on to something good.

I kept my head lowered. I'd actually succeeded in opening my constitutional history somewhere in the middle, but the corner of Dr Farvox was clearly visible under a heap of exercise books.

Bill reached my desk. 'But who knows,' he said, 'perhaps you love me too. Perchance you've been sitting there all morning just dreaming of a little home – just you and I. And later, perhaps some little ones. . . .'

A gasp of incredulous delight came from the other boys. This was Bill at his very best.

I looked up. It was no longer possible to pretend I thought he was talking to someone else.

'I'm sorry, sir,' I said, 'I was just smiling.'

Suddenly Bill pounced. He snatched up Dr Farvox.

'Cripes,' he said. 'What in the world have we here?

Ventriloquism in three weeks?

'Scholars,' he said, 'be so good as to listen to this.'

He read aloud: 'To imitate a Fly. Close the lips tight at one corner. Fill that cheek full of wind and force it through the aperture. Make the sound suddenly loud, and then softer, which will make it appear as though the insect were flying in different parts of the room. The illusion may be helped out by the performer chasing the imaginary fly, and flapping at it with his handkerchief.'

'Strewth,' said Bill. He looked round the class. 'We'd better get ourselves a little bit of this. Here am I taking up your time with the monotonies of constitutional history, while in this very room we have a trained performer who can imitate a fly.'

Suddenly he caught me by the back of the neck. 'Come,' he said, 'my little love, and let us hear this astounding impression.'

He dragged me down to the dais.

'Begin,' said Bill. 'Be so kind as to fill your cheek with wind and at all costs do not omit the flapping of the handkerchief.'

'Sir,' I said, 'that's animal noises. I haven't got that far yet.'

'Sir,' squeaked Bill in a high falsetto, 'that's animal noises. I 'aven't got that far yet.'

He surveyed the convulsed class calmly.

'Come, come,' he said, 'this art is not as difficult as I had imagined it to be. Did anyone see my lips move?'

They cheered him. They banged the lids of their desks. 'Try it again, sir,' they cried. 'It's splendid!'

Bill raised his hand. 'Gentlemen,' he said, 'I thank you for your kindness. I am, however, but an amateur. Am I not right in thinking we would like to hear something more from Professor Smallpox?'

They cheered again. Someone shouted, 'Make him sing a song, sir!'

Bill turned to me. 'Can you,' he said, 'Professor Smallpox, sing a song?'

It was the worst thing that had happened to me in my life. I tried to extricate myself.

'No, sir,' I said. 'I haven't mastered the labials yet.'

Bill started back. He pressed his hand to his heart.

'No labials?' he said. 'You have reached the age of fifteen without having mastered the labials. But, dear Professor Smallpox, we must look into this. Perhaps you would be so kind as to give us some outline of your difficulties?'

I picked up *Ventriloquism in Three Weeks*. There was no way out.

'There's a sentence here, sir, that goes "A pat of butter moulded into the shape of a boat".'

Bill inclined his head. 'Is there, indeed? A most illuminating remark. You propose to put it to music?'

'No, sir,' I said. 'I'm just trying to show you how hard it is. You see, you have to call that "A cat of gutter noulded into the shake of a goat".'

Bill fell right back into his chair.

'You have to call it *what*?' he said.

'A cat of gutter, sir, noulded into the shake of a goat.'

Bill's eyes bulged. 'Professor,' he said, 'you astound me. You bewilder me. A cat of gutter –' he repeated it reverently, savouring every syllable.

Then he sprang up. 'But we must hear this,' he cried. 'We must have this cat of gutter delivered by someone who knows what he is at. This – this is valuable stuff.'

He caught me by the ear. 'Professor,' he said, 'why does it have to be noulded into the shake of a goat?'

'Well, sir,' I said, 'if you say it like that you don't have to move your lips. You sort of avoid the labials.'

'To be sure you do,' said Bill. 'Why didn't I think of it myself? Well, now, we will have a demonstration.'

He turned to face the class. 'Gentlemen,' he said, 'Professor Smallpox will now say "a pat of butter moulded into the shape of a boat" *without moving the lips*. I entreat your closest attention. You have almost certainly never in your lives heard anything like this before.'

He picked up his heavy ebony ruler. His little pig-like eyes gleamed.

'And,' he went on, 'to make sure that Professor Smallpox will really give us of his best I shall make it my personal business to give Professor Smallpox a clonk on the conk with this tiny weapon should any of you see even the faintest movement of the facial muscles as he delivers his unforgettable message.'

Bill brought down the ruler with a sharp crack on my skull.

'Professor,' he said, 'it's all yours.'

I don't have to go into the next twenty-five minutes. The other boys yelled practically on every syllable. I got the meaningless words tangled up, and said 'A cack of rutter noulded into the gake of a shote.'

At times Bill was so helpless with laughter that he missed me with the ruler altogether.

When the bell went for the end of the hour he insisted on being helped out into the passage, wiping his eyes with the blackboard cloth.

After that, I gave it up, feeling no recurrence of interest even after reading Bill's observation on my end-of-term report. 'He ought to do well on the stage.'

CANNING, FRERE, AND ELLIS

The Rovers

PLOT

Rogero, son of the late Minister of the Count of Saxe Weimar, having, while he was at college, fallen desperately in love with Matilda Pottingen, daughter of his tutor, Doctor Engelbertus Pottingen, Professor of Civil Law; and Matilda evidently returning his passion, the Doctor, to prevent ill consequences, sends his daughter on a visit to her Aunt in Wetteravia, where she becomes acquainted with Casimere, a Polish Officer, who happens to be quartered near her Aunt's; and has several children by him.

Roderic, Count of Saxe Weimar, a Prince of a tyrannical and licentious disposition, has for his Prime Minister and favourite, Gaspar, a crafty villain, who had risen to his post by first ruining, and then putting to death, Rogero's father. Gaspar, apprehensive of the power and popularity which the young Rogero may enjoy at his return to Court, seizes the occasion of his intrigue with Matilda (of which he is apprized officially by Doctor Pottingen) to procure from his Master an order for the recall of Rogero from college, and for committing him to the care of the Prior of the Abbey of Quedlinburgh, a Priest, rapacious, savage, and sensual, and devoted to Gaspar's interests – sending at the same time private orders to the Prior to confine him in a dungeon.

Here Rogero languishes many years. His daily sustenance is administered to him through a grated opening at the top of a cavern, by the Landlady of the Golden Eagle at Weimar, with whom Gaspar contracts, in the Prince's name, for his support; intending, and more than once endeavouring, to corrupt the Waiter to mingle poison with the food, in order that he may get rid of Rogero for ever.

In the meantime Casimere, having been called away from the neighbourhood of Matilda's residence to other quarters, becomes enamoured of, and marries Cecilia, by whom he has a family; and whom he likewise deserts after a few years co-habitation, on pretence of business which calls him to Kamtschatka.

Doctor Pottingen, now grown old and infirm, and feeling the want of his daughter's society, sends young Pottingen in search of her, with strict injunctions not to return without her, and to bring with her either her present lover Casimere, or, should that not be possible, Rogero himself, if he can find him, the Doctor having set his heart upon seeing his children comfortably settled before his death. Matilda, about the same period, quits her Aunt's in search of Casimere; and Cecilia having been advertised (by an anonymous letter) of the falsehood of his Kamtschatka journey, sets out in the post-waggon on a similar pursuit.

It is at this point of time the Play opens – with the accidental meeting of Cecilia and Matilda at the Inn at Weimar. Casimere arrives there soon after, and falls in first with Matilda, and then with Cecilia. Successive *éclaircissements* take place, and an arrangement is finally made, by which the two Ladies are to live jointly with Casimere.

Young Pottingen, wearied with a few weeks' search. during which he has not been able to find either of the objects of it, resolves to stop at Weimar, and wait events there. It so happens that he takes up his lodging in the same house with Puddincrantz and Beefinstern, two English Noblemen, whom the tyranny of King John has obliged to fly from their country, and who, after wandering about the Continent for some time, have fixed their residence at Weimar.

The news of the signature of Magna Charta arriving, determines Puddincrantz and Beefinstern to return to England. Young Pottingen opens his case to them, and intreats them to stay to assist him in the object of his search. This they refuse, but coming to the Inn where they are to set off for Hamburg, they meet Casimere, from whom they had both received many civilities in Poland.

Casimere, by this time, tired of his 'Double Arrangement,' and having learnt from the Waiter that Rogero is confined in the vaults of the neighbouring Abbey *for love*, resolves to attempt his rescue, and to make over Matilda to him as the price of his deliverance. He communicates his scheme to Puddingfield and Beefington, who agree to assist him, as also does Young Pottingen. The Waiter of the Inn proving to be a *Knight Templar* in disguise, is appointed leader of the expedition. A band of Troubadours, who happen to be returning from the Crusades, and a Company of Austrian and Prussian Grenadiers returning from the Seven Years' War, are engaged as troops.

The attack on the Abbey is made with success. The Count of Weimar and Gaspar, who are feasting with the Prior, are seized and beheaded in the Refectory. The Prior

is thrown into the dungeon, from which Rogero is rescued.
Matilda and Cecilia rush in. The former recognizes Rogero,
and agrees to live with him. The Children are produced
on all sides – and Young Pottingen is commissioned to
write to his father, the Doctor, to detail the joyful events
which have taken place, and to invite him to Weimar to
partake of the general felicity.

Song by Rogero

Whene'er with haggard eyes I view
This dungeon that I'm rotting in,
I think of those companions true
Who studied with me at the U–
  –niversity of Gottingen–
  –niversity of Gottingen.

*Weeps, and pulls out a blue kerchief, with which he wipes
his eyes; gazing tenderly at it, he proceeds–*

Sweet kerchief, check'd with heav'nly blue,
Which once my love sat knotting in!
Alas! Matilda *then* was true!
At least I thought so at the U–
  –niversity of Gottingen–
  –niversity of Gottingen.

*At the repetition of this line Rogero clanks his Chains in
cadence*

Barbs! barbs! alas! how swift you flew
Her neat post-waggon trotting in!
Ye bore Matilda from my view;
Forlorn I languished at the U–
  –niversity of Gottingen–
  –niversity of Gottingen.

This faded form! this pallid hue!
This blood my veins is clotting in,
My years are many – they were few
When first I enter'd at the U–
    –niversity of Gottingen–
    –niversity of Gottingen.

There first for thee my passion grew,
Sweet! sweet Matilda Pottingen!
Thou wast the daughter of my Tu–
–tor, Law Professor at the U–
    –niversity of Gottingen–
    –niversity of Gottingen.

Sun, moon, and thou vain world, adieu,
That kings and priests are plotting in:
Here doom'd to starve on water–gru–
–el never shall I see the U–
    –niversity of Gottingen–
    –niversity of Gottingen.

*During the last Stanza Rogero dashes his head repeatedly
against the walls of his Prison; and, finally, so hard as to
produce a visible contusion. He then throws himself on
the floor in an agony. The Curtain drops – the Music still
continuing to play, till it is wholly fallen.*

Scene – the Abbey Gate, with Ditches, Drawbridges, and
Spikes.

Time – about an hour before Sunrise. The Conspirators
appear as if in ambuscade, whispering, and consulting together, in expectation of the Signal for attack. The WAITER
is habited as a Knight Templar, in the dress of his Order,
with the Cross on his breast, and the Scallop on his
shoulder. PUDDINGFIELD and BEEFINGTON armed with
Blunder-busses and Pocket-pistols; the GRENADIERS in their
proper Uniforms. The TROUBADOUR with his attendant
Minstrels, bring up the rear – martial Music – the Conspirators come forward, and present themselves before the
Gate of the Abbey. – Alarum – firing of Pistols – the Con-

vent appear in Arms upon the Walls – the Drawbridge is let down – a Body of Choristers and Lay-brothers attempt a Sally, but are beaten back and the Verger killed. The besieged attempt to raise the Drawbridge – PUDDINGFIELD and BEEFINGTON press forward with alacrity, throw themselves upon the Drawbridge, and by the exertion of their weight, preserve it in a state of depression – the other besiegers join them, and attempt to force the entrance, but without effect. PUDDINGFIELD makes the signal for the battering ram. Enter QUINTUS CURTIUS and MARCUS CURIUS DENTATUS, in their proper Military Habits, preceded by the Roman Eagle – the rest of their Legion are employed in bringing forward a battering ram, which plays for a few minutes to slow time, till the entrance is forced. After a short resistance, the besiegers rush in with shouts of Victory.

Scene changes to the interior of the Abbey. The inhabitants of the Convent are seen flying in all directions.

The COUNT OF WEIMAR and the PRIOR, who had been found feasting in the Refectory, are brought in manacled. The COUNT appears transported with rage, and gnaws his chains. The PRIOR remains insensible, as if stupefied with grief. BEEFINGTON takes the keys of the Dungeon, which are hanging at the PRIOR'S girdle, and makes a sign for them both to be led away into confinement.

Exeunt PRIOR and COUNT properly guarded. The rest of the Conspirators disperse in search of the Dungeon where ROGERO is confined.

HENRY CAREY

Chrononhotonthologos Sc. i.

Re-enter Rigdum-Funnidos and Aldiborontiphoscophornio
Rigdum The King's in a cursed Passion: Pray who is
    this
    Mr. *Somnus* he's so angry withal?

Aldiboronti   The Son of *Chaos* and of *Erebus*,*
Incestuous Pair! Brother of *Mors*† relentless,
Whose speckled Robe and Wings of blackest Hue,
Astonish all Mankind with hideous Glare;
Himself with sable Plumes to Men benevolent
Brings downy Slumbers and refreshing Sleep

Rigdum   This Gentleman may come of a very good Family, for aught I know : but I wou'd not be in his Place for the World.

Aldiboronti   But lo! The King his Footsteps this Way bends,
His cogitative Faculties immers'd
In Cogibundity of Cogitation;
Let Silence close our folding Doors of Speech,
Till apt Attention tell our heart the Purport
Of this profound Profundity of Thought.

Re-enter King and Attendants.

King   It is resolv'd – Now *Somnus* I defy thee,
And from Mankind ampute thy curs'd Dominion.
These Royal Eyes thou never more shall close.
Henceforth let no Man sleep, on Pain of Death :
Instead of Sleep, let pompous Pageantry,
And solemn Show, with sonorous Solemnity,
Keep all mankind eternally awake.
Bid *Harlequino* decorate the Stage
With all Magnificence of Decoration :
Giants and Giantesses, Dwarfs and Pigmies,
Songs, Dances, Musick in its amplest Order,

---

* *Erebus*. Son and husband of Chaos. Hence the 'incestuous pair' of the next line.

† *Mors*. Death, twin brother of Somnus, with whom he dwelt in Hades.

Mimes, Pantomimes, all all the magick
Motion
Of Scene deceptiovisive and sublime.

*An Entertainment of Singing, after the Italian Manner, by
Signor Scacciatinello and Signora Sicarina*
Enter Captain of the Guards.

Captain   To Arms! to Arms! great *Chrononhoton-
                   thologos!*
                   Th' *Antipodean* Pow'rs, from Realms below,
                   Have burst the solid Entrails of the Earth.
                   Gushing such *Cataracts* of *Forces* forth,
                   This World is too incopious to contain 'em:
                   Armies, on Armies, march in Form stupend-
                   ous;
                   Not like our Earthly Legions, Rank by Rank,
                   But Teer o'er Teer, high pil'd from Earth to
                   Heaven:
                   A blazing Bullet, Bigger than the Sun,
                   Shot from a huge and monstrous Culverin,
                   Has laid your Royal *Citadel* in Ashes.

King   Peace Coward! were they wedg'd like
                   Golden Ingots,
                   Or pent so close, as to admit no *Vacuum.*
                   One look from *Chrononhotonthologos*
                   Shall scare them into Nothing. *Rigdum Fun-
                   nidos,*
                   Bid *Bombardinion* draw his Legions forth,
                   And meet us in the Plains of *Queerumania.*
                   This very now ourselves shall there conjoin
                   him;
                   Mean Time, bid all the Priests prepare their
                   Temples
                   For Rites of Triumph: Let the Singing
                   Singers,
                   With vocal Voices, most Vociferous,'
                   In sweet Vociferation, out vociferize
                   Ev'n Sound itself; so be it as we have
                   order'd. *Exeunt*

LEWIS CARROLL

Alice in Wonderland

For a minute or two she stood looking at the house, and wondering what to do next, when suddenly a footman in livery came running out of the wood (she considered him to be a footman because he was in livery; otherwise, judging by his face only, she would have called him a fish) and rapped loudly at the door with his knuckles. It was opened by another footman in livery, with a round face, and large eyes like a frog, and both footmen, Alice noticed, had powdered hair that curled all over their heads. She felt very curious to know what it was all about, and crept a little way out of the wood to listen.

The Fish-Footman began by producing from under his arm a great letter, nearly as large as himself, and this he handed over to the other, saying in a solemn tone, 'For the Duchess. An invitation from the Queen to play croquet.' The Frog-Footman repeated, in the same solemn tone, only changing the order of the words a little, 'From the Queen. An invitation for the Duchess to play croquet.'

Then they both bowed, and their curls got entangled together.

Alice laughed so much at this, that she had to run back into the wood for fear of their hearing her; and, when she next peeped out, the Fish-Footman was gone and the other was sitting on the ground near the door, staring stupidly up into the sky.

Alice went timidly up to the door, and knocked.

'There's no sort of use in knocking,' said the Footman, 'and that for two reasons. First, because I'm on the same side of the door as you are: secondly, because they're making such a noise inside, no one could possibly hear you.' And certainly there was a most extraordinary noise going on within – a constant howling and sneezing, and every now and then a great crash, as if a dish or kettle had been broken to pieces.

'Please, then,' said Alice, 'how am I to get in?'

'There might be some sense in your knocking,' the Footman went on, without attending to her, 'if we had the door between us. For instance, if you were inside, you might knock, and I could let you out, you know.' He was looking up into the sky all the time he was speaking, and this Alice thought decidedly uncivil. 'But perhaps he ca'n't help it', she said to herself; 'his eyes are so very nearly at the top of his head. But at any rate he might answer questions. 'How am I to get in?' she repeated, aloud.

'I shall sit here,' the Footman remarked, 'till to-morrow —'

At this moment the door of the house opened, and a large plate came skimming out, straight at the Footman's head: it just grazed his nose, and broke to pieces against one of the trees behind him.

'— or next day, maybe,' the Footman continued in the same tone, exactly as if nothing had happened.

'How am I to get in?' asked Alice again, in a louder tone.

'Are you to get in at all?' said the Footman. 'That's the first question, you know.'

It was, no doubt; only Alice did not like to be told so. 'It's really dreadful,' she muttered to herself, 'the way all the creatures argue. It's enough to drive one crazy!'

The Footman seemed to think this a good opportunity for repeating his remark, with variations. 'I shall sit here,' he said, 'on and off, for days and days.'

'But what am I to do?' said Alice.

'Anything you like,' said the Footman, and began whistling.

'Oh, there's no use in talking to him,' said Alice desperately, 'he's perfectly idiotic!' And she opened the door and went in.

The door led right into a large kitchen, which was full of smoke from one end to the other, the Duchess was sitting on a three-legged stool in the middle, nursing a baby; the cook was leaning over the fire, stirring a large cauldron which seemed to be full of soup.

'There's certainly too much pepper in that soup!' Alice said to herself, as well as she could for sneezing.

There was certainly too much of it in the air. Even the Duchess sneezed occasionally; and as for the baby, it was sneezing and howling alternately without a moment's pause. The only two creatures in the kitchen that did not sneeze were the cook, and a large cat, which was lying on the hearth and grinning from ear to ear.

'Please would you tell me,' said Alice, a little timidly, for she was not quite sure whether it was good manners for her to speak first, 'why your cat grins like that?'

'It's a Cheshire Cat,' said the Duchess, 'and that's why, Pig!'

She said the last word with such sudden violence that Alice quite jumped; but she saw in another moment that it was addressed to the baby, and not to her, so she took courage, and went on again:

'I didn't know that Cheshire Cats always grinned; in fact, I didn't know that cats could grin.'

'They all can,' said the Duchess, 'and most of 'em do.'

'I don't know of any that do,' Alice said very politely, feeling quite pleased to have got into conversation.

'You don't know much,' said the Duchess, 'and that's a fact.'

Alice did not at all like the tone of this remark, and thought it would be as well to introduce some other subject of conversation. While she was trying to fix on one, the cook took the cauldron of soup off the fire, and at once set to work throwing everything within reach at the Duchess and the baby – the fire-irons came first; then followed a shower of saucepans, plates, and dishes. The Duchess took no notice of them even when they hit her, and the baby was howling so much already, that it was quite impossible to say whether the blows hurt it or not.

'Oh, please mind what you're doing!' cried Alice, jumping up and down in an agony of terror. 'Oh, there goes his precious nose!' as an unusually large saucepan flew close by it, and very nearly carried it off.

'If everybody minded their own business,' the Duchess said, in a hoarse growl, 'the world would go round a deal faster than it does.'

'Which would not be an advantage,' said Alice, who felt very glad to get an opportunity of showing off a little of her knowledge. 'Just think what work it would make with the day and night! You see, the earth takes twenty-four hours to turn round on its axis –'

'Talking of axes,' said the Duchess, 'chop off her head!'

Alice glanced rather anxiously at the cook, to see if she meant to take the hint, but the cook was busily stirring the soup, and seemed not to be listening, so she went on again, 'Twenty-four hours, I think; or is it twelve? I –'

'Oh, don't bother me!' said the Duchess. 'I never could abide figures!' And with that she began nursing her child again, singing a sort of lullaby to it as she did so, and giving it a violent shake at the end of every line:

> 'Speak roughly to your little boy,
> And beat him when he sneezes:
> He only does it to annoy,
> Because he knows it teases.'

CHORUS
(in which the cook and the baby joined):
'Wow! wow! wow!'

While the Duchess sang the second verse of the song, she kept tossing the baby violently up and down, and the poor little thing howled so that Alice could hardly hear the words:

> 'I speak severely to my boy,
> I beat him when he sneezes;
> For he can thoroughly enjoy
> The pepper when he pleases!'

CHORUS
'Wow! wow! wow!'

'Here! You may nurse it a bit, if you like!' the Duchess said to Alice, flinging the baby at her as she spoke. 'I must go and get ready to play croquet with the Queen,' and she hurried out of the room. The cook threw a frying-pan after her as she went, but it just missed her.

Alice caught the baby with some difficulty, as it was a queer-shaped little creature, and held out its arms and legs in all directions, 'just like a star-fish,' thought Alice. The poor little thing was snorting like a steam-engine when she caught it, and kept doubling itself up and straightening itself out again, so that altogether, for the first minute or two, it was as much as she could do to hold it.

As soon as she had made out the proper way of nursing it (which was to twist it up into a sort of knot, and then keep tight hold of its right ear and left foot, so as to prevent its undoing itself), she carried it out into the open air. 'If I don't take this child away with me,' thought Alice, 'they're sure to kill it in a day or two. Wouldn't it be murder to leave it behind?)' She said the last words out loud, and the little thing grunted in reply (it had left off sneezing by this time). 'Don't grunt,' said Alice; 'that's not at all a proper way of expressing yourself.'

The baby grunted again, and Alice looked very anxiously into its face to see what was the matter with it. There could be no doubt that it had a very turn-up nose, much more like a snout than a real nose; also its eyes were getting extremely small for a baby; altogether Alice did not like the look of the thing at all. 'But perhaps it was only sobbing,' she thought, and looked into its eyes again, to see if there were any tears.

No, there were no tears. 'If you're going to turn into a pig, my dear,' said Alice, seriously, 'I'll have nothing more to do with you. Mind now!' The poor little thing sobbed again (or grunted, it was impossible to say which) and they went on for some while in silence.

Alice was just beginning to think to herself, 'Now, what am I to do with this creature, when I get it home?' when it grunted again, so violently, that she looked down into its face in some alarm. This time there could be no mistake about it: it was neither more nor less than a pig, and she felt that it would be quite absurd for her to carry it any further.

So she set the little creature down, and felt quite relieved to see it trot away quietly into the wood. 'If it had grown up,' she said to herself, 'it would have made a dreadfully ugly child, but it makes rather a handsome pig, I think.' And she began thinking over other children she knew, who might do very well as pigs, and was just saying to herself 'if one only knew the right way to change them —' when she was a little startled by seeing the Cheshire Cat sitting on a bough of a tree a few yards off.

The Cat only grinned when it saw Alice. It looked good-natured, she thought; still it had very long claws and a great many teeth, so she felt that it ought to be treated with respect.

'Cheshire Puss,' she began, rather timidly, as she did not at all know whether it would like the name; however, it only grinned a little wider. 'Come, it's pleased so far,' thought Alice, and she went on. 'Would you tell me, please, which way I ought to go from here?'

'That depends a good deal on where you want to get to,' said the Cat.

'I don't much care where —' said Alice.

'Then it doesn't matter which way you go,' said the Cat.

'— so long as I get somewhere,' Alice added as an explanation.

'Oh, you're sure to do that,' said the Cat, 'if you only walk long enough.' Alice felt that this could not be denied, so she tried another question. 'What sort of people live about here?'

'In that direction,' the Cat said, waving its right paw round, 'lives a Hatter: and in that direction,' waving the other paw, 'lives a March Hare. Visit either you like;

they're both mad.'

'But I don't want to go among mad people,' Alice remarked.

'Oh, you ca'n't help that,' said the Cat, 'we're all mad here. I'm mad. You're mad.'

'How do you know I'm mad?' said Alice.

'You must be,' said the Cat, 'or you wouldn't have come here.'

Alice didn't think that proved it at all; however, she went on, 'And how do you know that you're mad?'

'To begin with,' said the Cat, 'a dog's not mad. You grant that?'

'I suppose so,' said Alice.

'Well, then,' the Cat went on, 'you see a dog growls when it's angry, and wags its tail when it's pleased. Now I growl when I'm pleased, and wag my tail when I'm angry. Therefore I'm mad.'

'I call it purring, not growling,' said Alice.

'Call it what you like,' said the Cat. 'Do you play croquet with the Queen to-day?'

'I should like it very much,' said Alice, 'but I haven't been invited yet.'

'You'll see me there,' said the Cat, and vanished.

Alice was not much surprised at this, she was getting so well used to queer things happening. While she was still looking at the place where it had been, it suddenly appeared again.

'Bye-the-bye, what became of the baby?' said the Cat. 'I'd nearly forgotten to ask.'

'It turned into a pig,' Alice answered very quietly, just as if the Cat had come back in a natural way.

'I thought it would,' said the Cat, and vanished again.

Alice waited a little, half expecting to see it again, but it did not appear, and after a minute or two she walked on in the direction in which the March Hare was said to live. 'I've seen hatters before,' she said to herself; 'the March Hare will be much the most interesting, and perhaps as this is May, it wo'n't be raving mad – at least not so mad as it was in March.' As she said this, she looked up, and there was the Cat again, sitting on a branch of a tree.

'Did you say "pig," or "fig"?' said the Cat.

'I said "pig",' replied Alice; 'and I wish you wouldn't keep appearing and vanishing so suddenly : you make one quite giddy!'

'All right,' said the Cat; and this time it vanished quite slowly, beginning with the end of the tail, and ending with the grin, which remained some time after the rest of it had gone.

'Well! I've often seen a cat without a grin,' thought Alice; 'but a grin without a cat! It's the most curious thing I ever saw in all my life!' She had not gone much farther before she came in sight of the house of the March Hare; she thought it must be the right house, because the chimneys were shaped like ears and the roof was thatched with fur. It was so large a house, that she did not like to go nearer till she had nibbled some more of the left-hand bit of mushroom, and raised herself to about two feet high; even then she walked up towards it rather timidly, saying to herself, 'Suppose it should be raving mad after all! I almost wish I'd gone to see the Hatter instead!'

There was a table set out under a tree in front of the house, and the March Hare and the Hatter were having tea at it; a Dormouse was sitting between them, fast asleep, and the other two were using it as a cushion, resting their elbows on it, and talking over its head. 'Very uncomfortable for the Dormouse,' thought Alice; 'only as it's asleep, I suppose it doesn't mind.' The table was a large one, but the three were all crowded together at one corner of it. 'No room! No room!' they cried out when they saw Alice coming. 'There's plenty of room!' Alice said indignantly, and she sat down in a large arm-chair at one end of the table.

'Have some wine,' the March Hare said in an encouraging tone.

Alice looked all round the table, but there was nothing on it but tea.

'I don't see any wine,' she remarked.

'There isn't any,' said the March Hare.

'Then it wasn't very civil of you to offer it,' said Alice angrily.

'It wasn't very civil of you to sit down without being invited,' said the March Hare.

'I didn't know it was your table,' said Alice: 'it's laid for a great many more than three.'

'Your hair wants cutting,' said the Hatter. He had been looking at Alice for some time with great curiosity, and this was his first speech.

'You should learn not to make personal remarks,' Alice said with some severity; 'it's very rude.'

The Hatter opened his eyes very wide on hearing this, but all he said was 'Why is a raven like a writing-desk?'

'Come, we shall have some fun now!' thought Alice. 'I'm glad they've begun asking riddles – I believe I can guess that,' she added aloud.

'Do you mean that you think you can find out the answer to it?' said the March Hare.

'Exactly so,' said Alice.

'Then you should say what you mean,' the March Hare went on.

'I do,' Alice hastily replied; 'at least – at least I mean what I say – that's the same thing, you know.'

'Not the same thing a bit!' said the Hatter. 'Why, you might just as well say that "I see what I eat" is the same thing as "I eat what I see!"'

'You might just as well say,' added the March Hare, 'that "I like what I get' is the same thing as "I get what I like"!'

'You might just as well say,' added the Dormouse, which seemed to be talking in its sleep, 'that "I breathe when I sleep" is the same thing as "I sleep when I breathe"!'

'It is the same thing with you,' said the Hatter, and here the conversation dropped, and the party sat silent for a minute, while Alice thought over all she could remember about ravens and writing-desks, which wasn't much. The Hatter was the first to break the silence. 'What day of the month is it?' he said, turning to Alice; he had taken his watch out of his pocket, and was looking at it uneasily, shaking it every now and then, and holding it to his ear.

Alice considered a little, and then said 'The fourth.'

'Two days wrong!' sighed the Hatter. 'I told you butter wouldn't suit the works!' he added, looking angrily at the March Hare.

'It was the best butter,' the March Hare meekly replied.

'Yes, but some crumbs must have got in as well,' the Hatter grumbled, 'you shouldn't have put it in with the bread-knife.'

The March Hare took the watch and looked at it gloomily, then he dipped it into his cup of tea, and looked at it again, but he could think of nothing better to say than his first remark, 'It was the best butter, you know.'

Alice had been looking over his shoulder with some curiosity. 'What a funny watch!' she remarked. 'It tells the day of the month, and doesn't tell what o'clock it is!'

'Why should it?' muttered the Hatter. 'Does your watch tell you what year it is?'

'Of course not,' Alice replied very readily, 'but that's because it stays the same year for such a long time together.'

'Which is just the case with mine,' said the Hatter.

Alice felt dreadfully puzzled. The Hatter's remark seemed to her to have no sort of meaning to it, and yet it was certainly English. 'I don't quite understand you,' she said, as politely as she could.

'The Dormouse is asleep again,' said the Hatter, and he poured a little hot tea upon its nose.

The Dormouse shook its head impatiently, and said,

without opening its eyes, 'Of course, of course, just what I was going to remark myself.'

'Have you guessed the riddle yet?' the Hatter said, turning to Alice again.

'No, I give it up,' Alice replied. 'What's the answer?'

'I haven't the slightest idea,' said the Hatter.

'Nor I,' said the March Hare.

Alice sighed wearily. 'I think you might do something better with the time,' she said, 'than wasting it in asking riddles that have no answers.'

'If you knew Time as well as I do,' said the Hatter, 'you wouldn't talk about wasting it. It's him.'

'I don't know what you mean,' said Alice.

'Of course you don't!' the Hatter said, tossing his head contemptuously.

'I dare say you never even spoke to Time!'

'Perhaps not,' Alice cautiously replied; 'but I know I have to beat time when I learn music.'

'Ah! That accounts for it,' said the Hatter. 'He wo'n't stand beating. Now, if you only kept on good terms with him, he'd do almost anything you like with the clock. For instance, suppose it were nine o'clock in the morning, just time to begin lessons: you'd only have to whisper a hint to Time, and round goes the clock in a twinkling! Half-past one, time for dinner!'

('I only wish it was,' the March Hare said to itself in a whisper.)

'That would be grand, certainly,' said Alice thoughtfully; 'but then – I shouldn't be hungry for it, you know.'

'Not at first, perhaps,' said the hatter: 'but you could keep it to half-past one as long as you liked.'

'Is that the way you manage?' Alice asked.

The Hatter shook his head mournfully. 'Not I!' he replied. 'We quarrelled last March – just before he went mad, you know –' (pointing with his teaspoon at the March Hare) '– it was at the great concert given by the Queen of Hearts, and I had to sing

'Twinkle, twinkle, little bat!
How I wonder what you're at!"

You know the song, perhaps?'

'I've heard something like it,' said Alice.

'It goes on, you know,' the Hatter continued, 'in this way:

"Up above the world you fly,
Like a tea-tray in the sky.
Twinkle, twinkle –"'

Here the Dormouse shook itself, and began singing in its sleep 'Twinkle, twinkle, twinkle, twinkle –' and went on so long that they had to pinch it to make it stop.

'Well, I'd hardly finished the first verse,' said the Hatter, 'when the Queen bawled out "He's murdering the time! Off with his head!"'

'How dreadfully savage!' exclaimed Alice.

'And ever since that,' the Hatter went on in a mournful tone, 'he wo'n't do a thing I ask! It's always six o'clock now.'

A bright idea came into Alice's head. 'Is that the reason so many tea-things are put out here?' she asked.

'Yes, that's it,' said the Hatter with a sigh, 'it's always tea-time, and we've no time to wash the things between whiles.'

'Then you keep moving round, I suppose?' said Alice.

'Exactly so,' said the Hatter: 'as the things get used up.'

'But what happens when you come to the beginning again?' Alice ventured to ask.

'Suppose we change the subject,' the March Hare interrupted, yawning. 'I'm getting tired of this, I vote the young lady tells us a story.'

'I'm afraid I don't know one,' said Alice, rather alarmed at the proposal.

'Then the Dormouse shall!' they both cried. 'Wake up, Dormouse!' And they pinched it on both sides at once.

The Dormouse slowly opened its eyes. 'I wasn't asleep,'

it said in a hoarse, feeble voice, 'I heard every word you fellows were saying.'

'Tell us a story!' said the March Hare.

'Yes, please do!' pleaded Alice.

'And be quick about it,' added the Hatter, 'or you'll be asleep again before it's done.'

'Once upon a time there were three little sisters,' the Dormouse began in a great hurry, 'and their names were Elsie, Lace, and Tillie, and they lived at the bottom of a well—'

'What did they live on?' said Alice, who always took a great interest in questions of eating and drinking.

'They lived on treacle,' said the Dormouse, after thinking a minute or two.

'They couldn't have done that, you know,' Alice gently remarked. 'They'd have been ill.'

'So they were,' said the Dormouse, 'very ill.'

Alice tried a little to fancy to herself what such an extraordinary way of living would be like, but it puzzled her too much: so she went on, 'But why did they live at the bottom of a well?'

'Take some more tea,' the March Hare said to Alice, very earnestly.

'I've had nothing yet,' Alice replied in an offended tone: 'so I ca'n't take more.'

'You mean you ca'n't take less,' said the Hatter, 'it's very easy to take more than nothing.'

'Nobody asked your opinion,' said Alice.

'Who's making personal remarks now?' the Hatter asked triumphantly.

Alice did not quite know what to say to this, so she helped herself to some tea and bread-and-butter, and then turned to the Dormouse, and repeated her question. 'Why did they live at the bottom of a well?'

The Dormouse again took a minute or two to think about it, and then said 'It was a treacle-well.'

'There's no such thing!' Alice was beginning very angrily, but the Hatter and the March Hare went 'Sh!

Sh!' and the Dormouse sulkily remarked, 'If you ca'n't be civil, you'd better finish the story for yourself.'

'No, please go on!' Alice said very humbly. 'I won't interrupt you again. I dare say there may be one.'

'One, indeed!' said the Dormouse indignantly. However, he consented to go on. 'And so these three little sisters – they were learning to draw, you know –'

'What did they draw?' said Alice, quite forgetting her promise.

'Treacle,' said the Dormouse, without considering at all, this time.

'I want a clean cup,' interrupted the Hatter, 'let's all move one place on.'

He moved on as he spoke, and the Dormouse followed him, the March Hare moved into the Dormouse's place, and Alice rather unwillingly took advantage from the change; and Alice was a good deal worse off than before, as the March Hare had just upset the milk-jug into his plate.

Alice did not wish to offend the Dormouse again, so she began very cautiously,

'But I don't understand. Where did they draw the treacle from?'

'You can draw water out of a water-well,' said the Hatter, 'so I should think you could draw treacle out of a treacle-well – eh, stupid?'

'But they were in the well,' Alice said to the Dormouse, not choosing to notice this last remark.

'Of course they were,' said the Dormouse, 'well in.'

This answer so confused poor Alice, that she let the Dormouse go on for some time without interrupting it.

'They were learning to draw,' the Dormouse went on, yawning and rubbing its eyes, for it was getting very sleepy, 'and they drew all manner of things – everything that begins with an M –'

'Why with an M?' said Alice.

'Why not?' said the March Hare.

Alice was silent.

The Dormouse had closed its eyes by this time, and was going off into a doze, but, on being pinched by the Hatter, it woke up again with a little shriek, and went on, '– that begins with an M, such as mousetraps, and the moon, and memory, and muchness – you know you say things are "much of a muchness" – did you ever see such a thing as a drawing of a muchness?'

'Really, now you ask me,' said Alice, very much confused, 'I don't think –'

'Then you shouldn't talk,' said the Hatter.

This piece of rudeness was more than Alice could bear; she got up in a great disgust, and walked off; the Dormouse fell asleep instantly, and neither of the others took the least notice of her going, though she looked back once or twice, half hoping that they would call after her; the last time she saw them, they were trying to put the Dormouse into the teapot.

'At any rate I'll never go there again!' said Alice, as she picked her way through the wood. 'It's the stupidest tea-party I ever was at in all my life!'

Just as she said this, she noticed that one of the trees had a door leading right into it. 'That's very curious!' she thought. 'But everything's curious to-day. I think I may as well go in at once.' And in she went. Once more she found herself in the long hall, and close to the little glass table. 'Now, I'll manage better this time,' she said to herself, and began by taking the little golden key, and unlocking the door that led into the garden. Then she set to work nibbling at the mushroom (she had kept a piece of it in her pocket) till she was about a foot high, then she walked down the little passage, and then she found herself at last in the beautiful garden, among the bright flower-beds and the cool fountains.

'Come on!' cried the Gryphon, and, taking Alice by the hand, it hurried off, without waiting for the end of the song.

'What trial is it?' Alice panted as she ran : but the

Gryphon only answered 'Come on!' and ran the faster, while more and more faintly came, carried on the breeze that followed them, the melancholy words:

'Soo-oop of the e-e-evening,
Beautiful, beautiful Soup!'

Through The Looking Glass

JABBERWOCKY

'Twas brillig, and the slithy toves
Did gyre and gimble in the wabe;
All mimsy were the borogoves,
And the mome raths outgrabe.

'Beware the jabberwock, my son!
The jaws that bite, the claws that catch!
Beware the Jubjub bird, and shun
The frumious Bandersnatch!'

He took his vorpal sword in hand;
Long time the manxome foe he sought —
So rested he by the Tumtum tree,
And stood awhile in thought.

And, as in uffish thought he stood,
The Jabberwock, with eyes of flame,
Came whiffling through the tulgey wood,
And burbled as it came!

One, two! One, two! And through and through
The vorpal blade went snicker-snack!
He left it dead, and with its head
He went galumphing back.

'And hast thou slain the Jabberwock?
Come to my arms, my beamish boy!
O frabjous day! Callooh! Callay!'
He chortled in his joy.

'Twas brillig, and the slithy toves
Did gyre and gimble in the wabe;
All mimsy were the borogoves,
And the mome raths outgrabe.

Tweedledee smiled gently, and began again:

'The sun was shining on the sea,
Shining with all his might;
He did his very best to make
The billows smooth and bright —
And this was odd, because it was
The middle of the night.

The moon was shining sulkily,
Because she thought the sun
Had got no business to be there
After the day was done —
"It's very rude of him", she said,
"To come and spoil the fun!"

The sea was wet as wet could be,
The sands were dry as dry.
You could not see a cloud, because
No cloud was in the sky;
No birds were flying overhead —
There were no birds to fly.

The Walrus and the Carpenter
Were walking close at hand;
They wept like anything to see
Such quantities of sand;
"If this were only cleared away,"
They said, "it would be grand!"

"If seven maids with seven mops
Swept it for half a year,
Do you suppose," the Walrus said,
"That they could get it clear?"
"I doubt it," said the Carpenter,
And shed a bitter tear.

"O Oysters, come and walk with us!"
The Walrus did beseech.
"A pleasant walk, a pleasant talk,
Along the briny beach;
We cannot do with more than four,
To give a hand to each."

The eldest Oyster looked at him,
But never a word he said;
The eldest Oyster winked his eye,
And shook his heavy head —
Meaning to say he did not choose
To leave the oyster-bed.

But four young Oysters hurried up,
All eager for the treat;
Their coats were brushed, their faces washed,
Their shoes were clean and neat —
And this was odd, because, you know,
They hadn't any feet.

Four other Oysters followed them,
And yet another four;
And thick and fast they came at last,
And more, and more, and more —
All hopping through the frothy waves,
And scrambling to the shore.

The Walrus and the Carpenter,
Walked on a mile or so,
And then they rested on a rock
Conveniently low;
And all the little Oysters stood
And waited in a row.

"The time has come," the Walrus said,
"To talk of many things:
Of shoes — and ships — and sealing wax —
Of cabbages — and kings —
And why the sea is boiling hot —
And whether pigs have wings."

"But wait a minute," the Oysters cried,
"Before we have our chat;
For some of us are out of breath,
And all of us are fat!"
"No hurry!" said the Carpenter.
They thanked him much for that.

"A loaf of bread," the Walrus said,
"Is what we chiefly need;
Pepper and vinegar besides
Are very good indeed —
Now, if you're ready, Oysters dear,
We can begin to feed."

"But not on us!" the Oysters cried,
Turning a little blue.
"After such kindness, that would be
A dismal thing to do!"
"The night is fine," the Walrus said.
"Do you admire the view?"

"It was so kind of you to come!
And you are very nice!"
The Carpenter said nothing but
"Cut us another Slice.
I wish you were not quite so deaf —
I've had to ask you twice!"

"It seems a shame," the Walrus said,
"To play them such a trick.
After we've brought them out so far,
And made them trot so quick!"
The Carpenter said nothing but
"The butter's spread too thick!"

"I weep for you," the Walrus said:
"I deeply sympathise."
With sobs and tears he sorted out
Those of the largest size,
Holding his pocket-handkerchief
Before his streaming eyes.

"O Oysters," said the Carpenter,
"You've had a pleasant run!
Shall we be trotting home again?"
But answer came there none –
And this was scarcely odd, because
They'd eaten every one.'

'I like the Walrus best,' said Alice; 'because he was a little sorry for the poor oysters.'

'He ate more than the Carpenter, though,' said Tweedledee. 'You see he held his handkerchief in front, so that the Carpenter couldn't count how many he took; contrariwise.'

'That was mean!' Alice said indignantly. 'Then I like the Carpenter best – if he didn't eat so many as the Walrus.'

'But he ate as many as he could get,' said Tweedledum.

'Well, what is the song, then?' said Alice, who was by this time completely bewildered.

'I was coming to that,' the Knight said. 'The song really is "A-sitting On a Gate"; and the tune's my own invention.'

So saying, he stopped his horse and let the reins fall on its neck; then, slowly beating time with one hand, and with a faint smile lighting up his gentle foolish face, as if he enjoyed the music of his song, he began. Of all the strange things that Alice saw in her journey Through The Looking-Glass, this was the one that she always remembered most clearly. Years afterwards she could bring the whole scene back again, as if it had been only yesterday – the mild blue eyes and kindly smile of the Knight – the setting sun gleaming through his hair, and shining on his armour in a blaze of light that quite dazzled her – the horse quietly moving about, with the reins hanging loose on his neck, cropping the grass at her feet – and the black shadows of the forest behind – all this she took in like a picture, as, with one hand shading her eyes, she leant against a tree, watching the strange pair, and listening, in a half-dream, to the melancholy music of the song.

'But the tune isn't his own invention,' she said to herself; 'it's "I give thee all, I can no more".' She stood and listened very attentively, but no tears came into her eyes.

'I'll tell thee everything I can;
There's little to relate.
I saw an aged aged man,
A-sitting on a gate.
"Who are you, aged man?" I said.
"And how is it you live?"
And his answer trickled through my head,
Like water through a sieve.

He said "I look for butterflies
That sleep among the wheat;
I make them into mutton-pies
And sell them in the street.
I sell them unto men," he said,
"Who sail on stormy seas;
And that's the way I get my bread —
A trifle, if you please."

But I was thinking of a plan
To dye one's whiskers green,
And always use so large a fan
That they could not be seen.
So, having no reply to give
To what the old man said,
I cried, "Come, tell me how you live!"
And thumped him on the head.

His accents mild took up the tale;
He said "I go my ways,
And when I find a mountain-rill,
I set it in a blaze;
And thence they make a stuff they call
Rowlands' Macassar-Oil —
Yet twopence-halfpenny is all
They give me for my toil."

'Don't you think we ought to have a *crescendo* series, as well?' said Lady Muriel. 'Only fancy being a hundred yards high! One could use an elephant as a paper-weight, and a crocodile as a pair of scissors!'

'And would you have races of different sizes communicate with one another?' I enquired. 'Would they make war on one another, for instance, or enter into treaties?'

'*War* we must exclude, I think. When you could crush a whole nation with one blow of your fist, you couldn't conduct war on equal terms. But anything, involving a collision of *minds* only, would be possible in our ideal world – for of course we must allow *mental* powers to all, irrespective of size. Perhaps the fairest rule would be that, the *smaller* the race, the greater should be its intellectual development!'

'Do you mean to say,' said Lady Muriel, 'that these manikins of an inch high are to *argue* with me?'

'Surely, surely!' said the Earl. 'An argument doesn't depend for its logical force on the *size* of the creature that utters it!'

She tossed her head indignantly. 'I would not argue with any man less than six inches high!' she cried. 'I'd make him *work!*'

'What at?' said Arthur, listening to all this nonsense with an amused smile.

'*Embroidery!*' she readily replied. 'What *lovely* embroidery they would do!'

'Pardon me,' said the pompous man, with lofty condescension. 'I had overlooked the noun. The *ladies*. We regret their absence. Yet we console ourselves. *Thought is free*. With them we are limited to *trivial* topics – Art, Literature, Politics, and so forth. One can bear to discuss *such* paltry matters with a lady. But no man, in his senses –' (he looked sternly round the table, as if defying contradiction) '– ever yet discussed WINE with a lady!' He sipped his glass of port, leaned back in his chair, and slowly raised it up to his eye, so as to look at it through it at the lamp. 'The vintage, my Lord?' he enquired, glancing at his host.

The Earl named the date.

'So I had supposed. But one likes to be certain. The *tint* is, perhaps, slightly pale. But the *body* is unquestionable. And as for the *bouquet* –'

Ah, that magic Bouquet. How vividly that magic word recalled the scene! The little beggar boy turning his somersault in the road – the sweet little crippled maiden in my arms – the mysterious evanescent nursemaid – all rushed tumultuously into my mind, like the creatures of a dream; and through this mental haze there still boomed on, like the tolling of a bell, the solemn voice of the great connoisseur of WINE.

Even *his* utterances had taken on themselves a strange and dream-like form. 'No,' he resumed – and *why* is it, I pause to ask, that in taking up the broken thread of a dialogue, one *always* begins with this cheerless monosyllable? After much anxious thought, I have come to the conclusion that the object in view is the same as that of the school-boy, when the sum he is working has got into a hopeless muddle, and when in despair he takes the sponge, washes it all out, and begins again. Just in the same way the bewildered orator, by the simple process of denying *everything* that has been hitherto asserted, makes a clean sweep of the whole discussion, and can 'start fair' with a fresh theory. 'No,' he resumed; 'there's nothing like cherry-jam, after all. That's what *I* say!'

'Not for *all* qualities!' an eager little man shrilly interposed. 'For *richness* of general tone I don't say that it *has* a rival. But for *delicacy* of modulation – for what one may call the "harmonics" of flavour – give *me* good old *raspberry*-jam!'

'Allow me one word!' The fat red-faced man, quite hoarse with excitement, broke into the dialogue. 'It's too important a question to be settled by Amateurs! I can give you the views of a *Professional* – perhaps the most experienced jam-taster now living. Why, I've known him fix the age of strawberry-jam, to a *day* – and we all know what a difficult jam it is to give a date to – on a single tasting! Well, I put to him the *very* question you are discussing. His words were "*cherry*-jam is best, for mere *chiaroscuro* of flavour; *raspberry*-jam lends itself to those unresolved discords that linger so lovingly on the tongue; but for rapturous *utterness* of saccharine perfection, it's *apricot-jam first and the rest nowhere*!" That was well put, wasn't it?'

'Consummately put!' shrieked the eager little man.

'I know your friend well,' said the pompous man. 'As a jam-taster, he has no rival! Yet I scarcely think –'

'But here the discussion became general; and his words were lost in a confused medley of names, every guest sounding the praises of his own favourite jam.

In stature the Manlet was dwarfish –
No burly big Blunderbore he;
And he wearily gazed on the crawfish
His Wifelet had dressed for his tea.
'Now reach me, sweet Atom, my gunlet,
    And hurl the old shoelet for luck;
Let me hie to the bank of the runlet,
    And Shoot thee a Duck!'

She has reached him his minikin gunlet
    She has hurled the old shoelet for luck
She is busily baking a bunlet
    To welcome him home with his Duck
On he speeds, never wasting a wordlet,
    Though thoughtlets cling, closely as wax,
To the spot where the beautiful birdlet
        So quietly quacks.

Where the Lobsterlet lurks, and the Crablet
    So slowly and sleepily crawls;
Where the Dolphin's at home, and the Dablet
    Pays long ceremonious calls;

Where the Grublet is sought by the Froglet;
  Where the Frog is pursued by the Duck;
Where the Ducklet is chased by the Doglet —
      So runs the world's luck!

He has loaded with bullet and powder;
  His footfall is noiseless as air;
But the Voices grow louder and louder,
  And bellow, and bluster, and blare.
They bristle before him and after,
  They flutter above and below,
Shrill shriekings of lubberly laughter,
      Weird wailings of woe!

They echo without him, within him;
  They thrill through his whiskers and beard;
Like a teetotum seeming to spin him,
  With sneers never hitherto sneered.
'Avengement,' they cry, 'on our Foelet!
  Let the Manikin weep for our wrongs!
Let us drench him, from toplet to toelet,
      With Nursery-Songs!

'He shall muse upon "Hey! Diddle! Diddle!"
  On the Cow that surmounted the Moon;
He shall rave of the Cat and the Fiddle,
  And the Dish that eloped with the Spoon;
And his soul shall be sad for the Spider,
  When Miss Muffet was sipping her whey,
That so tenderly sat down beside her
      And scared her away!

'The music of Midsummer-madness
  Shall sting him with many a bite,
Till, in rapture of rollicking sadness,
  He shall groan with a gloomy delight;
He shall swathe him, like mists of the morning,
  In platitudes luscious and limp,
Such as deck, with a deathless adorning
      The Song of the Shrimp!

'When the Ducklet's dark doom is decided
  We will trundle him home in a trice;
And the banquet, so plainly provided,
  Shall round into rose-buds and rice;
In a blaze of pragmatic invention
  He shall wrestle with Fate, and shall reign;
But he has not a friend fit to mention,
      So hit him again!'

He has shot it, the delicate darling!
  And the Voices have ceased from their strife;
Not a whisper of sneering or snarling,
  As he carries it home to his wife;
Then, cheerily champing the bunlet
  His spouse was so careful to bake,
He hies him once more to the runlet
      To fetch her the Drake!

'The day must come — if the world lasts long enough —'
said Arthur, 'when every possible tune will have been
composed — every possible pun perpetrated —' (Lady
Muriel wrung her hands, like a tragedy-queen) 'and, worse
than that, every possible *book* written! For the number
of *words* is finite.'

'It'll make very little difference to the *authors*,' I suggested. 'Instead of saying "*what* book shall I write?" an
author will ask himself "*which* book shall I write?" A
mere verbal distinction!'

Lady Muriel gave me an approving smile. 'But *lunatics*
would always write books, surely?' she went on. 'They
couldn't write the same books over again!'

'True,' said Arthur. 'But their books would come to an
end, also. The number of lunatic *books* is as finite as the
number of lunatics.'

'And *that* number is becoming greater every year,' said
a pompous man, whom I recognised as the self-appointed
showman on the day of the picnic.

'So they say,' replied Arthur. 'And, when ninety per

cent. of us are lunatics,' (he seemed to be in a wildly non-sensical mood) 'the asylums will be put to their proper use.'

'And that is –?' the pompous man gravely enquired.

'*To shelter the sane!*' said Arthur. '*We* shall bar ourselves in. The lunatics will have it all their own way, *outside*. They'll do it a little queerly, no doubt; steamers always blowing up; most of the towns will be burnt down; most of the ships sunk –'

'And most of the men *killed!*' murmured the pompous man, who was evidently hopelessly bewildered.

'Certainly,' Arthur assented. 'Till at last there will be *fewer* lunatics than sane men. Then *we* come out; they go in; and things return to their normal condition.'

The pompous man frowned darkly, and bit his lip, and folded his arms vainly trying to think it out. 'He is *jesting!*' he muttered to himself at last, in a tone of withering contempt, as he stalked away.

By this time the other guests had arrived; and dinner was announced. Arthur of course took down Lady Muriel; and *I* was pleased to find myself seated at her other side, with a severe-looking old lady (whom I had not met before, and whose name I had, as is usual in introduction, entirely failed to catch, merely gathering that it sounded like a compound-name) as my partner for the banquet.

She appeared, however, to be acquainted with Arthur, and confided to me in a low voice that he was 'a very argumentative young man'. Arthur, for his part, seemed well inclined to show himself worthy of the character she had given him, and, hearing her say 'I never take wine with my soup!' (this was not a confidence to me, but was launched upon Society, as a matter of general interest), he at once challenged a combat by asking her '*when* would you say that property *commences* in a plate of soup?'

'This is *my* soup,' she sternly replied: 'and what is before you is *yours*.'

'No doubt,' said Arthur; 'but *when* did I begin to own it? Up to the moment of its being put into the plate, it was

the property of our host; while being offered round the
table, it was, let us say, held in trust by the waiter; did
it become mine when I accepted it? Or when it was
placed before me? Or when I took the first spoonful?'

'*He is a very* argumentative young man!' was all the
old lady would say: but she said it audibly, this time,
feeling that Society had a right to know it.

> He thought he saw a Buffalo
>   Upon the chimney-piece;
> He looked again, and found it was
>   His Sister's Husband's Niece.
> 'Unless you leave this house,' he said,
>   I'll send for the Police!'
>
> He thought he saw a Rattlesnake
>   That questioned him in Greek;
> He looked again, and found it was
>   The Middle of Next Week.
> 'The one thing I regret,' he said,
>   Is that it cannot speak!'
>
> He thought he saw a Banker's Clerk
>   Descending from the bus;
> He looked again, and found it was
>   A Hippopotamus;
> 'If this should stay to dine,' he said
>   There won't be much for us!'
>
> He thought he saw a Kangaroo
>   That worked a coffee-mill;
> He looked again, and found it was
>   A Vegetable-Pill.
> 'Were I to swallow this,' he said,
>   I should be very ill!'
>
> He thought he saw a Coach-and-Four
>   That stood beside his bed;
> He looked again, and found it was
>   A Bear without a Head.

'Poor thing,' he said, 'poor silly thing!
   It's waiting to be fed!'

He thought he saw an Albatross
   That fluttered round the lamp;
He looked again, and saw it was
   A Penny-Postage-Stamp.
'You'd best be getting home,' he said:
   'The nights are very damp!'

He thought he saw a Garden-Door
   That opened with a key;
He looked again, and found it was
   A Double Rule of Three;
'And all its mystery', he said
   Is clear as day to me!'

He thought he saw an Argument
   That proved he was the Pope;
He looked again, and found it was
   A Bar of Mottled Soap.
'A fact so dread,' he faintly said
   Extinguishes all hope!'

ALAN COREN

Once I Put It Down, I Could Not Pick It Up Again

A couple of years ago, some organisation calling itself the Encyclopaedia Britannica sent me twenty-three books to review. Like any reviewer faced with such a task, I wasn't able, of course, to read any of them – just snatched a quick look at the titles on the spines and made a few shrewd guesses.

A. ANSTEY

F. Anstey, author of *Vice-Versa*, *The Brass Bottle*, and many other bestsellers, was one of the most famous figures in Victorian London. A. Anstey wasn't. This, indeed, was the nub of his personal disaster, a searing comment on nineteenth-century society, told for the first time in this splendid volume. A. Anstey was constantly being introduced at smart Victorian soirees to people whose instant reaction was 'Not *the* Anstey?' to which he would immediately answer 'No, just *a* Anstey, ha-ha-ha!' This pitiful little quip commended him to no-one, and was usually met with a sneering 'You mean *an* Anstey' and a snub. He endured this for eighteen years before finally hanging himself in a rented room just off Lewisham High Street.

ANT BALFE

When General Tom Thumb crowned a successful fairground tour with a command performance in front of Queen Victoria, the seal was set on a midget-vogue of staggering proportions. Country fairs and London theatres alike were filled with talented dwarfs, each tinier than the last. The smallest and indubitably the most adroit of these (he could play Mozart's four horn concertos on a drinking-straw while riding on a stoat) was Ant Balfe, so called because of his incredible diminutiveness. Who knows to what figurative heights he might not have risen, had he not, at his Drury Lane premiere, been trodden on by an inept autograph-hunter?

BALFOUR BOTH

A fascinating tale of Georgian surgery, this recounts the earliest known sex-change operation, on the unfortunate Geraldine (née Gerald) Balfour. It seemed successful at first, and the happy Geraldine took to signing herself G. Balfour (Miss), but subsequent developments proved this course to be premature, and soon she was sending letters of complaint to the General Medical Council signed G. Balfour (Both). Eventually, the name was changed by deed poll to Balfour-Both to avoid upsetting pre-permissive sensibilities. Beautifully illustrated.

BOTHA CARTHAGE

An exceptionally well-documented life of Hannibal, whose dying words give the book its intriguing title. His actual words, apparently, were 'Bugga Carthage!' but the publishers, I understand, felt that this might have meant rejection by W. H. Smith, and compromised accordingly.

CARTHUSIANS COCKCROFT

Subtitled 'An Edwardian Tragedy', this bitter book tells the story of Thomas Cockcroft, perhaps the most promising Senior Master in Charterhouse's history. He was due for appointment to the headmastership at the incredibly early age of thirty, when certain facts were made public by a disgruntled porter concerning the intimate teas to which Cockcroft would invite the smaller boys. Inevitably, the yellow press dubbed him Carthusians Cockcroft at his infamous trial (*The Daily Graphic* even tried to christen him Fag Cockcroft, but the multi-entendres were too much for its working-class readership), and upon his release from Brixton, he went off to the Congo to shoot porters. There is a statue of him in Chisholm St. Mary, erected in error.

COCKER DAIS

Perhaps the best loved of the East End flyweights, Cocker Dais at one time held the British, British Empire, and European titles. At the peak of his career, he fought an unknown American for the World title, and was knocked out in the second minute of the first round. His pub, *The Cocker Dais*, later became a famous dockside landmark for German bombers.

DAISY EDUCATIONAL

A poignant, heart-warming novel about an elderly schoolmistress in a tiny Welsh village. The influence of *How Green Was My Valley* is, of course, observable, but the presence of a black Druid boutique owner gives the book an essentially modern air.

EDWARD EXTRACT

I'm delighted that the publishers have seen fit to reprint this little-known eighteenth-century novel by Tobias Sterne, because it's a narrative gem of the first water. A bawdy, picaresque romp, it tells how postboy Edward Extract makes off with Square Weasell's buxom daughter Phyllis, loses her to a Turkish mercenary during the Battle of Blenheim, makes his way to Utrecht disguised as an alternative Pope, falls in love with Warty Eva of Bosnia, is press-ganged into the Hungarian navy, loses his leg at Malplaquet, seduces a lady-in-waiting to Queen Anne, becomes a Whig, loses his right arm at Sheriffmuir, gets Gräfin von Immel with child, goes deaf during the siege of Belgrade, abducts a Moorish slave-girl, and returns at last to his native Suffolk, where he knocks out his left eye on a broken wainshaft. Lusty, purgative, rollicking, and highly recommended.

EXTRADITION GARRICK

It is said that when Lord Chief Justice Sir Esmond Garrick (1789–1852) was refused his request to the Brazilian authorities to extradite Bloody Ned Magee on a charge of treason, he sailed personally to Sao Paulo, strode into the Court of Justice, decapitated the President of the Brazilian Supreme Court, and, turning to the other judges and waving his bloody sabre above his wig, cried: 'I would remind ye that English law is based on precedent, and I have just created one!' Magee was released forthwith, and duly hanged at the notorious Vile Assize of 1828. As Extradition Garrick, Sir Esmond pursued an inflexible hunt for refugee criminals, often giving up his holidays to root about in the stews of Marseilles and Cadiz, heavily disguised, in his inexorable search for what he called 'hanging fodder', frequently bringing them back to England in a gunny-sack. A thundering good read.

GARRISON HALIBUT

I was bored by this long, scholarly thesis on the Minne-

apolis dry-goods salesman who rose to be the Governor of
Minnesota and is chiefly remembered as the initiator of
off-street parking.

HALICAR IMPALA
If you like books that take the lid off the motor industry,
then this is for you! Spurred on by what they thought was
going to be the enormous success of the Ford Edsel, a
group of General Motors designers made a survey of what
the typical *female* customer wanted in a motor car, and
proceeded accordingly. After two years of research and
the expenditure of eighty million dollars, the first Halicar
Impala was built. The engine started well enough, but at
35 mph the linkage connecting the hair-drier to the eye-
level grill snapped, disconnected the telephone, and threw
the crib through the windscreen. Upon applying the
brakes, the driver inadvertently set the instant heel-bar in
motion, and was riveted to the wardrobe by a row of tin-
tacks. A second Impala was never built.

IMPATIENS JINOTEGA
Jose Ortega 'Impatiens' Jinotega was the father of modern
bullfighting. Until his appearance in 1919, the average
matador took eight hours to kill a bull, and there was only
one fight per afternoon. Impatient as his nickname suggests, Jinotega soon saw that strangling was a slow and
inept method, and, on his first appearance in the Barcelona
ring, he pulled a sword from beneath his cloak, and des-
patched six fighting bulls in the space of half an hour.
This book is a a magnificent tribute to a man who died as
he would have wished, gored by Ernest Hemingway during
a bar-brawl in Pamplona.

JIRASEK LIGHTHOUSES
A penetrating analysis of the great Czech film director,
Imry Jirasek, known in the West as Jirasek Lighthouses,
after his greatest film, a four-hour satirical study of the
life of a solitary wick-trimmer. *Lighthouses* was followed

by *An Old Bus*, *Jackets*, and the deeply disturbing *My Bath And Hat*. After vigorous appeals by Ken Tynan, Arnold Wesker, Vanessa Redgrave, George Melly and others, Jirasek was allowed to leave Prague for England. He left London almost immediately for Hollywood, where he now makes half a million dollars a year scripting *I Love Lucy*.

LIGHTING MAXIMILIAN
Sean Kenny's detailed account of his special effects work on the Peter Weiss/Peter Brook production of *The Manic Depression And Concomitant Hallucinations That Led To The Nervous Breakdown Of Emperor Maximilian Of Austro-Hungary As Performed By Members Of The Portuguese World Cup Team*.

MAXIMINUS NAPLES
The first Proconsul of what was, in the second century BC, still Calabrium, Maximinus is chiefly remembered for his habit of throwing political opponents into Vesuvius. His proconsulate was exceptionally stormy, corrupt and inefficient, and in 134 BC, Emperor Tiberius Gracchus demoted him to the proconsulate of Sicilia, where he is chiefly remembered for his habit of throwing political opponents into Etna. His significance is minimal, and my own opinion is that this dreary account was long underdue.

NAPOLEON OZONOLYSIS
The story of how Napoleon Ozonolysis rose from humble origins to become the wealthiest Greek shipowner in the world has, of course, all the fabulous ingredients of legend, and in this frank autobiography (as told to Bobby Moore), the amazing tycoon reveals all. Lavishly illustrated with photographs of colonels, the book also contains an extremely useful index of eligible American widows. Just the thing for a Hellenic cruise, or a short piano leg.

P–PLASTERING

I opened this volume with considerable trepidation, believing it to be just another Do-It-Yourself tract. Imagine my delighted surprise to discover that it was in fact a history of stammering! Packed with fascinating information – did you know, for example, that George Washington was unable to enunciate 'teaspoon,' or that *K-K-K-Katie* was not written by Gustav Mahler? – the book is a veritable mine of glottal arcana. The appendix on Regency hiccups is on no account to be missed.

PLASTICS RAZIN

If you like escapology as much as I do, then you'll find it hard to resist this vivid biography of The Great Razin (pronounced *Rah'tsin*). Louis Razin's career began astoundingly early: in the last stages of labour, his mother was rushed to hospital in Boston, Mass., by hansom cab, but by the time she arrived on the maternity ward, she was no longer pregnant. Hysterical, she was led back to the waiting cab by her doctor, only to find the infant Louis screaming on the back seat! By the age of fourteen, he was already The Great Razin and Doris (subsequently The Great Razin and Beryl, after Doris had failed to emerge from a cabinet on the stage of the Holborn Empire), and in 1923 he became the first man to escape from a strait-jacket on radio. When transatlantic flights became regular with the advent of the Super Clipper, Razin celebrated by eating an entire canteen of airline cutlery, and the nickname stuck. Plastics Razin is buried in Boston Cemetery, probably.

RAZOR SCHURZ

On the afternoon of September 8, 1926, a short, stocky man in a barathea coat and a pearl-grey fedora walked into a garage in South Side Chicago. When he walked out again, four minutes later, he left six men dead behind him, cut to ribbons. That was the beginning of the career of Razor Schurz, dreaded torpedo of the Capone gang and by

the time he was finally trapped in an alley beside the Rexo
Bowling Palace in Peoria, Illinois, early in 1937, and mown
down by the guns of J. Edgar Hoover — or was it the
hoovers of J. Edgar Gun? The print in my copy was tiny
and execrable — he had accounted for no less than sixty-
eight other hoodlums. This book, by the way, is now being
made into seven feature films.

SCHÜTZ SPEKE
Schütz speke (sometimes schützspeke) was an entirely
new language invented by embittered ex-Esperantist Wil-
helm Schütz, and was designed to be the greatest international medium of communication the world had ever
known. Unfortunately, the secret died with Schütz, and
since this volume is written in it, the publisher's motives
escape me. It may be a tax-loss, or something.

SPELMAN TIMMINS
This expensively produced facsimile edition of the diary
of a fourteenth-century warlock is not particulary interesting in itself, but it contains some interesting recipes
entirely new to me: I would recommend in particular his
tasty langues de crapauds au fin bec, even if it does, for
some mysterious reason, make your face come out in long
ginger hair.

TIMOLEON-VIETA
These collected love letters of young Timoleon, Prince of
Tyre, to Vieta, the beautiful fourteen-year-old daughter
of a Sidonian lunatic, make poignant reading. The two
lovers never touched, and saw one another only briefly,
just once, when Timoleon's carriage ran down Vieta's milk-
float early in 981 AD. Their tender and passionate affair
came to an abrupt end when palace Nubians employed
by Timoleon's tyrannical father seized the young prince
and cut off his allowance.

VIETNAM ZWORYKIN
If, like me, you find the radical-chic posturings of the

Zworykin family of New York extremely tiresome – tracts and polemica by Nat 'Cuba' Zworykin, Sharon 'Women's Lib' Zworykin, Chuck 'Legalise Acid' Zworykin, Sigmund 'Environment' Zworykin, and Dustin 'Kill the Pigs' Zworykin have all become best-sellers on both sides of the Atlantic – then this new tirade by the youngest member, Willy 'Vietnam' Zworykin, is not for you, despite its foreword by Gore Vidal, its addendum on Ulster by Edward Kennedy, its footnotes on the poor finish of the Sidewinder missile by Ralph Nader, and its jacket-blurb by Jane Fonda. The fact that the whole text can be pulled out to form a banner may be of interest to bibliophiles.

IVOR CUTLER

How To Make Friends

Do you find it difficult to make friends?

I am, at least I was, until I discovered how to do it.

First of all, take a large bucket of whitewash, then stand by the window and look out. When you see someone approaching whom you would like to know, wait until he is directly below, then empty the bucket over his head.

He will stop, and look up, and shout unspeakable language at you. You reply, 'Do come upstairs and clean yourself up' and throw him down the key.

He will pick up the key and enter your home, tramping whitewash into the carpet all the way up.

You will say, 'Come. Have a bath,' light the geyser and start running the water. He will take his clothes off, and as he is taking them off say, 'ah! You have a hole in your underwear. Let me mend it while you are having your bath.' He will say, 'Thank you. I am very grateful for this.'

While he is in the bath, sit there talking to him, darning his vest. It doesn't matter what kind of thread you use, it is the deed which is important. I myself use cobbler's thread, because when he wears the vest and feels the cobbler's thread against his skin, it is a constant reminder to him of our friendship and he thinks, 'I must phone this man again.'

When he is dry, and in your best red silk dressing-gown, with the dragons; then he can take his clothes, put them into the bath water and wash them, then hang them out of the window to dry.

Say to him, 'Come and sit with me and talk to me by the window while they are drying.' Then you talk, enjoying one another's conversation.

By this time the clothes are dry. Fetch them in and he will don them, thanking you for the darn of his vest.

As it is now lunch, you offer him a share of your dinner.

After dinner he says, Well, I must really go now, and as you go downstairs he notices with alarm the whitewash on the carpet and says, 'Goodness! Look what I have done to your carpet.' And you say, 'No, no! I only rent a room here. It is the landlord's carpet.' Then he says, 'We cannot let you get into bad odour with the landlord. Let us together clean this carpet.' So you clean the carpet, and this makes your friendship stronger than ever.

When you have cleaned the carpet, he says, 'Well, I must really go now, but I shall come and see you again tomorrow and we shall have another long talk.'

You have made a friend.

The False God

Crawl up! Crawl up! See the famous god!

Here you! Get down on your hands and knees! This is a god, you know!

Oh, no, not me mister. I don't get down on my hands and knees to anybody.

Well, you'll have to, or else you'll have to leave the tent.

I've paid my money sir, and I'm staying.

Come on now. Down on your hands and knees.

Look, there's no need for you to shout at me like that. I'm the only person in your tent.

Oh, all right, if you want to stand, keep right to the back, against the tent wall.

I'll do that. Now where's your god?

Take it easy. Don't be in such a hurry. It's behind this curtain.

Well, show me it. Come on, I'm in a hurry.

That's not the right attitude. Now you just stand quiet for a moment and I'll pull the curtain aside. There!

It looks like a gold brick.

It is a gold brick.

And you call that a god?

It's a good enough god for me.

Well it's not good enough for me. What else does it do besides sit there?

Oh, it talks to you.

Go on. Get it to talk to me.

All right. Wait a minute. Listen – did you hear it?

No. I heard nothing.

You probably weren't listening on the right frequency. What frequency do you listen on?

Any frequency from 32 to 12,000.

Ah! Now my god talks on 20 to 22,000.

That's a damn silly frequency to talk on. That means that nobody can hear it except bats.

That's right. Nobody hears it except bats.

Then what are you asking me to listen to it for?

Well, you might be a bat.

Do I look like a bat?

No, frankly you don't. You might be a bat in disguise though.

Well, I'm not a bat in disguise, I'm a gold brick in disguise. And I accuse you of being in possession of a false gold brick. Here, let me see it. Just as I thought. A big lump of cod painted over. No wonder I couldn't hear it.

PAUL DEHN

Schotto Bottled

Advertising in a recent issue of the *New Yorker*, Messrs Barton and Guestier (Wine Merchants Inc.) have undertaken the enlightened task of introducing their clientèle to certain European wines which many an American has either never heard of or (if we may credit rumour) is too frightened to order on the telephone for fear of mispronouncing. The advertisement contains the following list:

So tairn	Shah blee
May dock	Man kon
Bow Joe lay	Mawn rah shay
Poo yee Fweesay	Poe mahr
Schotto Neff du Pop	Grahv
Sant Ay mee lee on	

Literate Europeans and Orientals will, of course, recognize at once the titles of eleven comparatively well-known Drinking Songs. But I wonder how many Americans will know the words (or, indeed, the meaning) of these 'ditties' that Messrs Barton and Guestier are obviously recommending their clients to sing, while the unfamiliar bottle goes round the table. It is for their benefit that I take the liberty of adding an explanatory 'gloss' on some of the better-known songs.

So tairn became popular in Scotland about 1796:

So tairn frae yon stuir,
An' glaur me the tassie.
Wha helpit the puir
Nae gowaned a lassie!

Nae gowaned a mither
Wha whelpit a bairn!
We'll quecht it thegither,
So tairn, lassie, tairn!

(*Stuir*: mess. *glaur*: toss. *tassie*: utensil. *gowaned*: soli-
cited (*sc.* for advice). *quecht*: *turpitudinem alicui per vim
inferre*)

The ladies (or 'lassies') should courteously *turn* as each
man upends his individual utensil. The piece has been
translated into Lallans by Sydney Goodsir Smith, but the
original is the simpler version.

May dock is a 14th-century English wassail song. The
words of these often had very little relevance to the act
of drinking, until they resolved into the rollicking chorus
that was wassail's happiest convention:

Sith May dock blowe,
We schal have snowe
When bulluc lowe
Wid windes snell.

Ac fadeth May dock
In fold and padock,
Ne holt ne hadock
Moun swete smell

Then troll the boll, boteler ... etc.

(*snell*: painful. *hadock*: haycock; not (as Quiller-Couch in
The Oxford Book of English Verse) haddock.)

Bow Joe Lay is a straight 18th-century drinking shanty:

'Twere nor' nor' west from Port o' Brest
(Yare, yare and away!)
That hard abaft the scupper-tholes
Bow Joe lay.

With a ho, Joe! Blow, Joe!
Row me round the bay.
Fill us a tot and wet the spot
Where Bow Joe lay.

Bow Joe has never been satisfactorily identified. Some
hold that 'bow' refers to the shape of his limbs and is an
ellipsis for 'bow-legged Joe'; others, that it is a corruption
of Fr. *beau* and that, for a naval man, he was singularly
beautiful.

Poo-yee Fweesay is a Chinese *haiku* (circ. 5080 B.C.)
and should strictly be sung only when drinking wine that
has been distilled from rice:

Poo-yee fweesay,
Ori-tamae!
Nao, nao, hou han shi.
Shan, kuei fweesay, ho tsai yu.

Princess Poo-yee
Come down!
Nao, nao, blows the autumn wind.
I long for a royal lady, but dare not speak.
(tr. Arthur Waley)

The author, Po, is said to have died of drink.

Schotto Neff, Du, Pop? is a traditional Yiddish lament
still sung, over a glass of *klatsch* on the Sabbath, by the
descendants of those Jews who were driven from the
Great Ghetto of Neff by edict of Czar Nicholas at the turn
of the 19th century.

'Schotto Neff, du, Pop?
Schotto Neff, du, Pop?'
'Weh, weh, bontsche schnee!
Schot' woh' Neff dein Pop.'

'Dost remember Neff, thou, mine father?
Dost remember Neff, thou, mine father?'
'Woe, woe! Silent snow!
Remembers well Neff thine father.'

With the words of the remaining songs I am unfamiliar, though any reasonably experienced folklorist will recognize the titles.

Sant Ay, Mee Lee on was first sung in French by a group of 17th-century Catholic missionaries far from their home village ('St.Ay, white-roofed, still calls ...') and translated by their Hawaiian converts, whose descendants sing it to this very day – though its regional significance has long been forgotten and it is sung chiefly during beach-banquets arranged at moderate cost for the tourist trade. I am indebted to the *Guide Michelin* for a comprehensive note on modern St. Ay:

ST. AY Loiret. Ⓢ – Ⓢ – 620 h. Alt. 100
☞ **Bouguereau**

Shah Blee is a loyal toast from the 4th-century Persian; *Mah Kon*, a popular Siamese love-song; *Mawn Rah Shay*, a ritualistic Hindu invocation to Rah Shay (King Breath), which is not really a drinking song at all, unless Messrs Barton and Guestier have actually bottled the waters of the Ganges; *Poe Mahr* (more correctly *Po Mahr*: 'A little more!'), a *skjemtsang* (joke-song) in which second-year students of Upsala University induct freshmen into the joys of Aquavit; and *Grahv*, a Latvian dirge.

A good list, on the whole, though there are notable omissions. What of the Tibetan *Ahman Yak*? Or that festive group of Italo-Yugoslav *canzonette della frontiera* compositely called *Romanay Contee* (Tales of the Gipsies)? Or the bitter little Trinidad calypso, *Ma go!*? Or the ever-green *Arnjew*:

> Arnjew de kutiest
> Butiest frutiest
> Beibi –
> Arnjew?

But this, on second thoughts, is still in current usage among certain irredentist minorities all over America. The Vanderbilts are said to sing it in family conclave once yearly. New York (one so easily forgets) used to be Nieuw Amsterdam.

CHARLES DICKENS

from Nicholas Nickleby

'This is the first class in English spelling and philosophy, Nickleby,' said Squeers, beckoning Nicholas to stand beside him. 'We'll get up a Latin one, and hand that over to you. Now, then, where's the first boy?'

'Please, sir, he's cleaning the back parlour window,' said the temporary head of the philosophical class.

'So he is, to be sure,' rejoined Squeers. 'We go upon the practical mode of teaching, Nickleby; the regular education system. C-l-e-a-n, clean, verb active, to make bright, to scour. W-i-n, win, d-e-r, der, winder, a casement. When the boy knows this out of the book, he goes and does it. It's just the same principle as the use of the globes. Where's the second boy?'

'Please, sir, he's weeding the garden,' replied a small voice.

'To be sure,' said Squeers, by no means disconcerted. 'So he is. B-o-t, bot, t-i-n, n-e-y, bottinney, noun substantive, a knowledge of plants. When he has learned that bottinney means a knowledge of plants, he goes and knows 'em. That's our system, Nickleby; what do you think of it?'

'It's a very useful one, at any rate,' answered Nicholas.

'I believe you,' rejoined Squeers, not remarking the emphasis of his usher. 'Third boy, what's a horse?'

'A beast, sir,' replied the boy.

'So it is,' said Squeers. 'Ain't it, Nickleby?'

'I believe there is no doubt of that, sir,' answered Nicholas.

'Of course there isn't,' said Squeers. 'A horse is a quad-ruped, and quadruped's Latin for beast, as everybody that's gone through the grammar, knows, or else where's the use of having grammars at all?'

'Where, indeed!' said Nicholas abstractedly.

'As you're perfect in that,' resumed Squeers, turning to the boy, 'go and look after *my* horse, and rub him down well, or I'll rub you down. The rest of the class go and draw water up, till somebody tells you to leave off, for it's washing-day tomorrow, and they want the coppers filled.'

Kate looked very much perplexed, and was apparently about to ask for further explanation, when a shouting and scuffling noise, as of an elderly gentleman whooping, and kicking up his legs on loose gravel with great violence, was heard to proceed from the same direction as the former sounds; and, before they had subsided, a large cucumber was seen to shoot up in the air with the velocity of a sky-rocket, whence it descended, tumbling over and over, until it fell at Mrs. Nickleby's feet.

This remarkable appearance was succeeded by another of a precisely similar description; then a fine vegetable marrow, of unusually large dimensions, was seen to whirl aloft, and come toppling down; then, several cucumbers shot up together; finally, the air was darkened by a shower of onions, turnip-radishes, and other small vegetables which fell rolling and scattering, and bumping about, in all directions.

As Kate rose from her seat, in some alarm, and caught her mother's hand to run with her into the house, she felt herself rather retarded than assisted in her intention; and following the direction of Mrs. Nickleby's eyes, was quite terrified by the apparition of an old black velvet cap, which, by slow degrees, as if its wearer were ascending a ladder or pair of steps, rose above the wall dividing their garden from that of the next cottage (which, like their own, was a detached building), and was gradually followed by a very large head, and an old face in which were a pair of most extraordinary grey eyes; very wild, very wide open, and rolling in their sockets, with a dull, languishing leering look, most ugly to behold.

'Mama!' cried Kate, really terrified for the moment, 'why do you stop, why do you lose an instant? Mama, pray come in!'

'Kate, my dear,' returned her mother, still holding back, 'how can you be so foolish? I'm ashamed of you. How do you suppose you are ever to get through life, if you're such a coward as this! What do you want, sir?' said Mrs. Nickleby, addressing the intruder with a sort of simpering displeasure, 'How dare you look into this garden?'

'Queen of my soul,' replied the stranger, folding his hands together, 'this goblet sip!'

'Nonsense, sir,' said Mrs. Nickleby, 'Kate, my love, pray be quiet.'

'Won't you sip the goblet?' urged the stranger, with his head imploringly on one side, and his right hand on his breast. 'Oh, do sip the goblet!'

'I shall not consent to do anything of the kind, sir,' said Mrs. Nickleby. 'Pray, begone.'

'Why is it,' said the old gentleman, coming up a step higher, and leaning his elbows on the wall, with as much complacency as if he were looking out of a window, 'why is it that beauty is always obdurate, even when admiration is as honourable and respectful as mine?' Here he smiled, kissed his hand, and made several low bows. 'Is it owing to the bees, who, when the honey season is over, and they are supposed to have been killed with brimstone, in reality fly to Barbary and lull the captive Moors to sleep with their drowsy songs? Or is it,' he added, dropping his voice almost to a whisper, 'in consequence of the statue at Charing Cross having been lately seen on the Stock Exchange at midnight, walking arm-in-arm with the Pump from Aldgate, in a riding-habit?'

'Mama,' murmured Kate, 'do you hear him?'

'Hush, my dear!' replied Mrs. Nickleby, in the same tone of voice, 'he is very polite, and I think that was a quotation from the poets. Pray, don't worry me so – you'll pinch my arm black and blue. Go away, sir!'

'Quite away?' said the gentleman, with a languishing look. 'Oh! quite away?'

'Yes,' returned Mrs. Nickleby, 'certainly. You have no business here. This is private property, sir; you ought to know that.'

'I do know,' said the old gentleman, laying his finger on his nose, with an air of familiarity, most reprehensible, 'that this is a sacred and enchanted spot, where the most divine charms' – here he kissed his hand and bowed again – 'waft mellifluousness over the neighbours' gardens, and force the fruit and vegetables into premature existence. That fact I am acquainted with. But will you permit me, fairest creature, to ask you one question, in the absence of the planet Venus, who has gone on business to the Horse Guards, and would otherwise – jealous of your superior charms – interpose between us?'

'Kate,' observed Mrs. Nickleby, turning to her daughter, 'it's very awkward, positively. I really don't know what to say to this gentleman. One ought to be civil, you know.'

'Dear mama,' rejoined Kate, 'don't say a word to him, but let us run away, as fast as we can, and shut ourselves up till Nicholas comes home.'

Mrs. Nickleby looked very grand, not to say contemptuous, at this humiliating proposal; and, turning to the old gentleman, who had watched them during these whispers with absorbing eagerness, said, 'If you will conduct yourself, sir, like the gentleman I should imagine you to be, from your language and – and – appearance (quite the counterpart of your grandpapa, Kate, my dear, in his best days), and will put your question to me in plain words, I will answer it.'

If Mrs. Nickleby's excellent papa had borne, in his best days, a resemblance to the neighbour now looking over the wall, he must have been, to say the least, a very queer-looking old gentleman in his prime. Perhaps Kate thought so, for she ventured to glance at his living portrait with some attention, as he took off his black velvet cap, and, exhibiting a perfectly bald head, made a long series of bows, each accompanied with a fresh kiss of the hand. After exhausting himself, to all appearance, with this fatiguing performance, he covered his head once more, pulled the cap very carefully over the tips of his ears, and resuming his former attitude, said,

'The question is –'

Here he broke off to look round in every direction, and satisfy himself beyond all doubt that there were no listeners near. Assured that there were not, he tapped his nose several times, accompanying the action with a cunning look as though congratulating himself on his caution; and stretching out his neck, said in a loud whisper,

'Are you a princess?'

'You are mocking me, sir,' replied Mrs. Nickleby, making a feint of retreating towards the house.

'No, but are you?' said the old gentleman.

'You know I am not, sir,' replied Mrs. Nickleby.

'Then are you any relation to the Archbishop of Canterbury?' inquired the old gentleman with great anxiety. 'Or to the Pope of Rome? Or the Speaker of the House of Commons? Forgive me, if I am wrong, but I was told you were niece to the Commissioners of Paving, and daughter-in-law to the Lord Mayor and Court of Common Council, which would account for your relationship to all three.'

'Whoever has spread such reports, sir,' returned Mrs. Nickleby with some warmth, 'has taken great liberties with my name, and one which I am sure my son Nicholas, if he was aware of it, would not allow for an instant. The idea!' said Mrs. Nickleby, drawing herself up, 'Niece to the Commissioners of Paving!'

'Pray, mama, come away!' whispered Kate.

' "Pray, mama!" Nonsense, Kate,' said Mrs. Nickleby angrily, 'but that's just the way. If they had said I was niece to a piping bullfinch, what would you care! But I have no sympathy,' whimpered Mrs. Nickleby, 'I don't expect it, that's one thing.'

'Tears!' cried the old gentleman, with such an energetic jump that he fell down two or three steps and grated his chin against the wall. 'Catch the crystal globules – catch 'em – bottle 'em up – cork 'em tight – put sealing-wax on the top – seal 'em with a cupid – label 'em "Best quality" – and stow 'em away in the fourteen bin, with a bar of iron on the top to keep the thunder off.'

Pickwick Papers

'Heads, heads – take care of your heads!' cried the loquacious stranger, as they came out under the low archway, which in those days formed the entrance to the coachyard. 'Terrible place – dangerous work – other day – five children – mother – tall lady, eating sandwiches – forgot the arch – crash – knock – children look round – mother's head off – sandwich in her hand – no mouth to put it in – head of a family off – shocking, shocking! Looking at Whitehall, sir? – fine place – little window – somebody else's head off there, eh, sir? – he didn't keep a sharp lookout enough either – eh, sir, eh?'

'I am ruminating,' said Mr. Pickwick, 'on the strange mutability of human affairs.'

'Ah, I see – in at the palace door one day, out at the window the next. Philosopher, sir?'

'An observer of human nature, sir,' said Mr. Pickwick.

'Ah, so am I. Most people are when they've little to do and less to get. Poet, sir?'

'My friend Mr. Snodgrass has a strong poetic turn,' said Mr. Pickwick.

'So have I,' said the stranger. 'Epic poem – ten thousand lines – revolution of July – composed it on the spot – Mars by day, Apollo by night – bang the field-piece; twang the lyre.'

'You were present at that glorious scene, sir?' said Mr. Snodgrass.

'Present! think I was; fired a musket – fired with an idea

– rushed into wine shop – wrote it down – back again –
whiz, bang – another idea –wine shop again – pen and ink
– back again – cut and slash – noble time, sir. Sportsman,
sir?' abruptly turning to Mr. Winkle.

'A little, sir,' replied that gentleman.

'Fine pursuit, sir – fine pursuit. – Dogs, sir?'

'Not just now,' said Mr. Winkle.

'Ah! you should keep dogs – fine animals – sagacious
creatures – dog of my own once – Pointer – surprising
instinct – out shooting one day – entering enclosure –
whistled – dog stopped – whistled again – Ponto – no go;
stock still – called him – Ponto, Ponto – wouldn't move –
dog transfixed – staring at a board – looked up, saw an
inscription – "Gamekeeper has orders to shoot all dogs
found in this enclosure" – wouldn't pass it – wonderful
dog – valuable dog that – very.'

'Singular circumstance that,' said Mr. Pickwick. 'Will
you allow me to make a note of it?'

'Certainly, sir, certainly – hundred more anecdotes of
the same animal. – Fine girl, sir' (to Mr. Tracy Tupman,
who had been bestowing sundry anti-Pickwickian glances
on a young lady by the roadside).

'Very!' said Mr. Tupman.

'English girls not so fine as Spanish – noble creatures –
jet hair – black eyes – lovely forms – sweet creatures –
beautiful.'

'You have been in Spain, sir?' said Mr. Tracy Tupman.

'Lived there – ages.'

'Many conquests, sir?' inquired Mr. Tupman.

'Conquests! Thousands. Don Bolaro Fizzgig – Grandee
– only daughter – Donna Christina – splendid creature
– loved me to distraction – jealous father – high-souled
daughter – handsome Englishman – Donna Christina in
despair – prussic acid – stomach pump in my portmanteau – operation performed – old Bolaro in ecstasies –
consent to our union – join hands and floods of tears –
romantic story – very.'

'Is the lady in England now, sir?' inquired Mr. Tupman,

on whom the description of her charms had produced a powerful impression.

'Dead, sir – dead,' said the stranger, applying to his right eye the brief remnant of a very old cambric handkerchief. 'Never recovered the stomach pump – undermined constitution – fell a victim.'

'And her father?' inquired the poetic Snodgrass.

'Remorse and misery,' replied the stranger. 'Sudden disappearance – talk of the whole city – search made everywhere – without success – public fountain in the great square suddenly ceased playing – weeks elapsed – still a stoppage – workmen employed to clean it – water drawn off – father-in-law discovered sticking head first in the main pipe, with a full confession in his right boot – took him out, and the fountain played away again, as well as ever.'

'Will you allow me to note that little romance down, sir?' said Mr. Snodgrass, deeply affected.

Martin Chuzzlewit

'To be presented to a Pogram,' said Miss Codger, 'by a Hominy, indeed, a thrilling moment is in its impressiveness on what we call our feelings. But why we call them so, or why impressed they are, or if impressed they are at all, or if at all we are, or if there really is, O gasping one! a Pogram or a Hominy, or any active principle to which we give those titles, is a topic, Spirit-searching, light-abandoned, much too vast to enter on at this unlooked-for crisis.'

'Mind and matter,' said the lady in the wig, 'glide swift into the vortex of immensity. Howls the sublime, and softly sleeps the calm Ideal, in the whispering chambers of Imagination. To hear it, sweet it is. But then, outlaughs the stern philosopher, and saith to the Grotesque, "What ho! arrest for me that Agency. Go, bring it here!" And so the vision fadeth.'

H. F. ELLIS

Re Helicopters

To the Secretary of State for Air

Sir – I write to protest against the unwarrantable frequency with which I find myself rescued by your helicopters. On the first occasion on which I was snatched from the sea while enjoying a quiet float beyond the breakers I was prepared to make light of the incident. This is a normal holiday risk, which in my opinion it is the duty of members of the public to accept in the right spirit. But enough is as good as a feast. I have now three times been hoisted into the air and ferried to St Mawgan aerodrome, where everybody I have met has been most kind and attentive – too kind, if anything. Constant wrapping in warm blankets has brought my skin out in an irritating rash; nor am I a man who cares much for copious draughts of hot, sweet tea.

The pilot considers that my habit of floating very low in the water misleads holidaymakers ashore into thinking that I am waterlogged or in distress. That is as it may be. I cannot alter my centre of gravity or buoyancy co-efficient, to suit your convenience. Surely there is some alternative method of protecting the not-so-portly against the intrusive zeal of your Air Rescue Organisation?

August 5th.

Sir – It is no use saying that it is open to anyone not in immediate danger to refuse to be rescued. Quite apart from the question of good manners, if one attempts to ignore the machine or to brush the hoisting tackle aside the crew conclude that one is either unconscious or hysterical, and send a man down by rope-ladder to see about it. Only yesterday, while sunbathing in a small deserted cove, I attempted to move out of the shadow created by one of your infernal contraptions and found myself suddenly seized from behind and forcibly buckled into a kind of surcingle made of harsh webbing. It is ludicrous to suggest that I was in any danger of being cut off by the tide; but the pilot – not the one who generally rescues me, by the way; this was an altogether more domineering and self-sufficient type – would not listen to reason. He simply said that he had his orders and proposed to carry them out – with the result that I was late for lunch for the third day running, and dared not take my usual afternoon dip in case I missed a tennis engagement after tea.

I shall be obliged if you will take immediate steps to see that your rescue organisation turns its attention to some other holidaymaker, preferably one who stands in need of it.

August 7th.

Sir – After a momentary respite (due in part, I think, to my practice of laying out warning 'KEEP OFF' notices with strips of sheeting whenever I seek seclusion on the rocks and coast hereabouts) the situation has again worsened. I am now constantly attended by a large yellow helicopter, hired I believe by a London newspaper to take photographs of any further attempts that may be made to rescue me by air. The noise is indescribable, and whenever I try to escape it by taking refuge in a cave or holding my breath under water some busybody can be relied on to ring up St Mawgan and bring a second helicopter on the scene. I have noticed, too, that I am now kept dangling in the air, before being hauled into the rescue machine, for a longer period than was the case at the beginning of my holiday. This (though I cannot prove it) is done at the request of the photographers who seem to be hand in glove with the authorities at St Mawgan. I shall hold you entirely responsible if any harm comes to me through the almost perpetual draughts to which I am now exposed.

I re-open this letter to add that my wife has just returned in an RAF truck and in a very highly-strung condition from St Austell, of all places. It appears, so far as I can piece her story together, that she was violently scooped from the water *while actually sitting on an inflated horse* – an inexcusably careless mistake – and deposited, horse and all, on a makeshift aerodrome without any proper facilities for resuscitating people suffering from needless rescue. When I rang up St Mawgan to protest, they told me that their regular rescue craft was already out on a case (as if I needed to be told that!) when this second call came in. They had accordingly been compelled to ask Plymouth for assistance, and it might be that the pilot from there was *less experienced in rescue work than their own men* and had picked up the wrong bather by mistake. The italics are mine, but the responsibility, in my submission, remains yours.

August 8th.

Sir – You will see, from the enclosed cutting from a local paper headed 'HORSE RESCUED FROM SEA' something of the annoyance to which we as a family are almost daily subjected by the attentions of your rescue service. The very indifferent photograph of my wife does not help matters.

However, that is not the main purpose of this letter. I would like to inform you that, in a final attempt to obtain a little peace and privacy before returning to London on the 10th, I am tomorrow taking my wife, sister-in-law, two cousins, a Mrs. Winworth, and most of our children to Lundy Island in a hired motor-boat. We hope to be there by about 2.30 p.m. and have not, of course, thought it necessary to make any arrangements about the return journey.

We should like to reach St Mawgan not later than 7 p.m. If that would be convenient for you.

Yours faithfully,
H. F. Ellis

F

HERBERT FARJEON

Contract Bridge

Tabs part. Four players at card table: TWO MEN, TWO
WOMEN. *The last cards are being dealt as lights go up. The
players examine their hands. When they talk, they do not
look at each other, but concentrate entirely on their cards.*

FIRST MAN (*humming softly as he sorts*): Pom-pom-pom-
pom, pom-pom-pom, pom-pom-pom-pom, pom-pom-pom,
pom-pom-pom-pom –

SECOND MAN (*whistling through his teeth*): Ss, ss-ss-ss-ss,
ss-ss-ss, ss-ss-ss, ss-ss-ss, ss-ss-ss-ss –

FIRST LADY: Bub-bub-bub-bub –, bub-bub-bub-bub, bub-
bub, bub-bub-bub-bub – whose call?

SECOND LADY: Your callikins.

FIRST LADY (*still engrossed in her cards*): My little callikins, well, well, well – *my* little callikins. Let me see, then,
let me see – I think – I think – I think-a-pink-a-pink – no
bid.

SECOND LADY: Tch-tch-tch, tch-tch-tch, tch-tch, tch-tch,
tch-tch-tch, tch-tch-tch – no bid.

FIRST MAN: One cloob.

SECOND MAN (*dropping into Irish*): Did ye say one cloob?

FIRST MAN (*dropping into Irish*): I did that.

SECOND MAN: *Er hat ein cloob gesagen* (*singing*) *Er hat ein
cloob gesagen, er hat ein cloob* ... One hearty-party.

FIRST LADY: Two diminx.

SECOND LADY: No bid, no bid.

FIRST MAN: No bid-a-bid-bid

SECOND MAN: Two diminx, is it? Two naughty leetle diminx. This, I think demands a certain amount of *consideration.*
(*Drums fingers on table*). Yes, yes, my friends, *beaucoup de considération.*

SECOND LADY (*after a pause*): Your *call,* partner.

SECOND MAN: I know it, I know it, I know it, I know it. I know it, indeed, indeed, I know it. (*Clacks tongue*) I know it, I know it, I double two diminx.

SECOND LADY: He doubles two diminx.

FIRST MAN: He doubles two diminx.

SECOND MAN: I double, I double, I double two diminx.

FIRST LADY: Very well, then, have at you. Two no trumpets.

FIRST MAN: Ha, ha!

SECOND MAN: Ho, ho!

FIRST LADY: He, he!

SECOND LADY: H'm, h'm!

They revert to their pet noises as they consider their hands.

FLAUBERT

from Dictionary Of Accepted Ideas

Translated by Jacques Barzun

A

ABSINTHE. Extra, violent poison: one glass and you're dead. Newspapermen drink it as they write their copy. Has killed more soldiers than the Bedouin.

ACADEMY. Run it down but try to belong to it if you can.

ACHILLES. Add 'fleet of foot': people will think you've read Homer.

ACTRESS. The ruin of young men of good family. Are fearfully lascivious; engage in 'nameless orgies'; run through fortunes; end in the poorhouse. 'I beg to differ, sir: some are excellent mothers!'

ADVERTISING. Large fortunes are made by it.

ALABASTER. Its use is to describe the most beautiful parts of a woman's body.

ALBION. Always preceded by white,* perfidious or Positivist. Napoleon only failed by a hair's breadth to conquer it. Praise it: 'freedom-loving England.'

AMBITION. Always preceded by 'mad' unless it be 'noble'.

ANIMALS. 'If only dumb animals could speak! So often more intelligent than men.'

APARTMENT (BACHELOR'S). Always in a mess, with feminine garments strewn about. Stale cigarette smoke. A search would reveal amazing things.

ARCHIMEDES. On hearing his name, shout 'Eureka!' Or else: 'Give me a fulcrum and I will move the world.' There is also Archimedes' screw, but you are not expected to know what it is.

ARISTOCRACY. Despise and envy it.

ARMY. The bulwark of society.

ATHEISTS. 'A nation of atheists cannot survive.'

AUTHORS. One should 'know a few', never mind their names.

B

BACHELORS. All self-centred, all rakes. Should be taxed. Headed for a lonely old age.

BACK. A slap on the back can start tuberculosis.

BALLS. Use this word only as a swear word, and possibly not even then. (SEE DOCTOR).

BANDITS. Always 'fierce'.

BAYADÈRE. Word that stirs the fancy. All oriental women are bayadères. (SEE ODALISQUES).

BEDROOM. In an old château, Henry IV always spent one night there.

BIBLE. The oldest book in the world.

BILL. Always too high.

BILLIARDS. A noble game. Indispensable in the country.

BLONDES. Hotter than brunettes. (See BRUNETTES].

---

* Because of the white cliffs of Dover.

BODY. If we knew how our body is made, we wouldn't dare move.

BOOK. Always too long, regardless of subject.

BREAD. No one knows what filth goes into it.

BRUNETTES. Hotter than blondes. (See BLONDES).

BURIAL. Too often premature. Tell stories of corpses that had eaten an arm off from hunger.

C

CAMEL. Has two humps and the dromedary one; or the camel has one and the dromedary two – it *is* confusing.

CARTHUSIANS. Spend their time making chartreuse, digging their own graves and saying to one another, 'Brother, thou too must die'.

CASTLE. Has invariably withstood a great siege under Philip Augustus.

CATHOLICISM. Has had a good influence on art.

CAVALRY. Nobler than the infantry.

CEDAR (OF LEBANON). The one at the Botanical Garden was brought over in a man's hat.

CHAMPAGNE. The sign of a ceremonial dinner. Pretend to despise it, saying: 'It's really not a wine.' Arouses the enthusiasm of petty folk. Russia drinks more of it than France. Has been the medium for spreading French ideas throughout Europe. During the Regency people did nothing but drink champagne. But technically one doesn't drink it, one 'samples' it.

CHATEAUBRIAND. Best known for the cut of meat that bears his name.

CHEESE. Quote Brillat-Savarin's maxim: 'Dessert without cheese is like a beauty with only one eye.'

CHESS. Symbol of military tactics. All great generals good at chess. Too serious as a game, too pointless as a science.

CHIAROSCURO. Meaning unknown.

CHRISTIANITY. Freed the slaves.

CHRISTMAS. Wouldn't be Christmas without the pudding.

CIDER. Spoils the teeth.

CIRCUS TRAINERS. Use obscene practices.

CLARINET. Playing it causes blindness: all blind men play the clarinet.

CLASSICS. You are supposed to know all about them.

COCK. A thin man must invariably say: 'Fighting cocks are never fat!'

COGNAC. Most harmful. Excellent for certain diseases. A good swig of cognac never hurt anybody. Taken before breakfast, kills intestinal worms.

COMFORT. The most valuable discovery of modern times.

COMPOSITION. At school, a good composition shows application, whereas translation shows intelligence. Out in the world, scoff at those who were good at composition.

CONCERT. Respectable way to kill time.

CONCUPISCENCE. Priest's word for carnal desire.

CONFECTIONERS. All the inhabitants of Rouen are confectioners.

CONSERVATIVE. Politician with pot belly. 'A limited, conservative mind? Certainly! Limits keep fools from falling down wells.'

CONSTIPATION. All literary men are constipated. This affects their politics.

CONSTITUTIONAL (RULES). Are stifling us – under them it is impossible to govern.

CONTRALTO. Meaning unknown.

CONVICTS. Always look it. All clever with their hands. Our penitentiaries number many a man of genius.

COOKING. In restaurants, always bad for the system; at home, always wholesome; in the South, too much spice, or oil.

CORSET. Prevents childbearing.

COUNTERFEITERS. Always work below ground.

CRIMSON. Nobler word than red.

CRUCIFIX. Looks well above a bedstead – or the guillotine.

CYPRESS. Grows only in cemeteries.

D

DANCE. 'It isn't dancing any more, it's tramping about.'

DEBAUCHERY. Cause of all diseases in bachelors.

DECORATION. The Legion of Honour: make fun of it, but covert it. When you obtain it, say it was unsolicited.

DEICIDE. Wax indignant, despite the infrequency of the crime.

DEMOSTHENES. Never made a speech without a pebble in his mouth.

DERBY. Racing term: very swank.

DESERT. Produces dates.

DILETTANTE. Wealthy man who subscribes to the opera.

DINNER JACKET. In the provinces, the acme of ceremony and inconvenience.

DIPLOMA. Emblem of knowledge. Proves nothing.

DIVA. All women singers must be called divas.

DJINN. The name of an oriental dance.

DOCTOR. Always preceded by 'the good'. Among men, in familiar conversation, 'Oh! balls, doctor!' Is a wizard when he enjoys your confidence, a jackass when you're no longer on terms. All are materialists: 'You can't probe for faith with a scalpel.'

DOGE. Wedded the sea. Only one is known – Marino Faliero.

DOLMEN. Has to do with the old Gauls. Stone used for human sacrifice. Found only in Brittany. (Knowledge ends there).

DOLPHIN. Carries children on its back.

DOME. Tower with an architectural shape. Express surprise that it stays up. Two can be named: the Dome of the Invalides; that of St. Peter's in Rome.

DOMESTICITY. Never fail to speak of it with respect.

DOMINOES. One plays all the better for being tight.

DORMITORIES. Always 'Spacious and airy.' Preferable to single rooms for the morals of the pupils.

DUCKS. Always come from Rouen.

E

EARTH. Refer to its four corners since it is round.

EGG. Starting point for a philosophic lecture on the origin of life.

ELEPHANTS. Have remarkable memories; worship the sun.

EMBONPOINT. Sign of elegant leisure, of utter laziness. Disagree on the pronunciation of the word.

ENAMEL. The secret of this art is lost.

ENGLISH. All millionaires.

ENGLISHWOMEN. Express surprise that they can have good-looking children.*

ERECTION. Said only of monuments.

ETRUSCAN. All antique vases are Etruscan.

ETYMOLOGY. The easiest thing in the world, with a little Latin and ingenuity.

EXERCISE. Prevents all diseases. Recommend it at all times.

EXPIRE. Verb applied exclusively to newspaper subscriptions.

F

FACTORY. Dangerous neighbourhood.

FAME. 'Vanity of vanities.'

FARM. When visiting a farm, one must eat nothing but rye bread and drink nothing but milk. If eggs are added exclaim: 'Heavens, but they're fresh! Not a chance you'd find any like these in town!'

FARMERS. What would we do without them?

FENCING. Fencing masters know secret thrusts.

FEUDALISM. No need to have one single precise notion about it: thunder against.

FIGARO (MARRIAGE OF). Another of the causes of the Revolution!

FLAGRANTE DELICTO. Always use the Latin phrase. Applies only to cases of adultery.

FOETUS. Any anatomical specimen preserved in spirits of wine.

FOREHEAD. Wide and bald, a sign of genius, or of self-confidence.

---

* Until very recently, the stereotype of 'the Englishwoman' in France depicted a mountain climber of repellent aspect, disfigured by long teeth and wearing mannish clothes.

FREEMASONRY. Yet another cause of the Revolution. The initiation is a fearful ordeal. Cause of dissension among married pairs. Distrusted by the clergy. What can its great secret be?

FRENCH. The leading people in the world. 'It means only one more Frenchman'* (said the Comte d'Artois). How proud one is to be French when gazing at the Colonne Vendome.†

FRESCO PAINTING. No longer done.

FRICASSEE. Only good in the country.

FUGUE. Nobody knows what it consists in, but you must assert that it is extremely difficult and extremely dull.

G

GAIETY. Always preceded by 'mad'.

GARLIC. Kills intestinal worms and incites to amorous jousting. Henry IV's lips were rubbed with it at birth.

GENTLEMEN. There aren't any left.

GERMANS. Always preceded by 'blond', 'dreamy' – but how efficient their army! A people of metaphysicians (old-fashioned). 'It's no wonder they beat us, we weren't ready!'

GIAOUR. Fierce expression of unknown meaning, though it is known to refer to the Orient.

GIBBERISH. Foreigners' way of talking. Always make fun of the foreigner who murders French.

GLOBE. Genteel way of referring to a woman's breasts: 'May I be permitted to kiss those adorable globes?'

GOD. Voltaire himself admitted it: 'If God did not exist, it would be necessary to invent him.'

'GODDAM'. The essence of the English language, as Beaumarchais said.‡ Snicker patronizingly.

GOLDEN NUMBER, DOMINICAL LETTER, ETC. Shown on all calendars but nobody knows what they mean.

---

* Allusion to an apocryphal speech of the restored Bourbon prince in 1814: 'Nothing is changed; there is only one more Frenchman.'
† Monument made of enemy guns captured by Napoleon's armies.
‡ Allusion to *The Marriage of Figaro*, Act III, Sc. V.

GOTHIC. Architectural style which inspires religious feeling to a greater degree than others.

GOWN (A WOMAN'S). Disturbing to the fancy.

GRAPESHOT. The only way to make the Parisians shut up.

GROTTOES WITH STALACTITES. At some time or other a big banquet or notable party was given there. What you see is like organ pipes. During the Revolution, Mass was celebrated there in secret.

GUERRILLA. Does more harm to the enemy than the regular forces.

H

HAND. To govern France, must be of iron; to have a beautiful hand means to have a fine handwriting.

HANGMAN. Trade handed down from father to son.

HARE. Sleeps with its eyes open.

HARP. Gives out celestial harmonies. In engravings, is only played next to ruins or on the edge of a torrent. Showed off the arm and hand.

HASHEESH. Do not confuse with hash, which produces no voluptuous sensations whatsoever.

HEALTH. Excess of health causes illness.

HELOTS. Cite as a warning to your son, though you would be hard put to it to show him any.

HERMAPHRODITES. Arouse unwholesome curiosity. Try to see one.

HERNIA. Everybody has one without knowing it.

HIEROGLYPHICS. Language of the ancient Egyptians, invented by the priests to conceal their shameful secrets. 'Just think! There are people who understand hieroglyphics! But, after all, the whole thing may be a hoax ...'

HIPPOCRATES. Always to be cited in Latin because he wrote in Greek, except in the maxim: 'Hippocrates says Yes, but Galen says No.'

HOMER. Never existed. Famous for his laughter.

HOSPITALITY. Must be Scottish. Quote: 'In Scotland, hospitality when sought is given and never bought.'

HOSTILITIES. Hostilities are like oysters, they have to be

opened. 'Open hostilities' sounds as if one ought to sit down at table.

HOTELS. Are only good in Switzerland.

HUNCHBACKS. Are very witty. Much sought after by lascivious women.

HYDRA-HEADED (MONSTER). Of anarchy, socialism, and so on, of all alarming systems. We must try and conquer it.

I

ICE-CREAM MEN. All Neapolitans.

IDEALISM. The best of the philosophic systems.

IDEALS. Perfectly useless.

IDEOLOGISTS. Every newspaperman is an ideologist.

IDIOTS. Those who differ from you.

ILIAD. Always followed by 'Odyssey'.

IMAGINATION. Always 'lively'. Be on guard against it. When lacking in oneself, attack it in others. To write a novel, all you need is imagination.

IMPORTS. Canker at the heart of Trade.

INCOGNITO. The dress of princes on their travels.

INDOLENCE. Product of warm climates.

INFANTICIDE. Committed only by the lower classes.

INKWELL. The ideal gift for a doctor.

INQUISITION. Its crimes have been exaggerated.

INSPIRATION (POETIC). Brought on by: a sight of the sea, love, women, etc.

INSTITUTE. The members are all old men who wear green eye-shades.

INSULT. Must always be washed out in blood.

INTERVAL. Invariably too long.

INTRODUCTION. Obscene word.

ITALIANS. All musical. All treacherous.

ITALY. Should be seen immediately after marriage. Is very disappointing – not nearly so beautiful as people say.

J

JANSENISM. Meaning unknown, but any reference to it is swank.

JAPAN. Everything there is made of china.

JASPER. All vases in museums are of jasper.

JAVELIN. As good as a gun if one only knows how to throw it.

JEWS. 'Sons of Israel'. All Jews are spectacle vendors.

JUJUBE. Made of an unknown substance.

JUSTICE. Never worry about it.

K

KALEIDOSCOPE. Used only to describe picture exhibitions.

KEEPSAKE. Ought to be found on every drawing-room table.

KORAN. Book entirely about women, by Mohammed.

L

LACONIC. Idiom no longer spoken.

LACUSTRIAN (TOWNS). Deny their existence, since it is obviously impossible to live under water.

LADIES. Always come first. 'God bless them !' Never say : 'Your good lady is in the drawing-room.'

LADS. Never give a commencement address without referring to 'you young lads' (which is tautological).

LAGOON. City on the Adriatic.

LAKE. Have a woman with you when you sail on it.

LATHE. Indispensable for rainy days in the country. Have one in the attic.

LAUGHTER. Always 'Homeric'.

LAW (THE) Nobody knows what it is.

LEARNED (THE). Make fun of. All it takes to be learned is a good memory and hard work.

LEATHER. It all comes from Russia.

LEFTHANDED. Formidable fencers. Much more deft than those who use the right hand.

LENT. At bottom is only a health measure.

LIBERTINISM. Found only in big cities.

LIBRARY. Always have one at home, particularly if you live in the country.

LILAC. Delightful because it means summer is here.

LITERATURE. Idle pastime.

M

MACARONI. When prepared in the Italian style, is served with the fingers.

MACHIAVELLI. Though you have not read him, consider him a scoundrel.

MACKINTOSH. Scottish philosopher, invented the raincoat.

MAESTRO. Italian word meaning Pianist.

MAJOR (MILITARY). Only to be found in hotel dining rooms.

MALEDICTION. Always uttered by a father.

MANDOLIN. Indispensable for seducing Spanish women.

MARBLE. Every statue is of *Parian* marble.

MARSEILLES (PEOPLE OF). All great wits.

MARTYRS. All the early Christians were.

MATHEMATICS. Dry up the emotions.

MATTRESS. The harder the healthier.

MEDICINE. When in good health, make fun of it.

MELANCHOLY. Sign of a refined heart and elevated mind.

METALLURGY. Very swank.

METAMORPHOSIS. Make fun of the times when it was believed in. Ovid was the inventor.

METAPHORS. Always too many in poems. Always too many in anybody's writing.

METAPHYSICS. Laugh it to scorn: proof of your superior intellect.

METHOD. Of no use whatever.

MILK. Dissolves oysters, lures snakes; whitens the skin. Some women of Paris take milk baths daily.

MINUTE. 'Nobody has any idea how long a minute really is.'

MODELLING. In front of a statue, say: 'The modelling is not without charm.'

MONARCHY. 'A constitutional monarchy is the best of republics.'

MOOSE. Plural 'meese' – an old chestnut but always good for a laugh.

MOSAIC. The secret of the art is lost.

MOUNTEBANK. Always preceded by 'cheap'.

MUSCLES. The muscles of strong men are always of steel.

MUSHROOMS. Should not be bought except at the grocer's.
MUSIC. Makes one think of a great many things. Makes a
people gentle: e.g. 'La Marseillaise'.

N

NATURE. How beautiful is Nature! Repeat every time you
are in the country.
NEGRESSES. Hotter than white women. (See BLONDES and
BRUNETTES.)
NEGROES. Express surprise that their saliva is white and
that they can speak French.
NEOLOGISMS. The ruin of the French language.
NOSTRILS. When flaring, show lasciviousness.

O

OBSCENITY. All scientific words derived from Greek and
Latin conceal an obscenity.
ODALISQUES. All women in the Orient are odalisques. (See
BAYADERES).
ODOUR (FOOT). A sign of health.
OLDEST INHABITANTS. In times of flood, thunderstorm, etc.,
the oldest inhabitants cannot remember ever having seen
a worse one.
OLIVE OIL. Never good. You should have a friend in Mar-
seilles who sends you a small barrel of it.
OMEGA. Second letter of the Greek alphabet, since every-
body always says: 'The alpha and omega of ...'
OMNIBUS. Never a seat to be found. Were invented by Louis
XIV. 'Let me tell you, sir, that I can remember tricycles
when they had only three wheels.'
ORIGINAL. Make fun of everything that is original, hate it,
beat it down, annihilate it if you can.
OTTER. Created to make caps and waistcoats.

P

PAGANINI. Never tuned his violin. Famous for his long
fingers.
PAGEANTRY. Lends authority. Strikes the imagination of the

masses. We need more of it, more of it.

PAINTING ON GLASS. The secret of the art is lost.

PALMYRA. An Egyptian queen? Famous ruins? Nobody knows.

PAMPHLETEERING. No longer done.

PELICAN. Tears its breast to nourish its young. Symbol of the paterfamilias.

PERSPIRING (FEET). Sign of health.

PHILOSOPHY. Always snicker at it.

PHOENIX. Fine name for a Fire Insurance Company.

PHOTOGRAPHY. Will make painting obsolete.

PHYSICAL TRAINING. Cannot be overdone. Exhausting for children.

PIANO. Indispensable in a drawing-room.

PILLOW. Never use a pillow: it will make you into a hunchback.

PIMPLES. On the face or anywhere else, a sign of health and 'strong blood'. Do not try to get rid of them.

PITY. Always avoid feeling it.

POCK-MARKED. Pock-marked women are all lascivious.

POET. Pompous synonym for fool, dreamer.

POETRY. Entirely useless; out of date.

PORK-BUTCHER. Stories of pâtés made of human flesh. All pork-butchers have pretty wives.

POST. Always apply for one.

PRACTICAL JOKES. Always play practical jokes when going on a picnic with ladies.

PRAGMATIC SANCTION. Nobody knows what it is.

PREPSCHOOL. Swanker than 'boarding school'.

PRIAPISM. A cult of ancient times.

PRIESTS. Should be castrated. Sleep with their housekeepers and give them children whom they fob off as their nephews. 'Never mind! There are honest ones too.'

PRINTING. Marvellous invention. Has done more harm than good.

PROFESSOR. Always 'the learned'.

PROSE. Easier to write than verse.

PROSTITUTE. A necessary evil. A protection for our daughters and sisters, as long as we have bachelors. Should be harried without pity. It's impossible to go out with one's wife owing to the presence of these women on the boulevards. Are always poor girls seduced by wealthy bourgeois.

R

REDHEADS. See BLONDES, BRUNETTES and NEGRESSES.

REGARDS. Always the best.

RELATIVES. Always a nuisance. Keep the poor ones out of sight.

RELIGION. Part of the foundations of society. Is necessary for the common people. Yet we mustn't overdo it. 'The religion of our fathers ...' this must be uttered with unction.

RHYME. Never in accord with Reason.

S

SACRILEGE. It is sacrilege to cut down a tree.

SATRAP. Rich man of loose morals.

SCENERY (STAGE). Isn't real painting. The only skill required is to splash paint on the cloth and smear it with a broom – distance and lighting do the rest.

SCHOOLS. Polytechnique: every mother's dream for her boy (old-fashioned). Panic of the bourgeois during insurrections when he hears that Polytechnique sides with the workers (old-fashioned). Just say: 'At the School' and people will think you're a graduate. At St. Cyr: young aristocrats. At the School of Medicine: all subversives. At the School of Law: young men of good family.

SEA. Bottomless. Symbol of infinity. Induces deep thoughts. At the shore one should always have a good glass. While contemplating the sea, always exclaim: 'Water, water everywhere.'

SEASICKNESS. To avoid it, all you have to do is think of something else.

SECRET FUNDS. Incalculable sums with which the ministers buy men. Wax indignant.

SHELLS (ARTILLERY). Designed to make clocks and inkwells.

SHOES (WOODEN). All self-made men first arrived in Paris wearing wooden shoes.

SINGERS. Swallow a raw egg every morning to clear the voice. Tenors always have a 'golden, bewitching voice'; baritones a 'warm, well-placed voice'; basses 'a powerful organ'.

SNEEZE. After saying 'God bless you!' start discussing the origin of this custom. 'Sneezed': It is clever raillery to say: 'Russian and Polish are not spoken, they are sneezed.'

SOCIETY. Its enemies. What destroys it.

SOUTHERN COOKING. Always full of garlic. Thunder against.

SOUTHERNERS. All poets.

SPINACH. Acts on your stomach like a broom. Never forget to repeat M. Prudhomme's famous remark: 'I don't like it and am glad of it, because if I liked it I would eat it – and I can't stand it.' (Some people will find this sensible enough and won't laugh.)

STAR. Every one follows his own, like Napoleon.

STALLION. Always 'fiery'. A woman is not to know the difference between a stallion and a horse. A young girl must be told it is a larger type of horse.

STOCKBROCKERS. All thieves.

STOCK EXCHANGE. 'Barometer of public opinion.'

STOMACH. All diseases come from the stomach.

STUDENTS. All wear red berets and tight trousers, smoke pipes in the street – and never study.

SUICIDE. Proof of cowardice.

SUMMER. Always 'unusual'. (See WINTER).

SWAN. Sings just before it dies. Can break a man's leg with its wing. The Swan of Cambrai was not a bird but a man named Fenelon. The Swan of Mantua is Virgil. The Swan of Pesaro is Rossini.

SYBARITES. Thunder against.

SYPHILLIS. Everybody has it, more or less.

T

TEETH. Are spoiled by cider, tobacco, sweets, ices, drinking immediately after hot soup and sleeping with the mouth open. Eyeteeth: it is harmful to pull these out owing to their connection with the eye. 'Having teeth pulled is no fun.'

THUNDERBOLTS (FROM THE VATICAN). Laugh at them.

TIGHTS. Sexually exciting.

TOBACCO. The government brand is not so good as that which is smuggled in. Snuff suits studious men. Cause of all the diseases of the brain and spinal cord.

TOLERATED (HOUSE). Not one in which tolerant opinions are held.

TROUBADOUR. Fine subject for ornamental clock.

U

UNIVERSITY. The 'varsity'.

V

VIZIR. Trembles at the sight of a piece of string.

VOLTAIRE. Famous for his frightful grin or *rictus*. His learning superficial.

W

WAGNER. Snicker on hearing his name and joke about the music of the future.

WALTZ. Wax indignant about. A lascivious, impure dance that should only be danced by old ladies.

WAR. Thunder against.

WEATHER. Eternal topic of conversation. Universal cause of ailments. Always complain of the weather.

WINE. Topic of discussion among men. The best must be Bordeaux since doctors prescribe it. The worse it tastes, the more unadulterated it is.

WINTER. Always 'unusual' (See SUMMER). Is more healthful than the other seasons.

WITNESS. Always refuse to be a witness. You never know where you'll end up.

WOMEN. Member of the sex. One of Adam's ribs. Don't say 'the little woman' but 'my lady' or still preferable 'my better half.'

WORKMAN. Always honest – unless he is rioting.
WRITE. Dash things off – the excuse for errors of style or spelling.

MARJORY FLEMING

(Aged 7)

A Sonnet

O lovely O most charming pug
Thy gracefull air and heavenly mug
The beauties of his mind do shine
And every bit is shaped so fine
Your very tail is most devine
Your teeth is whiter than the snow
You are a great buck and a bow
Your eyes are of so fine a shape
More like a christians than an ape
His cheeks is like the roses blume
Your hair is like the ravens plume
His noses cast is of the roman
He is a very pretty weomen
I could not get a rhyme for roman
And was oblidged to call it weoman

PETER FLEMING

Implications Of An Incinerator

... To a literary man the possession of his own, personal incinerator opens possibilities which at first seem bright. When one of his books is translated into a foreign language he normally receives at least one and often as many as six copies of the new edition. He peruses it with a baffled complacency.

'Og tot inglanderskin schribblipholk', the blurb says, 'Strix e, par fillom sagasticom juddicibom, clamchowdit *doo manx phrilliposh, glarb ac dungsproodi. Burstnit en 1907 egg vom skeedlit iz Oxphordu....'* This sounds all right, though he cannot help wondering slightly about *'phrilliposh'.* Its off-white pages uncut, the book which has an indefinable air of being made of processed birch-bark, goes into the shelf on which his Works are arranged. The five spare copies of *Gliv og Tödlkippz* are left to find their own level in what, were his house a ship, would correspond to the bilge.

As time goes by these aimless symbols of his literary prowess in Ruritania and elsewhere accumulate. After the last war, when a succession of Germans, Danes and Spaniards did fleeting tours of duty in my kitchen, some of the translations were taken down from the shelves and may actually have been read as well as sprinkled with gravy. But there still remained, dotted about the place, deposits of redundant copies, and soon after the brick-kiln was relumed I cast into it three copies of *Seiklus Brasiilias* which thirty years ago took (for all I know) the literary world of Bucharest by storm, and with them no fewer than three dozen copies of a more recent pocket edition of the same work in German.

But that, although I am not a prolific writer, still leaves me with a shelf full of tawdry-looking volumes in French, German, Dutch, Polish, Italian, Spanish, Danish, Swedish, Norwegian and Rumanian, in more than half of which I could not, if I tried, read a single sentence. They are of no possible use to me; the right place for them is the kiln, but somehow they do not go there. I am puzzled by my reluctance to consign them to the flames.

It is not as if they were prominently displayed, ground-bait for the visitor's curiousity; nobody ever sees them except me. It is not that their format is elegant or even bizarre. What I suppose has happened is that they have got themselves taken on the strength of my *lares et penates*. They are at once trophies and curios. They are like Nanny's china ornament with 'A Present from Weymouth' on it, like the bunches of heather tied on to cars bound south from Scotland, like the obscure decoration conferred by some third-rate Power upon a former military attaché at its capital. They are, if not positively vulgar, valueless; yet I cannot quite bring myself to jettison them.

I wonder what the Giants of Literature do about a problem which must, be for them, attain almost sawdust-like dimensions? Are there on the Côte d'Azur great catacombs where the translated works of Mr. Maugham are stored in tier upon tier of shelves? Does the Inland Revenue allow Mr. Priestley to charge against his taxes the rent of a warehouse in Bradford? And what on earth will happen to these polyglot collections when their owners die? What, if it comes to that, will happen to *Gliv og Tödlkippz* and the rest of my humbler but equally useless hoard?

The only sensible answer is that these birch-bark books will be destroyed. I still don't quite know what restrains me from taking them up to the brick-kiln after luncheon.

Deuxièmes Hors de L'anneau!

Monsieur.

Mon attention a été tirée à une série de lettres publiées par le *Sunday Times*, dont les auteurs sont allés a grandes douleurs afin de se moquer de la langue française. La formule adoptée par ces gens se base sur la traduction littérale en francais de phrases anglaises appartenantes ou à l'argot ou aux activités – comme, par example, le *cricket* – malheureusement peu connues en France. Ce n'est guère difficile d'élever ainsi des rires bon marchées en confectionnant des phrases comme 'Il a cassé son canard' (*He has broken his duck*) ou 'Il était autrefois au assez utile vite chapeau melon' (*He used to be quite a useful fast bowler*).

J'espère, Monsieur, que personne ne me soupçonnera de tirer une ligne en faisant savoir à vos lecteurs que, presque dès ma naissance, j'ai parlé le français comme un indigène. Quoique ce soit une langue dont je tiens le plus haut avis, on doit admettre que c'est une langue plutôt ridicule. Chez nous, on a reconnu depuis longtemps que les étrangers (dont, naturellement, les Grenouilles) ont le droit de s'entretenir; et n'importe quel ane peut voir que c'est un peu trop d'espérer que les Francais apprendront tous l'anglais. Ce serait au delà d'eux, en tout cas. Mais fût-il vraiment nécessaire pour nos voisins d'outre-Manche de penser enhaut un tel petit déjeuner de chien d'une langue?

Voilà, malheureusement pour eux, ce qu'ils ont fait; les résultats suffisant pour faire rire un chat. Mais il devient les Anglais très malade de frapper un homme quand il est duvet; et c'est dans une pareille lumière qu'il faut regarder le triste état auquel sont reduits ceux qui, ne savant pas mieux, se sont débarqués eux-mêmes avec un tel baragouin. Les Français, néanmoins, portent en haut sous leur affliction avec un flegme tout à fait admirable. Pour moi, je leur ôte mon chapeau; et je le trouve un peu épais de traiter en Tante Sarah leur façon, si loin-menée qu'elle doit nous paraître, de parler.

Cependant que cela puisse étre, je m'étonne que personne ne semble avoir donné la pensée d'un moment aux conséquences quasi inéluctables de cette gôut-moins espièglerie. Ne l'a-t-on pas hissé dedans que ce jeu peut se jouer *l'autre voie rond*? Imaginez-vous, Monsieur, l'effet pénible qui se produiserait sur la colonie britannique en France si quelque loque parisienne se mettrait à imprimer des lettres dont l'objet serait de prendre le michel hors de la langue anglaise!

Il n'est que trop facile de se figurer les cheval-rires qui s'entendraient parmi les lecteurs de bêtises anglophobes telles que le suivante:

Sir,

What-that I have fear of entering the lists a bit in retard, maybe you will permit me to relieve the glove which the Editor of the *Sunday Times* has let to fall with a yellow smile? Person would deny that every tongue possesses attributes of which one can make a game of massacre. I am not of those who demand only gashes and bumps, and I do not love the quarrels of a German. But since several weeks this Editor has made with jokes about my birthly tongue a veritable rally-paper, and it seems to me that the quarter of an hour Rabelais has arrived. Well heard, all the world knows already that the majority of the sons of Albion speak French like a Spanish cow; but is it that this gives them the right to deconsider our national heritage? It is not the sea to drink to reverse the roles ....

Vous voyez, Monsieur, qu'aucune difficulté, ne confronte le régisseur d'une telle charade – éymologique; c'est aussi facile que de tomber d'une bûche. Je n'ai aucune hache à grincer dans cette affaire. Je ne demande que le foire-jeu pour une nation fière, affligeé (à travers nulle faute de son propre) avec une langue biscornue et alambiquée.

Parmi nous autres Anglais, soupire-t-il un homme à l'âme si morte qu'il ne s'est jamais – après avoir, peut-être, commandé 'un autre Martini, sivouplé' – donné un coup de pied pour laissant devenir rouillé son français? (Et la même chose, maintenant que je viens d'en penser, s'applique aux Anglaises, bénissez leures petites coeurs.)

Brutaliser, ainsi qu'ont tenté de faire les provocateurs auxquels le *Sunday Times* a donné la lumière verte, la langue française n'est simplement pas sur. Ce n'est pas fait. C'est pire que fusiller, dans le blé qui se dresse, une faisane assise.

J'espère, Monsieur, que vous saurez comment, dans les interêts du copain-navire mondial et tout ça, vous en servir de cette lettre.

Vôtre sincèrement,

STRIX

The Terrible Stone Boat

You often hear it said that letter-writing is a dead art, that nobody any longer sits down and lets their pen flow over page after page just for the hell of it.

I am sure that there is something in this generalisation, but I am equally sure that it does not apply to Mrs. P., a citizeness of the State of Ohio, from whom I have just received an envelope as long, as thick and nearly as heavy as a mackerel. I am unable for technical reasons to reproduce the missal-type illustrations with which Mrs. P. has embellished her text. Three of them are small snapshots of the writer, her son Homer and her daughter Ferne, but the others are crayon-and-ink sketches, done with considerable skill, of the strange events which she describes. For me these have have a quality at once dream-like and compelling, and in the hope that my readers will find her adventures, and her style, as interesting as I have I propose to summarise them here. I have retained the original spelling, but have here and there amended the punctuation, suppressing in particular my correspondent's tendency to use five exclamation marks in a row.

Mrs. P. begins by saying that she is a widow of 67 and is reading a book I wrote; she goes on to outline the genealogy of her family since they settled in America in 1732. It is not until we come to the details of her son's service in the United States Navy in the last war that her taste for the macabre begins to show itself. Homer was 'a coxswain aboard a Floating Dry Dock, and he was one of 20 Sailors that had to descend into the Ship *Huston* and bring out 20 dead Sailors (three months dead). After their Airship Carrier was raised from the Bottom those Sailors were not all in one piece. The boys were sent down into the Ship when it was nearly pumped out of sea water *naked as Adam* with White Canvas Bags to drop the Rotten legs, arms, torsoes and heads into, and the smell of death and Rot was overwhelming. The Ship's commander gave the 17 year old Temperate Church boys shots of whisky to Build up their Courage and some boys with drunking fathers had their first taste of booze and became (in time) plain drunks!'

After some more gruesome details Mrs. P. takes us

suddenly back to the First World War, when she was living on her father's farm in Vermont. 'One night in 1914 I heard the sound of motors running and I thought a doctor was coming to our place to inquire where someone lived: so I got up, thrust my feed in shoes and pulled a bath-robe over my nightdress and went out. I saw a hugh Zepplain pass over our house low, headed North. I could plainly hear a husky guttural voice speaking German over the Inter Comm. Next day the newspapers were full of reports that the Ottawa Canada House of Parlement buildings were bombed and burned. I was 1 of 17 people that saw that Zepplain that night....'

Yet more stirring events were to follow, and although Mrs. P. is too modest to claim that the leading part she played in them had a decisive effect on the outcome of the war, it sounds to me very much as if it did.

Soon after the appearance of the Zeppelin 'there was suddent changes in our neighbourhood.' Two men 'from Boston (said to be)' bought up all the surrounding farms. For some time they stood empty. 'Then suddenly early Spring we heard a great noise along the Road of teams, wagons, trucks and people in cars shouteing and yelling.' Many of the vehicles got stuck in the mud, 'and every man, woman, boy and girl all shouted at each other in German. Now it is the custome of our native Vermont to offer help to folks out for free, but theese folks were the pecul1arest people we had ever seen. They were unfriendly, sour-looking. They said: "Go vay mit use! Ve vont nodding to do mit use"! They extocted themselves from the mud-holes and chopped the road all up in the progress.'

Before long Mrs. P.'s father's farm was surrounded by a whole settlement of these horrible people. Mrs. P. herself lived in an old schoolhouse, and the newcomers harboured designs on this, for they had 'lots of Buppleys', or babies, and wanted a place to teach them in. The two nearest families began to turn the heat on Mrs. P.; their names were Lisky and Kribbouk.

Her faculties sharpened by their persecutions, Mrs. P.

became aware that there was something fishy about the
Kribbouks. Every evening at 4.30 p.m. they disappeared
into the woods behind her house with a team of horses
pulling a 'Stone Boat'. This, as far as I can make out, was a
wooden sledge used for carting rocks and stones off land
which was being reclaimed for cultivation.

But the Kribbouks' stone boat had several unusual
features. It had a 'Gasoline Engine on it and other
machinery: a Dynamo, a Transformer, a Telegraph Set
and other mechanical devices; and it was covered over
with a Brown Canvas laced down to rings in the Stone
Boat so the wind could not uncover the machinery.' Moreover on these expeditions, Kribbouk, his brother and his
sons carried rifles. One day when Mrs. P. took a short cut
she met them all dragging the stone boat along, and,
old Kribbouk shouted 'Don't you ever let me see you on
my land again, or I'll shoot you down dead.' 'I had never,'
Mrs. P. recalls, 'encountered a more hostile bunch of
people.'

One night, carrying a sleeping child on her shoulder,
she again took a short cut through the wood. But at the
end of every track a guttural *franc tireur* was stationed,
'so I pushed my way into a dense groath of bushes' –
only to stumble (believe it or not) on the stone boat.

'Old man Krübbouk was seated on a box with some ear-
phones over his ears and before him a telegraph set on a
box and some other mechanical devices I did not know
the names or uses of.' An aerial dangled from a spruce.
Mrs. P. hid in the roots of 'a blow-down tree, with my
sleeping son in my armes wripped in a Cashmere Shawl.
Soon he started up the gasoline engine. I heard the humming of the dynamo, and he began Thumping away on a
telegraph set. 'Not until dawn were the horses hitched to
the stone boat, the whole fiendish oufit dragged away,
and Mrs. P. and Homer released from their predicament.

As a result of all this '3 Government Men' came and
arrested the Kribbouks; the stone boat was 'confiscated'.
Mrs. P.'s brother was shortly afterwards found 'uncon-

scious and a hole in his side over his Appendix'. Though taken to 'a physician's office, he did not live but a short time.' Foul play was suspected.

But Mrs. P.'s endeavours had an important sequel. 'After these German Mountain Broadcasters were Arrested, the war with German ended quite suddenly. They supprised everyone and unexpectedly sued for peace. Before that they were knocking down our ships along the Gulf of Mexico faster than the US could build them!

Very Respectfully
Mrs. Charlotte P.'

I fear that this greatly condensed summary does less than justice to the original. But it does at least indicate that people are still able, and willing to the point of eagerness, to express themselves in letters. Superior minds may feel that Mrs. P.'s prose is not up to the highest traditions of this minor literary genre; but you cannot have everything, and although I have not seen the originals I am prepared to bet that Lord Chesterfield's celebrated epistles are nowhere embellished with pictures of a bright green dirigible gliding over his residence at chimney-top height.

SAMUEL FOOTE

The Great Panjandrum

So she went into the garden
to cut a cabbage-leaf
to make an apple pie;
and at the same time
a great she-bear, coming down the street,
pops its head into the shop.
What! no soap?
        So he died,
and she very imprudently married the Barber:
and there were present

the Picninnies,
    and the Joblillies,
        and the Garyulies,
and the great Panjandrum himself,
with the little round button at top;
and they all fell to playing the game of catch-as-catch-can
till the gunpowder ran out at the heels of their boots.

HARRY GRAHAM

Ruthless Rhymes

The Stern Parent
Father heard his Children scream,
So he threw them in the stream,
Saying, as he drowned the third,
'Children should be seen, *not* heard!'

Nurse's mistake
Nurse, who peppered baby's face
    (She mistook it for a muffin)
Held her tongue and kept her place,
    'Laying low and sayin' nuffin' ';
Mother, seeing baby blinded,
Said, 'Oh, nurse, how absent-minded!'

Jim : or, The Deserted Luncheon Party
When the line he tried to cross,
The express ran into Jim;
Bitterly I mourn his loss –
I was to have lunched with him.

Tender-heartedness
Billy, in one of his nice new sashes,
Fell in the fire and was burnt to ashes;
Now, although the room grows chilly,
I haven't the heart to poke poor Billy.

Impetuous Samuel
Sam had spirits nought could check,
And today, at breakfast, he
Broke his baby-sister's neck,
So he shan't have jam for tea!

Calculating Clara
O'er the rugged mountain's brow
Clara threw the twins she nursed,
And remarked, 'I wonder now
Which will reach the bottom first?'

The Perils of Obesity
Yesterday my gun exploded
When I thought it wasn't loaded;
Near my wife I pressed the trigger,
Chipped a fragment off her figure,
Course I'm sorry, and all that,
But she shouldn't be so fat.

Mr Jones
'There's been an accident!' they said,
'Your servant's cut in half; he's dead!'
'Indeed!' said Mr Jones, 'and please
Give me the half that's got my keys.'

Poetical Economy
What hours I spent of precious time,
    What pints of ink I used to waste,
Attempting to secure a rhyme
    To suit the public taste,
Until I found a simple plan
Which makes the lamest lyric scan!
When I've a syllable *de trop*,
    I cut it off, without apol.:

This verbal sacrifice, I know,
    May irritate the schol.;
But all must praise my dev'lish cunn.

Who realise that Time is Mon.
My sense remains as clear as cryst.,
   My style as pure as any Duch.
Who does not boast a bar sinist.
   Upon her fam. escutch.;
And I can treat with scornful pit.
The sneers of every captious crit.

I gladly publish to the pop.
A scheme of which I make no myst.,
And beg my fellow scribes to cop.
   This labour-saving syst.
I offer it to the consid.
Of every thoughtful individ.

The author, working like a beav.,
   His readers' pleasure could redoub.
Did he but now and then abbrev.
   The work he gives his pub.
(This view I most partic. suggest.
To A. C. Bens. and G. K. Chest.)

If Mr Caine rewrote *The Scape.*,
   And Miss Correll. condensed *Barabb.*,
What could they save in foolscap pape.
   Did they but cultivate the hab.
Which teaches people to suppress
All syllables that are unnec.!

If playwrights would but thus dimin.:
   The length of time each drama takes,
(*The Second Mrs Tanq.*, by Pin.
   Or even *Ham.*, by Shakes.)
We could maintain a watchful att.
When at a Mat. on Wed. or Sat.

Have done, ye bards, with dull monot.!
   Foll my examp., O Stephen Phill.,
O, Owen Seam., O, William Wat.,

O, Ella Wheeler Wil.,
And share with me the grave respons.
Of writing this amazing nons.!

H

JOEL CHANDLER HARRIS

The Tar Baby

'Didn't the fox *never* catch the rabbit, Uncle Remus?' asked the little boy the next evening.

'He come mighty nigh it, honey, sho's you bawn – Brer Fox did. One day arter Brer Rabbit fool 'im wid dat calamus root, Brer Fox went ter wuk en got 'im some tar, en mix it wid some turkentime, en fix up a contrapshun wat he call a Tar-Baby, en he tuck dish yer Tar-Baby en he sot 'er in de big road, en den he lay off in de bushes fer ter see wat de news wuz gwineter be. En he didn' hatter wait long, nudder, kaze bimeby here come Brer Rabbit pacin' down de road – lippity-clippity, clippity – lippity – des ez sassy ez a jay-bird. Brer Fox, he lay low. Brer Rabbit come prancin' 'long twel he spy de Tar-Baby, en den he fotch up on his behime legs like he wuz 'stonished. De Tar-Baby, she sot dar, she did, en Brer Fox, he lay low.

' "Mawnin'!" sez Brer Rabbit, sezee – "nice wedder dis mawnin'," sezee.

'Tar-Baby ain't sayin' nuthin', en Brer Fox he lay low.

' "How duz yo' sym'tums seem ter segashuate?" sez Brer Rabbit, sezee.

'Brer Fox, he wink his eye slow, en lay low, en de Tar-Baby, she ain't sayin' nuthin'.

' "How you come on, den? Is you deaf?" sez Brer Rabbit, sezee. "Kaze if you is, I kin holler louder," sezee.

'Tar-Baby stay still, en Brer Fox, he lay low.

' "Youer stuck up, dat's w'at you is," says Brer Rabbit,

sezee, "en I'm gwineter kyore you, dat's wa't I'm gwineter do,' sezee.

'Brer Fox, he sorter chuckle in his stummuck, he did, but Tar-Baby ain't sayin' nuthin'.

' "I'm gwineter larn you howter talk ter 'specttubble fokes ef hit's de las' 'act," sez Brer Rabbit, sezee. "Ef you don't take off dat hat en tell me howdy, I'm gwineter bus' you wide open," sezee.

'Tar-Baby stay still, en Brer Fox, he lay low.

'Brer Rabbit keep on axin' 'im, en de Tar-Baby, she keep on sayin' nuthin', twel present'y Brer Rabbit draw back wid his fis', he did, en blip he tuck 'er side 'er de head. Right dar's whar he broke his merlasses jug. His fis' stuck, en he can't pull loose. De tar hilt 'im. But Tar Baby, she stay still, en Brer Fox, he lay low.

' "Ef you don't lemme loose, I'll knock you agin," sez Brer Rabbit, sezee, en wid dat he fotch 'er a wipe wid de udder han', en dat stuck. Tar-Baby, she ain't sayin' nuthin', en Brer Fox, he lay low.

' "Tu'n me loose, fo' I kick de natal stuffin' outen you," sez Brer Rabbit, sezee, but de Tar-Baby, she ain't sayin' nuthin'. She des hilt on, en den Brer Rabbit lose de use er his feet in de same way. Brer Fox, he lay low. Den Brer Rabbit squall out dat ef de Tar-Baby don't tu'n 'im loose he butt 'er cranksided. En den he butted, en his head got stuck. Den Brer Fox, he sa'ntered fort', lookin' des ez innercent ez wunner yo' mammy's mockin'-birds.

' "Howdy, Brer Rabbit," sez Brer Fox. "You look sorter stuck up dis mawnin'," sezee, en den he roled on de groun', en laft en laft twel he couldn' laff no mo'. "I speck you'll take dinner wid me dis time, Brer Rabbit. I done laid in some calamus root, en I ain't gwineter take no skuse," sez Brer Fox, sezee.'

Here Uncle Remus paused, and drew a two-pound yam out of the ashes.

'Did the fox eat the rabbit?' asked the little boy to whom the story had been told.

'Dat's all de fur de tale goes,' replied the old man. 'He

mout, en den agin he moutent. Some say Jedge B'ar come
'long en loosed 'im – some say he didn't. I hear Miss Sally
callin'. You better run 'long.'

A. P. HERBERT

A Criminal Type

To-day I am MAKing aN inno6£vation. as you may already
have gessed, I am typlng this article myself Zz½ lnstead of
writing it, The idea is to save time and exvBKpense, also
to demonstyap demonBTrike= =damn, to demonstrato
that I can type /ust as well as any blessedgirl if I give
my mInd to iT"''' Typlng while you compose is realy
extraoraordinarrily easy, though composing whilr you
typE is more difficult. I rather think my typing style is
going to be different froM my u6sual style, but Idaresay
noone will mind that much. looking back i see that we
made rather a hash of that awfuul wurd
extraorordinnaryk? in the middle of a woRd like thaton
N-e gets quite lost? 2hy do I keep putting questionmarks
instead of fulstopSIwonder. Now you see i have put a
fulllstop instead Of a question mark it nevvvver reins but
it pours.

the typewriter to me has always been a mustery£?
and even now that I have gained a perfect mastery over
the machine in gront of me i have npt th3 faintest idea
hoW it workss% &or instance why does the thingonthetop
the klnd of lverhead Wailway arrange-ment move along
one pace afterr every word; I haVe exam aaa ined the
mechanism from all points of view but there seeems to
be noreason atall whyit shouould do t£is damn that £, it
keeps butting in: it is Just lik real life. then there are all
kinds oF attractive devisesand levers andbuttons of which
is amanvel in itself, and does someth15g useful without
lettin on how it does iT.

Forinstance on this machinE which is Ami/et a mije7
imean a mi/dgt, made of alumium,, and very light sothat

you caN CARRY it about on your £olidays (there is that
£ again) and typeout your poems onthe Moon
immmmediately, and there is onely one lot of keys for
capITals and ordinary latters; when you want to doa
Capital you press down a special key marked cap i mean
CAP with the lefft hand and yo7 press down the letter
withthe other, like that abcd, no, ABCDEFG. how jolly
that looks as a mattr of fact th is takes a little gettingintoas
all the letters on the keys are printed incapitals so now
and then one forgets topress downthe SPecial capit al key.
not often, though. on the other hand onceone£as got it
down and has written anice man e in capitals like
LLOYdgeORGE IT IS VERY DIFFICULT TO REmemBER
TO PUT IT DOWN AGAIN ANDTHE N YOU GET THIS
SORT OF THING WHICH SPOILS THE LOOK OF THE
HOLE PAGE. or els insted of preSSing down the key marked
CAP onepresses down the key m arked FIG and then
instead of LLOYDGEORGE you find that you have
written ½½96% :394:3. this is very dissheartening and
£t is no wonder that typists are sooften sououred in ther
youth.

Apart fromthat though the key marked FIG is rather
fun, since you can rite such amusing things withit, things
like % and @ and dear old & not to mention = and ¼
and ¾ and ! ! ! i find that inones ordinarry (i never get
that word right) cor orresponden£c one doesnt use
expressions like @@ and %%% nearly enough.
typewriting gives you a new ideaof possibilities o fthe
engli£h language; thE more i look at % the more beautiful
it seems to Be : and like the simple flowers of england itis
per£haps most beauti£ul when seen in the masss, Look atit

% % % % % % % % % % % %
% % % % % % % % % % % %
% % % £ % % % % % % % %
% % % % % % % % % % % %
% % % % % % % % % % £ %

how would thatdo for a BAThrooM wallpaper? it
could be produced verery cheaply and itcould be calld the

CHERRYdesigN damn, imeant to put all that in capitals.
Iam afraid this articleis spoilt now but butt bUt curse.
But perhaps the most excitingthing a£out this mac£ine is
that you can be presssing alittle switch suddenly writein
redor green instead of in black; I donvt understanh how £t
is done butit is very jollY? busisisness men us e the device
a great deal wen writing to their membersof PARLIAment,
in order to emphasasise the pointin wich the£r in£ustice
is worSe than anyone elses in£justice. wen they come to
WE ARE RUINED they burst out into red and wen they
come to WE w WOULD remIND YOU tHAT ATtHE
LAST E£ECTION youU UNDERTOOk they burst into
GReeN. thei r typists must enjoy doing those letters. with
this arrang ment of corse one coul d de allkinds of capital
wallpapers. for rinstance wat about a scheme of red £'s
and black %'s and gReen &'s? this sort of thing

          £ % £ % £ % £ % £ %
          & £ & £ & £ & £ & £
          £ % £ % £ % £ % £ %
          & £ & £ & £ & £ & £

Manya poor man would be glad to £ave that in his
parLour ratherthan wat he has got now. of corse, you
wont be ab?e to apreciate the fulll bauty of the design
since iunderst and that the retched paper which is going to
print this has no redink and no green inq either; so you
must £ust immagine that the £'s are red and the &'s are
green. it is extroarordinarry (wat a t erribleword ! ! !) how
backward in MAny waYs these uptodate papers are
www¼¼¼¼¼¼¼½ = ¾ now how did that happen
i won der; i was experimenting with the BACK SPACE
key; if that is wat it is for i dont thinq i shall use it again.
iI wonder if i am impriving at this½ sometimes i thinq i
am and so metimes i thinq iam not. we have not had so
many £'s lately but i notice that theere have been one or
two misplaced q's & icannot remember to write i in
capital s there is goes again.

Of curse the typewriter itself is not wolly giltless ½ike
all mac&ines it has amind of it sown and is of like passsions

with ourselves. i could put that into greek if only the machine was not so hopelessly MOdern. it's chief failing is that it cannot write m'sdecently and instead of h it will keep putting that confounded £. as amatter of fact ithas been doing m's rather better today butthat is only its cusssedusssedness and because i have been opening my shoul ders wenever we have come to an m; or should it be A m? who can tell; little peculiuliarities like making indifferent m's are very important & w£en one is bying a typewriter one s£ould make careful enquiries about themc; because it is things of that sort wich so often give criminals away. there is notHing a detective likes so much as a type riter with an idiosxz an idioynq damit an idiotyncrasy. for instance if i commit a murder i s£ould not thinq of writing a litter about it with this of all typewriters becusa because that fool ofa £ would give me away at once I daresay scotland Yard have got specimens of my trypewriting locked up in some pigeon-hole allready. if they £avent they ought to; it ought to be part of my dosossier.

i thinq the place of the hypewriter in ART is inshufficiently apreciated. Modern art i understand is chiefly sumbolical expression and straigt lines. a typwritr can do straight lines with the under lining mark) and there are few more atractive symbols thaN the symbols i have used in this articel; i merely thro out the sugestion

I dont tink i shal do many more articles like this it is tooo much like work? but I am glad I have got out of that £ habit;

A.P.£.

Love Lies Bleeding

(This drama, 'written by a Russian during his residence in Hammersmith', is from the Revue 'Riverside Nights', which Sir Nigel Playfair and I put together at the Lyric

Theatre, Hammersmith, in 1926. Mr Ridgeway had been running a season of Tchechov plays at the Barnes Theatre across the River. It is, I fear, a little like some of these modern plays.)

Characters

EBENEZER STEPHEN STEPHENSON, *a lunatic.*

THOMAS WILLIAM LOVE, *a footballer.*

HENRIETTA JOLLY, *an aunt.*

JONATHAN NATHANIEL JOLLY, *a gambler.*

ALICE MARGARET JOLLY, (*his daughter*), *a bride.*

HENRY HIGGINBOTTOM, *a steeplechaser.*

HARRIET ELIZABETH HIGGINBOTTTOM, *his mother.*

REGINALD ARTHUR FOSTER, *a best man.*

HEZEKIAH TOPLEY, *a newspaper seller.*

SCENE: *A room in the house of the* JOLLYS, *Blythe Road, Hammersmith. The furniture crowded against the walls. One table with white tablecloth, glasses, etc., being an attempt at a buffet.*

At a small table (right) sits STEPHENSON, *who is very old and untidy. He wears a most ancient second-hand frock-coat which is too large for him, and a straw hat with a hat-guard. He has his back to the room, and seems to be writing, referring now and then to a pile of papers and a number of great books, some of which have overflowed from his table to the floor. He looks woebegone and works feverishly, muttering. Indeed, he seems a little mad, and sometimes chews a cucumber.*

On the other side of the room (left) sits LOVE, *who is young and sulky. He is dressed in a football jersey and shorts, for he is a footballer, and plays goal for Chelsea. His boots and shorts are muddy, and one would say that he had been playing for Chelsea quite recently.*

He is sitting in front of a wireless set, with loudspeaker, and is tinkering with the controls. He wears an expression of profound discontent.

STEPHENSON (*not looking up*) What is the time, Thomas William Love?

LOVE (*after a pause – and with a shrug of utter disillusionment*) What does it matter?

HENRIETTA *drifts, or rather staggers, into the room; she is extremely old, though not as old as* EBENEZER; *she looks as if at any moment she might die, not from ill-health or age, but from concentrated melancholy. She carries a plate with some cake on it.*

HENRIETTA Here is the seed cake for the wedding breakfast. There is something peculiar about this house. The pork sandwiches have gone bad.

STEPHENSON *looks at her suspiciously and mutters;* LOVE *pays no attention to her; she puts the plate down and drifts out again.*

LOVE I admire pork. (*sighing*) It is a quarter past three, Ebenezer Stephen Stephenson.

STEPHENSON (*not looking up*) Morning – or afternoon?

LOVE *shrugs hopelessly.*

STEPHENSON (*turning round – darkly*) As a matter of fact, when you come to think of it, it matters to a quite extraordinary degree. At half-past three the 3.30 is run; and you know what that means to the head of this house. (*Confidential*) And then, you must be aware, Friday is the end of the financial year, and I am still at Schedule A. (*Wildly*) A fortnight! Only a fortnight to fill up all my forms! The forms of a whole family! (*Fiercely*) Oh, my forms! My beautiful forms! *He buries his face in them, sobbing, as though they were roses.*

LOVE (*is not much affected by this sad scene – but continues to tinker with the wireless*) As for me, I have never been able to share your enthusiasm for the Income Tax. But then, there is absolutely no seriousness in me. All my life I have been a failure, and yet, as you see (*looking very lugubrious*) I am as gay as a spark. Even now, look at me (STEPHENSON *does not*) I sit here trying to extract music from the ether with this utterly ridiculous machine, and, do you know, I simply do not care whether I succeed or not?

HENRIETTA *drifts in again from the other side of the room with a plate of sandwiches and a small teapot.*

HENRIETTA The gold-fish are swimming round in circles, Alice Margaret's canary is lying dead in its cage. It would not surprise me if something quite unusual took place in this strange house. (*Going over to* STEPHENSON *in a humouring voice*) Dear Uncle Ebenezer Stephen Stephenson! It is good of you to calculate the assessments for us all. But this is a day of joy ... You should have put on your black clothes like the others and gone to the church. *She lays a hand on his shoulder.*

STEPHENSON (*starting violently, covers his forms protectively with his hands*) Don't touch me! Keep away! (*Cunningly – looks at her searchingly, as if seeing her in a new light*) Are you a relative incapacitated by age or infirmity, Henrietta Jolly, or a daughter upon whose services the individual depends by reason of old age or infirmity, where the said relative, widowed mother, or daughter is maintained by the individual? (*Beating his forehead*) So much depends on that! (*Confidential*) But listen, Henrietta Jolly – if Love Lies Bleeding does not win the 3.30, then even I cannot save your brother. Oh, my forms! (*He returns to them*).

HENRIETTA (*wringing her hands*) Oh, this house is dreadful – dreadful! My poor brother! Yesterday he was misinformed by a gypsy at Sandown, and today his daughter is married to a steeplechaser. Oh!

Suddenly, behind her LOVE's *labours are rewarded, and a gay dance-tune pours from the loudspeaker.* LOVE *sits listening to it with an expression of abject sorrow.*

HENRIETTA (*turning – horrified*) Stop it, Thomas William Love (*He stops the music*) And why are you in fancy dress?

LOVE (*rising, with more vigour*) Will you have the goodness to tell me, Henrietta Jolly, the name of the detestable individual who is at this moment marrying your brother's daughter, Alice Margaret?

HENRIETTA (*wearily*) I forgot whether his name is Foster or Higginbottom. It is all the same.

STEPHENSON (*wildly – to himself – reading from his forms and tearing his hair*) Wear and tear of machinery and plant!

HENRIETTA But excuse me, why are you not playing in the cup-tie, Thomas William Love?

LOVE To be perfectly accurate, I am. Or, rather, shall we say, I was. I will tell you what happened –

STEPHENSON (*vaguely – as he works*) Nine-tenths of the amount of such earned income (subject to a maximum additional allowance of £45).

LOVE (*annoyed by the interruption, resumes*) I was standing in goal. The score, as we say, was five goals each (and half the game to go). Five times the ball had passed me and entered the net. (*Bitterly*) That is the sort of man I am. The centre-forward of the other side was running straight for me with the ball. He had passed the backs – there was nothing between him and me. Suddenly, at that moment, I realized the utter futility of my whole existence. What in the world, I reflected, does it matter whether a goal is scored or not, by one side or the other? Will anybody be wiser, more beautiful, have more elevated ideals? Besides, now that all things are held in common, is it right for one brother to have more goals than the rest? Some of the crowd, it is true, will cheer louder, and some will utter blasphemy and threats. But what, after all, is the crowd? What are they *for*?

STEPHENSON (*muttering*) Retirement, bankruptcy, death, etcetera.

LOVE Well, you will understand, Henrietta Jolly, that, having reached that conclusion, there was only one thing for me to do. Without so much as another glance at the advancing centre-forward, I turned on my heel, walked away from the goal, and came to this house.

STEPHENSON (*who seems to have been listening all the time, looks up, but not round*) Did he score a goal?

LOVE (*indifferently*) I did not notice.

HENRIETTA This is a very peculiar house (*With her woman's intuition*) It is evident from what you have said that you are in love with Alice Margaret.

LOVE (*shrugs, hopelessly*) Could anyone love a person so exceptionally second-rate as myself? (*He returns to the wireless*)

Clatter, conversation, and wedding-bells outside.

HENRIETTA Here they come, and now I dare say the tea is cold (*She pours out tea, etc.*)

LOVE *turns on the wireless, and another dance-tune is heard as the wedding party enter.*

The BRIDE (ALICE MARGARET JOLLY) *and the* BRIDEGROOM (HENRY HIGGINBOTTOM) *come in hand in hand. She is slight, pinched, and intense; she wears a very dingy wedding-dress, worn by her great-grandmother in the year?? He is in a very horsy black-and-white check suit, with breeches, and has bow legs. The* BRIDE *looks as if she has been crying, or is just about to. The* BRIDEGROOM *looks like death. The other three are dressed almost entirely in black.* JONATHAN NATHANIEL JOLLY, *the father of the bride, is a robust, florid, hearty, and cheerful person in a long frock-coat and brown boots.*

HARRIET ELIZABETH HIGGINBOTTOM, *the mother of the bride-groom, is stout and short of breath. She wears a good deal of jet, sequins, and lace. She carries smelling-salts and a fan.* REGINALD ARTHUR FOSTER, *the best man, is natty and perky and efficient – perhaps a clerk or young salesman. He is supporting* MRS HIGGINBOTTOM, *who seems much exhausted.*

LOVE *sits tinkering with the wireless, and* STEPHENSON *goes on with his work. Neither looks at the party.*

The BRIDE, *as soon as she sees* LOVE, *detaches her hand from* HIGGINBOTTOM'S *and goes quickly up to* LOVE, *who looks up and stops the wireless. The others make for the refreshment table.*

FOSTER Perhaps a little tea, Mrs Higginbottom?

MRS HIGGINBOTTOM (*nigh spent*) Tea? I could drain a samovar! (*Sinks into a chair*).

She and FOSTER *are at one side,* MR JOLLY *and* HIGGIN-BOTTOM *at the other.*

HENRIETTA *carts refreshments about.*

ALICE MARGARET (*intensely*) Thomas William, I cannot endure my married life. My husband sings in church. We have never been to church together before. It is dreadful. I detest music. What am I to do?

LOVE *looks darkly over her shoulder and takes a revolver from the pocket of his shorts.*

LOVE (*laughing sardonic-like*) And now I suppose you expect me to gratify your absurd passion for me by killing your husband? But let me tell you, young lady, you have come to the wrong shop. For I shall certainly miss him.

ALICE MARGARET (*putting her arms round him*) Do not be morbid, Thomas William. I have always loved you, but I married him to please my father, because he said he could spot winners.

They embrace passionately, a little hampered by the revolver. None of the others seems to observe these goings-on.

JONATHAN (*comfortably – having had a little wine – looking at the clock*) They should be off by now, Henry Higginbottom. You still have faith in Love Lies Bleeding?

HIGGINBOTTOM (*pontifical*) Mr Jolly, the horse that beats Love Lies Bleeding will win.

STEPHENSON (*totters to his feet and feebly waves a form or two at them*) If Love Lies Bleeding does not win (*He sinks back into his seat*).

JONATHAN Ha! I tell you what it is. I believe I am the most extraordinary character alive. I have absolutely no influence over a single human being. I say to one 'Come!' and he goes, 'Do this' and he does exactly the opposite. But when it comes to horses, I have the power of an archangel. Put me on the back of a horse and it becomes possessed of a devil, flies over mountains, jumps hedges, plunges into ponds. Put my money on a horse, and it stops dead. I do not believe that in all the world there is an animal so mild and swift that I cannot turn it into a wild beast by sitting on its back, or convert it into a lumbering cart-horse by putting half a crown on the creature. I have

only to draw a horse in a sweepstake, and it bursts out
coughing or swells at the knees. (*Drinking*) Ha! Truly a
remarkable power! (*to* HIGGINBOTTOM) But now that *you*
are a member of the family – we shall see a change, eh,
Henry Higginbottom?

HIGGINBOTTOM *nods, and they drink together.*

STEPHENSON (*pricking up his ears, totters over to* HIGGIN-
BOTTOM) A new member of the family? Then naturally
you will want your forms filled up?

(*Taking his arm, he leads the bridegroom over to the table,
delighted, still croaking*).

HIGGINBOTTOM, *humouring him, goes quietly.*

JONATHAN (*looking at his watch*) Go, Henrietta Susan Jolly,
and buy an evening paper.

HENRIETTA (*going out*) As you will, Jonathan Jolly, but I
never yet knew any good to come out of an evening paper.
There is something very queer about this party. (*She drifts
out*).

Enter, right, along the street, an old NEWSPAPER SELLER,
drunk.

NEWSPAPER SELLER Paper! Paper! All the losers! (*Highly
amused*) He! He! The trouble about me is that half the
time I yearn after beauty and the other half I drink gin.
Paper! He! He! I remember when there were larks singing
in the Broadway. Did anyone want an evening paper
then? Everyone was content with his own misfortunes –
his own and his neighbour's. But nowadays a man bears
on his back the calamities of the whole world. Earthquakes
and murders with his breakfast; floods, strikes and
railway-smashes on his way to work. He! He! (*Waving
his papers*). And, not satisfied with so much misery in the
morning, he must needs have another dose of disaster in
the evening. He! He! (*To* HENRIETTA JOLLY, *who now
approaches*) Paper, miss? I tell you what it is, miss, there's
more joy in Fleet Street over one sinner that cuts his
sweetheart's throat than over the ninety and nine just men
who marry and live happily ever after. (*Going off*) I never
sell one of these things without thinking I've made another

fellow-creature miserable. But I keep on doing it! He! He! Paper! All the losers! (*Exit*).

MRS HIGGINBOTTOM (*panting and puffing*) It is difficult to see why people continue to get married in this country, Mr Foster, for sooner or later they go mad or have a baby, and then everything begins all over again.

JONATHAN, *meanwhile, has closed his eyes, and is humming drunkenly to himself.*

REGINALD FOSTER At home, Mrs Higginbottom, I have a tame salamander, which continually stands on its hind legs. I have sometimes wondered why.

THE BRIDE (*who all this time has been locked in* LOVE's *arms whispers tensely*) Let me go! Someone will see us!

LOVE *releases her, and she sits down by the wireless. He stands fingering his revolver, and gazing darkly at the inoffensive* FOSTER.

HENRIETTA *then bounces into the room with an evening paper – saying almost gaily* Did I not tell you that some misfortune would befall us?

ALL What is it?

STEPHENSON *and* HIGGINBOTTOM *turn in their chairs (right),* JONATHAN *jumps up and looks over* HENRIETTA's *shoulder at the paper.* FOSTER *pushes over and stands centre.* MRS HIGGINBOTTOM *waddles over to the paper group. The* BRIDE *and* LOVE *remain where they are (left).*

JONATHAN (*reading – in sepulchral tones*) 'Loves Lies Bleeding fell dead at the starting-gate.'

THE BRIDE (*gives a little scream*) Oh! And he promised it should win!

Silence – broken at last by a rending sound. It is STEPHENSON, *tragically tearing up the forms on which he has laboured so long. All gaze straight in front of them. Perhaps by accident, the* BRIDE *turns the appropriate lever, and dance-music again issues from the loud-speaker.*

Then LOVE *moves a step, and raising his revolver, shoots* FOSTER *through the head.* FOSTER *falls to the ground. No one at first appears to notice the incident.* LOVE *stands over*

the body and shoots it again. The BRIDE *stops the wireless.*
LOVE, *to make quite sure, fires another shot at the defunct*
FOSTER.
THE BRIDE What are you doing, Thomas William Love?
The others slowly begin to take things in.
LOVE (*with an eloquent gesture towards the body*) Well,
at any rate you will admit that we can now be married,
and live happily ever after.
THE BRIDE But that is not my husband. That is the best
man.
LOVE (*throwing down his revolver, with a shrug*) Now *that*
is just the sort of thing that happens to me.

CURTAIN.

SAMUEL HOFFENSTEIN

Poems in Praise of Practically Nothing

You buy some flowers for your table;
You tend them tenderly as you're able;
You fetch them water from hither and thither —
What thanks do you get for it all? They wither.

—

Only the wholesomest foods you eat;
You lave and you lave from your head to your feet;
The earth is not steadier on its axis
Than you in the matter of prophylaxis;
You go to bed early and early you rise;
You scrub your teeth and you scour your eyes —
What thanks do you get for it all? Nephritis,
Pyorrhhea, appendicitis,
Renal calculus and gastritis.
You hire a cook, but she can't cook yet;
You teach her by candle, bell, and book yet;
You show her, as if she were in her cradle,
Today, the soup, tomorrow, a ladle.
Well, she doesn't learn, so though you need her,

You decide that somebody else should feed her —
But you're kind by birth; you hate to fire her;
To tell a woman you don't require her —
So you wait and wait, and before you do it,
What thanks do you get? She beats you to it!

From *A Garden of Verses for the Little Ones, Including Orphans and Step-children, and their Parents and Guardians Also.*

When the wind is in the tree,
It makes a noise just like the sea,
As if there were not noise enough
To bother one, without that stuff.

—

Sleep, my darling baby, sleep:
The French eat frogs; Australians, sheep.

Today will go, tomorrow come;
I'll bake a cake and give you some.

Angels through your slumber sing!
A kangaroo's a funny thing.

A kangaroo will make you laff,
But not so much as a giraffe —

Not so much as a giraffe;
I'll bake a cake and give you haff —

A chocolate cake and a gooseberry tart;
Sleep, my darling; have a heart!

Don't you worry; ma will keep —
You yelled all day and now you sleep!

Progress

They'll soon be flying to Mars, I hear —
But how do you open a bottle of beer?

A flash will take you from Nome to New York –
But how the hell do you pull a cork?

They'll rocketeer you to Hibernia –
But open a window and get a hernia.

They've stripped space from the widow'd blue –
But where is the lace that fits a shoe?

Where is the key that fits a lock?
Where is the garter that holds a sock?

They'll hop to the moon and skip to the stars,
But what'll stay put are the lids on jars.

The mighty telescope looks far
But finds no place to park a car.

The world crackles with cosmic minds
Tangled up in Venetian blinds.

One day they'll resurrect the dead,
Who'll die again of colds in the head.

Spiritual

I got a complex; you got a complex –
All God's chillun got things.
You are neurotic; I got suppressions;
She's idiotic; they owe money –
All God's chillun got things.
Heb'n! Heb'n!
M'yeh, Heb'n!

I got a summons; you got sinus trouble –
All God's chillun got things.
You are a book-keeper; I am worse off;
She *can't* get married; he *got* married –
All God's chillun got things.
Heb'n! Heb'n!
Go tell papa!

Anon

The man in the wilderness asked me
How many strawberries grow in the sea?
I answered him as I thought good
As many as herrings grow in the wood

—

There are men in the village of Erith
Whom nobody seeth or heareth,
And there looms, on the marge
Of the river, a barge
That nobody roweth or steereth

—

Hector Protector was dressed all in green;
Hector Protector was sent to the Queen.
The Queen did not like him, no more did the King,
So Hector Protector was sent back again.

—

Sally go round the moon, Sally,
Sally go round the sun;
Sally go round the omnibus
On a Sunday afternoon.

—

Up came the doctor, up came the cat,
Up came the devil with a white straw hat.
Down went the doctor, down went the cat,
Down went the devil in a white straw hat.

OLIVER WENDELL HOLMES

*A Visit To The Asylum For Aged And Decayed
Punsters*

The charter provides for the support of 'One hundred aged
and decayed Gentlemen-Punsters'. On inquiry if there was
no provision for *females*, my friend called my attention
to this remarkable psychological fact, namely:

THERE IS NO SUCH THING AS A FEMALE PUNSTER.

This remark struck me forcibly, and, on reflection, I
found that *I never knew nor heard one* though I have once
or twice heard a woman make a *single detached* pun, as
I have known a hen to crow.

On arriving at the south gate of the Asylum grounds, I
was about to ring, but my friend held my arm and begged
me to rap with my stick, which I did. An old man, with a
very comical face, presently opened the gate and put out
his head.

'So you prefer *Cane to A Bell*, do you?' he said, and
began chuckling and coughing at a great rate.

My friend winked at me.

'You're here still, Old Joe, I see,' he said to the old man.

'Yes, yes; and it's very odd, considering how often I've
bolted, nights.'

He then threw open the double gates for us to ride
through.

'Now,' said the old man, as he pulled the gates after us,
'You've had a long journey.'

'Why, how is that, Old Joe?' said my friend.

'Don't you see?' he answered; 'there's the *East hinges*
on one side of the gate, and there's the *West hinges* on
t'other side – haw! haw! haw!'

We had no sooner got into the yard than a feeble little
gentleman, with a remarkably bright eye, came up to us,
looking very serious, as if something had happened.

'The town has entered a complaint against the asylum

as a gambling establishment,' he said to my friend the Director.

'What do you mean?' said my friend.

'Why, they complain that there's a *lot o' rye* on the premises,' he answered, pointing to a field of that grain, and hobbled away, his shoulders shaking with laughter, as he went.

On entering the main building we saw the Rules and Regulations for the Asylum conspicuously posted up. I made a few extracts, which may be interesting.

SECT. I. OF VERBAL EXERCISES.

5. Each Inmate shall be permitted to make Puns freely, from eight in the morning until ten at night, except during Service in the Chapel and Grace before Meals.

6. At ten o'clock the gas will be turned off, and no further Puns, Conundrums, or other play on words, will be allowed to be uttered, or to be uttered aloud.

9. Inmates who have lost their faculties, and cannot any longer make Puns, shall be permitted to repeat such as may be selected for them by the Chaplain out of the work of Mr. *Joseph Miller*.

19. Violent and unmanageable Punsters, who interrupt others when engaged in conversation, with Puns, or attempts at the same, shall be deprived of their *Joseph Millers*, and, if necessary, placed in solitary confinement.

SECT. III. OF DEPORTMENT AT MEALS.

4. No Inmate shall make any Pun, or attempt at the same, until the Blessing has been asked and the company are decently seated.

7. Certain Puns having been placed on the *Index Expurgatorius* of the Institution, no Inmate shall be allowed to utter them, on pain of being debarred the perusal of *Punch* and *Vanity Fair*, and, if repeated, deprived of his *Joseph Miller*.

Among these are the following:

Allusions to *Attic salt*, when asked to pass the salt-cellar.

Remarks on the Inmates being *mustered*, &c, &c.

Personal allusions in connection with *carrots* and *turnips*.

Attempts upon the word *tomato*, &c.

The following are also prohibited, excepting to such Inmates as may have lost their faculties, and cannot any longer make Puns of their own:

'– your own *hair* or a wig;' 'it will be *long enough*,' &c. &c.

'little of its age,' &c. &c. also playing upon the following words:

hospital, *mayor*, *pun*, *pitied*, *bread*, *sauce*, *sole*, &c, &c, &c

See INDEX EXPURGATORIUS, *printed for use of Inmates*.

The Superintendent, who went round with us, had been a noted punster in his time, and well known in the business world, but lost his customers by making too free with their names – as in the famous story he set afloat in '29 of *forgeries* attaching to the names of a noted Judge, an eminent lawyer, the Secretary of the Board of Foreign Mission, and the well-known Landlord at Springfield. One of the *four Jerries*, he added, was of gigantic magnitude.

The Superintendent showed some of his old tendencies as he went round with us.

'Do you know' – he broke out all at once – 'why they don't takes steppes in Tartary for establishing Insane Hospitals?'

We both confessed ignorance.

'Because there are *normal* people to be found there,' he said, with a dignified smile.

He proceeded to introduce us to different Inmates. The first was a middle-aged, scholarly man, who was seated at a table with a Webster's Dictionary and a sheet of paper before him.

'Well, what luck to-day, Mr. Mowzer?' said the Superintendent.

He turned to his notes and read:

'Don't you see Webster *ers* in the words cent*er* and theat*er*?'

'If he spells leather *lether*, and feather *fether*, isn't there danger that he'll give us a *bad spell of weather?*'

'Besides, Webster is a resurrectionist; he does not allow *u* to rest quietly in the *mould.*'

'And again, because Mr. Worcester inserts an illustration in his text, is that any reason why Mr. Webster's publishers should hitch one on in their appendix? It's what I call a *Connect-a-cut* trick.

'Why is his way of spelling like the floor of an oven? Because it is *under bread.*'

'Mowzer!' said the Superintendent – 'that word is on the Index!'

'I forgot,' said Mr. Mowzer – 'please don't deprive me of *Vanity Fair*, this one time, sir.'

'These are all, this morning. Good day, gentlemen.' Then to the Superintendent – 'And you, sir!'

The next Inmate was a semi-idiotic-looking old man. He had a heap of block-letters before him, and, as we came up, he pointed, without saying a word, to the arrangements he had made with them on the table. They were evidently anagrams, and had the merit of transposing the letters of the words employed without addition or subtraction. Here are a few of them:

TIMES	SMITE
POST	STOP!
TRIBUNE	TRUE NIB
WORLD	DR. OWL
ADVERTISER	{ RES VERI DAT { IS TRUE. READ!
ALLOPATHY	ALL O' TH'PAY
HOMOEOPATHY	O, THE – ! O! O, MY! PAH!

RICHARD HUGHES

Living in W'ales

Once there was a man who said he didn't like the sort of houses people lived in, so he built a model village. It was not really like a model village at all, because the houses were all big enough for real people to live in, and he went about telling people to come and Live in W'ales.

There was also living in Liverpool a little girl who was very nice. So when all the people went off with the man to live in W'ales, she went with them. But the man walked so fast that presently some of them got left behind. The ones who were left behind were the little girl, and an Alsatian dog, and a very cross old lady in a bonnet and black beads, who was all stiff, but had a nice husband, who was left behind too.

So they all went along till they came to the sea; and in the sea was a whale. The little girl said, 'That was what he meant, I suppose, about living in W'ales. I expect the others are inside; or, if not, they are in another one.'

So they shouted to know if they might come in, but the whale didn't hear them. The nice husband said that if that was what living in W'ales meant, he would rather go back to Liverpool; but the horrid old lady said, 'Nonsense! I will go and whisper in its ear.'

But she was very silly, and so instead of whispering in its ear she went and tried to whisper in its blowhole. Still the whale didn't hear; so she got very cross and said, 'None of this nonsense, now! Let us in at once! I won't have it, do you hear? I simply won't have it!' and she began to stir in his blowhole with her umbrella.

So the whale blew, like an enormous sneeze, and blew her right away up into the sky on top of the water he blew out of his hole, and she was never seen again. So then the nice husband went quietly back to Liverpool.

But the little girl went to the whale's real ear, which

was very small and not a bit like his blowhole, and whispered into it, 'Please, nice whale, we would so like to come in, if we may, and live inside.' Then the whale opened his mouth, and the little girl and the Alsatian dog went in.

When they got right down inside, of course, there was no furniture. 'He was quite right,' said the little girl. 'It is certainly not a bit like living in a house.'

The only thing in there was a giant's wig that the whale had once eaten. So the little girl said, 'This will do for a door-mat.' So she made it into a door-mat, and the Alsatian dog went to sleep on it.

When he woke up again he started to dig holes; and of course it gave the whale most terrible pains to have holes dug by such a big dog in his inside, so he went up to the top of the water and shouted to the Captain of a ship to give him a pill. On board the ship there was a cold dressed leg of mutton that the Captain was tired of, so he thought, 'That will make a splendid pill to give the whale.' So he threw it to the whale, and the whale swallowed it; and when it came tobogganing down the whale's throat the Alsatian dog, who was very hungry, ate it, and stopped digging holes; and when the dog stopped digging holes the whale's pain went away. So he said, 'Thank you', to the Captain. 'That was an excellent pill.'

The Captain was very surprised that his pill had made the whale well again so soon; he had really only done it to get rid of the cold mutton.

But the poor little girl wasn't so lucky as the Alsatian dog. *He* had a door-mat to sleep on, and something to eat. But there was no bed, and the little girl couldn't sleep without a bed to sleep on possibly, and she had nothing to eat; and this went on for days and days.

Meanwhile the whale began to get rather worried about them. He had swallowed them without thinking much about it; but he soon began to wonder what was happening to them, and whether they were comfortable. He knew nothing at all about little girls. He thought she would probably want something to eat by now, but he didn't know at all what. So he tried to talk down into his own inside, to ask her. But that is very difficult; at any rate *he* couldn't do it. The words all came out instead of going in.

So he swam off to the tropics, where he knew a parrot, and asked him what to do. The parrot said it was quite simple, and flew off to an island where there was a big snake. He bit off its head and bit off its tail, and then flew back to the whale with the rest of it. He put most of the snake down the whale's throat, so that one end just came up out of its mouth.

'There,' he said, 'now you have got a speaking tube. You speak into one end of the snake, and the words will go down it inside you.'

So the whale said, 'Hallo' into one end of the snake, and the little girl heard 'Hallo' come out of the other.

'What do you want?' said the whale. 'I want something to eat,' said the little girl. The whale told the parrot, 'She wants something to eat. What do little girls eat?'

'Little girls eat rice pudding,' said the parrot. He had one in a big glass bowl, so he poured it down the snake too, and it came down the other end and the little girl ate it.

When she had eaten it she caught hold of her end of the snake, and called 'Hallo!' up it.

'Hallo!' said the whale.

'May I have a bed?' said the little girl.

'She wants a bed,' the whale said to the parrot.

'You go to Harrod's for that,' said the parrot, 'which is the biggest shop in London,' and flew away.

When the whale got to Harrod's he went inside. One of the shopwalkers came up to him and said, 'What can I do for *you*, please?' which sounded very silly.

'I want a bed,' said the whale.

'Mr. Binks, BEDS!' the shopwalker called out very loud, and then ran away. He was terribly frightened, because there had never been a whale in the shop before.

Mr. Binks the Bed Man came up and looked rather worried.

'I don't know that we have got a bed that will exactly fit you, sir,' he said.

'Why not, silly?' said the whale. 'I only want an ordinary one.'

'Yes, sir,' said the Bed Man, 'but it will have to be rather a large ordinary one, won't it?'

'Of course not, silly,' said the whale. 'On the contrary it will have to be rather a small one.'

He saw a very nice little one standing in a corner.

'I think that one will just about fit me,' he said.

'You can have it if you like' said the Bed Man. 'But I think it is you who are the silly to think a little bed like that will fit you!'

'I want it to fit me *inside*, of course,' said the whale, 'not *outside*! – Push!' and he opened his mouth.

So they all came and pushed, and sure enough it did just fit him. Then he ate all the pillows and blankets he could find, which was far more than was needed really, and when it all got down inside, the little girl made the bed and went to sleep on it.

So the whale went back to the sea. Now that the little girl and the Alsatian dog both had had something to eat and somewhere to sleep, they said:

'The man was right, it really is much more fun living in W'ales than living in houses.'

So they stayed on.

P.S. The parrot went on feeding them, not always on rice pudding.

LEIGH HUNT

The Fish, The Man, And the Spirit

To a Fish

You strange, astonished-looking, angle-faced,
  Dreary-mouthed, gaping wretches of the sea,

Gulping salt-water everlastingly,
Cold-blooded, though with red your blood be graced,
And mute, though dwellers in the roaring waste;
And you, all shapes beside, that fishy be –
Some round, some flat, some long, all devilry,
Legless, unloving, infamously chaste:

O scaly, slippery, wet, swift, staring wights,
What is't ye do? What life lead? Eh, dull goggles?
How do ye vary your vile days and nights?
How pass your Sundays? Are ye still but joggles
In ceaseless wash? Still naught but gapes, and bites,
And drinks, and stares, diversified with boggles?

A Fish Answers

Amazing monster! that, for aught I know,
With the first sight of thee didst make our race
For ever stare! O flat and shocking face,
Grimly divided from the breast below!
Thou that on dry land horribly dost go
With a split body and most ridiculous pace,
Prong after prong, disgracer of all grace,
Long – useless – finned, haired, upright, unwet, slow!

O breather of unbreathable, sword-sharp air,
How canst exist? How bear thyself, thou dry
And dreary sloth? What particle canst thou share
Of the only blessed life, the watery?
I sometimes see of ye an actual *pair*
Go by! linked fin by fin! most odiously.

The Fish Turns Into a Man, and then Into a Spirit, and Again Speaks

Indulge thy smiling scorn, if smiling still,
O man! and loathe, but with a sort of love;
For difference must its use by difference prove,
And in sweet clang, the spheres with music fill.

One of the spirits am I, that at his will
Live in whate'er has life – fish, eagle, dove –
No hate, no pride, beneath nought, nor above,
A visitor of the rounds of God's sweet will.

Man's life is warm, glad, sad, 'twixt loves and graves
Boundless in hope, honoured with pangs austere,
Heaven-gazing; and his angel-wings he craves:
The fish is swift, small-needing, vague yet clear,
A cold, sweet, silver life, wrapped in round waves,
Quickened with touches of transporting fear.

NORMAN HUNTER

From Professor Branestawm's Dictionary

Aaron	What a wig has.
abandon	What a hat has.
abundance	A waltz for cakes.
accord	A piece of thick string.
addition	What a dinner table has.
administer	A clergyman in a television commercial.
aftermath	The next lesson after arithmetic.
Aldershot	A tree killed in action.
already	Completely crimson.
angler	Someone good at geometry.
bandeau	Forbidden French water.
bicycle	Purchase a thing for cutting long grass.
boycott	Bed for a male baby.
buoyant	Male insect.
cabaret	Row of taxis.
Caerphilly	How to cross a road in Wales.
cantilever	Is the gentleman not able to go away from the lady?
capsize	How large a hat you wear.

carnation	Race of people who live in motor cars.
cartridge	Made by a cart wheel.
climax	An alpenstock.
copper nitrate	What policemen get paid for working overtime in the evenings.
cross purposes	Bad-tempered fish.
Defoe	The enemy author.
diploma	The man who comes to mend a burst water pipe.
dozen	Opposite of what one does.
during	Did you use the bell?
enchant	A female chicken's song.
enterprise	Come in, award.
euphonium	Italian request to get someone on the telephone.
expunge	Cake made with eggs.
farthingale	A cheap blast of wind
fungi	A comedian
furlong	The coat of a Persian cat.
gable	A jolly male cow.
hirsute	Lady's costume.
hyacinth	Familiar greeting for Cynthia.
igloo	An Eskimo's toilet.
jargon	The vase is no longer here.
juggernaut	An empty jug.
khaki	A thing for starting a motor car.
knapsack	Sleeping bag.
liability	Capacity for telling untruths.
macadam	The first Scotsman.

meander	Myself and girl friend.
non-iron shirt	One made of brass.
offal	Terrible.
out of bounds	A frog too tired to leap.
oxide	Leather.
pasteurize	Across your vision.
pulpit	A Yorkshireman's instruction to pound something to paste.
quota	Report what the lady said.
rampage	Attendant on a male sheep.
ramshackle	Handcuff for a male sheep.
raucous	Uncooked swear word.
rheumatic	An apartment at the top of a house.
robust	A line of knitting that has come undone.
sediment	What he announced he had in mind.
sesame	I say, said by a foreigner.
settee	Lay the afternoon meal.
shamble	Imitation male cow.
soldier	Caused you to buy.
sonata	Not long afterwards.
staple	Tower of an Irish church.
statue	Enquiry as to whether it is yourself.
supersede	Very good thing for growing flowers from.
testimony	Bad-tempered coins.
Triton	See if the coat fits.
twain	What you twavel in on the wailway.
tyro	A line of neckwear.
urchin	The lower part of the lady's face.

velocity	We mislaid the hot drink.
versatile	Poetry on the roof.
vertigo	In which direction did he proceed?
whose	A Scottish residence.
Windsor	Did you succeed at your game, guv'nor?

II

EUGENE IONESCO

The Bald Prima Donna

MR SMITH: (*still with his paper*) Well, well, well! According to this, Bobby Watson's dead.

MRS SMITH: Good Heavens! Poor fellow! When did it happen?

MR SMITH: What are you looking so surprised about? You knew perfectly well he was dead. He died about two years ago. You remember, we went to the funeral, about eighteen months ago, it must be.

MRS SMITH: Of course, I remember perfectly. It came back to me at once; but I fail to understand why you had to look so surprised to see it in the paper.

MR SMITH: It wasn't in the paper! It must be three years ago now since there was talk of his passing away. I was reminded of it by an association of ideas.

MRS SMITH: What a shame it was! He was so very well preserved.

MR SMITH: He made the best-looking corpse in Great Britain! And he never looked his age. Poor old Bobby! He'd been dead for four years and he was still warm. A living corpse if ever there was one. And how cheerful he always was!

MRS SMITH: Little Bobby, poor darling!

MR SMITH: What do you mean, 'Poor darling'?

MRS SMITH: I was thinking about his wife. Her name was Bobby, like his. As they had the same name, when you saw them together, you could never tell one from the other. It was really only after he died that you could tell which was which. But fancy, even now, there are still people who mix her up with her dead husband when they offer their condolences. Did you know her, dear?

MR SMITH: I only saw her once, quite by chance, at Bobby's funeral.

MRS SMITH: I've never seen her. Is she nice-looking?

MR SMITH: She has regular features, but you can't call her beautiful. She's too tall and too well-built. Her features are rather irregular, but everyone calls her beautiful. A trifle too short and too slight perhaps. She teaches singing. (*The clock strikes five times*)

MRS SMITH: And when are they thinking of getting married, the two of them?

MR SMITH: Next spring, at the latest.

MRS SMITH: We can't possibly get out of going to their wedding.

MR SMITH: We shall have to give them a wedding present. I wonder what.

MRS SMITH: Why shouldn't we offer them one of the silver trays we were given when we were married and which have never been the slightest use to us? It's sad for her to have been widowed so young.

MR SMITH: Lucky they didn't have any children.

MRS SMITH: Oh! That would have been too much! Children! What on earth would she have done with them?

MR SMITH: She's still a young woman. She may quite well marry again. Anyway, mourning suits her extremely well.

MRS SMITH: But who will take care of the children? They've a girl and a boy, you know. How do they call them?

MRS SMITH: Bobby and Bobby – like their parents. Bobby Watson's uncle, old Bobby Watson, has pots of money and he's very fond of the boy. He could very easily take over Bobby's education.

MRS SMITH: Yes, it's what one would expect. And in the same way Bobby Watson's aunt, old Bobby Watson, could very easily take over the education of Bobby Watson, the daughter of Bobby Watson. Then, if that happened Bobby, the mother of Bobby Watson, could marry again. Has she anyone in view?

MR SMITH: Yes, a cousin of Bobby Watson's.

MRS SMITH: Who? Not Bobby Watson?

MR SMITH: To which Bobby Watson are you referring?

MRS SMITH: Why, to Bobby Watson, the son of old Bobby Watson, the other uncle of the Bobby Watson who's just died.

MR SMITH: No, it's not that one. It's another one. It's the Bobby Watson who's the son of old Bobby Watson, the aunt of the Bobby Watson who's just died.

MRS SMITH: Oh! You mean Bobby Watson, the commercial traveller?

MR SMITH: They're *both* commercial travellers.

MRS SMITH: What a hard job that is! They do well out of it, though!

MR SMITH: Yes, when there's no competition.

MRS SMITH: And when isn't there any competition?

MR SMITH: Tuesdays, Thursdays and Tuesdays.

MRS SMITH: Ah! Three days in the week? And what does Bobby Watson do on those days?

MR SMITH: He has a rest; he sleeps.

MRS SMITH: But if there's no competition on those days, why doesn't he work?

MRS SMITH: You can't expect me to know everything. I can't answer all your silly questions!

MRS SMITH: (*hurt*) You said that just to upset me!

MR SMITH: You know perfectly well I didn't.

MRS SMITH: You men are all alike! There you sit, all day long, with a cigarette in your mouth, making your face up with lipstick and powder fifty times a day, that is if you can take the time off from drinking!

MR SMITH: I'd like to know what you'd say if men car-

ried on as women do! Smoking all day long, sticking
powder and lipstick all over their faces and gulping
down the whisky!

MRS SMITH: You can say what you like! I don't care!
But if you're saying that just to get my goat, well ... I
I don't like that kind of a joke, you know perfectly
well I don't *(She hurls the socks away and shows her
teeth. She gets up.)*

MR SMITH: *(also coming to his feet and going towards his
wife tenderly)*. Why are you spitting fire like that, my
little roast chicken? You know I only said it for fun.
(He takes her by the waist and kisses her.) What a
ridiculous couple of old lovebirds we are! Come along
now, we'll put the lights out and go bye-byes!

(Enter MARY)

MARY: I am the maid. I have just spent a very pleasant
afternoon. I went to the pictures with a man and saw
a film with some women. When we came out of the
cinema we went and drank some brandy and some
milk, and afterwards we read the newspaper.

MRS SMITH: I hope you spent a pleasant afternoon. I hope
you went to the pictures with a man and drank some
brandy and some milk.

MR SMITH: And the newspaper!

MARY: Your guests, Mr and Mrs Martin, are waiting at
the door. They were waiting for me. They were afraid
to come in on their own. They were meant to be dining
with you this evening.

MRS SMITH: Ah yes. We were expecting them. And we
were hungry. As they showed no sign of coming, we
went and dined without them. We'd had nothing to
eat all day long. You shouldn't have gone off like that,
Mary.

MARY: But you gave me your permission!

MR SMITH: We didn't do it on purpose!

MARY: *(bursts into laughter, then into tears. Smiling)* I've
bought myself a chamber-pot.

MRS SMITH: Dear little Mary will you be so good as to

open the door, please, and let Mr and Mrs Martin in. We'll go and get dressed quickly.

(MR *and* MRS SMITH *go off right,* MARY *opens the door left, and* MR *and* MRS MARTIN *come in*)

MARY: What do you mean by being so terribly late? It's not polite. You must arrive punctually. Understand? Still, now you're here, you might as well sit down and wait. (*She goes out*).

J

PAUL JENNINGS

Cornish Jungle

One of the curious pleasures of being alive in England today is a sort of surprise at our own immortality. While
one part of us regrets the nineteenth-century gunboats,
another part is entranced by the huge timeless tableau, for
instance, of Gandhi and Nehru at one side of a table, Halifax and Cripps on the other, gravely playing celestial chess
with a sub-continent. Coloured students throng London;
we are still here, but with a strange lightheadedness, as if
in a country where all the physical laws have altered,
where things are lighter, where a man could pick up a
house.

It is like dying and finding one is more alive than ever
before. Yet things *look* the same. We are only halfway
between iron and aluminium. The vast masonry of banks
and factories, so accepted a part of our Victorian prag-
matism, is now seen in a strange new light, as evidence of
a mercantilism that is more exciting, more perilous, less
taken for granted. We are at once more insular and more
international. From Land's End, where England comes to
a point, limited and small, we widen out, becoming more
real, over the broad countires, eastwards to London, to the
great reality.

At the same time that we have ceased to take foreigners
for granted, we have become more delicately conscious of
the mystery of our own country. Land's End, Cornwall,
that strange thinning-out into the sea. Perhaps it's all more

exotic than we think, more exotic than Delhi or Zanzibar or Tonga. If not, how is one to account for the following, which I swear is exhibited in foot-high letters over a shop at the entrance to Fleet Street, just where the road narrows down from the wide, public Strand into the narrow sounding-board of England?

CORNISH FLEXIBLE EARTH

FROM THE CORNISH JUNGLE

WHERE STRAWBMATS ARE MADE

AND BRITISH BAMBOOS ARE GROWN.

No, it can't be true. Let us hold on to reality. A *jungle*? Why, it's all moors and cromlechs in Cornwall. I've been there myself. Sure, England gets a bit thin, but there are still half signs and cafes.

No, wait a minute. When you come to think of it, there *is* something tropical and humid about the Cornish legend of Tristram and Iseult. And what about that dance they have – the Furry Dance? People monstrously covered with fur, jiggling all day in a bright High Street; antlers and strange feline faces mumping among the hat-shops. Can it be that something is going on, has been going on for centuries in Cornwall, of which practical London knows nothing, even though it be blatantly announced to Fleet Street?

They have Druids in Cornwall. What if their ancient wisdom is the real thing, and our vast metropolitan, nay, our world planning, has been a dream? Down there in Cornwall, these Druids have discovered the secret of the Flexible Earth, of the magical kink in space–time that has always haunted mystics. We stand watching the Furry Dance, and suddenly we feel a quiver, an expansion, a released, disembodied feeling – and we *are* in the Cornish jungle.

Gone are the cream teas and the artists' cottages. We are in a strange Douanier Rousseau country. Girls part the tall reeds, and dance among the monstrous flowers. They are dressed in strawbmats, a kind of Cornish grass skirt. To thin, Atlantis piping they move about, they prepare a barbaric feast – yam rolls, gosky patties, truro fruit – for King Mark's party, whose ship approaches endlessly across the crimson sea.

Meanwhile, the strange temple of the twin gods Pol and Pen, built of baked strawbmats, guarded by Druids who play booming conch music, is being prepared. The drums throb, the people come out of their strawbmat houses, they sail out to meet King Mark in their strawb-mat canoes. (Indeed, it is quite possible that the original words was *strawboat* – a kind of Celtic coracle, built on a frame of British bamboo. *Strawbmat* is the kind of word a typewriter produces out of the subconscious of the machine age, like *electricticy*, *atmopshere* and *Hampsetad Hetha*. These Druids, pecking away on their unfamiliar typewriters, their beads catching in the keys, as they worded the draft of the announcement to Fleet Street, in-tended to write *strawboat*, but *strawbmat* is how it came out.) And yet, in some way, it is still British, this jungle. In this thin, bright light, it is not hot. The British bamboo trees provide shelter from the bodiless sun of dreams.

Fleet Street, Janus-faced, looks outward, with its oracu-lar foreign corespondents, and inward, with its hundreds of second-floor rooms umbilically linked to some British town, to some local newspaper, to the inner dream of an ancient people; but even if Fleet Street does not know about the Cornish jungle, England does.

Report on Resistentialism

It is the peculiar genius of the French to express their philosophical thought in aphorisms, sayings hard and tight as diamonds, each one the crystal centre of a whole constellation of ideas. Thus, the entire scheme of seventeenth-century intellectual rationalism may be said to branch out from that single, pregnant saying of Descartes, *cogito ergo sum* – I think, therefore I am. Resistentialism, the philosophy which has swept present-day France, runs true to this aphoristic form. Go into any of the little cafés or *horlogeries* on Paris' Left Bank (make sure the Seine is flowing *away* from you, otherwise you'll be on the Right Bank, where *no* one is *ever* seen) and sooner or later you will hear someone say, '*Les choses sont contre nous.*'

'Things are against us.' This is the nearest English translation I can find for the basic concept of Resistentialism, the grim but enthralling philosophy now identified with bespectacled, betrousered, two-eyed Pierre-Marie Ventre. In transferring the dynamic of philosophy from man to a world of hostile Things, Ventre has achieved a major revolution of thought, to which he himself gave the name 'Resistentialism'. Things (*res*) resist (*résister*) man (*homme*, understood). Ventre makes a complete break with traditional philosophic method. Except for his German precursors, Freidegg and Heidansiecker, all previous thinkers from the Eleatics to Marx have allowed at least some legitimacy to human thought and effort. Some, like Hegel or Berkeley, go so far as to make man's thought the supreme reality. In the Resistentialist cosmology, that is now the intellectual rage of Paris, Ventre offers us a grand vision of the Universe as One Thing – the Ultimate Thing (*Derniere Chose*). And it is against us.

Two world wars have led to a general dissatisfaction with the traditional Western approach to cosmology, that of scientific domination. In Ventre's view, the World-Thing, to which he sometimes refers impartially as the Thing-World, opposes man's partial *stealing*, as it were, of consciousness – of his dividing it into the separate 'minds' with which human history has made increasingly fatal attempts to create a separate world of men. Man's increase in this illusory domination over Things has been matched, pari passu, by the increasing hostility (and greater force) of the Things arrayed against him. Medieval man, for instance, had only a few actual Things to worry about – the lack of satisfactory illumination at night, the primitive hole in the roof blowing the smoke back and letting the

rain in, and one or two other small Things like that.
Modern, domesticated Western man has far more oppor-
tunities for battle-losing against Things — can-openers,
collar-studs, chests of drawers, open manholes, shoe-
laces....

Now that Ventre has done it for us, it is easy to see that
the reaction against nineteenth-century idealism begun by
Martin Freidegg and Martin Heidansiecker was bound
eventually to coalesce with the findings of modern physics
in a philosophical synthesis for our time. Since much stress
has been laid on the 'scientific' basis of Resistentialism, it
will not be out of place here, before passing on to a more
detailed outline of Ventre's thought, to give a brief account
of those recent developments in physical science which
have so blurred the line that separates it from metaphysics. It is an account which will surprise those whose
acquaintance with Ventre is limited to reading reviews of
his plays and who, therefore, are apt to think that Resistentialism is largely a matter of sitting inside a wet sack
and moaning.

A convenient point of departure is provided by the
famous Clark-Trimble experiments of 1935. Clark-Trimble
was not primarily a physicist, and his great discovery of
the Graduated Hostility of Things was made almost accidentally. During some research into the relation between
periods of the day and human bad temper, Clark-Trimble,
a leading Cambridge psychologist, came to the conclusion
that low human dynamics in the early morning could not
sufficiently explain the apparent hostility of Things at the
breakfast table — the way honey gets between the fingers,
the unfoldability of newspapers, etc. In the experiments
which finally confirmed him in this view, and which he
demonstrated before the Royal Society in London, Clark-
Trimble arranged four hundred pieces of carpet in ascending degrees of quality, from coarse matting to priceless
Chinese silk. Pieces of toast and marmalade, graded,
weighed and measured, were then dropped on each piece
of carpet, and the marmalade-downwards incidence was

statistically analyzed. The toast fell right-side-up every time on the cheap carpet, except when the cheap carpet was screened from the rest (in which case the toast didn't know that Clark-Trimble had other and better carpets), and it fell marmalade-downwards every time on the Chinese silk. Most remarkable of all, the marmalade-downwards incidence for the intermediate grades was found to vary *exactly* with the quality of carpet.

The success of these experiments naturally switched Clark-Trimble's attention to further research on *resistentia*, a fact which was directly responsible for the tragic and sudden end to his career when he trod on a garden rake at the Cambridge School of Agronomy. In the meantime, Noys and Crangenbacker had been doing some notable work in America. Noys carried out literally thousands of experiments, in which subjects of all ages and sexes, sitting in chairs of every conceivable kind, dropped various kinds of pencils. In only three cases did the pencil come to rest within easy reach. Crangenbacker's work in the social-industrial field, on the relation of human will-power to specific problems such as whether a train or subway will stop with the door opposite you on a crowded platform, or whether there will be a mail box anywhere on your side of the street, was attracting much attention.

Resistentialism, a sombre, post-atomic philosophy of pagan, despairing nobility, advocates complete withdrawal from Things. Now that Ventre has done the thinking for us it is easy to see how the soil was prepared for Resistentialism in the purely speculative field by the thought of Martin Freidegg (1839–1904) and Martin Heidansiecker (1850–1910), both well-known anti-idealists and anti-intellectualists. It is in the latter's *Werke* (Works) published at Tübingen in 1894, that the word *Resistentialismus* first appears, although it has not the definite meaning assigned to it by Ventre. It is now possible to trace a clear line of development to Ventre from Goethe, who said, with prophetic insight into the hostility of one Thing, at least, 'Three times has an apple proved fatal. First to the human race, in the fall of Adam; secondly to Troy, through the gift of Paris; and last of all, to science through the fall of Newton's apple' (*Werke* XVI, 17). Later we find Heidan-siecker's concept of *Dingenhass*, the hatred of Things. But in the confused terminology of this tortured German mystic we are never sure whether it is the Things who hate us, or we who hate the Things.

To the disillusioned youth of post-war France there was an immediate appeal in Ventre's relentlessly logical concept of man's destiny as a *néant*, or No-Thing, and it was the aesthetic expression of this that gave Resistentialism such great popular currency outside the philosophical textbooks. Ventre himself is an extraordinarily powerful dramatist; his first play, *Puits Clos*, concerns three old men who walk round ceaselessly at the bottom of a well. There are also some bricks in the well. These symbolise Things, and all the old men hate the bricks as much as they do each other. The play is full of their pitiful attempts to throw the bricks out of the top of the well, but they can, of course, never throw high enough, and the bricks always fall back on them. *Puits Clos* has only recently been taken off at the little Theatre Jambon to make room for another Resistentialist piece by Blanco del Huevo, called *Comment Sont Les Choses?* Del Huevo is an ardent young disciple of Ventre, and in this play, which is also running in London under the title *The Things That Are Caesar*, he makes a very bold step forward in the application of Resistentialist imagery to the theatre. He has made Things the characters, and reduced the human beings to what are known in Resistentialist language as *poussés*. The nearest English translation that suggests itself for this philosophical term is 'pushed-arounds'.

The chief 'characters' in *Comment Sont Les Choses?* are thus a piano and a medicine cabinet; attached to the piano is *Poussée* Number One – no human beings are given actual names, because names are one of the devices by which man has for so long blinded himself to his fundamental inability to mark himself out from the Universe

(*Dernière Chose*). *Poussé* Number One is determined to play the piano, and the piano is determined to resist him. For the first twenty minutes of Act I, he plays a Beethoven sonata up to a certain bar, which always defeats him. He stops, and plays this bar over a hundred times, very slowly. He begins the sonata again, and when he gets to this bar he makes the very same mistake. He pours petrol on the piano, and is just about to set it on fire when he hears a huge crash from the bathroom, also visible to the audience on the other side of a stage partition.

All this time the medicine cabinet has been resisting the attempts of *Poussé* Number Two to fix it on the wall, and it has now fallen into the bath. *Poussé* Number One who is in love, naturally, with *Poussé* Number Two's wife, *Poussée*, mimes his derision at the woeful lack of manhood of one who cannot even dominate Things to the extent of fixing a medicine cabinet. While he does so, the piano, with the tragic irony of a Greek chorus, speaks of *Poussé* Number One's own *hubris* and insolence in imagining that he can master the piano. *Poussé* Number Two is too busy to retaliate, as he is sweeping up the mess of camphorated oil, essence of peppermint, hair cream, calamine lotion, and broken glass towards the plug end of the bath, meaning to swill them out with hot water. He is desperately anxious to get this done before *Poussée* arrives home. She comes, however, while he is still trying ignominiously to get the bits of glass off one sticky hand with the other sticky hand, the glass then sticking to the other sticky hand and having to be got off with the first sticky hand (a good example of *choses corélatives* in the Resistentialist sense). *Poussée* expresses her scorn and asks her husband, all in mime, why he can't play the piano like *Poussé* Number One (who has persuaded her that he can). Eventually she goes out with *Poussé* Number One, and *Poussé* Number Two, exhausted by his labours at the bath, falls into it and into a deep coma.

Act II is extremely unconventional, and although some critics have hailed it as a great attempt to break down the modern separation between players and audience it seems to me to be the weakest part of the play, the nearest to a mere philosophical treatise. The curtain simply goes up on a Resistentialist exhibition, and the audience are invited to walk around. While they are examining the exhibits, which contain not only Resistentialist paintings but also what Ventre as well as Del Huevo calls *objets de vie* (chests of drawers, toothpaste caps, collar buttons, etc.), the stage manager comes on in his shirt sleeves and reads the chapter on sex from Ventre's *Résistentialisme*. Ventre takes a tragic view of sex, concerned as it is with the body, by which the World-Thing obtains its mastery over human territory. In so far as man is not merely a body he is only a pseudo-Thing (*pseudo-chose*), a logical 'monster'. Ventre sees woman, with her capacity for reproduction indefinitely prolonging this state of affairs, as the chief cause of humanity's present dilemma of Thing-separation and therefore Thing-warfare. Love between humans, i.e. between Man (Not-woman) and Woman (Not-man), perpetuates bodies as Things, because a man, in being a Not-woman, shows the capacity of all things for being only *one* Thing (it is all much clearer in the French, of course). Just as a man is a Not-woman, he is also a Not-sideboard, a Not-airplane. But this is as far as man can go in Thing-ness, and if it were not for women we could all die and be merged comfortably in the Universe or Ultimate Thing.

In Act III, the action, if one can call it that, is resumed. When the curtain goes up *Poussé* Number Two is discovered still lying in the bath. The tragedy of man's futile struggle against the power of Things begins to draw towards its fatal climax as we hear a conversation between the piano and the medicine cabinet in which the Piano suggests an exchange of their respective *Poussés*. The piano, realising that *Poussée* doesn't know anything about music anyway and will probably accept *Poussé* Number One's word that he can play, queering the pitch for Things, with this ambivalent concept of love, wishes to lure

Number Two on instead. (In Ventre's system, Things are quite capable of emanations and influences by reason of their affinity with man's Thing-body or Not other). Accordingly, when *Poussé* Number Two wakes up in the bath he feels a compulsive desire to play the piano, forgetting that his fingers are still sticky – and of course it is not his piano anyway. The piano, biding its time, lets him play quite well. (In Resistentialist jargon, which unashamedly borrows from the terminology of Gonk and others when necessary, the resistance of the I-Thing is infinite and that of the Thou-Thing is zero – it is always my bootlaces that break – and of course *Poussé* Number Two thinks he is playing *Poussé* Number One's Piano.) Number Two only leaves the instrument when he hears the others coming back. He goes to the bathroom and listens through the partition with a knowing smile as *Poussé* Number One begins to play for *Poussée*. Naturally, his fingers stick to the keys the piano being an I-Thing for him, or so he thinks. This makes *Poussé* Number Two feel so good that he actually manages to fix the medicine cabinet. *Poussée*, returning to him disillusioned from the pseudo-pianist, flings herself into his arms, but it is too late. He has cut an artery on a piece of the broken glass sticking out of the medicine cabinet. In despair she rushes back to the music room, where *Poussé* Number One has just lit a cigarette to console himself and think out the next move. ('As if that mattered,' says the piano scornfully.) As she comes in there is a great explosion. *Poussé* Number One has forgotten the petrol he had poured on the piano in Act I.

The drama is not the only art to have been revivified in France (and therefore everywhere) by Resistentialism. This remorseless modern philosophy has been reflected in the work of all the important younger composers and painters in Paris. Resistentialist music, based on acceptance of the tragic Thing-ness, and therefore limitation, of musical instruments, makes use of a new scale based on the Absolute Mathematical Reluctance of each instrument. The A.M.R. of the violin, for instance, is the critical speed beyond which it is impossible to play it because of the strings' melting. The new scale is conceived, says Dufay, as 'a geometric rather than a tonic progression. Each note is seen as a point on the circumference of a circle of which the centre is the A.M.R. The circle must then be conceived as *inside-out*'. Dufay has expressed in mathematical terms that cosmic dissatisfaction of the artist with the physical medium in which he is forced to work. Kodak, approaching the problem from a different angle, has taken more positive steps to limit the 'cosmic offence-power' of the conventional scale by *reducing* the number of notes available. His first concerto, for solo tympanum and thirty conductors, is an extension of the argument put forward some years ago, in remarkable anticipation of Resistentialism, by Ernest Newman, music critic of the London *Sunday Times*, who said that the highest musical pleasure was to be derived much more from score-reading than from actual performance. Kodak is now believed to be working on a piece for conductors only.

I have left Resistentialism in painting to the end because it is over the quarrel between Ventre and Agfa, at one time his chief adherent among the artists, that the little cafés and bistros of the Quartier Latin are seething to-day. When Agfa first came under Ventre's influence he accepted the latter's detachment, not so much Franciscan as Olympic, from Things. His method was to sit for hours in front of a canvas brooding over disasters, particularly earthquakes in which Things are hostile in the biggest and most obvious way. Sometimes he would discover that the canvas had been covered during his abstraction, sometimes not. At any rate, Agfa enjoyed a *succès fou* as a painter of earthquakes and recently he has shown himself impatient of the thoroughgoing *néantisme* (no-thingery) of Ventre, who insists relentlessly that to conform completely to the pure Resistentialist ideal a picture should not only have no paint but should be without canvas and without frame, since, as he irrefutably points out, these Things are all Things (*ces choses sont toutes des choses*).

The defection of Agfa and of other 'moderates' among the Resistentialists has been brought to a head by the formation, under a thinker named Qwertyuiop, of a neo-Resistentialist group. The enthusiasm with which medieval students brawled in the streets of Paris over the Categories of Being has lost none of its keenness today, and the recent pitched battle between Ventristes and followers of Qwertyuiop outside the Café aux Fines Herbes, by now famous as Ventre's headquarters, has, if nothing else, demonstrated that Paris still maintains her position as the world's intellectual centre. It is rather difficult to state the terms of the problem without using some of the Resistentialists' phraseology, so I hope I may be pardoned for briefly introducing it.

Briefly, the issue is between Ventre, the pessimist, and Qwertyuiop, the optimist. Ventre, in elaborating on his central aphorism, *les choses sont contre nous*, distinguishes carefully between what he calls *chose-en-soi*, the Thing in itself, and *chose-pour-soi*, the Thing for itself. *Chose-en-soi* is his phrase for Things existing in their own right, sublimely and tragically independent of man. In so far as Ventre's pregnant terminology can be related to traditional western categories, *chose-en-soi* stands for the Aristotelean outlook, which tends to ascribe a certain measure of reality to Things without reference to any objective Form in any mind, human or divine. There are even closer parallels with the later, medieval philosophy of Nominalism, which says, roughly, that there are as many Things as we can find names for; Ventre has an interesting passage about what he calls inversion (*inversion*) in which he exploits to the full the contrast between the multiplicity of actions which Things can perform against us – from a slightly overhanging tray falling off a table when the removal of one lump of sugar over-balances it, to the atomic bomb – and the paucity of our vocabulary of names on such occasions.

The third great concept of Ventre is *le neant* (the No-

Thing). Man is ultimately, as I have said, a No-Thing, a metaphysical monster doomed to battle, with increasing non-success, against real Things. Resistentialism, with what Ventre's followers admire as stark, pagan courage, bids man abandon his hopeless struggle.

Into the dignified tragic, Olympian detachment of Ventre's 'primitive' Resistentialism the swarthy, flamboyant Qwertyuiop has made a startling, meteoric irruption. Denounced scornfully by the Ventristes as a plagiarist, Qwertyuiop was, indeed, at one time a pupil of Ventre. He also asserts the hostility of Things to man – but he sees grounds for hope in the concept of *chose-pour-soi* (the Thing for itself) with which it is at least possible to enter into relationship. But he is more a dramatist than a philosopher, and what enrages the Ventristes is the bouncing optimism of his plays and also the curious symbolic figure of the *géant* or giant which appears in them all. This *géant* is a kind of Resistentialist version of Nietzsche's superman, a buskined, moustachioed figure who intervenes, often with great comic effect, just when the characters in the play are about to jump down a well (the well is, of course, a frequent Resistentialist symbol – cf. Ventre's own *Puits Clos*).

The Ventristes point out acidly that in the first edition of *Résistentialisme* the word *geant* appears throughout as a misprint for *néant*. Friction between the two groups was brought to a head by Qwertyuiop's new play *Messieurs, Les Choses Sont Terribles*, (loosely, *Gentlemen, Things are Terrible*). On the first night at the Théâtre des Somnambules, the Ventristes in the gallery created an uproar and had to be expelled when, at the end of the second act, the inevitable *géant* had stepped in to prevent three torturings, seven betrayals, and two suicides. The battle was renewed later with brickbats and bottles when Qwertyuiop and his followers interrupted one of Ventre's *choseries*, or Thing-talks, at the Café aux Fines Herbes. Five of the moderates and two Ventristes were arrested by the gendarmerie and

later released on bail. All Paris is speculating on the outcome of the trial, at which many important literary figures
are expected to give evidence.

It is, however, not in the law courts that the influence
of Resistentialism on our time will be decided. It is in
the little *charcuteries* and *épiceries* of the Left Bank. It is
in the stimulating mental climate of Paris that the artists
and dramatists will decide for themselves whether there
is any future for art in the refined philosophical at-
mosphere to which Ventre's remorseless logic would have
them penetrate. Although Qwertyuiop has succeeded in
attracting many of Ventre's more lukewarm followers
among the arts, who had begun to rebel against the Master's uncompromising insistence on pictures without paint
and music without instruments, without any Things at
all, there seems no doubt that Ventre is the greater thinker,
and it is an open question whether he will achieve his
object of persuading the world to abandon Things without the indispensable help of the artistic confraternity in
moulding public opinion.

There is no doubt, either, that Ventre's thought strikes a
deep chord in everyone during these sombre, post-atomic
times. Ventre has, I think, liberated the vast flood of
creative hatred which makes modern civilization possible.
My body, says Ventre, is *chose-en-soi* for me, a Thing which
I cannot control, a Thing which uses me. But it is *chose-
pour-soi* for the Other. I am thus a Hostile Thing to the
Other, and so is he to me. At the same time it follows (or
it does in the French) that I am a No-Thing to the world.
But I cannot be united or merged with the World-Thing
because my Thing-Body, or Not-Other, gives me an illicit
and tragically deceptive claim on existence and 'happiness'.
I am thus tragically committed to extending the area of
my always illusory control over the Thing-Body – and as
the 'mind' associated with my Thing-Body is merely the
storing up of recollected struggles with Things, it follows
that I cannot know the Other except as one of the weapons

with which the World-Thing has increased its area of hostile action.

Resistentialism thus formalizes hatred both in the cosmological and in the psychological sphere. It is becoming generally realized that the complex apparatus of our modern life – the hurried meals, the dashing for trains, the constant meeting of people who are seen only as 'functions' – the barman, the wife, etc. – could not operate if our behaviour were truly dictated by the old, reactionary categories of human love and reason. This is where Ventre's true greatness lies. He has transformed, indeed reversed the traditional mechanism of thought, steered it away from the old dogmatic assumption that we could use Things, and cleared the decks for the evolution of the Thing-process without futile human opposition. Ventre's work brings us a great deal nearer to the realization of the Resistentialist goal summed up in the words, 'Every Thing out of Control.'

JOHN KEATS

A Song about Myself

There was a naughty Boy,
  A naughty boy was he,
He would not stop at home,
  He could not quiet be –
    He took
    In his Knapsack
    A Book
    Full of vowels
    And a shirt
    With some towels –
    A slight cap
    For night cap –
    A hair brush,
    Comb ditto,
    New Stockings
    For old ones
    Would split O!
    This Knapsack
    Tight at's back
    He rivetted close
And followed his Nose
    To the North,
    To the North,
And followed his nose
    To the North

II

There was a naughty boy
  And a naughty boy was he
For nothing would he do
  But scribble poetry —
    He took
    An ink stand
    In his hand
    And a pen
    Big as ten
    In the other,
    And away
    In a Pother
    He ran
    To the mountains
    And fountains
    And ghostes
    And Postes
    And witches
    And ditches
    And wrote
    In his coat
    When the weather
    Was cool,
    Fear of gout
    And without
    When the weather
    Was warm —
    Och the charm
    When we choose
To follow one's nose
  To the north,
  To the north,
To follow one's nose
  To the north!

IV

There was a naughty Boy,
    And a naughty Boy was he,
He ran away to Scotland
        The people for to see –
        Then he found
        That the ground
        Was as hard,
        That a yard
        Was as long
        That a song
        Was as merry,
        That a cherry
        Was as red –
        That lead
        Was as weighty
        That fourscore
        Was as eighty,
        That a door
        Was as wooden
        As in England –
So he stood in his shoes
    And he wonder'd,
    He wonder'd,
He stood in his shoes
    And he wonder'd

L

RING LARDNER

Dinner Bridge

Characters
CROWLEY, *the foreman*
AMOROSI, *an Italian labourer*
TAYLOR, *a Negro labourer*
CHAMALES, *a Greek labourer*
HANSEN, *a Scandinavian labourer*
LLANUZA, *a Mexican labourer*
THE INQUISITIVE WAITER
THE DUMB WAITER

Programme note
This playlet is an adaptation from the Wallachian of
Willie Stevens. For a great many years, Long Islanders and
Manhattanites have been wondering why the Fifty-ninth
Street Bridge was always torn up at one or more points.
Mr Stevens heard the following legend: that Alexander
Woolcott, chief engineer in charge of the construction of
the bridge, was something of a practical joker; that on the
day preceding the completion of the bridge, he was invited to dinner by his wife's brother; that he bought a
loaded cigar to give his brother-in-law after the meal and
that the cigar dropped out of his pocket and rolled under
the unfinished surface planking. Ever since, gangs of men
have been ripping up the surface of the bridge in search
of the cigar, but an article the shape of a cigar is apt to
roll in any and all directions. This is what has made it so

difficult to find the lost article, and the (so far) vain search is the theme of Mr Steven's playlet. – *Adapter*

SCENE: An area under repair on the Fifty-ninth Street Bridge.

Part of the surface has been torn up, and, at the curtain's rise, three of the men are tearing up the rest of it with picks. Shovels, axes, and other tools are scattered around the scene. Two men are fussing with a concrete mixer. Crowley is bossing the job. Crowley and the labourers are dressed in dirty working clothes. In the foreground is a flat-topped truck or wagon. The two waiters, dressed in waiters' jackets, dickies, etc., enter the scene, one of them carrying a tray with cocktails and the other with a tray of caviar, etc. The labourers cease their work and consume these appetisers. The noon whistle blows. The waiters bring in a white table cloth and spread it over the truck or wagon. They also distribute place cards and six chairs, or camp stools, around the truck, but the 'table' is left bare of eating implements.

FIRST WAITER *to* CROWLEY: Dinner is served.

(*Crowley and the labourers move toward the table*)

TAYLOR *to* AMOROSI: I believe I am to take you in.

(AMOROSI *gives* TAYLOR *his arm and* TAYLOR *escorts him to the table. The labourers all pick up the place cards to find out where they are to sit.*)

CROWLEY *to* AMOROSI: Here is your place, Mr Amorosi. And Taylor is right beside you.

(*Note to producer: Inasmuch as* TAYLOR *and* AMOROSI *do most of the talking, they ought to face the audience. In spite of their nationalities, the labourers are to talk in correct Crowninshield dinner English, except that occasionally, say every fourth or fifth speech, whoever is talking suddenly bursts into dialect, either his own or Jewish or Chinese or what you will.*

All find their places and sit down. *The two waiters now re-enter, each carrying one dinner pail. One serves* CROWLEY *and the other serves* AMOROSI. *The serving is done by the waiter's removing the cover of the pail and holding it in front of the diner. The latter looks into the pail and takes out some viand with his fingers. First, he takes out, say, a sandwich. The waiter then replaces the cover on the pail and exits with it. All the labourers are served in this manner, two at a time, from their own dinner pails. As soon as one of them has completed the sandwich course, the waiter brings him the pail again and he helps himself to a piece of pie or an apple or orange. But the contents of all the pails should be different, according to the diner's taste. The serving goes on all through the scene, toward the end of which everyone is served with coffee from the cups on top of the pails).*

CROWLEY (*to* AMOROSI): Well, Mr Amorosi, welcome to the Fifty-ninth Street Bridge.

AMOROSI: Thank you, I really feel as if this is where I belonged.

HANSEN (*politely*): How is that?

AMOROSI: On account of my father. He was among the pioneer Fifty-ninth Street Bridge destroyers. He had the sobriquet of Giacomo 'Rip-Up-the-Bridge' Amorosi.

TAYLOR (*sotto voce, aside to* HANSEN): This fellow seems to be quite a card!

LLANUZA: I wonder if you could tell me the approximate date when your father worked here.

AMOROSI: Why, yes. The bridge was completed on the fifth day of August, 1909. So that would make it the sixth day of August, 1909, when father started ripping it up.

TAYLOR (*aside to* HANSEN, *in marked Negro dialect*): I repeats my assertation that this baby is quite a card!

AMOROSI (*in Jewish dialect*): But I guess it must be a lot more fun nowadays, with so much motor traffic to pester.

TAYLOR: And all the funerals. I sure does have fun with the funerals.

CROWLEY (*in Irish brogue*): Taylor has a great time with the funerals.

HANSEN, CHAMALES and LLANUZA (*in unison*): Taylor sure has a grand time with the funerals.

AMOROSI (*to* TAYLOR): How do you do it?

TAYLOR (*in dialect*): Well, you see, I'm flagman for this outfit. When I get out and wave my flag, whatever is coming, it's got to stop. When I see a funeral coming, I let the hearse go by and stop the rest of the parade. Then when I see another funeral coming, I stop their hearse and let the rest of *their* procession go on. I keep doing this all morning to different funerals and by the time they get to Forest Hills, the wrong set of mourners is following the wrong hearse. It generally winds up with the friends and relatives of the late Mr Cohen attending the final obsequies of Mrs Levinsky.

CROWLEY, HANSEN, *and* CHAMALES (*in unison*): Taylor has a great time with the funerals.

AMOROSI: I'm a *trumpet* medium myself.

TAYLOR (*aside to* HANSEN): This boy will turn out to be quite a card!

LLANUZA: Why do you always have to keep repairing it?

AMOROSI: What do you mean, what's the matter?

LLANUZA: Why do they always have to keep repairing it?

AMOROSI: Perhaps Mr Crowley has the repairian rights.

TAYLOR (*guffawing and slapping* HANSEN *or* CHAMALES *on the back*): What did I tell you?

LLANUZA: (*in dialect*): But down in Mexico, where I come from, they don't keep repairing the same bridge.

AMOROSI (*to* LLANUZA): If you'll pardon a newcomer. Mr –, I don't believe I got your name.

LLANUZA: Llanuza.

AMOROSI: If you'll pardon a newcomer, Mr Keeler, I want to say that if the United States isn't good enough for you, I'd be glad to start a subscription to send you back to where you came from.

LLANUZA: I was beginning to like you, Mr Amorosi.

AMOROSI: You get that right out of your mind, Mr Barrows. I'm married; been married twice. My first wife died.

HANSEN: How long were you married to her?

AMOROSI: Right up to the time she died.

CHAMALES (*interrupting*): Mr Amorosi, you said you had been married twice.

AMOROSI: Yes, sir. My second wife is a Swiss girl.

HANSEN: Is she here with you?

AMOROSI: No, she's in Switzerland, in jail. She turned out to be a murderer.

CROWLEY: When it's a woman, you call her a murderess.

TAYLOR: And when it's a Swiss woman, you call her a Swiss-ess.

(*One of the waiters is now engaged in serving* AMOROSI *with his dinner pail*).

WAITER, *to* AMOROSI: Whom did she murder?

(WAITER *exits hurriedly without seeming to care to hear the answer*).

AMOROSI (*after looking wonderingly at the disappearing* WAITER): What's the matter with *him*?

TAYLOR: He's been that way for years – a born questioner but he hates answers.

CROWLEY: Just the same, the rest of us would like to know whom your wife murdered.

TAYLOR, HANSEN, CHAMALES *and* LLANUZA (*to* CROWLEY): Speak for yourself. We don't want to know.

CROWLEY: Remember, boys, I'm foreman of this outfit. (*Aside to* AMOROSI) Who was it?

AMOROSI: (*Whispers name in his ear*).

CROWLEY: I don't believe I knew him.

AMOROSI: Neither did my wife.

CROWLEY: Why did she kill him?

AMOROSI: Well, you see, over in Italy and Switzerland, it's different from, say, Chicago. When they find a man murdered over in those places, they generally try to learn who it is and put his name in the papers. So my wife was curious about this fellow's identity and she figured that the easiest way to get the information was to pop him.

TAYLOR: I'm a *trumpet* medium myself.

(WAITER *enters and serves one of the labourers from his dinner pail*).

WAITER: How long is she in for?

(WAITER *exits hurriedly without waiting for the answer.* AMOROSI *again looks after him wonderingly*).

HANSEN (*to* AMOROSI): Did you quarrel much?

AMOROSI: Only when we were together.

TAYLOR: I was a newspaper man once myself.

LLANUZA (*sceptically*): You! What paper did you work on?

TAYLOR: It was a tabloid – the Porno-graphic.

(WAITER *enters to serve somebody*).

WAITER TO TAYLOR: Newspaper men must have lots of interesting experiences.

(*Exits without waiting for a response*).

AMOROSI: I suppose you've all heard this story –

THE OTHER LABOURERS (*in unison*): Is it a golf story?

AMOROSI: No.

THE OTHERS (*Resignedly*): Tell it.

AMOROSI (*In dialect*): It seems there was a woman went into a photographer's and asked the photographer if he took pictures of children.

(WAITER *enters to serve somebody*).

WAITER: How does it end? (WAITER *exits hurriedly*).

AMOROSI: The photographer told her yes, that he did take pictures of children. 'Why, yes, madam,' replied the photographer –

TAYLOR: He called her 'madam'.

AMOROSI: The photographer told her yes, that he did take pictures of children. 'And how much do you charge?' inquired the madam, and the photographer replied, 'Three dollars a dozen.' 'Well,' said the woman, 'I guess I'll have to come back later. I've only got eleven.'

(*The other labourers act just as if no story had been told*).

LLANUZA: Down in Mexico, where I come from, they don't keep repairing the same bridge.

TAYLOR (*to* HANSEN): Can you imitate birds?

HANSEN: No.

TAYLOR (*to* CHAMALES): Can you imitate birds?

CHAMALES: No.

TAYLOR: Can anybody here imitate birds?

THE OTHER LABOURERS (*in unison*): No.

TAYLOR: *I* can do it. Long before I got a job on this bridge, while I was helping tear up the crosstown streets, I used to entertain the boys, imitating birds.

AMOROSI: What kind of birds can you imitate?

TAYLOR: All kinds.

AMOROSI: Well, what do you say we play some other game?

CROWLEY (*rising*): Gentlemen, we are drawing near to the end of this dinner and I feel we should not leave the table till someone has spoken a few words of welcome to our newcomer, Mr Amorosi. Myself, I am not much of a talker. (*Pauses for a denial*).

TAYLOR: You said a full quart.

CHAMALES: Therefore, I will call on the man who is second to me in length of service on the Fifty-ninth Street Bridge, Mr Harvey Taylor. (*Sits down*).

TAYLOR (*rising amid a dead silence*): Mr Foreman, Mr Amorosi, and gentlemen: Welcoming Mr Amorosi to our little group recalls vividly to my mind an experience of my own on the levee at New Orleans before Prohibition. (*He bursts suddenly into Negro dialect, mingled with Jewish*). In those days my job was to load and unload those great big bales of cotton and my old mammy used always to be there at the dock to take me in her lap and croon me to sleep.

(*WAITER enters, serves somebody with coffee*).

WAITER: What was the experience you was going to tell? (*Exit hurriedly*).

TAYLOR: It was in those days that I studied bird life and learned to imitate the different bird calls. (*Before they can stop him, he gives a bird call*). The finch. (*The others pay no attention. He gives another bird call*). A Dowager. (*TAYLOR is pushed forcibly into his seat*).

AMOROSI (*rising to respond*): Mr Foreman and gentlemen: I judge from Mr Taylor's performance that the practice of imitating birds is quite common in America. Over where I come from we often engage in the practice of mimicking public buildings. For example (*he gives a cry*). The American Express Company's office at Rome. (*He gives another cry*). The Vatican. (*He gives another cry*) Hotel McAlpin. (*A whistle blows, denoting that the dinner hour is over*).

CROWLEY (*rising*): Shall we join the ladies?

(*All rise and resume the work of tearing up the bridge. The waiters enter to remove the table cloth and chairs*).

WAITER (*the more talkative one*): How many Mack trucks would you guess had crossed this bridge in the last half-hour? (*He exits without waiting for a reply*).

CURTAIN

Clemo Uti – 'The Water Lilies.'

Characters

PADRE, *a Priest*

SETHSO
GETHSO *both twins*

WAYSHATTEN, *a shepherd's boy*

TWO CAPITALISTS

WAMA TAMISCH, *her daughter.*

KLEMA, *a janitor's third daughter.*

KLEVELA, *their mother, afterwards their aunt.*

(TRANSLATOR'S NOTE: *This show was written as if people were there to see it*).

ACT I

The outskirts of a Parchesi Board. People are wondering what has become of the discs. They quit wondering and sit up and sing the following song.

CHORUS: What has become of the discs?
What has become of the discs?
We took them at our own risks,
But what has become of the discs?

(WAMA *enters from an exclusive waffle parlour. She exits as if she had waffles*)

ACTS II & III

(These two acts were thrown out because nothing seemed to happen)

ACT IV

A silo. Two RATS *have got in there by mistake. One of them seems diseased. The other looks at him. They both go out. Both* RATS *come in and wait for a laugh. They don't get it, and go out.* WAMA *enters from an off-stage barn. She is made up to represent the Homecoming of Casanova. She has a fainting spell. She goes out.*

KEVELA: Where were you born?

PADRE: In Adrian, Michigan.

KEVELA: Yes, but I thought I was confessing to you.

(The Padre goes out on an old-fashioned high-wheel bicycle. He acts as if he had never ridden many of them. He falls off and is brought back. He is in pretty bad shape)

ACT V

A COUPLE OF SALESMEN *enter. They are trying to sell Portable Houses. The rest of the cast don't want Portable Houses.*

REST OF THE CAST: We don't want Portable Houses.

(The SALESMEN *become hysterical and walk off-stage left).*

KEVELA: What a man!

WAYSHATTEN *(the Shepherd's Boy)*: Why wasn't you out there this morning to help me look after my sheep?

CHORUS OF ASSISTANT SHEPHERDS:

Why did you lay there asleep
When you should of looked after his sheep?
Why did you send telegrams
When you should have looked after his lambs?
Why did you sleep there, so old,
When you should have looked after his fold?

SETHSO: Who is our father?

GETHSO: What of it? We're twins, ain't we?

WAMA: Hush, clemo uti *(the Water Lilies).*

(Two queels enter, overcome with waterlilies. They both

make fools of themselves. They don't seem to have any self-control. They quiver. They want to play the show over again, but it looks useless).

SHADES

I Gaspiri — (The Upholsterers)

A DRAMA IN THREE ACTS

Adapted from the Bukovinian of Casper Redmonda
Characters

IAN OBRI, *a blotter salesman.*
JOHAN WASPER, *his wife.*
GRETA, *their daughter.*
HERBERT SWOPE, *a nonentity.*
FFENA, *their mother, later their wife.*
EGSO, *a pencil guster.*
TONO, *a typical wastebasket.*

ACT I

A public street in a bathroom. A man named Tupper has evidently just taken a bath. A man named Brindle is now taking a bath. A man named Newburn comes out of the faucet which has been left running. He exits through the exhaust. Two strangers meet each other on the bath mat.

FIRST STRANGER : Where was you born?

SECOND STRANGER : Out of wedlock.

FIRST STRANGER : That's a mighty pretty country around there.

SECOND STRANGER : Are you married?

FIRST STRANGER : I don't know. There's a woman living with me, but I can't place her.

(Three outsiders named Klein go across the stage three times. They think they are in a public library. A woman's cough is heard off-stage left).

A NEW CHARACTER : Who is that cough?

TWO MOORS : That is my cousin. She died a little while ago in a haphazard way.

A GREEK : And what a woman she was!

(*The curtain is lowered to denote the lapse of a week*)

ACT III

The Lincoln Highway. Two bearded glue lifters are seated at one side of the road. (Translator's Note : The principal industry in Phlace is hoarding hay. Peasants sit alongside of a road on which hay wagons are likely to pass. When a hay wagon does pass, the hay hoarders leap from their points of vantage and help themselves to a wisp of hay. On an average a hay hoarder accumulates a ton of hay every four years. This is called Mah Jong).

FIRST GLUE LIFTER : Well, my man, how goes it?

SECOND GLUE LIFTER (*Sings 'My Man,' to show how it goes*).

(*Eight realtors cross the stage in a friendly way. They are out of place*).

CURTAIN

STEPHEN LEACOCK

Boarding-house Geometry

Definitions and Axioms

All Boarding-houses are the same boarding-house.

Boarders in the same boarding-house and on the same flat are equal to one another.

A single room is that which has no parts and no magnitude.

The landlady of a boarding-house is a parallelogram – that is, an oblong angular figure, which cannot be described, but which is equal to anything.

A wrangle is the disinclination for each other of two boarders that meet together but are not in the same line.

All the other rooms being taken, a single room is said to be a double room.

Postulates and Propositions

A pie may be produced any number of times.

The landlady can be reduced to her lowest terms by a series of propositions.

A bee line may be made from any boarding-house to any other boarding-house.

The clothes of a boarding-house bed, though produced ever so far both ways, will not meet.

Any two meals at a boarding-house are together less than two square meals.

If from the opposite ends of a boarding-house a line be drawn passing through all rooms in turn, then the stove-pipe which warms the boarders will lie within that line.

On the same bill and on the same side of it there should not be two charges for the same thing.

If there be two boarders on the same flat, and the amount of side of the one be equal to the amount of side of the other, each to each, and the wrangle between one boarder and the landlady be equal to the wrangle between the landlady and the other, then shall the weekly bills of the two boarders be equal also, each to each. For if not, let one bill be the greater.

Then the other bill is less than it might have been – which is absurd.

A, B and C

The Human Element in Mathematics

The student of arithmetic who has mastered the first four rules of his art, and successfully striven with money sums and fractions, finds himself confronted by an unbroken expanse of questions known as problems. These are short stories of adventure and industry with the end omitted, and, though betraying a strong family resemblance, are not without a certain element of romance.

The characters in the plot of a problem are three people called, A, B, and C. The form of the question is generally of this sort:

'A, B, and C do a certain piece of work. A can do as much work in one hour as B in two, or C in four. Find how long they work at it.'

Or thus:

'A, B, and C are employed to dig a ditch. A can dig as much in one hour as B can dig in two, and B can dig twice as fast as C. Find how long, etc. etc.'

Or after this wise:

'A lays a wager that he can walk faster than B or C. A can walk half as fast again as B, and C is only an indifferent walker. Find how far, and so forth.'

The occupations of A, B, and C are many and varied. In the older arithmetics they contented themselves with doing 'a certain piece of work'. This statement of the case, however, was found too sly and mysterious, or possibly lacking in romantic charm. It became the fashion to define the job more clearly and to set them at walking matches, ditch-digging, regattas, and piling cord-wood. At times they became commercial and entered into partnership, having with their old mystery a 'certain' capital. Above all they revel in motion. When they tire of walking matches, A rides on horseback, or borrows a bicycle and competes with his weaker-minded associates on foot. Now they race on locomotives; now they row; or again they become historical and engage stage-coaches; or at times they are aquatic and swim. If their occupation is actual work they prefer to pump water into cisterns, two of which leak through holes in the bottom and one of which is water-tight. A, of course, has the good one; he also takes the bicycle, and the best locomotive, and the right of swimming with the current. Whatever they do they put money on it, being all three sports. Always wins.

In the early chapters of arithmetic, their identity is concealed under the names John, William and Henry, and they wrangle over the division of marbles. In algebra they are often called X, Y and Z. But these are only their Christian names, and they are really the same people.

Now to one who has followed the history of these men

through countless pages of problems, watched them in their leisure hours dallying with cord-wood, and seen their panting sides heave in the full frenzy of filling a cistern with a leak in it, they become something more than mere symbols. They appear as creatures of flesh and blood, living men with their own passions, ambitions, and aspirations like the rest of us. Let us view them in turn. A is a full-blooded blustering fellow, of energetic temperament, hot-headed and strong-willed. It is he who proposes everything, challenges B to work, makes the bets, and bends the others to his will. He is a man of great physical strength and phenomenal endurance. He has been known to walk forty-eight hours at a stretch, and to pump ninety-six. His life is arduous and full of peril. A mistake in the working of a sum may keep him digging a fortnight without sleep. A repeating decimal in the answer might kill him.

B is a quiet, easy-going fellow, afraid of A and bullied by him, but very gentle and brotherly to little C, the weakling. He is quite in A's power, having lost all his money in bets.

Poor C is an undersized, frail man, with a plaintive face. Constant walking, digging, and pumping have broken his health and ruined his nervous system. His joyless life has driven him to drink and smoke more than is good for him, and his hand often shakes as he digs ditches. He has not the strength to work as the others can; in fact, as Hamlin Smith has said, 'A can do more work in one hour than C in four.'

The first time that ever I saw these men was one evening after a regatta. They had all been rowing in it, and it had transpired that A could row as much in one hour as B in two, or C in four. B and C had come in dead fagged and C was coughing badly. 'Never mind, old fellow,' I heard B say, 'I'll fix you up on the sofa and get you some hot tea.' Just then A came blustering in and shouted, 'I say, you fellows, Hamlin Smith has shown me three cisterns in his garden and he says we can pump them until tomorrow night. I bet I can beat you both. Come on. You can pump in your rowing things, you know. Your cistern leaks a little, I think, C.' I heard B growl that it was a dirty shame and that C was used up now, but they went, and presently I could tell from the sound of the water that A was pumping four times as fast as C.

Four years after that I used to see them constantly about town and always busy. I never heard of any of them eating or sleeping. Then, owing to a long absence from home, I lost sight of them. On my return I was surprised to no longer find A, B, and C at their accustomed tasks; on inquiry I heard that work in this line was now done by M, N, and O, and that some people were employing for algebraical jobs four foreigners called Alpha, Beta, Gamma, and Delta.

Now it chanced one day that I stumbled upon old D, in the little garden in front of his cottage, hoeing in the sun. D is an aged labouring man who used occasionally to be called in to help A, B, and C. 'Did I know 'em, sir?' he answered, 'why, I knowed 'em ever since they was little fellows in brackets. Master A, he were a fine lad, sir, though I always said, give me Master B for kind-hearted-ness-like. Many's the job as we've been on together, sir, though I never did no racing nor aught of that, but just the plain labour, as you might say. I'm getting a bit too old and stiff for it nowadays, sir – just scratch about in the garden here and grow a bit of a logarithm, or raise a common demoninator or two. But Mr. Euclid he use me still for them propositions, he do.'

From the garrulous old man I learned the melancholy end of my former acquaintances. Soon after I left town, he told me, C had been taken ill. It seems that A and B had been rowing on the river for a wager, and C had been running on the bank and then sat in a draught. Of course the bank had refused the draught and C was taken ill. A and B came home and found C lying helpless in bed. A shook him roughly and said 'Get up, C, we're going to pile wood.' C looked so worn and pitiful that B said, 'Look here, A, I won't stand this, he isn't fit to pile wood tonight.' C smiled feebly and said, 'Perhaps I might pile a little if I sat up in bed.' Then B, thoroughly alarmed, said 'See here, A, I'm going to fetch a doctor; he's dying.' A flared up and answered, 'You've no money to fetch a doctor.' 'I'll reduce him to his lowest terms,' B said firmly, 'that'll fetch him.' C's life might even then have been saved but they made a mistake about the medicine. It stood at the head of the bed on a bracket and the nurse accidentally removed it from the bracket without changing the sign. After the fatal blunder C seems to have sunk rapidly. On the evening of the next day, as the shadows deepened in the little room, it was clear to all that the end was near. I think that even A was affected at the last as he stood with bowed head, aimlessly offering to bet with the doctor on C's laboured breathing. 'A', whispered C, 'I think I'm going fast.' 'How fast do you think you'll go, old man?' murmured A. 'I don't know,' said C, 'but I'm going at any rate.' The end came soon after that. C rallied for a moment and asked for a certain piece of work that he had left downstairs. A put it in his arms and he expired. As his soul sped heavenward, A watched its flight with melancholy admiration. B burst into a passionate flood of tears and sobbed, 'Put away his little cistern and the rowing clothes he used to wear, I feel as if I could hardly ever dig again.' The funeral was plain and unostentatious. It differed in nothing from the ordinary, except that out of deference to sporting men and mathematicians, A engaged two hearses. Both vehicles started at the same time, B driving the one which bore the sable parallelopiped containing the last remains of his ill-fated friend. A on the box of the empty hearse generously consented to a handicap of a hundred yards, but arrived first at the cemetery by driving four times as fast as B. (Find the distance to the cemetery.) As the sarcophagus was lowered, the grave was surrounded by the broken figures of the first book of Euclid. It was noticed that after the death of C, A became a changed man. He lost interest in racing with B, and dug but languidly. He finally gave up his work and settled down to live on the interest of his bets. B never recovered from the shock of C's death; his grief preyed upon his intellect and it became deranged. He grew moody and spoke only in monosyllables. His disease became rapidly aggravated, and he presently spoke only in words whose spelling was regular and which presented no difficulty to the beginner. Realizing his precarious condition he voluntarily submitted to be incarcerated in an asylum, where he abjured mathematics and devoted himself to writing the History of the Swiss Family Robinson in words of one syllable.

The Old Men's Page

A Brand-new Feature in Journalism

I observe that nowadays far too much of the space in the newspapers is given up to children and young people. Open almost any paper, published in any British or American city, and you may find a children's page and a girl's page and a women's page – special columns for tiny tots, poetry by high-school girls, notes for boy scouts, fashion notes for young women, and radio hints for young men.

This thing is going too far – unless the old men get a chance. What the newspapers need now is a special page for old men. I am certain that it would make an enormous hit at once.

Let me try to put together a few samples of what ought to go on such a page. My talented readers can carry it on themselves.

Notes for Old Men Scouts

A general field meeting of the (newly established) Old Men Scouts will be held next Saturday. The scouts will assemble at the edge of the pine woods about seven miles out of town. Every scout will tell his chauffeur to have the car ready for an early start, not later than 10.30. The scout will see that the chauffeur brings, a full kit of cooking utensils and supplies. A good chauffeur can easily carry 150 pounds and the scout will see that he does it.

Each scout is to have a heavy greatcoat and a thick rug and folding camp-chair strapped together in a bundle and will see to it personally that these are loaded on the chauffeur.

Each scout, in advancing into the woods, will carry his own walking stick and will smoke his own cigar.

In passing through the woods, the scout is expected to recognize any trees that he knows, such as pine trees, lilac trees, rubber trees, and so forth. If in any doubt of the nature or species of a tree, the scout may tell the chauffeur to climb it and see what it is.

The scouts will also recognize and remark any species or genera of birds that are sitting on the path which are familiar to them, such as tame canaries, parrots, partridges, cooked snipe, and spring chicken.

Having arrived at an open glade, the scouts will sit about on their camp-chairs, avoiding the damp, while the chauffeurs kindle a fire and prepare lunch. During this time the Scout Master, and other scouts in order of seniority, may relate stories of woodcraft, or, if they can't think of any stories of woodcraft, they may tell any other kind that they know.

As exercise before lunch, the scouts may open the soda-water bottles.

After lunch, each scout will place his rug and cushion under a suitable tree and smoke a cigar while listening in silence for any especial calls and woodnotes of birds, bees and insects, such as cicada, the rickshaw, the gin-ricki, and others that he has learned to know. Should he see any insect whose call is not familiar to him, he should crawl after it and listen to it, if he prefers, tell his chauffeur to follow it up.

At five p.m. the scouts should reload the chauffeurs and themselves, and, when all are well loaded, drive to any country club for more stories of woodcraft.

Every old man – being really just a boy in a disguised form – is naturally interested in how to make things. One column in the old men's page therefore ought to contain something in the way of

HINTS ON MECHANICS

Carpentry for Old Men

How to Make a Rustic Table – Get hold of any hard-working rustic and tell him to make a table.

How to Make a Camera Stand – Put right on the table. It will stand.

How to Tell the Time by the Sun – First look at your watch to see what time it is. Then step out into the sunlight with your face towards the sun and hold the watch so that the hour hand points directly at the sun. This will be the time.

How to Make a Book-case – Call up any wood factory on the telephone and tell them to cut you some plain boards, suitable for making a book-case. Ask them next where you can get nails. Then send your chauffeur to bring the board and nails. Then advertise for a carpenter.

To stain your table, when it is complete, a good method is to upset soda water on it.

Homer and Humbug

My plan is so to transpose the classical writers as to give, not the literal translation word for word, but what is really the modern equivalent. Let me give an odd sample or two to show what I mean. Take the passage in the *First Book of Homer* that describes Ajax the Greek dashing into the battle in front of Troy. Here is the way it runs (as nearly as I remember) in the usual word-for-word translation of the classroom, as done by the very best professor, his spectacles glittering the literary rapture of it.

'Then he too Ajax on the one hand leaped (possibly jumped) into the fight wearing on the other hand yes certainly a steel corset (or possibly a bronze under-tunic) and on his head of course yes without doubt he had a helmet with a tossing plume taken from the mane (or perhaps extracted from the tail) of some horse which once fed along the banks of the Scamander (and it sees the herd and raises its head and paws the ground) and in his hand a shield worth a hundred oxen and on his knees too especially in particular greaves made by some cunning artificer (or perhaps blacksmith) and he blows the fire and it is hot. Thus Ajax leapt (or, better, was propelled from behind) into the fight.'

Now, that's grand stuff. There is no doubt of it. There's a wonderful movement and force to it. You can almost see it move, it goes so fast. But the modern reader can't get it. It won't mean to him what it meant to the early Greek. The setting, the costume, the scene has all got to be changed in order to let the reader have real equivalent to judge just how good the Greek verse is. In my translation I alter it just a little, not much, but just enough to give the passage a form that reproduces the proper literary value of the verses, without losing anything of the majesty. It describes, I may say, the Directors of the American Industrial Stocks rushing into the Balkan War cloud:

'Then there came rushing to the shock of war
Mr. McNicoll of the C.P.R.
He wore suspenders and about his throat
High rose the collar of a sealskin coat,
He had on gaiters and he wore a tie,
He had his trousers buttoned good and high,
About his waist a woollen undervest
Bought from a sad-eyed farmer of the West,
(And every time he clips a sheep he sees
Some bloated plutocrat who ought to freeze),
Thus in the Stock Exchange he burst to view,
Leaped to the post, and shouted, "Ninety-two".'

There! That's Homer, the real thing! Just as it sounded to the rude crowd of Greek peasants who sat in a ring and guffawed at the rhymes and watched the minstrel stamp it out into 'feet' as he recited it!

Or let me take another example from the so-called *Catalogue of the Ships* that fills up nearly an entire book of Homer. This famous passage names all the ships, one by one, and names the chiefs who sailed on them, and names the particular town or hill or valley that they came from. It has been much admired. It has that same majesty of style that has been brought to an even loftier pitch in the *New York Business Directory* and the *City Telephone Book*. It runs along, as I recall it, something like this:

'And first indeed Oh yes was the ship of Homistogetes the Spartan, long and swift, having both its masts covered with cowhide and two rows of oars. And he, Homistogetes, was born of Hermogenes and Ophthalmia and was at home in Syncope beside the fast flowing Paresis. And after him came the ship of Preposterus the Eurasian, son of Oasis and Hysteria' – and so on endlessly.

Instead of this I substitute, with the permission of the New York Central Railway, the official catalogue of their locomotives taken almost word for word from the list compiled by their superintendent of works. I admit that he wrote in hot weather. Part of it runs:

Out in the yard and steaming in the sun
Stands locomotive engine number forty-one.
Seated beside the windows of the cab
Are Pat McGaw and Peter James McNab.
Pat comes from Troy and Peter from Cohoes,
And when they pull the throttle off she goes,
And as she vanishes there comes to view
Steam locomotive engine number forty-two.
Observe her mighty wheels, her easy roll,
With William J. Macarthy in control.
They say her engineer some time ago
Lived in a farm outside of Buffalo,

Whereas his fireman Henry Edward Foy
Attended school in Springfield, Illinois.
Thus does the race of man decay or rot:
Some men can hold their jobs and some can not.

Please observe that if Homer had actually written that last line it would have been quoted for a thousand years as one of the deepest sayings ever said. Orators would have rounded out their speeches with the majestic phrase, quoted in sonorous and unintelligible Greek verse, 'Some men can hold their jobs and some can not'; essayists would have begun their most scholarly dissertations with the words, 'It has been finely said by Homer that (in Greek) "some men can hold their jobs" '; and the clergy in mid-pathos of a funeral sermon would have raised their eyes aloft and echoed, 'Some men can not!'

This is what I should like to do. I'd like to take a large stone and write on it in very plain writing: 'The classics are only primitive literature. They belong to the same class as primitive machinery and primitive music and primitive medicine,' and then throw it through the windows of a University and hide behind a fence to see the professors buzz!

EDWARD LEAR

The Pobble Who Has No Toes

The Pobble who has no toes
Had once as many as we;
When they said, 'Some day you may lose them all';
He replied, 'Fish fiddle de-dee!'
And his Aunt Jobiska made him drink
Lavender water tinged with pink,
For she said, 'The World in general knows
There's nothing so good for a Pobble's toes!'

The Pobble who has no toes,
Swam across the Bristol Channel;
Before he set out he wrapped his nose
In a piece of scarlet flannel,
For his Aunt Jobiska said, 'No harm
Can come to his toes if his nose is warm;
And it's perfectly known that a Pobble's toes
Are safe – provided he minds his nose.'

The Pobble swam fast and well,
And when boats or ships came near him
He tinkledy-binkledy-winkled a bell,
So that all the world could hear him.
And all the Sailors and Admirals cried,
When they saw him nearing the further side,
'He has gone to fish, for his Aunt Jobiska's
Runcible Cat with crimson whiskers!'

But before he touched the shore,
The shore of the Bristol Channel.
A sea-green Porpoise carried away
His wrapper of scarlet flannel,
And when he came to observe his feet,
Formerly garnished with toes so neat,
His face at once became forlorn
On perceiving that all his toes were gone!

And nobody ever knew
From that dark day to the present,
Whoso had taken the Pobble's toes,
In a manner so far from pleasant.
Whether the shrimps or crawfish gray,
Or crafty Mermaids stole them away –
Nobody knew; and nobody knows
How the Pobble was robbed of his twice five toes!

The Pobble who has no toes,
Was placed in a friendly Bark,
And they rowed him back, and carried him up
To his Aunt Jobiska's Park.

And she made him a feast at his earnest wish
Of eggs and buttercups fried with fish;
And she said, 'It's a fact the whole world knows,
That Pobbles are happier without their toes.'

To Make Gosky Patties

Take a Pig, three or four years of age, and tie him by the off hind leg to a post. Place 5 pounds of currants, 3 of sugar, 2 pecks of peas, 18 roast chestnuts, a candle, and 6 bushels of turnips within his reach; if he eats these, constantly provide him with more.

Then procure some cream, some slices of Cheshire cheese, four quires of foolscap paper, and a packet of black pins. Work the whole into a paste, and spread it out to dry on a sheet of clean brown waterproof linen.

When the paste is perfectly dry, but not before, proceed to beat the Pig violently, with the handle of a large broom. If he squeals, beat him again.

Visit the paste and beat the Pig alternately for some days, and ascertain if at the end of that period the whole is about to turn into Gosky Patties.

If it does not, then it never will; and in that case the Pig may be let loose, and the whole process may be considered as finished.

The Courtship of the Yonghy-Bonghy Bo

On the Coast of Coromandel
Where the early pumpkins blow,
In the middle of the woods
Lived the Yonghy-Bonghy-Bo.
Two old chairs, and half a candle,
One old jug without a handle –
These were all his worldly goods:
In the middle of the woods,

These were all the worldly goods,
Of the Yonghy-Bonghy-Bo,
Of the Yonghy-Bonghy-Bo.

Once, among the Bong-trees walking
Where the early pumpkins blow,
To a little heap of stones
Came the Yonghy-Bonghy-Bo.
There he heard a Lady talking,
To some milk-white Hens of Dorking –
''Tis the Lady Jingly Jones!
On that little heap of stones
Sits the Lady Jingly Jones!'
Said the Yonghy-Bonghy-Bo,
Said the Yonghy-Bonghy-Bo.

'Lady Jingly! Lady Jingly!
Sitting where the pumpkins blow,
Will you come and be my wife?'
Said the Yonghy-Bonghy-Bo.
'I am tired of living singly
On this coast so wild and shingly,
I'm a-weary of my life;
If you'll come and be my wife,
Quite serene would be my life!'
Said the Yonghy-Bonghy-Bo,
Said the Yonghy-Bonghy-Bo.

'On this Coast of Coromandel,
Shrimps and watercresses grow,
Prawns are plentiful and cheap,
Said the Yonghy-Bonghy-Bo.
'You shall have my chairs and candle,
And my jug without a handle!
Gaze upon the rolling deep
(Fish is plentiful and cheap);
As the sea, my love is deep!'
Said the Yonghy-Bonghy-Bo,
Said the Yonghy-Bonghy-Bo.

Lady Jingly answered sadly,
And her tears began to flow,
'Your proposal comes too late,
Mr. Yonghy-Bonghy-Bo!
I would be your wife most gladly!'
(Here she twirled her fingers madly),
'But in England I've a mate!
Yes! you've asked me far too late,
For in England I've a mate,
Mr. Yonghy-Bonghy-Bo!
Mr. Yonghy-Bonghy-Bo!'

'Mr. Jones (his name is Handel,
Handel Jones, Esquire, & Co.)
Dorking fowls delights to send,
Mr. Yonghy-Bonghy-Bo!
Keep, O keep your chairs and candle,
And your jug without a handle,
I can merely be your friend!
– Should my Jones more Dorkings send,
I will give you three, my friend!
Mr. Yonghy-Bonghy-Bo!
Mr. Yonghy-Bonghy-Bo!'

'Though you've such a tiny body,
And your head so large doth grow,
Though your hat may blow away,
Mr. Yonghy-Bonghy-Bo!
Though you're such a Hoddy Doddy –
Yet I wish that I could modi –
fy the words I needs must say!
Will you please to go away?
That is all I have to say –
Mr. Yonghy-Bonghy-Bo!
Mr. Yonghy-Bonghy-Bo!'

The Quangle Wangle's Hat

On the top of the Crumpetty Tree
The Quangle Wangle sat,
But his face you could not see,
On account of his Beaver Hat.
For his Hat was a hundred and two feet wide,
With ribbons and bibbons on every side,
And bells, and buttons, and loops, and lace,
So that nobody ever could see the face
Of the Quangle Wangle Quee.

The Quangle Wangle said
To himself on the Crumpetty Tree,
'Jam; and jelly; and bread;
Are the best of food for me!
But the longer I live on this Crumpetty Tree,
The plainer than ever it seems to me
That very few people come this way,
And that life on the whole is far from gay!'
Said the Quangle Wangle Quee.

But there came to the Crumpetty Tree,
Mr. and Mrs. Canary;
And they said, 'Did ever you see
Any spot so charmingly airy?
May we build a nest on your lovely Hat?
Mr. Quangle Wangle, grant us that!
O please let us come and build a nest
Of whatever material suits you best,
Mr. Quangle Wangle Quee!'

And besides, to the Crumpetty Tree
Came the Stork, the Duck, and the Owl;
The Snail and the Bumble-Bee,
The Frog, and the Fimble Fowl
(The Fimble Fowl, with a Corkscrew leg);
And all of them said, 'We humbly beg,

We may build our homes on your lovely hat,
Mr. Quangle Wangle, grant us that!
Mr. Quangle Wangle Quee!'

And the Golden Grouse came there,
And the Pobble who has no toes,
And the small Olympian bear,
And the Dong with a luminous nose.
And the Blue Baboon, who played the flute,
And the Orient Calf from the Land of Tute,
And the Attery Squash, and the Bisky Bat,
All came and built on the lovely Hat
Of the Quangle Wangle Quee.

And the Quangle Wangle said
To himself on the Crumpetty Tree,
'When all these creatures move
What a wonderful noise there'll be!'
And at night by the light of the Mulberry moon
They danced to the Flute of the Blue Baboon
On the broad green leaves of the Crumpetty Tree,
And all were as happy as happy could be,
With the Quangle Wangle Quee.

The Dong With a Luminous Nose

When awful darkness and silence reign
Over the great Gromboolian plain,
Through the long, long wintry nights;
When the angry breakers roar
As they beat on the rocky shore;
When Storm-clouds brood on the towering heights
Of the Hills of the Chankly Bore:
Then, through the vast and gloomy dark,
There moves what seems a fiery spark,
A lonely spark with silvery rays
Piercing the coal-black night,

A meteor strange and bright:
Hither and thither the vision strays,
A single lurid light.

Slowly it wanders, pauses, creeps,
Anon it sparkles, flashes and leaps;
And ever as onward it gleaming goes
A light on the Bong-tree stems it throws.
And those who watch at that midnight hour
From Hall or Terrace, or lofty Tower,
Cry, as the wild light passes along,
'The Dong! – the Dong!
The wandering Dong through the forest goes!
The Dong! – the Dong!
The Dong with a luminous Nose!'

Long years ago
The Dong was happy and gay,
Till he fell in love with a Jumbly Girl
Who came to those shores one day.
For the Jumblies came in a Sieve, they did,
Landing at eve near the Zemmery Fidd
Where the Oblong Oysters grow,
And the rocks are smooth and gray.
And all the woods and the valleys rang
With the Chorus they daily and nightly sang,
'Far and few, far and few,
Are the lands where the Jumblies live;
Their heads are green, and their hands are blue,
And they went to sea in a sieve.'

Happily, happily passed those days!
While the cheerful Jumblies staid;
They danced in circlets all night long,
To the plaintive pipe of the lively Dong,
In moonlight, shine, or shade.
For day and night he was always there
By the side of the Jumbly Girl so fair,
With her sky-blue hands, and her sea-green hair.

Till the morning came of that hateful day
When the Jumblies sailed in their sieve away,
And the Dong was left on the cruel shore
Gazing, gazing for evermore,
Ever keeping his weary eyes on
That pea-green sail on the far horizon,
Singing the Jumbly Chorus still
As he sate all day on the grassy hill,
'*Far and few, far and few,*
Are the lands where the Jumblies live;
Their heads are green, and their hands are blue,
And they went to sea in a sieve.'

But when the sun was low in the West
The Dong arose and said,
'What little sense I once possessed
Has quite gone out of my head!'
And since that day he wanders still
By lake and forest, marsh and hill,
Singing – 'O somewhere, in valley or plain
Might I find my Jumbly Girl again!
For ever I'll seek by lake and shore
Till I find my Jumbly Girl once more!'
Playing a pipe with silvery squeaks,
Since then his Jumbly Girl he seeks,
And because by night he could not see,
He gathered the bark of the Twangum Tree
On the flowery plain that grows.
And he wove him a wondrous Nose,
A Nose as strange as a Nose could be!
Of vast proportions and painted red,
And tied with cords to the back of his head.
In a hollow rounded space it ended
With a luminous lamp within suspended,
All fenced about
With a bandage stout
To prevent the wind from blowing it out;
And with holes all round to send the light,
In gleaming rays on the dismal night.

And now each night, and all night long,
Over those plains still roams the Dong;
And above the wail of the Chimp and Snipe
You may hear the squeak of his plaintive pipe
While ever he seeks, but seeks in vain
To meet with his Jumbly Girl again;
Lonely and wild, all night he goes,
The Dong with a luminous Nose!
And all who watch at the midnight hour,
From Hall or Terrace, or lofty Tower,
Cry, as they trace the Meteor bright,
Moving along through the dreary night,
'This is the hour when forth he goes,
The Dong with a luminous Nose!
Yonder – over the plain he goes;
He goes!
He goes;
The Dong with a luminous Nose!'

The Owl And The Pussy-Cat

The Owl and the Pussy-Cat went to sea
In a beautiful pea-green boat,
They took some honey, and plenty of money,
Wrapped up in a five-pound note,
The Owl looked up to the stars above,
And sang to a small guitar,
'O lovely Pussy! O Pussy, my love,
What a beautiful Pussy you are,
You are,
You are!
What a beautiful Pussy you are!'

Pussy said to the Owl, 'You elegant fowl!
How charmingly sweet you sing!
O let us be married! too long we have tarried:
But what shall we do for a ring?'

They sailed away for a year and a day,
To the land where the Bong-tree grows,
And there in a wood a Piggy-wig stood,
With a ring at the end of his nose,
His nose,
His nose,
With a ring at the end of his nose.

'Dear Pig, are you willing to sell for one shilling
Your ring?' Said the Piggy, 'I will.'
So they took it away, and were married next day
By the Turkey who lives on the hill.
They dined on mince, and slices of quince,
Which they ate with a runcible spoon;
And hand in hand, on the edge of the sand,
They danced by the light of the moon,
The moon,
The moon,
They danced by the light of the moon.

The Jumblies

They went to sea in a Sieve, they did,
In a Sieve they went to sea:
In spite of all their friends could say,
On a winter's morn, on a stormy day,
In a Sieve they went to sea!
And when the Sieve turned round and round,
And everyone cried, 'You'll all be drowned!'
They called aloud, 'Our Sieve ain't big,
But we don't care a button! We don't care a fig!
In a Sieve we'll go to sea!'
Far and few, far and few,
Are the lands where the Jumblies live;
Their heads are green, and their hands are blue.
And they went to sea in a Sieve.

They sailed away in a Sieve, they did,
In a Sieve they sailed so fast,
With only a beautiful pea-green veil
Tied with a riband by way of a sail,
To a small tobacco-pipe mast;
And everyone said, who saw them go,
'O won't they be soon upset, you know!
For the sky is dark, and the voyage is long,
And happen what may, it's extremely wrong
In a Sieve to sail so fast!'
Far and few, far and few,
Are the lands where the Jumblies live;
Their heads are green, and their hands are blue,
And they went to sea in a Sieve.

The water it soon came in, it did,
The water it soon came in;
So to keep them dry, they wrapped their feet
In a pinky paper all folded neat,
And they fastened it down with a pin.
And they passed the night in a crockery-jar,
And each of them said, 'How wise we are!
Though the sky be dark, and the voyage be long,
Yet we never can think we were rash or wrong,
While round in our Sieve we spin!'
Far and few, far and few,
Are the lands where the Jumblies live;
Their heads are green, and their hands are blue,
And they went to sea in a Sieve.

And all night long they sailed away;
And when the sun went down,
They whistled and warbled a moony song
To the echoing sound of a coppery gong,
In the shade of the mountains brown.
'O Timballo! How happy we are,
When we live in a sieve and a crockery-jar,
And all night long in the moonlight pale,
We sail away with a pea-green sail,

In the shade of the mountains brown!'
Far and few, far and few,
Are the lands where the Jumblies live
Their heads are green, and their hands are blue,
And they went to sea in a Sieve.

They sailed to the Western Sea, they did,
To a land all covered with trees,
And they bought an Owl, and a useful Cart,
And a pound of Rice, and a Cranberry Tart,
And a hive of silvery Bees.
And they bought a Pig, and some green Jack-daws,
And a lovely Monkey with lollipop paws,
And forty bottles of Ring-Bo-Ree,
And no end of Stilton Cheese.
Far and few, far and few,
Are the lands where the Jumblies live;
Their heads are green, and their hands are blue,
And they went to sea in a Sieve.

And in twenty years they all came back,
In twenty years or more,
And everyone said, 'How tall they've grown!
For they've been to the Lakes, and the Terrible Zone,
And the hills of the Chankly Bore';
And they drank their health, and gave them a feast
Of dumplings made of beautiful yeast;
And everyone said, 'If we only live,
We too will go to sea in a Sieve,
To the hills of the Chankly Bore!'
Far and few, far and few,
Are the lands where the Jumblies live;
Their heads are green, and their hands are blue,
And they went to sea in a Sieve.

There was a Young Person of Smyrna,
Whose grandmother threatened to burn her;
But she seized on the cat,

And said, 'Granny, burn that!
You incongruous old woman of Smyrna!'

—

There was a Young Lady of Tyre,
Who swept the loud chords of a lyre;
At the sound of each sweep
She enraptured the deep,
And enchanted the city of Tyre.

—

There was an Old Man who said, 'Hush!
I perceive a young bird in this bush!'
When they said, 'Is it small?'
He replied, 'Not at all!
It is four times as big as the bush!'

—

There was a Young Person whose History
Was always considered a Mystery;
She sate in a Ditch,
Although no one knew which,
And composed a small treatise on History.

—

There was an Old Man of Spithead,
Who opened the window, and said,
'Fil-jomble, fil-jumble,
Fil-rumble-come-tumble!'
That doubtful Old Man of Spithead.

—

There was an Old Man of Thermopylae,
Who never did anything properly;
But they said, 'If you choose
To boil Eggs in your Shoes,
You shall never remain in Thermopylae.'

—

There was an Old Man with a gong,
Who bumped at it all the day long;
But they called out, 'Oh law!
You're a horrid old bore!'
So they smashed that Old Man with a gong.

—

There was an Old Man who said, 'Well!
Will *nobody* answer this bell?
I have pulled day and night,
Till my hair has grown white,
But nobody answers this bell!'

—

There was an Old Person of Dutton,
Whose head was as small as a button;
So, to make it look big,
He purchased a wig,
And rapidly rushed about Dutton.

—

There was a Young Lady in Blue,
Who said, 'Is it you? Is it you?'
When they said, 'Yes, it is,'
She replied only, 'Whizz!'
That ungracious Young Lady in Blue.

—

There was a Young Lady in White
Who looked out at the depths of the Night;
But the birds of the air,
Filled her heart with despair,
And oppressed that Young Lady in White.

—

There was an Old Person of Barnes,
Whose Garments were covered with Darns;
But they said, 'Without doubt,
You will soon wear them out,
You luminous Person of Barnes!'

—

There was an Old Person of Shoreham,
Whose habits were marked with decorum;
He bought an Umbrella,
And sate in the cellar,
Which pleased all the people of Shoreham.

—

There was an Old Man with a beard,
Who said 'It is just as I feared!
Two Owls and a Hen,
Four Larks and a Wren,
Have all built their nests in my beard!'

—

There was a Young Lady of Ryde,
Whose shoe-strings were seldom untied;
She purchased some clogs,
And some small spotty dogs,
And frequently walked about Ryde.

—

There was a Young Lady of Dorking,
Who bought a large bonnet for walking;
But its colour and size
So bedazzled her eyes,
That she very soon went back to Dorking.

—

There was an Old Man of Cape Horn,
Who wished he had never been born;
So he sat on a chair,
Till he died of despair,
That dolorous Man of Cape Horn.

—

There was an Old Man of Corfu,
Who never knew what he should do;
So he rushed up and down,
Till the sun made him brown,
That bewildered Old Man of Corfu.

—

There was an Old Man of the Nile,
Who sharpened his nails with a file;
Till he cut off his thumbs,
And said calmly, 'This comes
Of sharpening one's nails with a file!'

—

There was an Old Person of Cromer,
Who stood on one leg to read Homer;
When he found he grew stiff,
He jumped over the cliff,
Which concluded that Person of Cromer.

—

There was an Old Man on some rocks,
Who shut his wife up in a box;
When she said, 'Let me out,'
He exclaimed, 'Without doubt,
You will pass all your life in that box.'

—

There was a Young Lady of Troy,
Whom several large flies did annoy;
Some she killed with a thump,
Some she drowned at the pump,
And some she took with her to Troy.

—

There was an Old Person of Tartary,
Who divided his jugular artery;
But he screeched to his wife,
And she said, 'Oh, my life!
Your death will be felt by all Tartary!'

—

There was an Old Lady of Prague,
Whose language was horribly vague;
When they said, 'Are these caps?'
She answered, 'Perhaps!'
That oracular Lady of Prague.

—

There was an Old Person of Burton,
Whose answers were rather uncertain;
When they said, 'How d'ye do?'
He replied, 'Who are you?'
That distressing Old Person of Burton.

—

There was an Old Man of Aosta,
Who possessed a large Cow, but he lost her;
But they said, 'Don't you see,
She has rushed up a tree?
You individious Old Man of Aosta!'

How Pleasant to Know Mr Lear

'How pleasant to know Mr Lear!'
    Who has written such volumes of stuff!
Some think him ill-tempered and queer,
    But a few think him pleasant enough.

His mind is concrete and fastidious,
  His nose is remarkably big;
His visage is more or less hideous,
  His beard it resembles a wig.

He has ears, and two eyes, and ten fingers,
  Leastways if you reckon two thumbs;
Long ago he was one of the singers,
  But now he is one of the dumbs.

He sits in a beautiful parlour,
  With hundreds of books on the wall;
He drinks a great deal of Marsala,
  But never gets tipsy at all.

He has many friends, laymen and clerical,
  Old Foss is the name of his cat:
His body is perfectly spherical,
  He weareth a runcible hat.

When he walks in a waterproof white,
  The children run after him so!
Calling out, 'He's come out in his night-
  gown, that crazy old Englishman, oh!'

He weeps by the side of the ocean,
  He weeps on the top of the hill;
He purchases pancakes and lotion,
  And chocolate shrimps from the mill.

He reads but he cannot speak Spanish,
  He cannot abide ginger-beer:
Ere the days of his pilgrimage vanish
  How pleasant to know Mr Lear!

JOHN LENNON

I Remember Arnold

I remember Kakky Hargreaves
As if 'twer Yestermorn'
Kakky, Kakky Hargreaves
Son of Mr Vaughan.

He used to be so grundie
On him little bike
Riding on a Sundie
Funny little tyke

Yes, I remember Kathy Hairbream
As if 'twer yesterday
Katthy, Kathy Hairbream
Son of Mr May.

Arriving at the station
Always dead on time
For his destination
Now He's dead on line
(meaning he's been got by a train or something)

And so we growt and bumply
Till the end of time,
Humpty dumpty bumply
Son of Harry Lime.

 Bumbleydy Hubledy Humbley
 Bumdley Tum. (Thank you)

Scene Three Act One

(Scene) A broadshouldered room containing huge fireplace facing a large windy, a giant-size desk is covered in all type of many business paper and great disorder to look on. There are three or four or five chairs faceing the desk. One are occupied by a scruddy working clog, cap in hook

what is gesticulated greatly but humble toward a big fat catipalyst boss. A white man carefully puts coal on the fire and steps back toward a giant door which seems to lead somewhere else. A cat smarting in the corner by the fire leaps up and smiles all on the carpet. A photy of of Fieldimarcher Loud Montgammery solv ing a prodlem looks down on the two men, each of them looking up at it trying to place him.

A dog is quietly gnawing at a pigmy under the giant desk. The time is half past three on the old grandbladder clock by the windy.

Fatty: 'It's harf parst three Taddpill, and the men haven't done a strike. Why can't we settle this here and now without resorting to a long union discussion and going through all that bit about your father.'

Scruddy: 'Why don't yer shut yer gob yer big fat get or I'll kick yer face in. Yer all the same you rich fat Bourgies, workin' uz poor workers to death and getting all the gelt and going to France for yer 'olidays.'

Fatty: (*going all red and ashen*)
'But listen Taddpill you're only working two hours a day now, and three days a week and we're losing money as it is, and here you are complaining again about screw screwing and I'm trying to help you. We could have built our factory somewhere else where men like to work, but Ho no here we are government-sponsored and all that.'

Scruddy: 'Why don't yer shut yer gob yer big fat get or I'll kick yer face in. Yer all the same you rich fat Bourgies, workin' uz poor workers to death and getting all the gelt and going to France for yer 'olidays.'

(*Enter a coloured woman singing a coloured song. On her back is a bundle.*)

Mammy: 'Pope dat barge, left that bail'

(*She unloads her bundle on the right of the desk.*)

Fatty: (*Impatiently*)
'What is it Mammy, can't you see I'm haveing a prodlem with Taddpill and you come in here all black and singing? And get that bundle of ruddish away from my big desk!'

Mammy: 'O.K. Kimu sahib bwana, massa.'
(*she lifts the bundle and eats it*)
'Sho' was naice'.
Fatty: 'Anyway what was it mammy?'
Mammy: 'Dat was yo' little daughter, by yo secind wife
KIMU SAHIB'.
Fatty: (*colouring*) 'But I'm not married, old Mammy'
(*Mammy clasps her hands to her head horryfried*)
'Oh Lord, I've jes' eaten a bastard!'
(*She runs round the room crossing herself, and singing
another verse. Scruddy stands up replacing his cap firmly
on his head – walking toward the door he half turns like in
the films and shakes his fist.*)
'Get this black woman out of this factory before the men
find out, or yer'll have a strike on yer fat Bourgie 'ands.
I'm tellin yer that fer nothin' yer old bum!'
(*Scruddy walks out of the room leaving Fatty – Mammy
and fourteen little Jewish children all singing together a
kind of hymn.*)

THE END

Alec Speaking

He is putting it lithely when he says
Quobble in the Grass,
Strab he down the soddieflays
Amo amat amass;
Amonk amink a minibus,
Amarmylaidie Moon,
Amikky mendip multiplus
Amighty midgey spoon.
And so I traddled onward
Careing not a care
Onward, Onward, Onward.
Onward, my friends to victory and glory for the
thirtyninth.

(The same in French; translated by

Alec Vous Cause

Il parle d'or lorsqu'il dit
Copulez dans l'Herbe,
Embaquez le de pamprelis
Amo amas amerbe;
Ami amok a minibus,
Amarmalade amouches,
Amarche amor habens minus
En vide pein la bouche
Ainsi je bipède en avant
Comme un chien d'une pomme
En avant, En avant, En avant,
En avant, marche enfants de la carrière abreuve
    nos sillons.

LIMERICKS

There was a young man at the War Office,
Whose brain was an absolute store office.
 Each warning severe
 Went in at one ear,
And out at the opposite orifice.

J. W. Churton

A certain young gourmet of Crediton
Took some pâté de foie gras and spread it on
 A chocolate biscuit,
 Then murmured, 'I'll risk it.'
His tomb bears the date that he said it on.

Charles Inge

Evangelical vicar in want
Of a portable, second-hand font,
 Would dispose of the same
 For a portrait (in frame),
Of the Bishop-Elect of Vermont.

Ronald Knox

There was a young man who said, 'Damn!
At last I've found out that I am
    A creature that moves
    In determinate grooves,
In fact not a "bus but a tram".'

Unknown

There once was a man who said, 'God
Must think it exceedingly odd
    If He finds that this tree
    Continues to be
When there's no one about in the Quad.'

Ronald Knox

and an equally famous reply –
Dear Sir, your astonishment's odd;
I am always about in the Quad
    And that's why this tree
    Continues to be,
Since observed by, Yours faithfully, God.

A tiger, by taste anthropophagous
Felt a yearning within his oesophagus
    He spied a fat Brahmin
    And said 'there's no harm in
A peripatetic sarcophagus.'

There was an old party of Lyme
Who married three wives at one time.
    When asked, 'Why the third?'
    He replied, 'One's absurd,
And bigamy, sir, is a crime!'

Fr. Valentine

There was an Archdeacon who said,
'May I take off my gaiters in bed?'
    But the Bishop said, 'No,
    Wherever you go
You must wear them until you are dead.'

F. H. Cozens

There was a young lady of Kent,
Who said that she knew what it meant
     When men asked her to dine,
     Gave her cocktails and wine,
She knew what it meant – but she went!

Anon

There was a young boy of Quebec,
Who fell into the ice to his neck,
     When asked, 'Are you friz?'
     He replied, 'Yes, I is,
But we don't call this cold in Quebec.'

Rudyard Kipling

A rare old bird is the Pelican,
His beak holds more than his belican.
     He can take in his beak
     Enough food for a week.
I'm darned if I know how the helican!

Dixon Merritt

There was an old man of St. Bees,
Who was stung in the arm by a wasp,
     When asked, 'Does it hurt?'
     He replied, 'No, it doesn't,
I'm so glad it wasn't a hornet.'

W. S. Gilbert

There was a young lady named Psyche,
Who was heard to ejaculate, 'Pcryche!'
     For, when riding her pbych,
     She ran over a ptych,
And fell on some rails that were pspyche.

A fly and a flea in a flue
Were imprisoned, so what could they do?
     Said the fly, 'Let us flee!'
     'Let us fly!' said the flea,
So they flew through a flaw in the flue.

A tutor who taught on the flute
Tried to teach two young tooters to toot.
 Said the two to the tutor,
 'Is it harder to toot, or
To tutor two tooters to toot?'

Said a man to his wife, down in Sydenham,
'My best trousers — where have you hydenham?
 It is perfectly true
 That they weren't very new,
But I foolishly left half-a-quidenham.'

P. L. Mannock

There once was a man of Calcutta
Who spoke with a terrible stuttter.
 At breakfast he said,
 'Give me b-b-b-bread,
And b-b-b-b-b-b-butter.'

There was a young dancer of Ipswich,
Who took most astonishing skips, which
 So delighted a miss
 She said, 'Give me a kiss!'
He replied, 'On the cheek or the lips, which?'

There was a young lady of Riga,
Who went for a ride on a tiger;
 They returned from the ride
 With the lady inside,
And a smile on the face of the tiger.

The same in Latin
Puella Rigensis ridebat,
Quam tigris in tergo vehebat,
 Externa profecta
 Interna revecta,
Sed risus cum tigre manebat.

There was a young man of Japan,
Who wrote verse that never would scan.
 When they said, 'But the thing

Doesn't go with a swing,'
He said, 'Yes, but I always like to get as many
words into the last line as I possibly can.'

There was an old man of Peru,
Who dreamt he was eating his shoe.
    He woke in the night
    In a terrible fright,
And found it was perfectly true.

There was a young lady of Lynn,
Who was so uncommonly thin
    That when she essayed
    To drink lemonade,
She slipped through the straw and fell in.

There was a young lady of Lancashire,
Who once went to work as a bank cashier,
    But she scarcely knew
    $1 + 1 = 2$
So they had to revert to a man cashier.

There was a young lady of Twickenham,
Whose boots were too tight to walk quickenham.
    She bore them awhile,
    But at last, at a stile,
She pulled them both off and was sickenham.

There was a young man of Herne Bay,
Who was making some fireworks one day;
    But he dropped his cigar
    In the gunpowder jar.
There *was* a young man of Herne Bay.

Two gluttonous youngsters of Streatham
Bought fifty-five doughnuts and eatham.
    The coroner said,
    'No wonder they're dead,
How unwise of their parents to leatham!'

There was an old man of Madrid,
Who ate sixty-five eggs for a quid.
> When they asked, 'Are you faint?'
> He replied, 'No, I ain't,
But I don't feel as well as I did.'

There was a faith-healer of Deal
Who said, 'Although pain isn't real,
> If I sit on a pin
> And it punctures my skin
I dislike what I fancy I feel.'

The world's worst limerick (sent into a Tit-Bits competition)

I met a smart damsel at Copenhagen
With her pretty face I was very much taken.
> 'What!' she said. 'Turned-up trousers – a London
> man!
> Fall in love with a crank I never can.'
She turned up her nose and away she ran.

There was an old man in a trunk
Who enquired of his wife, 'Am I drunk?'
> She replied with regret
> 'I'm afraid so, my pet,'
And he answered, 'It's just as I thunk.'

Ogden Nash

When they said to a Fellow of Wadham
Who had asked for a ticket to Sodom,
> 'Oh sir, we don't care
> To send people there'
He said 'Don't call me Sir, call me Modom.'

and a few more –

Said Lot, 'I've escaped from Gomorrah,
That city of sin, shame and horrah;
> It wasn't my fault
> That my wife turned to salt
So I'll marry my daughter tomorrah.'

An LSE graduate said
'As a student, of course, I was red;
    But now I'm with Shell
    Let the proles go to hell,
My pension is safe till I'm dead.'

The statesman's great art, that of fixn'
Would have been more effective in Nixn
    If he'd understood
    That the bad and the good
Are for keeping apart, not for mixn.

O girls, you've no glamour or glitter
Until you find footwear that's fitter
    What on earth is the good
    Of those huge heels of wood?
While you teeter and totter, we titter.

... and a final word –

Beware of the limerick bore;
From a seemingly infinite store
    He trots out more verse
    Where the scansion gets worse
But the subject's the same as before.

M

RICHARD MALLETT

A Mystery Explained

It is now some time since a little elderly man who said he was a licensed horse-slaughterer (but he may have been boasting) told me this story. If it were longer ago than that I might have forgotten it, but you can't have everything.

This man, who had two sons, one a very able grocer's-boy, declared that he and he alone could explain the mystery of the *Marie Celeste*.

'It was a flat calm,' he began. 'In the middle of the broad Atlantic, we –'

'You were on board?'

'Certainly I was on board. You want me to drown? Of course I was on board. Though I had, I admit, only just come up after being sent below to count the barnacles. You know the old song – "The *Marie Celeste* was barnacled and green as grass below beelow, beelow, whoa-oh-ho-ho, listen to the JAIRZ come"' –

'How many were there?' I interrupted.

'Barnacles? Oh, a fairish number,' said the man. 'That's what I told the captain. "There's a fairish number of barnacles down there, captain," I said. He replied "What do I care so long as I have my strength?"'

'The captain of the *Marie Celeste*?'

'Oh, bless you, no,' said the man. 'This was a friend of mine, a little fat feller we used to call "the captain" because he'd been an Army captain's baptain, or, as it is now called, *batman*, in the Peninsular War, and wore an armlet to prove it – a savoury armlet he said it was. As for the captain of the ship, I told him there weren't *any* barnacles, because if I'd said there were any he'd have had me down there scraping them off before you could say H. Robinson Cleaver or Freeman, Willis and Crofts. So he said "Fine! Fine! I can't abide a barnacle."'

'Really?'

'Well, I admit what he really said was "I can't abarn a bidacle," but we were as loyal a set of men as ever sailed the seven seas and we guessed what he meant. Well, we went on in our flat calm, busying ourselves in various ways. I remember I busied myself with a scheme for stepping the mainmast out to starboard so that the wind would go on into the mainsail after leaving the foresail, instead of blowing away and being wasted. I explained it to the mate. "Look at this, Mister," I said. He very kindly pointed out that it wouldn't do, because when there was any wind it wouldn't be needed and when there wasn't it wouldn't be any use. I saw his point.'

'I see it myself,' I said. 'But by the way, what were you on board?'

'Even then I was a horse-slaughterer.'

'But there weren't any horses on the *Marie* –'

'No,' said the man. 'That's just it. Think of the confusion if there had been! It was my duty to get rid of any that might turn up. Bless me, how do you suppose the captain would have managed with a lot of beastly great horses cluttering up the place? Horses on a ship! Bless me, you make me tired. I never heard of anything so ridiculous.'

'Look,' I said. 'What about this mystery you were going to explain?'

'Ah, the mystery. I'll tell you. All of a sudden a stiff breeze got up, and we forged ahead. We bowled along. We bowled *merrily* along. Well, after we'd been bowling merrily along for a bit a great clamour arose from the cook's galley. The cook was kicking up a fuss because he'd lost his best colander. "I've been robbed!" he shouted again and again. So the police were called at once.'

'The what?'

'I didn't say they *came*, did I? Then the captain called us all together in the third-class lounge. "Men," he said, "I have a grave duty. Our popular and efficient cook has lost his pet colander. I must ask the man who appropriated it to come forward frankly," said the captain. Nobody moved. What was to be done?'

'I wish you'd get to the point,' I said.

'Impatience,' said the man reprovingly, 'butters no parsnips. What, I repeat, was to be done? Well, none of us could think, and evidently the captain couldn't either, for he dismissed us to our various tasks with a heavy heart. From that day to this, nobody else has known what became of the cook's colander. But as it happens I know, and for a very good reason. *It was I,*' said the man, '*that threw it overboard.*'

'What for?'

'I took a dislike to it. All those silly little holes!' he said, and there was a long pause.

'And the mystery?' I asked at length.

'That was the mystery.'

'But the *famous* mystery – why the *Marie Celeste* was found abandoned, with food on the tables and –'

'Oh, that. That would have been after I left the dear old ship. Ah, me!'

'Who?'

'Me.'

'Oh.'

ARCHIBALD MARSHALL

The Hermit

Once there was a rich man who had committed a lot of sins. And when he was getting rather old he said I am tired of committing sins but I don't seem to be able to help it, I think I had better go and be a hermit.

Well he had a wife who hadn't committed as many sins as he had, but she wasn't very nice and he didn't like her much, but he had to tell her about being a hermit. And he didn't much like doing it because she was often so rude to him, but he thought he'd better.

So one morning he said to his wife look here, what do you think of me being a hermit?

Well she wasn't feeling very well that morning and was rather snappy. So she said what do you think of me being a cockatoo?

And he said well you are one.

So she was angry at that and told him to get out, and he got out.

Well afterwards he was sorry he had said she was a cockatoo, though she was rather like one. And he said there now, I keep on committing sins, though I'd much rather not, I feel sure the only thing for me is to be a hermit.

So he went to his wife again and he said I really must go and be a hermit, I'm sure it's the only thing.

And she said well then for goodness sake go and be a hermit but you must leave me all your money.

And he said well I don't mind that because I shan't want any of it when I'm a hermit.

So then she let him go, and she didn't even see him off because she went out somewhere and forgot.

Well he had a good meal to start with because he didn't know when he should get any more to eat, and he went to a wood a little way off and made himself a nice hut out of the branches of trees and started being a hermit.

And he liked it very much at first, but the wood was rather lonely and nobody came to see him or brought him anything.

And he didn't have anything to eat except a few acorns which he didn't like, and after a week he said I really must go home and get something to eat.

So he went home, and his wife said oh here you are, well I did think I'd got rid of you at last, but of course I knew you didn't really mean it.

And he said oh yes I did but I must make another start, and this time I think I will take a little food with me in my wallet.

And she said well I don't mind that, you can have a cold chicken, but for goodness sake don't come back again just yet because I like having the house to myself.

Well this wasn't very kind, but he didn't say anything about it but he had a nice meal and started off again.

Well this time he went a long way off, and he came to another wood. And he told some people that he was thinking of setting up as a hermit there. And they said they thought it was a very good idea and they would bring him some food sometimes.

Well he found a very nice cave with a fountain just outside it and he settled down there as a hermit.

And he was very happy, because it was easier not to commit sins there. And the animals and birds made friends with him and he was never unkind to them or took their eggs.

And he said this is much better than being rich and I wish I had been a hermit before.

Well he stopped there for a long time and became very holy. And the people all round were proud of him because he was so holy, and he didn't mind being cold in the winter and never grumbled if they forgot to bring him food sometimes, and they all loved him.

So presently everybody got to know about him, and then they brought him too much food.

Well one Christmas Day he had a really lovely dinner of turkey and beef and ham and sausages and plum-pudding and cheese and almonds and raisins and three different kinds of wine, which different people had brought him. And he enjoyed it very much because nobody had brought him anything for a few days because they had all been getting ready for Christmas and had forgotten. But the next morning he was very sorry he had enjoyed it so much, and he said there now, I have committed another sin just when I thought I was getting over it, I really can't go on like this, it won't do.

So he put what was left of his Christmas dinner into his wallet and went away without telling anybody.

Well he went a long way this time and then he found another cave, but it was not so nice as the last one. But he said I don't mind that, it will be better for not committing sins in. And he said I shan't let people bring me any food here, I shall go and fetch it myself.

So he used to go round begging, and he asked them not to give him things that were too nice, but they were always trying to because he was so holy and they all loved him.

Well that went on for some time and then his wife said well he hasn't come back after all and I wasn't very nice to him, I think I will go and find him. So she went and found him, because everybody knew about him now and told her where to go.

And when she saw him sitting outside his cave she said I think you'd better come home now, I'm sure this cave is damp, and you look as if you wanted a bath and a good meal and I'm rather tired of being alone.

And he said well I think I won't if you don't mind, because I don't want to commit any more sins if I can help it and this cave is very good for that. So she was rather offended and went home again.

And soon after she had gone he said well I don't think I have been very kind, I don't want to go home but perhaps I had better for a little.

So he went home, and his wife was very pleased to see him, but he said I'm afraid I can't stay long.

And she said oh very well but stay as long as you can.

Well he found he quite liked being at home again because his wife was much nicer to him. And everybody knew now that he had become very holy, so they were nice to him too and didn't try to make him eat and drink a lot or be too comfortable.

Well that went on for a little and then he said to his wife this is very nice but I can't stay here for ever. I shall begin committing sins again if I do. And she said well why not stop here in the winter and go and be a hermit in the summer?

So he said oh very well perhaps that will be best as I am getting rather old for it in the winter, and I think I'm better at not committing sins than I was, at any rate I can try it.

So he stayed at home in the winter, and in the summer he went back to his cave and was a real hermit. And all the people loved him because he was so holy and kind to their children.

But they were very glad he didn't spend the winter in his cave any more because they said it was really too much for him at his age, and besides if he was ill his wife could look after him.

JAMES MICHIE

Out Of A Hot Lapis Lazuli Sky
by Pia Holst

(Written in hospital, and containing more than one ana-gram on that word).

> PILOT HAS CRASHED, HITS PALO ALTO.
> SHIP TAIL HOPS MILE, DIGS STREETWIDE PIT.
> SHOAL OF DEAD BODIES! headline screamed.
> I, Osip, survived. Condemned to phials
> Of Pathosil and to palish tea,
> Hot pails of it (pah, lots!) – I take
> A loth sip, it's like opal shit,
> Pith also (if I may lisp oath) –
> I'm in ward I, St Olaph's Clinic,
> Potash, L.I. Being spoilt? Ah, no.
> Dr Philotas lit a posh
> Cigar and growled, 'Your femur's split.
> Oh, a bad case. You've lost a hip.'
> I spot Hal, his assistant. 'Pish,

A lot you know, Plato!' (His first name).
'Tho' a lip's gashed, I shall mend,' I said.
'Sh! Ailpot!' Doc barked. 'Hop it, Sal!'
(A pi sloth, a hot slip of a nurse,
To Phil, as to his pal, a slave).
'Pat his 'ol back, slap it. Ho! Cough please.
Phlegm like Po silt — ha! ha! Op. list?
Ta. Polish the knife, soap hilt and spit.
Hola! We lop this.' A leg goes — mine.
His plot a fact at last, I hop,
A lame, halt Osip; so Lapith did
Hamstrung by Centaur's fierce lap-hoist.
I ask you, is P.T. a hol
In hospital? Ah, pistol, end me!
Lo, ashpit yawns! Hail, post-existence!
A dark one? It may hap so, 'til
God's halo tips my soil-path trudged.
P.S. A litho, 'Th'Oil Spa'
By Hals, I opt to leave to my holist
Pa, T. A. Hislop. Ha, I'l stop.

Notes

There are 59 anagrams of *hospital*.

Ship: = *plane*, as often.

Pathosil: A drug to relieve suffering (*pathos*), unknown, alas, to modern medicine and me.

Pith: The oath, or crude word, is of course piss.

St. Olaph: Correctly spelt *Olaf*. But surely the name can be *Olaph* in some language? cf. *Adolf* and *Adolph*.

Potash: Concussed, Osip makes a mistake. The town of Potash is in fact in La (Louisiana), damn it.

Ailpot: Valetudinarian. Cf. *fusspot*.

Op.: Operation.

Spit: For luck.

Hola!: Not in English dictionaries, but in all French ones. The Greek doctor was doubtless trained at the Sorbonne.

P.T. physical training; therapeutic exercises for the disabled.

Post-existence: In the dictionary. The hyphen, though, is a pity. *Post hoc* life?

God's halo &c.: The meaning is 'rewards my earth-journey completed.' Very Browningesque.

Th'Oil Spa: It is assumed that in seventeenth-century Holland natural oil springs were resorted to for health purposes.

Holist: A follower of holism, the philosophy of General Smuts.

I'l stop: Sorry, unavoidable. Or Shavian spelling.

SPIKE MILLIGAN

Tales of Men's Shirts

WALLACE:	This is the BBC. After the news there will be a talk on Early Christian Plastic Knees, and the first broadcast of a piece of knotted string. If you would like a piece of knotted string, send three rust-proof shillings to 'Honest' Wal Greenslade of Weybridge. Ta.
NED:	Hello folks, hello folks, and in that order!
WALLACE:	Ta. That voice comes from inside a short fat round blob, namely Neddie of Wales.
NED:	My first impression will be of Peter Sellers.
PETER:	Hello folks.
	Sudden Burst of Cheering
NED:	Stop! My next impression will be of Spike Milligan saying 'Thynne'.
SPIKE:	Thynneeeeeeeeeeeeeeeeeeeeeeee!
	Orchestra & Omnes: Thynneeeeeeeeeeeee eeeeeeee!
	Orchestra: Thynneeeeeeeeeeeeeeeeeeeeeee!

NED:	That's thin enough! Remember, folks, saying 'Thynneeeee' cures you of monkeys in the knees.
PETER:	Yes, if you've got monkeys on the knees, just say –
SPIKE:	Thynneeeeeeeeeeeeeeeeeeeee!
PETER:	And they are only three and six a box.
SPIKE:	Yes, I swear by them. One morning I woke up and there they were – monkeys on the knees!

At the Word 'Monkeys' Add Sound Of Monkeys In a Temper

SPIKE:	Then I said the cure word – Thynneeeeeeeeeeeeeee!

Speed Up and Fade Record of the Monkeys At High Speed

WALLACE:	Ta. The Monkeys were played by professional apes.
NED:	That was Wallace Greenslade saying words.
WALLACE:	Mr Seagoon, stand by to take part in an adventure story entitled –

Orchestra: Timpani Roll Soft – Held Under Speech

PETER:	'Tales of Men's Shirts' – a story of down under.

Orchestra: Concluding Chords
Morse Code Comes out of the Music

WALLACE:	1938 – but from the continent come ominous rumblings.

Rumbling and Bubbling Cauldron.

BLOODNOK:	Oh, this Spanish food! Waiter! One brandy – and pronto.
SPIKE (Jim):	One brandy and pronto coming up!
WALLACE:	Those were the last words said at peace. At that moment Germany declared war in all directions.
PETER:	Bang!

BLOODNOK: Bang? War!!! I must write me
                    memoirs.
                    Typewriter
BLOODNOK: The day war broke, I said to Allen-
                    brooke, 'You fool ...'
NED: England was mobilized.
PETER: Recruits were rushing to the recruiting
                    depots at the rate of one a year.
WALLACE: We join the story in 1942, a critical
                    year for Britain, with British Generals
                    slaving away at their autobiographies.
                    Dozens of Typewriters
PETER (*American*): While across the Channel, the German
                    High Command were welding a master
                    plan.
                    Typewriters
HARRY: Achtung, gentlemen! Be seated. We
                    must have a halt on our war memoirs
                    and go to war. Our scientists have just
                    invented a liquid that will win der war.
                    This chemical, when applied to the tail
                    of a military soldier shirt, is tasteless,
                    colourless and odourless.
SPIKE: What good is that on the tail of a shirt,
                    hein?
HARRY: The moment the wearer sits down, the
                    heat from his body causes the chemical
                    to explode. This way, the soldier will
                    be neutralized.
SPIKE: It will be worse than that.
PETER: Is einer wonderschön Gerhimmel!
HARRY: Speak English, you swine, there are no
                    sub-titles in this scene. Now zen, this is
                    my plan of attack.
SPIKE: It looks like a nail.
HARRY: No, it's a tack. Ho ho ho ho – who said
                    we Germans haven't got a sense of
                    humour?

SPIKE: Just about everybody.

HARRY: Oberlieutenant Schatz! You will take
              ten men, each one carrying a spray-gun
              full of the exploding shirt-tail fluid. You
              will be dropped near Leicester and there
              you will gain entrance to the Great
              British Military Shirt Factory. The rest
              is up to you. We shall call the operation
              'Burnbaum'.
              Orchestra: German Chords

WALLACE: The effect of this deadly plan was soon
              felt. The first discovery was made at
              Whitehall, where they were working
              at their memoirs.
              Typewriters

BLOODNOK: Halt! Now gentlemen – be seated.
              *Series of Shirt-Tail Explosions and
              Shouts of Rage*

BLOODNOK: Ohhhhhh – quick, nurse, the screens!

WALLACE: Portions of the charred shirt-tails were
              soon at a Military Forensic Laboratory,
              where they were forensicked.

NED: Mmmm, yes, there's been severe com-
              bustion all right. Hard to say what type
              – what do you think, sir?

MATE: Ooo, I don' know, mate, I'm only the
              kleener around 'ere.

NED: Oh, I'm sorry, I thought you were one
              of us.

MATE: No, no – I'm one of them, mate.

NED: You don't look like one of them. I
              mean, why are you dressed like an ad-
              miral?

MATE: Well, I don't like people ter think I'm
              just a kleener. I mean, I went to a good
              school, mate – Eton.

NED: How long were you there?

MATE: Oh, about five minutes. I was deliverin'

	the groceries.
NED :	You were a greengrocer?
MATE :	Not quite green, more of a dirty yellow colour – ha ha ha ...
NED :	Very good, now just step out of this thirteenth-storey window.
MATE :	No thanks, I'm trying to give 'em up.
NED :	I wish I could – hup!
MATE :	(*dramatic*) So sayin', he stepped aht – *Long Fading Screammmmmmmmmm* (*Very Long Indeed*)
NED :	Yes, I always travel by window, folks, it's the quickest way down. I was on my way to the Quarter-Master-General, Nick Nock Nokkity Nok.
CRUN :	Come in, Pnick Pnock Pnokkity Pnok.
NED :	It's me – Lieutenant Seagoon – from the body of the same name.
CRUN :	Oh, Ned. Here, let me take your window – eh – did you hear they're sending up a rocket to photograph the other side of you?
NED :	All lies, all lies! I'm losing weight – I've dropped three stone.
	Lump of Iron Goes Clang on the Ground
NED :	There's one now.
MINNIE :	Hello, sailor.
NED :	What's this, then?
MINNIE :	My name is Bannister.
NED :	Didn't I see you on the stairs?
MINNIE :	Don't bother me ...
	Typewriter
MINNIE :	'I was Churchill's Wet Nurse', Chapter One. I was standing in Piccadilly when ...
NED :	Now, Mr. Crun, I want to borrow a stock military shirt for an experiment. But

	first, Geldray and his famed Dutch Conk!
MAX:	These are my wartime Conk memoirs. Ploogie!
	Max & Orchestra: Music
WALLACE:	'Tales of Men's Shirts', Part Two.
	Orchestra: Dramatic Descending Chords with Distant Bugle and Drum Crowd of Men Chatting and Type-writers
PETER:	*(loud and soft voice)*
	Eyes front, ears to the side! Stop these memoirs!
	Orderly officer ...
	Slur Record of Chatting Down
PETER:	All correct and present, sir. Thynneee!
NED:	Thank you, and *Thynneee*. Right, at ease, men.
	Immediate Snoring – Fade Under
NED:	Gentlemen, all you officers have been selected because of your high standard of intelligence.
ECCLES:	You sure of dat?
NED:	Someone has blundered. Private Eccles, I've got bad news.
ECCLES:	Private? I'm a Captain.
NED:	That's the bad news. Now, just stand in this shallow grave and wait for the next death. Gentlemen, there has been an outbreak of exploding shirt-tails in the British Army. We suspect sabotage.
SPIKE:	*(gabbles a rubbishy question)*
NED:	Not when the train is standing in the station.
SPIKE:	Blast!
NED:	Now, gentlemen, this a matter of life and death. I want a volunteer to wear this shirt and make notes on the way it

behaves. In fact, try everything to make that shirt-tail explode. Who will volunteer?

Omnes: Pause – Light, Nervous Singing Starts – Gets Louder and Louder

Orchestra: All Gradually Join In the Singing

NED: Stop this! I appreciate your love of singing and cowardice – if you won't volunteer, we must draw lots. Eccles? Write your name on a piece of paper and put it in this hat.

ECCLES: Dere.

NED: Now draw it out and read it.

ECCLES: Mrs. Phyllis Quott.

NED: You imposter, you're not Mrs. Quott.

ECCLES: Wait, I know the ideal volunteer for you – he's had more experience with shirt-tails than anybody – his name is –

Orchestra: Bloodnok Theme

Typewriter

BLOODNOK: So I said to Winnie, 'Allenbrooke and Montgomery are ideal lads –'

The Shirt-Tail Explosion

BLOODNOK: Oh Oh – Abdul! Quick, a new shirt – it's happened again.

NED: Nickity Knock Knock oh nock!

BLOODNOK: Nickity Knock Knock oh nock? That's my private number. Come in within.

NED: Thank you. Major Bloodnok?

BLOODNOK: I have been called worse. Yes? Now what can I do for you? Better still, *get out*!!!!!!!!!!

NED: Major, I'm here to offer you money.

BLOODNOK: Ohhhh, come in Ned, warm yourself by this woman. She's just coming to the boil.

Grams: Kettle With Steam Whistle

BLOODNOK: There she goes!!!

NED: I've been told that you have more experience with exploding shirt-tails than any man alive.

BLOODNOK: True. I feel no pain. But what of the rewards?

NED: Several plastic OBEs and a drip-dry statue of Diana Dors and a ticket to Hampstead Fairground.

BLOODNOK: Ohhhh, none but the brave deserve the fair. I accept!

NED: Come, Bloodnok, on with this military test shirt.

BLOODNOK: Let's drink to the success of the venture — here's mud in yer eye.

NED: (*puzzled*) So saying, he threw a plate of mud at me.
Orchestra: Dramatic Chords

WALLACE: Neddy's next move was to actually get into Germany and try to find out the enemy's secret.

NED: At dawn, a ship hove to at Portsmouth Ho.
Seagulls. Bosun's Whistle. Ship Making Up Steam
Typewriter

MORIARTY: 'How I Saved De Gaulle And Told Mark-Clarke Where To Get Off ...' (*Sings*) A life on the ocean waveee, is the key to a watery grave.

THYNNE: Happy, Moriarty?

MORIARTY: Aye aye, Captain.

NED: Ahoy there!

THYNNE: Ahoy, Ned! Come aboard.
Splash

THYNNE: You must wait for the gangplank — ups-a-daisy.
Man Pulled Out of Water

NED:	Jove, that water was taller than me!
THYNNE:	It's older, that's why. Welcome to the Good Ship Lollipop.
NED:	My name is Lieutenant Seagoon.
THYNNE:	A better name for a twit I've yet to hear. Ned, this man in the red football jersey and one white sock is an old French sailor.
MORIARTY:	Aye, mate, I've got the sea in my blood.
NED:	(*giggles*) And you can see where it gets in.
MORIARTY:	Mind how you speak to me. Do you know who I am?
NED:	Can't you remember?
MORIARTY:	I am Comte della Robbia Moriarty, the Duke of Orange, an old naval family.
NED:	So, folks, he comes from a long line of naval oranges – ha ha ha ha. Laugh and the world laughs with you, they say.
THYNNE:	You've proved them wrong, haven't you?
SPIKE:	(*Jim*) We're ready to sail, Jim, ready to saillllllllll.
THYNNE:	Thank you, Jimmmmmm! Cast off fore and aft and ift.

Omnes: *Sea Shouts*
Ship's Telegraph
Orchestra: *Dramatic Seascape Music*

WALLACE:	A heavy sea mist descended, demanding constant vigilance by seamen in the chart-room.
BLUEBOTTLE:	Aft by fore aft ... Six bells and all's well on the dog. (*Sings*)
NED:	Everything all right, Seaman Bottle?
BLUEBOTTLE:	Everything is Bristol fashion and shipn-shanke.
NED:	Aye aye.

B.N.—M

BLUEBOTTLE: Aye aye to *you*, sir. De de de (*sings*) de de de de de.

NED: What's that rough sailor song you sing, Seaman?

BLUEBOTTLE: I'm singing this map ... (*Ad libs tune*) All those brown parts are the land, and the blue bits with the little lines on are the seasssssssssss, all the green is where the forest is, Sherwood Forest nine miles long ...

NED: (*singing with Bottle*)
                Ahh lad, they don't write maps like that any more. I say, this fog is getting thick.
                Distant Fog Horn. Bloodnok's 'Ohhhhhh'

NED: What's that?

BLUEBOTTLE: Sounds like Major Bloodnok.

NED: No, it can't be. He's never had it that bad ... Is Eccles in the crow's nest?

BLUEBOTTLE: Yes ...

NED: Eccles?

ECCLES: Yer.

NED: Can you see ahead?

ECCLES: Yer, a big bald one.

NED: Is it one of ours?

ECCLES: Ray Ellington on the cardboard bow!

RAY: Man! I don't know how they get away with it.
                The Ray Ellington Quartet: Music

WALLACE: That was Mr Ray Ellington, who now uses the blue whitener. Part Three of 'Tales of Men's Shirts'. Thynneeeee!
                Orchestra: Dramatic Return-to-Story Chords

NED: At dawn we came to off the coast of Germany. We prepared to swim ashore by electric plunging drawers.

THYNNE:	No you don't! Hands up, little Ned of Wales.
NED:	What's the meaning of this?
THYNNE:	*This* means you're a prisoner of the German Navy.
NED:	So that's what *this* means. I've often wondered. You traitor, Thynne.
THYNNE:	My name is Horne.
NED:	Traitor Horne! *Orchestra: Ta Raa Cymbal*
NED:	They don't come any older.
THYNNE:	Moriarty, clap this lot in irons. *Typewriters*
THYNNE:	Chapter Two: 'How I Captured a British Idiot in Drawers'.
MORIARTY:	Come on, you – spotty Herbert.
BLUEBOTTLE:	Take your hands of me! Do you think you take Bluebottle alive? Fixes Moriarty with hypnotic gaze – toot toot toot … *Old Fashioned Silent Movie Piano – Tension Music*
BLUEBOTTLE:	My man, I was trained in Judo by the Great Bert. Using the body as a counter-pivot to displace the opponent, I use the Great Bert's method of throwing the opponent to his death. Be warned, Moriarty, one false move and you die by Bert's method.
MORIARTY:	Take that! *Thwack on Bottle's Head*
BLUEBOTTLE:	Owwwww! (*Cries*) Wait till I see that twit Bert …
ECCLES:	You hit my friend Bottle again and see what happens. *Terrific Slapstick*
BLUEBOTTLE:	Owwwwwww!

ECCLES :	See? Dat's what happens!
	Orchestra: Dramatic Descending Chords
	Typewriter
WALLACE :	'The Greenslade War Memoirs', Chapter
	One. I said to Allenbrooke, 'How dare
	you ...'
	Behind Dialogue: Silent Film Piano –
	Sad
WALLACE :	The whole plot has misfired. Lieutenant
	Seagoon has somehow been betrayed.
	The destroyer transferred them to a U-
	boat that took them to the POW camp
	at Rhinegold Castle.
SPIKE :	The prison was full of British Officers
	who had sworn to die rather than be
	captured.
NED :	It was winter when we arrived and the
	snow lay heavy on the slopes of Brigitte
	Bardot.
VON ARLONE :	Nowzen, Englanders, my name is von
	Arlone.
ECCLES :	(*sings*) Von Aloneeeeee ter be –
	Slapstick
ECCLES :	Owwww, you'll pay fer dat.
	Half A Crown Thrown Down Onto the
	Pavement
ECCLES :	Ta. Want another go?
NED :	Shut up, Eccles. Now then, von Arlone,
	what do you intend to do with us?
VON ARLONE :	You will be incarcerated.
NED :	Ahemmm. I hope I heard right.
VON ARLONE :	Perhaps if you were to tell us what your
	mission is, we could ...
NED :	Never – I won't tell you!
VON ARLONE :	Do you know what happens to British
	spies?
NED :	No.
VON ARLONE :	So, you won't even tell us *that*? Throw

them in Stalag Ten – Eleven – and Twelve!

Orchestra: Dramatic Chords

Iron Door Slams. Heavy Key in Lock. Pair of Gaolers' Footsteps Walk Away

BLUEBOTTLE: I don't like this game. I don't like all these hairy Germans, they hitted me. Hitttt ... Hitttt ... Hitteeeeeeee, they went.

NED: Don't worry men. I have a plon of a plan. When the German guard comes in with our dinner, let him have it!

BLUEBOTTLE: Den what are we going to eat?

NED: I mean, let him have this iron bar on his nut, then we'll change uniforms and pretend to be Huns. Trouble is, I can't speak the language. Eccles, how's your German?

ECCLES: He's fine, how's yours?

MATE: (*approaching, singing*) Deutschland, Deuescher land uber the alles, mate.

NED: Listen – a German speaking fluent Cockney.

Iron Gate Opening

MATE: Here's yer breakfast, mates.

Great Heavy Rock Thuds on The Floor

MATE: Boiled egg, I'll be bound, ha ha –

Iron Bar Across His Nut

MATE: Oh, I been sponned – from the film of the same nameeeeee. Ohhhhhh.

Feeble Typewriter

MATE: (*very feeble*) Chapter One: 'How I was Sponned in Action'. I said to Alanbrooke, 'You twit ...'

NED: Wait – this isn't a German, this is Sewerman Sam! What are you doing dressed as a German General?

MATE: I told yer, I don't like people to know I

	does the sewers.
NED :	You come with us. You may come in useful – you can say odd lines.
MATE :	Odddd Linessssss! Odd Lines! Yer, I can.
	Orchestra : Dramatic Chords
WALLACE :	Ned and his party made their way to the great German Chemical Works at Schattz. By using the short-wave cardboard secret horse-hair and mattress telephone, they were able to contact London by speech.
	Typewriter on Distort
BLOODNOK :	(*distorted*) Hello, hello – Lieutenant Seagoon, about artillery –
NED :	What about it?
BLOODNOK :	One 'l' or two?
NED :	Two 'l'.
BLOODNOK :	To 'ell with you, too.
NED :	We've escaped from the German nick.
BLOODNOK :	German Nick? That swine, he and Belgian Tom!
	Now listen, we've discovered the name of the chemical that explodes our shirttails. It's called Gershattzer.
NED :	Gerschattzer? How do you spell it?
BLOODNOK :	I – T
NED :	(*over writing FX*)
	I – T, pronounced Gerschattzer ... Thanks. Now, will you do us a favour?
BLOODNOK :	What's her name?
NED :	Women – women – is that all you think of?
BLOODNOK :	(*meditatively*) By Jove, I do believe it it. Naughty Dennis.
NED :	Listen, I remember in the First World War that an English Officer hid in a cupboard from the Germans. So could you

have three cupboards dropped to us?

BLOODNOK: At once.
Crash Crash Crash

NED: Thank you. Now men, the moment you see any Germans approaching, swallow your uniforms, get inside the cupboards, and do an impression of a suit – the shabbier the better.

BLUEBOTTLE: Can I be a pin-stripe, Captain?

NED: No, I want the pin-stripe – I'm senior.

ECCLES: I'll be a morning suit so I can have the afternoon off.

BLOODNOK: I'll be a dinner jacket – I'm hungry.

NED: Bloodnok! Come out of that cupboard!

BLOODNOK: Has her husband gone, then?

NED: This is not the time to think of women.

BLOODNOK: Well, let me know when it is and I'll be off again. OOOOOOh.
Chickens Clucking

NED: (*dry*) Look – a patrol of Germans disguised as chickens.

BLOODNOK: Nonsense – they're disguised as pigeons.

NED: So that's why we've all been spotted.

BLOODNOK: Shh! Look, they're digging in behind that tree. I *hope* they're digging in behind that tree.

NED: Shhh ... Keep quiet. They know we're here. I wonder why they're holding their fire.

ECCLES: Perhaps they haven't got a fireplace.
Slapstick

SPIKE: Listen, Englanders – we know you are dere.

NED: Gad, it's Spike Milligan with a bad German accent.

SPIKE: Listen, we make bargain – we let you all go free if you hand over Major Bloodnok.

BLOODNOK:	Never! You hear? We'd rather die than hand him over.
NED:	You speak for yourself.
BLOODNOK:	I am. I'll make a bargain with you! Take all these lads and I'll let Major Bloodnok go free. What do you say?
SPIKE:	Dis is our answer.
	Great Outbreak of Firing
BLOODNOK:	Speak English, you swine!
	American Bugle Call and Approach of Cavalry.
	Shooting
NED:	Look – the American Fifth Cavalry! Saved!
	Orchestra: Ta Raa
WALLACE:	That was ending Number One. And now here is happy ending Number Two.
	Orchestra: Alto and Rhythm Play 'Laura'
	Door Opens
NED:	Cynthia? Cynthia darling, it's me – Tom.
PETER:	Tom darling! You're back!
NED:	Yes. I've been a fool about you.
PETER:	Don't say that, darling.
NED:	This parcel – it's – it's for you.
PETER:	Ohh – what is it?
	Unwrapping
NED:	Darling, this thing is bigger than both of us.
PETER:	Oh, Tom, it's – it's an elephant!
NED:	Yes – I'm not waiting any longer, we're getting married tonight.
WALLACE:	And so, that night, Neddie Seagoon married an elephant. Goodnight.
	Orchestra: Old Comrades March

N

OGDEN NASH

Who Did Which? or Who Indeed?

Oft in the stilly night,
When the mind is fumbling fuzzily,
I brood about how little I know,
And know that little so muzzily.
Ere slumber's chains have bound me,
I think it would suit me nicely,
If I knew one tenth of the little I know,
But knew that tenth precisely.

O Delius, Sibelius,
And What's-his-name Aurelius,
O Manet, O Monet,
Mrs Siddons and the Cid!
I know each name
Has an oriflamme of fame,
I'm sure they all did something,
But I can't think what they did.

Oft in the sleepless dawn
I feel my brain is hominy
When I try to identify famous men,
Their countries and anno Domini.
Potemkin, Pushkin, Ruskin,
Velásquez, Pulaski, Laski;
They are locked together in one gray cell,
And I seem to have lost the pass key.

O Tasso, Picasso,
O Talleyrand and Sally Rand,
Elijah, Elisha,
Eugene Aram, Eugène Sue,
Don Quixote, Donn Byrne,
Rosencrantz and Guildenstern,
Humperdinck and Rumpelstiltskin,
They taunt me, two by two.

At last, in the stilly night,
When the mind is bubbling vaguely,
I grasp my history by the horns
And face it Haig and Haigly.
O, Austerlitz fought at Metternich,
And Omar Khayyam wrote Moby Dick,
Blücher invented a kind of shoe,
And Kohler of Kohler, the Waterloo;
Croesus was turned to gold by Minos,
And Thomas à Kempis was Thomas Aquinas.
Two Irish Saints were Patti and Micah,
The Light Brigade rode at Balalaika,
If you seek a roué to irk your aunt,
Kubla-Khan but Immanuel Kant,
And no one has ever been transmogrified
Until by me he has been biogrified.

Gently my eyelids close;
I'd rather be good than clever;
And I'd rather have my facts all wrong
Than have no facts whatever.

First Child ... Second Child

FIRST

Be it a girl, or one of the boys,
It is scarlet all over its avoirdupois,
It is red, it is boiled; could the obstetrician
Have possibly been a lobstertrician?

His degrees and credentials were hunky-dory,
But how's for an infantile inventory?
Here's the prodigy, here's the miracle!
Whether its head is oval or spherical,
You rejoice to find it has only one,
Having dreaded a two-headed daughter or son;
Here's the phenomenon all complete,
It's got two hands, it's got two feet,
Only natural, but pleasing, because
For months you have dreamed of flippers or claws.
Furthermore, it is fully equipped :
Fingers and toes with nails are tipped;
It's even got eyes, and a mouth clear cut;
When the mouth comes open the eyes go shut,
When the eyes go shut the breath is loosed
And the presence of lungs can be deduced.
Let the rockets flash and the cannon thunder,
This child is a marvel, a matchless wonder.
A staggering child, a child astounding,
Dazzling, diaperless, dumfounding,
Stupendous, miraculous, unsurpassed,
A child to stagger and flabbergast,
Bright as a button, sharp as a thorn,
And the only perfect one ever born.

SECOND

Arrived this evening at half-past nine.
Everybody is doing fine.
Is it a boy, or quite the reverse?
You can call in the morning and ask the nurse.

The Private Dining-room

Miss Rafferty wore taffeta,
Miss Cavendish wore lavender.
We ate pickerel and mackerel
And other lavish provender.

Miss Cavendish was Lalage,
Miss Rafferty was Barbara.
We gobbled pickled mackerel
And broke the candelabara,
Miss Cavendish in lavender,
In taffeta, Miss Rafferty,
The girls in taffeta lavender,
And we, of course, in mufti.

Miss Rafferty wore taffeta,
The taffeta was lavender,
Was lavend, lavender, lavenderest,
As the wine improved the provender.
Miss Cavendish wore lavender,
The lavender was taffeta.
We boggled mackled pickerel,
And bumpers did we quaffeta.
And Lalage wore lavender,
And lavender wore Barbara,
Rafferta taffeta Cavender Lavender
Barbara abracadabra.

Miss Rafferty in taffeta,
Grew definitely raffisher.
Miss Cavendish in lavender
Grew less and less stand-offisher.
With Lalage and Barbara
We grew a little pickereled,
We ordered Mumm and Roederer
Because the bubbles tickereled
But lavender and taffeta
Were gone when we were soberer.
I haven't thought for thirty years
Of Lalage and Barbara.

The Wild Jackass

Have ever you harked to the jackass wild,
Which scientists call the onager?
It sounds like the laugh of an idiot child,
Or a hepcat on a harmoniger.
But do not sneer at the jackass wild,
There is method in his hee-haw,
For with maidenly bush and accent mild
The jenny-ass answers, shee-haw.

The Wendigo*

The Wendigo,
The Wendigo!
Its eyes are ice and indigo!
Its blood is rank and yellowish!
Its voice is hoarse and bellowish!
Its tentacles are slithery,
And scummy,
Slimy,
Leathery!
Its lips are hungry blubbery.
And smacky,
Sucky,
Rubbery!
The Wendigo,
The Wendigo!
I saw it just a friend ago!
Last night it lurked in Canada;
To-night, on your veranada!
As you are lolling hammockwise
It contemplates you stomachwise.

---

* *Wendigo*. In the mythology of the northern Algonquians, an evil spirit; one of a fabulous tribe of cannibals. Webster's Unabridged *Dictionary*.

You loll,
It contemplates,
It lollops,
The rest is merely gulps and gollops.

DENIS NORDEN

I Think, Therefore I Am

Although 'I Think, Therefore I Am' was the line on which Descartes achieved his meteoric rise to stardom, that was not the line he actually wrote. So I can't tell you how much pleasure it gives me to put the record straight, if only for poor René's sake.

René, as some of you may have heard, was the unfortunate Christian name of that eminent 17th century philosopher, and even though the French pronounce it Renay it was still one hell of a liability for a growing lad in those rough times. The other burden under which poor Descartes laboured was that he had this real granite-block of a wife. Although Madame Descartes brought some property to the marriage, the truth is she was several years older, had the disposition of an untipped taxi-driver and was an incurable picture-straightener. Every time Descartes sat down to deliver himself of a crystalline aphorism, in she'd come in her rollers and – 'I'm sorry, I need this room for a social occasion.' Or, 'if you don't mind, kindly shift your philosophy kit to the shed.'

It's hard to think of a way in which she wasn't a dead loss to an aspiring philosopher. Even in their more intimate moments, when he was endeavouring to make love to her, her invariable response was the phrase which George Gershwin later put to such profitable use – 'Descartes take that away from me.'

You may well wonder, then, how it was that under such miserable working conditions René managed to reach Number One among philosophy's all-time chart-toppers.

Well, as I've indicated, it was all due to the widespread misunderstanding about his line 'I Think, Therefore I Am.' And to trace the *exact* origin of that I must take you, by the magic of radio, back to the New Year's Eve party which Madame Descartes threw to celebrate the advent of 1636.

She'd decided that as it was to be an informal affair what she'd serve would be a 'buffet' (a French word meaning 'we've got more people than chairs'). As she also intended it to be a late do, with the guests not arriving until around 11 o'clock, she ran up an enormous bunch of that Gallic imitation of bacon-and-egg flan they call 'Quiches.' Not the large catering-size ones, but those small individual versions affectionately celebrated by Yvette Guilbert ('Just a leetle love, a leetle quiche, etc.').

However – and you'll be glad to know we're getting somewhere near the point – Madame made it clear to René that although the quiches would be put out on the sideboard in advance – 'what I *don't* want is people helping themselves all evening and treading their crumbs into the Aubusson. So I'm relying on you to see to it that nobody starts digging into them until at least an hour after we've seen the New Year in. Then they can take plates and eat properly!'

Ironic, isn't it? The founder of the Cartesian School relegated to the position of Securicor for bacon-and-egg flans. As he said to Father Dinet – I haven't mentioned him, but he was a Jesuit priest who was about René's only real mate at that time – as he said to him, 'I can't think this is in any way advancing my career. Being sat down here at the sideboard till one o'clock in the morning, no way will there be any philosophising done tomorrow. I'll be like a limp rag.'

To which the good Father rejoined an extremely practical rejoinder. 'Then why don't you use this as *working* time? Take a pen and write while you're sitting here, set your mind for lofty thoughts and if any arrive, jot them down on a paper serviette.'

'Not a bad idea at all,' said Descartes. 'Give us a borrow of your quill.'

So it was that for the next hour or so, there by the sideboard the two friends sat and Descartes was able to get off quite a few zingers relating to corporeal rationality. It was while he was putting into shape an eternal verity on adventitious volition that he glanced up and, to his horror, saw that Father Dinet had absent-mindedly helped himself to a quiche and was quietly munching it.

About to open his mouth and exclaim 'watch it! They're not supposed to be eaten yet,' he became aware of something else. There, not two metres away – well within earshot – stood his wife!

There was only one thing to do. Stealthily, Descartes took another serviette, scribbled out his warning, then equally furtively, pushed the serviette under Father Dinet's nose.

So it was that the whole 300-year-old misunderstanding originated. That message – the one which Father Dinet was later to publish to the world as 'I Think Therefore I Am' – all it referred to was the time-ban on the bacon-and-egg flans.

The truth is, what Descartes actually wrote was *I think they're for 1 a.m.*

BARRY PAIN

The Poets At Tea

I. Macaulay, Who Made It.
    Poûr, varlet, pour the water,
      The water steaming hot!
    A spoonful for each man of us,
      Another for the pot!
    We shall not drink from amber,
      No Capuan slave shall mix
    For us the snows of Athos
      With port at thirty-six;
    Whiter than snow the crystals
      Grown sweet 'neath tropic fires,
    More rich the herb of China's field,
    The pasture-lands more fragrance yield;
    For ever let Britannia wield
      The teapot of her sires!

II. Tennyson, Who Took It Hot.
    I think that I am drawing to an end:
    For on a sudden came a gasp for breath,
    And stretching of the hands, and blinded eyes,
    And a great darkness falling on my soul.
    O Hallelujah! ... kindly pass the milk.

III. Swinburne, Who Let It Get Cold.
    As the sin that was sweet in the sinning
      Is foul in the ending thereof,

As the heat of the summer's beginning
Is past in the winter of love;
O purity, painful and pleading!
O coldness, ineffably grey!
Oh hear us, our handmaid unheeding,
And take it away!

IV. Cowper, Who Thoroughly Enjoyed It.

The cosy fire is bright and gay,
The merry kettle boils away
And hums a cheerful song
I sing the saucer and the cup;
Pray, Mary, fill the teapot up,
And do not make it strong.

V. Browning, Who Treated It Allegorically.

Tst! Bah! We take as another case —
    Pass the pills on the window-sill; notice the capsule
(A sick man's fancy, no doubt, but I place
    Reliance on trade-marks, Sir) so perhaps you'll
Excuse the digression — this cup which I hold
    Light-poised — Bah, it's spilt in the bed! — well, let's
                                              on go —
Held Bohea and sugar, Sir; if you were told
The sugar was salt, would the Bohea be Congo?

VI. Wordsworth, Who Gave It Away.

'Come, little cottage girl, you seem
    To want my cup of tea;
And will you take a little cream?
    Now tell the truth to me.'

She had a rustic, woodland grin,
    Her cheek was soft as silk,
And she replied, 'Sir, please put in
    A little drop of milk.'

'Why, what put milk into your head?
   'This cream my cows supply;'
And five times to the child I said,
   'Why, pig-head, tell me, why?'

'You call me pig-head,' she replied;
   'My proper name is Ruth.
I called that milk' – she blushed with pride –
   'You bade me speak the truth.'

VII. *Poe, Who Got Excited Over It.*
   Here's a mellow cup of tea – golden tea!
   What a world of rapturous thought its fragrance
                                       brings to me
      Oh, from out the silver cells
      How it wells!
      How it smells!
   Keeping tune, tune, tune, tune
   To the tintinnabulation of the spoon.

   And the kettle on the fire
   Boils its spout off with desire,
   With a desperate desire
   And a crystalline endeavour
   Now, now to sit, or never,
   On the top of the pale-faced moon,
   But he always came home to tea, tea, tea, tea, tea,
      Tea to the nth.

VIII. *Rossetti, Who Took Six Cups Of It.*
      The lilies lie in my lady's bower
         (O weary mother, drive the cows to roost).
      They faintly droop for a little hour;
      My lady's head droops like a flower.

      She took the porcelain in her hand
         (O weary mother, drive the cows to roost).
      She poured; I drank at her command;

Drank deep, and now – you understand!
(O weary mother, drive the cows to roost).

IX. *Burns, Who Liked It Adulterated.*

Weel, gin ye speir, I'm so inclined,
Whusky or tay – to state my mind
   For ane or ither;
For, gin I tak the first, I'm fou,
And gin the next, I'm dull as you,
   Mix a' thegither.

X. *Walt Whitman, Who Didn't Stay More Than a Minute.*
One cup for my self-hood,
Many for you. *Allons, camerados*, we will drink
   together
O hand-in-hand! That tea-spoon, please, when
   you've done with it.
What butter-coloured hair you've got. I don't want
   to be personal.
All right, then, you needn't – you're a stale –
   cadaver.
Eighteenpence if the bottles are returned,
Allons, from all bat-eyed formules.

Dukes

My friends are always complaining to me about my dukes.
They say that I have too many, that I ought not to allow
them in the house, and that they are very ill-mannered.
There may, perhaps, be something in the complaints, but
what can I do? I own between thirty and forty dukes,
and although they are safely locked up in an old shed
during the night they simply will get into the house in
the daytime. As a rule, I do not think that they do much
harm; most of them are good-tempered, and all of them
are quite clean, for I have them well washed with carbolic
soap once every fortnight. But there are, of course, ex-

ceptional cases. Now, some time ago I bought a large duke
who had been in an American novel and got his temper
spoiled. I have told my servants time after time that I
will not have this animal in the drawing-room – that they
may make as much fuss with him as they like in the
kitchen, but that on no account is he to be allowed to go
any further than the kitchen. I have tried, too, to make
the duke himself see that the kitchen is his proper place.
But it is all of no use. However careful my servants are,
and however often I thrash him for his disobedience, he
is certain to break bounds; and then, of course, there is
unpleasantness. It is not very nice for a visitor, just
ushered into the drawing-room, to find a great fat duke
asleep on the hearth-rug in front of the fire; and it is
especially unpleasant when the beast uncurls himself, sits
up, and begins to talk about his order. I really hardly know
what to do with him. He has a way of saying 'Noblesse
oblige', and not caring where he says it. Then, again, there
was a duke in 'Sir Percival'; I do not know if you remember him. I bought him; he was expensive, but I do not care
what I give for a really good duke. He was well marked,
with a broad blue ribbon, as it were, across his chest; and
when he passed through the market-place, he would speak
many a gracious word. The first suspicion that I had of
his temper was when the butler complained about him.
It appeared that he had formed a habit of smelling every
cork that was drawn, and carefully examining both ends;
he would then shrug his shoulders, frown, and completely
lose the drift of the conversation. As the butler pointed out
to me, no one in the kitchen could possibly stand such
manners. I was reluctant to lose the animal, and tried to
break him of the habit by keeping him on Apollinaris. It
was of no use, and shortly afterwards the poor thing's
sense of its social status became so acute, that it was no
kindness to keep him alive any longer. Another of my
failures was also a novel duke. He had been in Mr. Craw-
ford's 'Dr. Claudius.' He was quite simple, wore cheap
clothes, and seemed able to forget that he had any par-

ticular rank. The simplicity and forgetfulness were a little ostentatious, perhaps, but he had no serious vices; he did not, for instance, drop many a gracious word. Yet an accident compelled me to get rid of him. He had gone into the garden in the dusk, to get strawberry leaves, and I mistook him for the gardener. Unfortunately the gardener got to hear of it, and was much hurt. So, to prevent the mistake occurring again, I sold the duke.

I have been asked whether I recommend English or foreign dukes. Either do very well if you can only conquer their passion for social aggrandisement. As a rule, the English duke has the greater property, and the foreign duke has the darker moustache; the foreign duke is more of a villain, and the English duke is more of a bore; but these distinctions only hold in the case of novel-bred dukes. Novel-bred dukes are more satisfactory than the other kind, although I myself keep both. I have only got one literary duke, and I cannot remember at the present moment whether he is novel-bred or not. But he is always shedding articles about the house, and I hardly know what to do with them. If only we had some monthly review which made a speciality of ducal articles, without much regard to their inward merit, I could send them there; but, of course, there is nothing of the sort in existence. As it is, I find these articles lying all over the house – one on the mantelpiece, another on the carpet, and a third very likely on the income tax. But, as I have already said, the main difficulty is to put a stop to their social ambitions. Few dukes, at any rate very few of my collection, are willing to stop down-stairs in the kitchen; and yet if they come up-stairs, one's friends begin to complain at once. I often think, cynically enough, when I got to feed my dukes or to superintend their fortnightly bath, that probably at least half of the beasts consider themselves to be every bit as good as I am. The duke that I got from 'Dr. Claudius', however, was quite different. He had a proper sense of shame. I've known him run off into the garden, scratch up a hole, and bury all his titles and family estates in it; then he would come back, and put his cold nose into my hand, and fawn on me, and try to make me believe that he was his butler. It was a pretty and pathetic incident, and a pleasing contrast to the conduct of some of my other dukes, who will go running after American heiresses. Of course, they only get snubbed for their pains.

Yes, in spite of what my friends may say, I love my dukes. It is the natural sympathy of the strong for the weak. The poor animals have been terribly handicapped in the race of life, and I feel for them, and, I think, they are happy with me. The strict discipline, plain living, plain speaking, and carbolic soap, are good for them, and they know it. Occasionally one of them will so far forget himself as to drop a gracious word; and, of course, I have had to put up with the exceptional cases that I have already mentioned; but on the whole they are getting to be very well trained – I had almost said civilised. They will never, I am afraid, be quite as common as canaries, but I do not see any reason why every middle-class household should not own at least one of them. The prejudice which exists against them at present is perfectly senseless, but it has prevented fanciers from devoting proper attention to them. And do not be misled by silly stories about their appetite; they eat very little, if any, more than ordinary people.

Babies

Babies are various. They resemble invalids in their habits of browsing on milk; political programmes in their absence of any decided features; type-writers in their refusal to work; and steam-whistles in the gentle cooing sounds which they are said to produce. But, in spite of these minor points of resemblance, naturalists are probably correct in regarding them as a kind of serpent. Nor have they come to this conclusion merely on the ground that both babies and serpents require warmth; that is merely a point which they have in common with soup, the affections, and many other things. There is more evidence than that. Notice the gliding, undulatory motion of a large baby as it crosses the nursery carpet; notice, too, the wicked looks of the hooded variety, or listen to their terrible rattle; or throw a number of school-girls into the cage in which your baby is placed, and see the deadly fascination which it exercises over the poor creatures. There they stand, under his glassy, hypnotic stare, swaying a little to and fro; they cannot escape, even though you leave the cage-door wide open; presently their terror causes a partial paralysis of the vocal organs; they are no longer able to speak articulate English, and their efforts only result in gibberish; then they draw nearer and nearer to the crouching baby, and in another minute they are in its clutches. The scene is too painful for further description, but enough has been said to show what the real nature of these reptiles is. Still a few school-girls more or less do not matter, and where babies are properly under the control of adults they are not really dangerous. The great point is not to let them see that you are afraid of them. If you are going to kiss them, or to punish them in any other way, you must simply show a little pluck. Some young men shirk kissing babies, and afterwards allow themselves to be led into it. That is not right; there should be no hesitation. I find that the best way is to shut the eyes, hold the breath, and take a short run at it. I mean that this way suits me the best, personally; I own that it generally produces in the baby that gentle cooing sound to which I have already referred, and nursemaids say rather bitter things about me afterwards.

Any number of middle-aged bachelors who are anxious to have a baby in their chambers to pet have written to ask me where a fat one-year-old specimen can generally be found. Well, there are many places; although, of course, they have one or two special haunts. You will find two or three babies, as a rule, on the edge of any precipice. Or you can ride a bicycle through a suburb and afterwards brush a dozen or so off the spokes of the machine; the chief objection to this is that they sometimes get soiled or even broken in the process. The simplest way is to look in any smoking compartment. There you will never be disappointed. If there is a mother attached to the child, it is usual to throw her out of window. Even after you have found a baby, it is just possible that you may not know what to do with it. It is not necessary to slightly compress a baby's back in order to make it say 'pap!' In fact, by so doing you may damage its works; the mistake is generally made by those who have recollections of youthful experiences in toy-shops. The proper way is to put your own nose within an inch of such nose as the baby possesses, made a bad face, and then distinctly mispronounce the word. Another mistake was made by one of my dukes – I think it was the duke I got out of 'Sir Percival'. He was congratulating himself on the idea that only the upper classes in London possessed babies. He was deceived, of course, by a mere difference of nomenclature. Byebies are the same as babies – just as the tinned peaches of the grocer are precisely the same as the *pêches en compôte* of the Italian restaurant.

I have been asked why young babies have hair so short as to be almost imperceptible. It is to make up for the excessive length of their clothes at the other end. This is the law of compensation which we notice working everywhere in nature. Often when I have seen some poor baby wearing its feet where its waist should have been, it has comforted me to think that, after all, it need never brush its hair. Natural laws prevail everywhere; if you drop your baby out of the window it will fall as far as the pavement, and then it will stop. It was Sir Isaac Newton who first made this experiment. But I must not linger any longer upon these deep and philosophical reflections; if, however, you are not sufficiently educated to understand them, they will, at any rate, show you that one may take the keenest interest in home pets, and yet have a cultured mind.

Those who are less philosophical and more practical

have often urged that babies are unprofitable pets, that one gets nothing out of them. This is not altogether fair. They have many pretty tricks which it is interesting to watch. Did you ever see a baby cut a tooth? It begins on the outside edge, and ends on the high G. Or, if tricks are not practical enough to please these captious critics, I may point out that babies taste very much like young dairy-fed pork. They make, in fact, a capital breakfast dish, as every epicure knows.

S. J. PERELMAN

De Gustibus Ain't What Dey Used To Be

A girl and the four walls she lives in can get mighty tired of each other. Especially in mid-winter. Well, here are twenty-five transfusions which, with a minimum invest-ment of time and money, will repay sparkling dividends. They're as effective as the dozen roses someone once sent you just for fun, as easy as a birthday telephone call. Most of them don't even demand that you roll up your sleeves. 1. Invest in eight small white pots of ivy to range on your window-sills. 2. *Paint* a gaily fringed rug on a wooden floor. 3. Rent an original picture from a painting rental library. (Between $2 and $35 will let you live with a masterpiece for two months.) 4. Put a bowl of glittering goldfish on your coffee-table. 5. Partition a room with fish-net running on a ceiling track. 6. Get a kitten. 7. Cover your loose cushions with polka-dot cotton – perhaps white dots on black, black dots on white – variously sized and spaced. 8. Get a mobile to grace your room with motion – or better, make one yourself. 9. Slip cover your couch in dark denim – navy, brown or charcoal, maybe – de-pending on your colour scheme. 10. If your living-room walls are plain – on a Sunday, wallpaper just one wall. 11. Give houseroom to a *tree* in a big wooden tub. 12. Paste golden notary seals in an all-over design on your white window shade. 13. Wallpaper the insides of your cabinets and drawers with a flower print. 14. Have a favourite drawing photostated up as big as they'll make it; then hang it on your wall. 15. Forget polishing for ever and spray all your metal surfaces with a new plastic preservative. 16. Buy a new shower curtain – and make it SILLY. 17. Make a new table-cloth out of irresistible cotton yard goods. 18. Draw outline pictures of your kitchen utensils on the wall right where each should hang. 19. Dye your mother's white damask tablecloths in brilliant shades. If they're huge, cut the surplus up into squares and hem them for napkins. 20. Put silk fringe along the bottoms of window shades. 21. Get yards of fake leopard skin to throw over your studio couch. 22. Make a cork bulletin board. 23. Cover your lampshades in wallpaper to match your papered walls. 24. Find some cutlery boxes to keep your jewellery lucid in the drawers. 25. Invest in flowered china or glass door-knobs. ... *And if you're still yearning for a change; Spend an evening by candlelight.*

– Glamour.

SCENE: *A one-room apartment in Manhattan occupied by April Monkhood, a young career woman. At some time prior to rise, April and her four walls have tired of each other, and she has called in Fussfeld, a neighbourhood decorator, to give the premises the twenty-five transfusions recommended above. Fussfeld, a lineal descendant of Brigadier-General Sir Harvey Fussfeld-Gorgas, the genius who pacified the Sudan, has attacked the assignment with the same zeal that characterised his famous relative. He has placed at stage centre a magnificent specimen of Bechtel's flowering crab, the boughs of which are so massive that it has been necessary to stay them with cables and turnbuckles. This has perforce complicated the problem of the fish-net partitions on their ceiling tracks, but, fortunately, most of these have ripped off and now depend from the branches, supplying a romantic effect akin to that of Spanish moss. What with the hodge-podge of damask,*

*yard goods, fake leopard skin, floral wallpaper, silk fringe,
and notary seals, it is difficult at first to distinguish any
animate object. Finally, though, the eye picks out a rather
scrawny kitten, licking its lips by an overturned goldfish
bowl. A moment later, April Monkhood enters from the
kitchenette, practically on all fours. She is a vivacious
brownette in knee-hugging poltroons, with a retroussé nose
which she wears in a horsetail. Behind her comes Fussfeld,
a small, haggard gentleman with a monocle he affects for
chic. However, since he is constantly losing it in the decor
and scrabbling about for it, he fails to achieve any impressive degree of sang-froid.*

FUSSFELD (*dubiously*): I'm not so sure it's advisable, dusting spangles over the gas stove like that. The pilot light –
APRIL: Now, Mr. Feldpot, don't be an old fuss – I mean
stop worrying, will you? It's gay, it's chintzy. It's a whiff
of Mardi Gras and the storied Vieux Carré of New Orleans.
FUSSFELD (*with a shrug*): Listen, if you want to run down
a fire escape in your night-gown, that's your privilege.
(*Looking around*). Well, does the job suit you O.K.?
APRIL: Mad about it, my dear – simply transported. Of
course, it doesn't quite have a feeling of being lived in ...
FUSSFELD: I'd sprinkle around a few periodicals, or a can
of salted peanuts or so. Anyway, a place gets more homey
after your friends drop around.
APRIL: Golly, I can't wait to have my housewarming. Can
you imagine when people step off the dumbwaiter and see
this room by candlelight?
FUSSFELD (*faintly*): You – er – you're hoisting them up
here?
APRIL: How else? We'll be using the stairs outside to eat on.
FUSSFELD: M-m-m. I'm trying to visualise it.
APRIL: I thought of Basque place-mats, two on each stair,
and sweet little favours made of putty. Don't you think
that would be amusing?
FUSSFELD: Oh, great, great. (*Produces a statement*) I got
everything itemised here except what you owe the paper-

hanger. When he gets out of Bloomingdale, he'll send you a separate bill.

APRIL (*frowning*): Sixteen hundred and ninety-three dollars. Frankly, it's a bit more than I expected.

FUSSFELD: Well, after all, you can't pick up this kind of stuff for a song. Those notary seals, for instance. We used nine dozen at fifty cents apiece. The guy at the stationery store had to witness each one.

APRIL: I know, but you list four hundred dollars for structural work.

FUSSFELD: We had to raise the ceiling to squeeze in the tree. The plumber was here three days changing the pipes around.

APRIL: (*gaily tossing aside the bill*) Ah, well, it's only money. I'll mail you a cheque shortly.

FUSSFELD: No hurry – any time in the next forty-eight hours. (*Carelessly*) You still work for the same concern, don't you?

APRIL: Certainly. Why?

FUSSFELD: In case I have to garnishee your pay. (*A knock at the door. April crosses to it, admits Cyprian Voles. The associate editor of a pharmaceutical trade journal, he is a rabbity, diffident young man with vague literary aspirations. He is at present compiling* The Pleasures of Shag, *an anthology of essays relative to smoking, which will contain excerpts from Barrie's* My Lady Nicotine, *Machen's* The Anatomy of Tobacco, *etc., and which will be remaindered within thirty days of publication*).

CYPRIAN: Am I too early? You said six-thirty.

APRIL: Of course not, dear. Cyprian, this is my decorative-relations counsel, Mr. Fussfeld – Mr. Voles.

FUSSFELD: Likewise. Well, I got to be running along, Miss Monkhood. About that cheque –

APRIL: Just as soon as my ship comes in.

FUSSFELD: I'll be studying the maritime news. (*Exits. Cyprian, meanwhile, has backed into a mobile of fish and chips suspended overhead and is desperately fighting to disengage it from his hat*)

APRIL: (*thirsting for approval*): Isn't the flat delectable? Have you ever in your whole life seen anything so cosy?

CYPRIAN: Yes, it – it's stunning. It's really *you* – it captures the inner essence – that is, the outer inwardness –

APRIL: You don't think it's overdone, do you?

CYPRIAN: Overdone? Why, it's stark! You couldn't omit one detail without damaging the whole composition.

APRIL (*hugging him*) You old sorcerer. You know just the words to thaw a woman's heart. Now, I've an inspiration. Instead of going out for dinner, let's have powdered snails and a bottle of Old Rabbinical under the crab.

CYPRIAN (*fingering his collar*) Er – to tell you the truth, I – I find it a little close in here. You see, I fell into a grain elevator one time when I was small –

APRIL: Nonsense, it'll be heaps of fun. I loathe those big, expensive restaurants. Sit ye doon while I mix us an aperitif. (*She thrusts him backward on to the studio couch, almost decapitating him with a guy wire, then whisks a bottle from a cabinet*) Who do you suppose called me today? My husband, of all people.

CYPRIAN: Hanh? You never told me you were married.

APRIL: Oh, Sensualdo and I've been separated for years. He's a monster – an absolute fiend.

CYPRIAN: Is he a Mexican?

APRIL: Uh-uh – Peruvian. One of those insanely jealous types, always opening your mail and accusing you of carrying on with his friends. He tried to stab a man I was having a coke with. That's what broke up our marriage.

CYPRIAN: W-where is he now?

APRIL: Right here in New York. His lawyers are trumping up evidence for a divorce – What's the matter?

CYPRIAN: (*he has risen and sways dangerously*) I feel faint ... spots before the eyes ...

APRIL: Lie down, I'll get you some water –

CYPRIAN (*panting*): No, no. I've got to get out of here. The walls are closing in. (*He becomes entangled in a pile of mill-end remnants and flounders hopelessly. Simultaneously, a peremptory knock at door.*)

VOICE (*off scene*): Open up there!

CYPRIAN (*in an agonised whisper*): Who's *that*?

APRIL: I don't know, unless –

ANOTHER VOICE (*off scene*): Open the door, you tramp, else we break eet down!

APRIL (*biting her lip*): Damnation. It's Sensualdo. (*Grabbing Cyprian's arm*) Quick, into the bathroom – no, wait a second, stand over there! (*She snatches a handful of notary seals from a shelf, and, moistening them, begins pasting them at random on his face*).

CYPRIAN: (*struggling*): What are you doing?

APRIL: Sh-h-h, never mind – help me! Stick them on your clothes, anywhere! (*Pandemonium at the door as Sensualdo attempts to kick in the panels. April, in the meantime, has found a heavy iron ring – conveniently included in the props by the stage manager – and now arranges it to dangle from Cyprian's outstretched hand*). There. Now lean forward and try to look like a hitching post. That's perfect – don't budge! (*She runs to the door, yanks it open. Sensualdo, an overwrought Latin in the world's most expensive vicuña coat, erupts in, flanked by two private detectives*).

SENSUALDO (*roaring*): Where is thees animal which he is defiling my home? (*He and his aides halt in stupefaction as they behold the apartment*).

APRIL: Get out! How dare you barge in without a warrant? Help! Police!

FIRST SHAMUS (*ignoring her*): Holy cow! What kind of a joint is this?

SECOND DITTO: It's a thrift shop. Look at that statue with a ring in its hand.

FIRST SHAMUS (*to Sensualdo*): Hey, Bright Eyes, we didn't hire out to break in no store. I'm takin' a powder.

SENSUALDO: Eeet's a trick! Search in the closets, the bathroom –

SECOND SHAMUS: And lay in the workhouse ninety days? No sirree. Come on, Havemeyer. (*The pair exit. Sensualdo, his hood engorged with venom, turns on April*).

SENSUALDO : You leetle devil. One day you go too far.

APRIL (*tremulously*) : Oh, darling, don't – you mustn't. I'm so vulnerable when you look at me like that.

SENSUALDO: (*seizing her roughly*): Do not play pelota weeth my heart, woman. You mean you are still caring for me?

APRIL : Passionately, joyously. With every fibre of my being. Take me, hold me, fold me. (*Her eyeballs capsize*). To kiss anyone else is like a moustache without salt.

SENSUALDO : Ah-h-h, *Madre de Dios*, how you set my blood on fire anew. Let me take you out of all thees – to a hilltop in Cuzco, to the eternal snows of the Andes –

APRIL (*simply*) : Geography don't matter, sugar. With you I could be happy in a hallway. (*They depart, absorbed in each other. Cyprian holds his pose a few seconds, and then, straightening, tiptoes after them as warily as the goldfish bowl on his foot permits. His face at the moment is inscrutable, but, broadly speaking, he has the look of a man hellbent on completing an anthology on the joys of the weed.*)

CURTAIN

PLUCK

Examination Papers for Candidates At Oxford and Cambridge in 1836

Translate the following into your worst Ionic, in the style of Herodotus.

In the Atlantic Ocean, and nigh upon Cornwall, are some islands called anciently Cassiterides, or the tin islands, but now named Silly, which are much to be admired for their wonderful use and excellence. For therein does grow tin in such plenty that the inhabitants pass a most loveable life, being ever able to pay their debts, from having plenty of tin. These islands were first discovered according to tradition, by a man of Cambridge, who being plucked on a time, and having likewise great debts, determined nobly to go in search of them upon the bare report. Therefore, letting himself down at night from his college window, while the porter slept, and being armed with an Ainsworth's dictionary for defence, he descended to the Cam, and taking a skiff went along with the stream, through much wild and barbarous country, as was to be expected in those times; till in the end, after ten days' travel, he reached the sea coast, with much danger from savages, which nevertheless he escaped bravely, by wielding of his dictionary. From the coast he proceeded by land till he came opposite to a small island, which having reached by swimming, he found thereon much tin, lying in heaps of sovereigns along the shore. Likewise the trees had for leaves bank notes, whereof some were of five pound and others of ten pound, according to their age. Seeing which, he stuffed his pockets, not excepting even his fob, with the last mentioned, wisely neglecting the first. But perceiving the islanders to approach, he was forced to flee, and thus escaping to land by swimming, reached Cambridge in thirteen days, where he paid all his own debts besides those of his friends, albeit not a few of the notes had been destroyed by salt water. Since his time many undergraduates in debt have gone on the same journey, but as yet no one hath succeeded, which is much to be lamented.

A True and Faithful Account of the Cassiterides, or Tin Islands, by Herodotus Britannicus, in his History of Undergraduates.

Explain the use of the word Brick in the following sentences: As fast as a brick. As slow as a brick. As idle as a brick. To read like a brick. To run like a brick. To swear like a brick. To ride like a brick. To be as drunk as a brick. As hungry as a brick. An old brick. A young brick. Do you suppose this phrase to be borrowed from ancient authors? If so, what author is it who uses the corresponding Latin or Greek term in the same manner?

Soft fades the sun: the moon is sunk to sleep
Through heaven's blue fringe the stars serenely peep.
An azure calm floats o'er the breathing sky.
Like Memory brooding over days gone by
And while the owls in tender notes complain,
Grim Silence holds her solitary reign.

From which of the Oxford or Cambridge Prize Poems are these lines taken? Explain their beauties, and give parallel passages.

Has any Prize Poem appeared for the last ten years at Oxford or Cambridge, without the sun, moon, or stars in it? Explain the use of these great auxiliaries to verse-making, and shew how inferior the ancients are to the moderns in the number of their suns, moons, and stars.

Are you acquainted with any other use of the sun and moon besides this use of helping writers of prize poems? Give reasons why these authors have not made use of comets, especially when modern science has discovered that there are so many of them to spare.

Translate the following into your worst English.
Oh fortunatos nimium sua si bona norint
Sleevatos bachelors! neque enim sub sidere nightae
Ad bookas sweatant; nec dum Greattomia quartam
Lingua horam strikat, saveall sine candle tenentes,
Ad beddam creepunt semisleepi; nec mane prima
Scoutus adest saevus tercentum knockibus instans
Infelix wakare caput. Sed munera mater
Ipsa dot Alma illis, keepuntque secantque chapellam
Quandocunque volunt. Si non velvete minaci
Ornati incedunt, non pisces ad table higham
Quaque die comedunt, ast illis cuttere semper
Quemque licit tutorem, illis lectura nec ulla,
At secura quies, et nescia pluckere vita*

---

* Semi-translation: Oh, if only the sleeved Bachelors knew how lucky they are! For they do not sweat over books at night; nor when Great Tom strikes four do they creep half-asleep to bed, holding a saveall (a special candlestick which burns the candle

All members of the University wear caps and gowns,
Some ladies wear caps and gowns;
Therefore some ladies are members of the University.
Prove the correctness of this syllogism; also of the following:
A man in a skiff has got sculls in the water,
Sculls contain brains,
Therefore a man in a skiff has got water in the brains

> from PLUCK EXAMINATION PAPERS by 'Scriblerus
> Redivivus' (Henry Slatter, Oxford, 1836)

PUNCH

Elegy On The Porpoise

Dead, is he? Yes, and wasn't I glad when they carried
    away his corpus?
A great, black, oily, wallowing, walloping, plunging,
    ponderous porpus.
What call had Mr Frank Buckland, which I don't deny
    his kindness,
To take and shove in my basin a porpoise troubled with
    blindness?
I think it was like his impudence, and praps a little
    beyond,
To poke a blubbering brute like that in a gentle-fish's
    private pond,
Did he know as I am the King of Fish, and written down in
    histories

---

down to the end) without a candle : nor at the crack of dawn does
a savage scout arrive to rouse their weary heads from sleep with
three hundred insistent knocks. But instead, Alma Mater loads
them with gifts, and they can attend or cut chapel whenever they
wish. If they do not come in adorned with the velvet hood, they
don't have to eat fish at their high table, and it is perfectly all
right for them to cut any tutorial they like. For them no lectures,
just peace and quiet and a life where plucking is unknown.

As meat for his master, that is to say, for Victoria the
    Queen, his mistress,
And, if right was done, I shouldn't be here, but be sent in
    a water-parcel
To swim about in a marble tank in the gardings of
    Windsor Castle:
And them as forgets the law of the land which is made
    to rule and control,
And keeps a Royal Fish to themselves, may find themselves
    in a hole.
Is a King like me, I umbly ask, to be put in a trumpery
    puddle,
For Fellows to walk about and spy and talk zoological
    muddle,
And swells to come for a Sunday lounge, with French,
    Italians, and Germans.
Which would be better to stop at home and think of the
    morning sermons?
And then of a Monday to be used in a more obnoxious
    manner,
Stared at by tags and rags and bobtails as all come in
    for a Tanner?
Mr Kingfisher Buckland, Sir, I think you might be ashamed
    of yourself.
And then I can't be left alone, but you come and stick
    in a big
Blind blustering snorting oily beast which is only an old
    Sea-Pig.
I'm heartily glad he is dead, the pig: I was pleased, to my
    very marrow,
To see the keeper wheel him away in that dirty old
    garding barrow.
And though it was not flattering, last Sunday as ever
    were,
To hear the swells as had read the *Times* come rushing
    up for a stare,
And crying Bother the Sturgeon, it's the Porpus I want
    to see,

And going away in a state of huff because there was only
    Me,
It was pleasant (and kings has right divine to feel a little
    malicious)
To see 'em sent to behold his cops in the barrow behind
    the fish-house.
So when Mr Buckland next obtains a porpus as wants
    a surgeon.
Perhaps he won't insert that pig beside of a Royal
    Sturgeon.
I've heard the Tench is a curing fish and effects a perfect
    cure
Of other fish put into his pond, which he's welcome to
    do, I'm sure,
But don't bring sick porpuses up to me, I'm kin to the
    old Sea-Devil,
And though a king I'm not inclined to be touching fish
    for the evil.
Besides, a porpus isn't a fish, but a highly deweloped man,
Improved, of course, with a tail and fins, on the famous
    Westiges plan,
The Phocoena Rondoletii, though his scent in this
    sultry weather
Was not like rondoletia nor frangipanni neither,
But that is neither here nor there, and as I previously said,
From the bottom of both my heart and my pond I'm
    glad the Porpus is dead.

Poetic Classics For Prosaic Readers

The first King of Rome was called Romulus.
His position was slightly anomalous,
Him we cannot esteem, as
He killed brother Remus
For reading him cynical homilies.

The second was Numa Pompilius.
His subjects were really so silly as
To believe he was taught
By a nymph whom he caught
In a grot. Let's be glad we know *melius*.*

The third was named Tullus Hostilius.
It's uncertain of whom he was *filius*†;
But certain his vows
Brought down fire on his house,
For his incense made Jupiter bilious.

The fourth he was called Ancus Martius,
Who was full of most laudable vartues;
His Majesty's action
Gave much satisfaction,
And he probably wore fine moustarchios.

The fifth was Tarquinius and Priscus
He was proud of his wife and his whiskers;
Two Princes he'd chiselled
(When Ancus had mizzled)
Took and broke his old head with a discus

The sixth he was called Servius Tullius;
On reforms he could speak quite as dully as
Any Taylor, or Odger‡
Or Democrat codger
Of that sort, who stands up to bully us.

---

* better.
† son.
‡ George Odger (1820–77), became in 1862 secretary of the London trades union. He made five unsuccessful attempts to enter Parliament, and in 1864 organised the meeting which led to the formation of the Working Men's International Association, and was its president in 1870.

The Last was Tarquinius Superbus
(His wife o'er her father drove her bus),
He turned out such a brute
That Rome upped with her foot
And cried, 'There! No more Kings shall disturb us.'

MONTY PYTHON

The London Casebook Of Detective René Descartes

The acrid scent of stale cigarette smoke hung wearily in
the air of the dingy Whitehall office. The only sound was
the querulous buzz of a prying bluebottle indolently hopping among the familiar dun box files clustered above the
fireplace occupied by the regulation Scotland Yard electric
fire, one bar of which flickered hesitantly in a perfunctory
attempt to warm the November gloom.

Detective-Inspector René 'Doubty' Descartes absent-
mindedly flicked grey-white ash from the sleeve of his
only vicuña jacket and stared moodily across the pigeon-
violated rooftops of Whitehall. 'I muse,' he thought.
'Therefore ...'

The ginger telephone shrilled its urgent demand. Descartes, rudely awakened from his reverie, snatched the
receiver to his ear.

'Descartes here,' he posited.

'Sorry to interrupt, sir.' The familiar tones of Sergeant
Warnock floated down the line. 'Sergeant Warnock here.'

'How can you be sure?'

'I think I am Sergeant Warnock, therefore I am Sergeant
Warnock,' replied Sergeant Warnock confidently. Some
of Doubty's thinking was beginning to rub off.

'But if you thought you were Marcus Aurelius would
you therefore be Marcus Aurelius?' parried the forensic
savant deftly.

'Er ... probably not,' admitted the trusty servant, trust-
ing his arm. When the Detective-Inspector was in moods

like this, routine business could take days.

'So simply because you think you are Sergeant Warnock, it does not necessarily follow that you are,' his postulate continued.

'But, sir, you said, "You think something therefore you are something".'

'No, no, sergeant, you haven't got it at all.'

'Well, sir,' the stalwart gamely countered, 'there must be a strong probability that I am Sergeant Warnock. Couldn't we on this occasion proceed on that assumption.'

'I'm afraid that it is this "beyond all reasonable doubt" philosophy that has bedevilled the reputation of police thinking since the days of that woolly pragmatist Peel.'

'But this is an urgent matter, sir. The Prime Minister is on the other line.'

'My dear putative sergeant, this problem of your identity is something we are going to have to sort out sooner or later.'

'But it's the *Prime Minister*, sir.'

'But how do we *know* that it is the Prime Minister?'

'Oh Christ.'

'This is a perfect illustration of my theme, Warnock . . .'

'Aha!'

'. . . if that is indeed to whom I am speaking. If I cannot be sure of the Warnockness of the person or apparent person with whom I am at present speaking, how *a fortiori* can I accept an authentication from this source of a third party of whom my direct and verifiable experience is even further removed?'

'He's rung off anyway, sir.'

'If indeed he was ever there.'

'Well if he was, sir, then he almost definitely asked you to call him back. Can I get him for you, sir?'

'Not so fast, sergeant, for I will assume for the moment that that is who you are.'

'Thank you very much, sir.'

'If I now call the Prime Minister, how is he for certain to know that he is speaking to *me*?'

'Ah but that's *his* problem, sir.'

'But how shall I know that I am speaking to *him*?'

'You're calling him, sir.'

'But suppose I speak to someone, thinking him to be the Prime Minister when in fact he is not, *then* the Prime Minister will be disclosing what may well be state secrets to another party, believing him to be me.'

'But surely, sir, just because *you're* speaking to a third party it does not follow as a necessary consequence that the P.M. is speaking to anyone at all.'

Descartes sucked thoughtfully at his familiar thumb. '...Good work, sergeant. Get him *toute suite*.' Then replacing the receiver he ruefully swung round on the familiar leather trapeze and stared wistfully out of the window. 'Funny old London,' he thought. At least the pouring rain had stopped. Or rather, it certainly seemed there was no entity a, such that 'x is rainy and pouring' was true when x was a, but not otherwise.

CHAPTER 2

The door of Number Ten shut and he found himself once again in the oddly unpleasant driving sleet and hail to which his fourteen years in London had still not accustomed him. Setting off briskly across the street, dodging the swishing taxis, he hurried towards the warm and beckoning portals of New Scotland Yard. Why was it, he mused, that the Prime Minister always lost his temper with him? How could the P.M. become so agitated about a country whose very existence had never been properly established? Let alone the intentions of its supposed inhabitants to obtain what the Prime Minister had persisted in referring to as 'secrets'. 'Relative secrets' Doubty could have accepted subject only to a few minor qualifications but his attempts to point out this terminological slackness had received alarming rebuffs from the Prime Minister, a man at the best of times inclined to leap to unsatisfactorily substantiated conclusions, but on this occasion made positively foolhardy by the presence of a man he clearly believed to be the president of the United States of America, on no better evidence, as far as Doubty could deduce, than an exact but superficial physical resemblance to the man normally referred to by the American people as the President, the presence of a couple of hundred alleged 'bodyguards', a so-called Vice-President and a small cavalcade. The last three items, as he had dutifully pointed out, could have been easily faked by a reasonably competent organiser and were in no way contingent upon the Presidentness of the Nixon-like person, while the appearance of the latter, although at first sight impressive to the untrained mind, was still explicable in terms of a twin, a 'double', a highly sophisticated working model, an ordinary optical illusion occurring simultaneously to the apparent Prime Minister and himself, a hallucination caused by the possible presence of certain substances in the Downing Street tea, or, and this was the possibility that Doubty had found increasingly attractive, an oleograph. And it was after all in an attempt to discount this last suspicion that he had struck the putative oleograph the light blow across the top of the head that had caused all the trouble. But why, mused a curious Doubty as he absent-mindedly picked slivers of Prime Ministerial telephone from his scalp, should he now be sent to Tonga in the guise of an ordinary police constable and for an unspecified length of time?

Was *this* to be the Big One?

CHAPTER 3

The acrid scent of stale coconut milk hung wearily in the air of the sun-drenched Tongan beach. The only sound was the insistent lapping of the prying waves indolently hopping among the familiar dun rock piles clustered about the bay occupied by the regulation Tongan Government-issue catamaran, one float of which glistened hesitantly in a perfunctory attempt to out-shine the August glare. Police Constable René 'Doubty' Descartes absent-mindedly flicked the familiar coconut shells from the sleeve of his only vicuña swimming trunks and stared pointlessly across the crab-befouled beaches of White-bay. 'I stare pointlessly,' he thought, 'therefore I ...' But his reverie was rudely interrupted by the sharp gurgle of a passing flying fish and turning on his familiar heel he picked his way briskly through the swirling lobsters towards the beckoning head of the beach and the equally beckoning cool of the familiar majestic New Reichenbach Falls so many feet above his head and slightly to one side.

As he mounted the ginger path leading to the bridge which so precariously straddled the churning, tumultuous uproar of this watery object, he mentally summarised the past fourteen months.

'Not much, really,' he opined to himself. 'Very little paper-work; very little paper; none at all actually; which is why I am summarizing my thoughts mentally.' Pleased with this conclusion he strode perfunctorily through the driving sunshine past the enchanting pink-shuttered office of the cheery waterfall-keeper, hardly noticing the cluster of blazing bougainvillaea just beyond, that reminds one so strongly of the cluster of blazing bougainvillaea that one sees just outside Harry's bar, at the corner of Victoria Street and A. A. Milne Crescent, in the main square of Tonga's sleepy capital Tongatapu, where I have been, as you can tell from this description.

By now P.C. Descartes had cautiously stepped out on to the unfamiliar wildly swaying bakelite footbridge which alone stood between him and a watery grave with some bits of rock in it. Staring down into the frothy cascading vortex he nonchalantly flicked the familiar ice-cold spume from his navy-blue vicuña helmet. 'I muse,' he mused, 'therefore I am about to be interrup–'

But his muse was interrupted by the lisping bark he had somehow half-expected.

'Good morning.' Edward de Bono, his arch enemy, and notoriously lateral thinker stood on the bridge, in a mysterious sideways position. 'Good morning,' he rasped angrily. No response ... 'Good morning,' he re-rasped fiercely, mentally sidling a little. The bakelite bridge seemed to rattle the more violently in reply. Descartes stood his bakelite and mused on the awesome de Bono's existence with all the power he could muster. De Bono, seeing the familiar tell-tale beads of sweat stand out on Doubty's forehead sensed victory. 'Snap!' the bakelite seemed to muse, and a second later, moving laterally, sent the two combatants in an unexpected direction and a probably watery grave respectively.

'A long way down,' the inspector commented inwardly, disbelieving de Bono's existence to the last as he apparently plummeted.

'Somewhere in the distance one could hear the faint familiar cry of an eloping litter-bin,' yelled de Bono, thinking laterally to the last. There was a sickening crash, followed by a sickening cry, then two sickening splashes, a sickening crunch and then three sickening noises that are very difficult to describe.

'So ... I am dead,' thought Doubty. 'Wait a minute ... I'm thinking ... I think, therefore I....'

With one logical bound he was.

Monty Python's Big Red Book

A LOOSE COVER FOR YOU! Yes! At last we can offer a complete range of home-knitted loose covers, made to fit yourself or any relative. These are a MUST for people who tend to remain stationary for long periods. STOPS dust getting into the cracks and crevices that Nature left unprotected. Fit a loose cover over yourself today! Lamprey Loose Covers, Ltd., The Dales, Wonersh.

WHY NOT be different this Christmas? Why not send your friends a lump of cold sick? It may cost less than you think! Write to: 'VOM-IT' Products, 13 Elgarth Road, Preston, Lancs. Sole Props: Mr. & Mrs. Ernie Scrotem.

PIANOS repaired and put in little cardboard boxes. WE ARE EXPERTS. A family business since 1869. Avoid all imitations. The Pianos Into Little Cardboard Boxes Ltd., 268 Dagworth Ave. Bolton.

HOLIDAYS ARE FUN in our new range of exciting swimwear. Yes! You too can be the sensation of the beach this Summer for *Only 39/6*. Also please come home Marjorie, the kids miss you – love Ted. (Managing Director, SWIM-MEX SWIMWEAR LTD.)

POETS! Poets are needed by a reputable publisher to fill a new annual of poems for this year. Why not send your poems for a critical appreciation and the chance of World-Wide publication to: Sanitary Poetical Undertakings Ltd., Rip St. Government Surplus Town, Sussex.

THE DELILAH Body-Building Course ... Put on muscles in interesting places. James Cagney of Altringham writes: 'I never knew I had a muscle there until I took your DELILAH body-building course, and now I have two. I can also pick up a mug of cocoa with my left ear.' Write TODAY: Delilah Body-Building, Brighton.

FOR SALE: tin of boot polish, part-used. Willing to exchange for 1964 Rolls Royce in Maroon or Royal Blue. Must have M.O.T. Write: Ron Hopeful, The Cut, Bishop's Stortford.

FOR SALE: Desirable property in Neasden. Immaculate condit. Blonde hair. Will do anything. Write: c/o The Halifax Building Soc. Upper Bute St.

WHY throw away those unwanted undergarments? Why not send them direct to: Reg Cattermole, 136 The Buildings, Prestatyn.

FOR SALE: Large bed-ridden female, keen on astrology and the reestablishment of diplomatic relations with Communist China. Will part-exchange for slim brunette with slightest interest in development of trade with emergent African nations. PO Box ZZZZZZZ

FOR SALE : Parrot. Likes children, but will make do with cuttlefish and a bit of grass seed. Write : Box 15263645373-8475647585756474859029857625341635271827364538 1.

HOLIDAY in Spain? Why not come to Cleethorpes? We've got everything the bloody Dagos have got, plus you don't have to learn their stupid language. 'Cleethorpes – a good place for liberal intellectuals.'

WINDOWS BROKEN : Deposit accounts smeared with lard! Ring Ted & Arthur Irresponsible, 2785481.

NOW! the OFFER you have been WAITING FOR : Fighter bombers for only £40. Will carry nuclear payload. Ring : Mrs Lewis 048 39719 after 6 p.m.

1958 Morris for sale. Really VERY GOOD. Although it doesn't sound it, I must say. But really it's QUITE ALRIGHT. Oh I know the back door doesn't shut properly, but once you've got the knack it's fairly easy. It's only £80 after all. Oh alright £70. Ring : Sid Letchworth 0000001. Oh alright £60.

Small brown and green thing for sale. Could be Vermeer. £5 O.N.D. BOX 213.

TOP PRICES PAID for anything. Ring : J. R. Silly 068 7564 54.

BUZZ ALDRIN MODELS. Have a life-sized model of America's No. 2 Spaceman in your living room! Says, 'Hi! I'm Buzz,' and produces sample of Moon rock. Ring : NASA, HOUSTON, TEXAS, Houston 2435645345 After 7.30 p.m.

DON'T THROW AWAY your old jam-jars. Send them to Mrs. Betty Dago, 18a Leytonstone High St., and she will throw them away.

SURPRISE YOUR FRIENDS. Burn their houses down. The British League of Arsonists needs urgent help.

3rd nymphomaniac girl required to share student mini-bus to Cairo. No middle class. Dead Butch Adventure Tours Ltd., Earls Court Rd.

WELSH DRESSER for disposal. Ex-BBC. Would share digs with ex-theatrical. Ring Benny the Bent, Porthcawl 2000.

FOR YOU AT 65! A dozen haddocks. Write NOW to: The Imperial Consolidated But Rather Fish-Orientated Insurance Co.

SEND NO MONEY to the Extremely Poor Society.

NEW MEMBERS urgently required for Suicide Club. Watford Area.

DO YOU SUFFER FROM upset stomach, bad breath, poor digestion, heartburn, heat rash and indigestion? Eurgh.

WELSHMAN will exchange 1927 mint condition bronze halfpenny for one exactly the same. Pointless Swaps Ltd., Swansea.

The Big Fight

Already it's been dubbed 'Fight of the Fortnight'.

KEN CLEAN-AIR SYSTEM

Height	6 foot 5
Weight	15 stone
Reach	36 inches
Inside leg	34 inches
Previous fights	24

ELAINE GRIFFITHS

Height	5 foot
Weight	7 stone
Reach	25 inches
Inside leg	24 inches
Previous fights	none

Ken is interested in gravel, and collects housebricks Elaine is a southpaw and is keen on Cliff Richard records.

Can Ken do it?

by A. PUNDIT

The great white hope of British boxing takes to the ring tonight with a record of 24 fights and only three convictions. He's fighting fit again now that an operation has removed the small particle of brain that was lodged in his skull. Dubbed 'invincible' by his mother, each morning now for several months Ken has got up at 3 a.m. to jog the 15 miles from his 2 bedroomed, 6 bath-roomed, 4 up, 2 down, 3 to go luxury house in Reigate to the Government's Pesticide Research Centre at Shoreham. Nobody knows why. Tonight he takes on Elaine Griffiths, the plucky little Birmingham schoolgirl who's just turned professional after one amateur fight. (A draw against Myra Robinson.) Can Ken do it? Personally I think he can. I think Ken has the experience and the know-how to batter this young schoolgirl to the ground in a bloody pulp within ten rounds to give British Boxing the shot in the arm I so badly need.

Norman Mailer Himself on the big fight

Norman Mailer writes about his ego.

Tonight Ken will be swimming down subterranean rivers of exhaustion, staring at the light of his own death in the self-fulfilling process of his ego-consciousness, travelling the crossroads of karma, past the yawning appeals of the swooning catacombs of oblivion, experiencing the psychologically incomprehensible, the ultimately immense incommunicable oneness of a thousand dollar a paragraph, syndicated with repeats.

Norman Mailer will be Resumed as Soon as Possible.

Short Poem

Po

SIR ARTHUR QUILLER-COUCH

The Famous Ballad Of The Jubilee Cup

You may lift me up in your arms, lad, and turn my face
    to the sun,
For a last look back at the dear old track where the Jubilee
    Cup was won;
And draw your chair to my side, lad – no, thank ye, I feel
    no pain –
For I'm going out with the tide, lad, but I'll tell you the
    tale again.

I'm seventy-nine, or nearly, and my head it has long turned
    grey,
But it all comes back as clearly as though it was yester-
    day–
The dust, and the bookies shouting around the clerk of the
    scales,
And the clerk of the course, and the nobs in force, and 'Is
    'Ighness, the Pr*nce of W*les.

Twas a nine-hole thresh to wind'ard, but none of us cared
    for that,
With a straight run home to the service tee, and a finish
    along the flat.
'Stiff?' Ah, well you may say it! Spot-barred, and at five–
    stone–ten!
But at two and a bisque I'd ha' run the risk; for I was a
    greenhorn then.

So we stripped to the B. Race signal, the old red swallow-
tail–
There was young Ben Bolt, and the Portland colt, and
Aston Villa, and Yale;
And W. G., and Steinitz, Leander, and The Saint,
And the German Emperor's Meteor, a-looking as fresh as
paint;

John Roberts (scratch), and Safety Match, The Lascar, and
Lorna Doone,
Oom Paul (a bye), and Romany Rye, and me upon Wooden
Spoon;
And some of us cut for partners, and some of us strung to
baulk,
And some of tossed for stations – But there, what use to
talk?

Three-quarter-back on the Kingsclere crack was station
enough for me,
With a fresh jackyarder blowing and the Vicarage goal
a-lee!
And I leaned and patted her centre-bit, and eased the quid
in her cheek,
With a 'Soh, my lass!' and a 'woa, you brute!' – for she
could do all but speak.

She was geared a thought too high, perhaps; she was
trained a trifle fine;
But she had the grand reach forward! I never saw such a
line!
Smooth-bored, clean-run, from her fiddle head with its
dainty ear half-cock,
Hard-bit, *pur sang*, from her overhang to the heel of her
off hind sock.

Sir Robert he walked beside me as I worked her down to
the mark;
'There's money on this, my lad,' said he, 'and most of 'em's
running dark;

But ease the sheet if you're bunkered, and pack the scrim-
 mages tight,
And use your slide at the distance, and we'll drink to your
 health to-night!'

But I bent and tightened my stretcher. Said I to myself,
 said I,
'John Jones, this here is the Jubilee Cup, and you have to
 do or die.'
And the words weren't hardly spoken when the umpire
 shouted 'Play!'
And we all kicked off from the Gasworks end with a
 'Yoicks!' and a 'Gone away!'

And at first I thought of nothing, as the clay flew by in
 lumps,
But stuck to the old Ruy Lopez, and wondered who'd call
 for trumps,
And luffed her close to the cushion, and watched each one
 as it broke,
And in triple file up the Rowley mile we went like a trail
 of smoke.

The Lascar made the running: but he didn't amount to
 much,
For old Oom Paul was quick on the ball, and headed it
 back to touch;
And the whole first flight led off with the right, as The
 Saint took up the pace,
And drove it clean to the putting green and trumped it
 there with an ace.

John Roberts had given a miss in baulk, but Villa cleared
 with a punt;
And keeping her service hard and low, The Meteor forged
 to the front,
With Romany Rye to windward at dormy and two to
 play,
And Yale close up – but a Jubilee Cup isn't run for every
 day.

We laid our course for the Warner – I tell you the pace
    was hot!
And again off Tattenham Corner a blanket covered the lot.
Check side! Check side! Now steer her wide! and barely
    an inch of room,
With the lascar's tail over our lee rail, and brushing
    Leander's boom!

We were running as strong as ever – eight knots – but it
    couldn't last;
For the spray and the bails were flying, the whole field
    tailing fast;
And the Portland colt had shot his bolt, and Yale was
    bumped at the Doves,
And The Lascar resigned to Steinitz, stale-mated in fifteen
    moves.

It was bellows to mend with Roberts – starred three for a
    penalty kick:
But he chalked his cue and gave 'em the butt, and Oom
    Paul scored the trick –
'Off-side – no-ball – and at fourteen all! Mark cock! and
    two for his nob!'
When W.G. ran clean through his lee, and yorked him
    twice with a lob.

He yorked him twice on a crumbling pitch, and wiped his
    eye with a brace,
But his guy-rope split with the strain of it, and he dropped
    back out of the race;
And I drew a bead on The Meteor's lead, and challenging
    none too soon,
Bent over and patted her garboard strake, and called upon
    Wooden Spoon.

She was all of a shiver forward, the spoondrift thick on
    her flanks,
But I'd brought her an easy gambit, and nursed her over
    the banks;

She answered her helm the darling! – and woke up now
    with a rush,
While the Meteor's jock he sat like a rock – he knew we
    rode for his brush!

There was no one else left in it. The Saint was using his
    whip,
And Safety Match, with a lofting catch, was pocketed
    deep at slip;
And young Ben Bolt with his niblick took miss at Leander's
    lunge,
But he topped the net with the ricochet, and Steinitz threw
    up the sponge.

But none of the lot could stop the rot – nay, don't ask *me*
    to stop! –
The Villa had called for lemons, Oom Paul had taken his
    drop,
And both were kicking the referee. Poor fellow! he done
    his best;
But, being in doubt, he'd ruled them out – which he
    always did when pressed.

So, inch by inch, I tightened the winch, and chucked
    the sandbags out–
I heard the nursery cannons pop, I heard the bookies
    shout:
'The Meteor wins!' 'No, Wooden Spoon!' 'Check!'
    'Vantage!' 'Leg before!'
'Last lap!' 'Pass Nap!' At his saddle-flap I put up the helm
    and wore.

You may overlap at the saddle-flap, and yet be loo'd on the
    tape:
And it all depends upon changing ends, how a seven-year-
    old will shape;
It was tack and tack to the Lepe and back – a fair ding-
    dong to the Ridge,
And he led by his forward canvas yet as we shot 'neath
    Hammersmith Bridge.

He led by his forward canvas – he led from his strongest
    suit –
But along we went on a roaring scent, and at Fawley I
    gained a foot.
He fisted off with his jigger, and gave me his wash – too
    late!
Deuce – vantage – check! By neck and neck we rounded
    into the straight.

I could hear the 'Conquering 'Ero' a-crashing on Godfrey's
    band,
And my hopes fell sudden to zero, just there with the race
    in hand –
In sight of the Turf's Blue Ribbon, in sight of the umpire's
    tape,
As I felt the tack of her spinnaker crack, as I heard the
    steam escape!

Had I lost at that awful juncture my presence of mind? ...
    but no!
I leaned and felt for the puncture, and plugged it there
    with my toe ...
Hand over hand by the Members' Stand I lifted and eased
    her up,
Shot – clean and fair – to the crossbar there, and landed
    the Jubilee Cup!

'The odd by a head, and leg before,' so the Judge he gave
    the word:
And the Umpire shouted 'Over!' but I neither spoke nor
    stirred.
They crowded round: for there on the ground I lay in a
    dead-cold swoon,
Pitched neck and crop on the turf atop of my beautiful
    Wooden Spoon.

Her dewlap tire was punctured, her bearings all red-hot;
She'd a lolling tongue, and her bowsprit sprung, and her
    running gear in a knot;

And amid the sobs of her backers, Sir Robert loosened
    her girth
And led her away to the knacker's. She had raced her last
    on earth!

But I mind me well of the tear that fell from the eye of
    our noble Pr*nce,
And the things he said as he tucked me in bed – and I've
    lain there ever since;
Tho' it all gets mixed up queerly that happened before my
    spill,
But I draw my thousand yearly : it'll pay for the doctor's
    bill.

I'm going out with the tide, lad. You'll dig me a humble
    grave,
And whiles you will bring your bride, lad, and your sons
    (if sons you have),
And there, when the dews are weeping, and the echoes
    murmur 'Peace!'
And the salt, salt tide comes creeping and covers the
    popping-crease,
In the hour when the ducks deposit their eggs with a
    boasted force,
They'll look and whisper 'How was it?' and you'll take
    them over the course,
And your voice will break as you try to speak of the
    glorious first of June,
When the Jubilee Cup, with John Jones up, was won upon
    Wooden Spoon.

ℝ

RUDOLPH ERICH RASPE
'BARON MUNCHAUSEN'

The Surprising Adventures of Baron Munchausen

... My first visit to England was about the beginning of
the present King's reign. I had occasion to go down to
Wapping, to see some goods shipped, which I was sending
to some friends at Hamburg: after that business was over,
I took the Tower Wharf in my way back. Here I found
the sun very powerful; and I was so much fatigued that
I stepped into one of the cannon to compose me, where
I fell fast asleep. This was about noon; it was the fourth
of June: exactly at one o'clock these cannon were all
discharged, in memory of the day: they had been all
charged that morning, and having no suspicion of my
situation I was shot over the houses on the opposite side
of the river, into a farmer's yard, between Bermondsey
and Deptford, where I fell upon a large haystack, without
waking, and continued there in a sound sleep till hay
became so extravagantly dear (which was about three
months after) that the farmer found it to his interest to
send his whole stock to market: the stack I was reposing
upon was the largest in the yard, containing above five
hundred loads; they began to cut that first. I waked (with
the voices of the people who had ascended the ladders to
begin at the top) and got up, totally ignorant of my situation; in attempting to run away, I fell upon the farmer
to whom the hay belonged, and broke his neck, yet received no injury myself! I afterwards found, to my great

consolation, that this fellow was a most detestable character, always keeping the produce of his ground for extravagant markets.

... Upon this Island of Cheese grows great plenty of corn, the ears of which produce loaves of bread, ready made, of a round form like mushrooms. We discovered, in our rambles over this cheese, seventeen other rivers of milk, and ten of wine.

After thirty-eight days' journey we arrived on the opposite side to that on which we landed; here we found some blue mould, as cheese-eaters call it, from whence spring all kinds of rich fruit : instead of breeding mites it produced peaches, nectarines, apricots, and a thousand delicious fruits which we are not acquainted with. In these trees, which are of an amazing size, were plenty of birds' nests: amongst others was a kingfisher's, of prodigious magnitude; it was at least twice the circumference of the dome of St. Paul's Church in London; upon inspection, this nest was made of huge trees, curiously joined together; there were, let me see (for I make it a rule always to speak within compass), there were upwards of five hundred eggs in this nest, and each of them was as large as four common hogsheads, or eight barrels, and we could not only see but hear the young ones chirping within. Having, with great fatigue, cut open one of these eggs, we let out a young one un-feathered, considerably larger than twenty full-grown vultures. Just as we had given this youngster his liberty, the fisher lighted, and seizing our captain, who had been active in breaking the egg, in one of his claws, flew with him above a mile high, and then let him drop into the sea, but not till she had beaten all his teeth out of his mouth with her wings.

Dutchmen generally swim well; he soon joined us, and we retreated to our ship. On our return we took a different route, and observed many strange objects. We shot two wild oxen, each with one horn, also, like the inhabitants, except that it sprouted from between the eyes of these

animals; we were afterwards concerned at having destroyed them, as we found by inquiry they tamed these
creatures, and used them as we do horses, to ride upon and
draw their carriages; their flesh, we were informed, is
excellent, but useless where people live upon cheese and
milk. When we had reached within two days' journey of
the ship we observed three men hanging to a tall tree by
the heels: upon inquiring the cause of their punishment,
I found they had all been travellers, and upon their return
home had deceived their friends, by describing places they
never saw, and relating things that never happened: this
gave me no concern, *as I have ever confined myself to
facts.*

As soon as we arrived at the ship we unmoored, and set
sail from this extraordinary country, when, to our astonishment, all the trees upon the shore, of which there were
a great number, very tall and large, paid their respects to
us twice, bowing to exact time, and immediately recovered their former posture, which was quite erect.

By what we could learn of this Cheese, it was considerably larger than the continent of all Europe!

After sailing three months we knew not where, being
still without compass, we arrived in a sea which appeared
to be almost black; upon tasting it, we found it most
excellent wine, and had great difficulty to keep the sailors
from getting drunk with it. However, in a few hours we
found ourselves surrounded by whales, and other animals
of an immense magnitude, one of which appeared to be
too large for the eye to form a judgment of: we did not
see him till we were close to him. This monster drew our
ship, with all her masts standing, and sails bent, by suction,
into its mouth between its teeth, which were much larger
and taller than the masts of a first-rate man-of-war. After
we had been in his mouth some time he opened it pretty
wide, took in an immense quantity of water, and floated
our vessel, which was at least five hundred tons' burthen,
into his stomach; here we lay as quiet as at anchor in a
dead calm. The air, to be sure, was rather warm, and very

offensive. We found anchors, cables, boats and barges in abundance, and a considerable number of ships, some laden and some not, which this creature had swallowed. Everything was transacted by torchlight: no sun, no moon, no planet to make observations from. We were all generally afloat and aground twice a day: whenever he drank it became high water with us, and when he evacuated we found ourselves aground. Upon a moderate computation he took in more water at a single draught than is generally to be found in the Lake of Geneva, though that is about thirty miles in circumference.

On the second day of our confinement in these regions of darkness I ventured at low water, as we called it, when the ship was aground, to ramble with the Captain and a few of the other officers, with lights in our hands: we met with people of all nations, to the amount of upwards of ten thousand; they were going to hold a council how to recover their liberty; some of them having lived in this animal's stomach several years, there were several children here who had never seen the world, their mothers having lain in repeatedly in this warm situation. Just as the chairman was going to inform us of the business upon which we were assembled, this plaguey fish, becoming thirsty, drank in his usual manner: the water poured in with such impetuosity that we were all obliged to retreat to our respective ships immediately, or run the risk of being drowned; some were obliged to swim for it, and with difficulty saved their lives. In a few hours after we were more fortunate; we met again just after the monster had evacuated. I was chosen chairman, and the first thing I did was to propose splicing two main-masts together, and the next time he opened his mouth to be ready to wedge them in, so as to prevent his shutting it. It was unanimously approved. One hundred stout men were chosen upon this service. We had scarcely got our masts properly prepared when an opportunity offered: the monster opened his mouth. Immediately the top of the mast was placed against the roof, and the other end pierced his tongue, which

effectually prevented him from shutting his mouth. As
soon as everything in his stomach was afloat we manned
a few boats, who rowed themselves and us into the world.
The daylight, after — as near as we could judge — three
months' confinement in total darkness, cheered our spirits
surprisingly. When we had all taken our leave of this
capacious animal we mustered just a fleet of ninety-five
ships, of all nations, who had been in this confined situation.

JAMES REEVES

Oh, grim and gloomy,
So grim and gloomy
Are the caves beneath the sea.
Oh, rare but roomy
And bare and boomy
Those salt sea caverns be.

Oh slim and slimy
Or grey and grimy
Are the animals of the sea.
Salt and oozy
And safe and snoozy
The caves where those animals be.

Hark to the shuffling,
Huge and snuffling,
Ravenous, cavernous, great sea-beasts!
But fair and fabulous,
Tintinnabulous,
Gay and fabulous are their feasts.

Ah, but the queen of the sea,
The querulous, perilous sea!
How the curls of her tresses
The pearls on her dresses,
Sway and swirl in the waves,

How cosy and dozy,
How sweet sing-a-rosy
Her bower in the deep-sea caves!

Oh, rare but roomy
And bare and boomy
Those caverns under the sea,
And grave and grandiose,
Safe and sandiose
The dens of her denizens be.

E. V. RIEU

The Lady of Leigh

'Misery me!'
Said the Lady of Leigh,
As she queued for a bus in the Strand,
And callous conductresses, weary of work,
Drifted disdainfully into the murk
With a laugh at her lily-white hand.
'Oh the ladylike ease at Leigh on the Sea!
The curtains and comfort, the toast and the tea!
There goes another one – misery me!
Misery me!'
Said the Lady of Leigh.

ANTHONY ROBERTSON

How To Do And Say In England

A Chest Party

LORD SMITH   This year, winter makes itself percep-
tible.
LORD ROBINSON   I would winter past.

VISCOUNT BROWN   It frostles. Last night it rimed. Let us rap us warmly up.

LORD SMITH   The river is chockblocked with pieces of ice. Freezing! Thick enough sufficiently to be bearing.

LORD ROBINSON   What about a skate? Can I get a pair of skate lent?

VISCOUNT BROWN   Nay. One feels well only by the stove or not at all. Let us therefor commence a sporty party at Chest.

LORD SMITH   Where is the Chest board? I challenge at Chest!

LORD ROBINSON   I shall strive against you. Shall you direct the white Pieces? Very well, then, I select the blacks. You putsch first! On!

VISCOUNT BROWN   I shall adjudge the contest. Play fair! Do not act like not a gentleman with low-hand tricks and sly shoves!

(Play commences)

LORD SMITH   Finely putsched! You have intricated the game anew.

LORD ROBINSON   You mock.

LORD SMITH   It is chequ-mate. You have gained the party. I am incensed. I do violence to my feelings!

LORD ROBINSON   Don't violence to your feelings! It is only a game! I gained it! How happy I am! How delightful! Charming!

VISCOUNT BROWN   How pleasant are these games in the winter season, when one cannot sport about without!

W. ST. LEGER

A False Gallop of Analogies

'*The Chavender, or Chub*' – Izaak Walton

There is a fine stuffed chavender,
   A chavender, or chub,
That decks the rural pavender,
   The pavender, or pub,
Wherein I eat my gravender,
   My gravender, or grub.

How good the honest gravender!
   How snug the rustic pavender!
From sheets as sweet as lavender,
   As lavender, or lub,
I jump into my tavender,
   My tavender, or tub.

Alas! for town and clavender,
   For business and club!
They call me from my pavender
   Tonight; ay, there's the ravender
Ay, there comes in the rub!
   To leave each blooming shravender,
Each Spring-bedizened shrub,
   And meet the horsey savender,
The very forward sub
At dinner at the clavender,
And then at billiards dravender,

At billiards roundly drub
The self-sufficient cavender,
  The not ill-meaning cub,
Who me a bear will davender,
  A bear unfairly dub,
Because I sometimes snavender,
  Not too severely snub
His setting right the clavender,
  His teaching all the club!

Farewell to peaceful pavender,
  My river-dreaming pub,
To bed as sweet as lavender,
To homely, wholesome gravender,
And you, inspiring chavender,
Stuff'd chavender, or chub

OWEN SEAMAN

A Song of Renunciation
(after Swinburne)

In the days of my season of salad,
  When the down was as dew on my cheek,
And for French I was bred on the ballad,
  For Greek on the writers of Greek,
Then I sang of the rose that is ruddy,
  Of 'pleasure that winces and stings',
Of white women and wine that is bloody,
  And similar things.

Of Delight that is dear as Desi-er
  And Desire that is dear as Delight;
Of the fangs of the flame that is fi-er,
  Of the bruises of kisses that bite;
Of embraces that clasp and that sever,
  Of blushes that flutter and flee
Round the limbs of Dolores, whoever
  Dolores may be.

I sang of false faith that is fleeting
   As froth of the swallowing seas,
Time's curse that is fatal as Keating
   Is fatal to amorous fleas;
Of the wanness of woe that is whelp of
   The lust that is blind as a bat –
By the help of my Muse and the help of
   The relative THAT.

Panatheist, bruiser and breaker
   Of kings and the creatures of kings,
I shouted on Freedom to shake her
   Feet loose of the fetter that clings;
Far rolling my ravenous red eye,
   And lifting a mutinous lid,
To all monarchs and matrons I said I
   Would shock them – and did.

Thee I sang, and thy loves, O Thalassian,
   O 'noble and nude and antique!'
Unashamed in the 'fearless old fashion'
   Ere washing was done by the week;
When the 'roses and rapture' that girt you
   Were visions of delicate vice,
And the 'lilies and languors of virtue'
   Not nearly so nice.

O delights of the time of my teething,
   Félise, Fragoletta, Yolande!
Foam-yeast of a youth in its seething
   On blasted and blithering sand!
Snake-crowned on your tresses and belted
   With blossoms that coil and decay,
Ye are gone; ye are lost; ye are melted
   Like ices in May.

Hushed now is the bibulous bubble
   Of 'lithe and lascivious' throats;
Long stript and extinct is the stubble
   Of hoary and harvested oats;

From the sweets that are sour as the sorrel's
  The bees have abortively swarmed;
And Algernon's earlier morals
  Are fairly reformed.

I have written a loyal Armada,
  And posed in a Jubilee pose;
I have babbled of babies and played a
  New tune on the turn of their toes;
Washed white from the stain of Astarte,
  My books any virgin may buy;
And I hear I am praised by a party
  Called Something Mackay!

When erased are the records, and rotten
  The meshes of memory's net;
When the grace that forgives has forgotten
  The things that are good to forget;
When the trill of my juvenile trumpet
  Is dead and its echoes are dead;
Then the laurel shall lie on the crumpet
  And crown of my head!

An Ode To Spring In The Metropolis

(After Richard le Gallienne)

Is this the Scine?
And am I altogether wrong
About the brain,
Dreaming I hear the British tongue?
Dear Heaven! what a rhyme!
And yet 'tis all as good
As some that I have fashioned in my time,
Like *bud* and *wood*;
And on the other hand you couldn't have a
      more precise or neater
Metre.

Is this, I ask, the Seine?
And yonder sylvan lane,
Is it the *Bois*?
Ma foi!
Comme elle est chic, my Paris, my grisette!
Yet may I not forget
That London still remains the missus
Of this Narcissus.

No, No! 'tis not the Seine!
It is the artificial mere
That permeates St. James's Park.
The air is bosom-shaped and clear;
And, Himmel! do I hear the lark,
The good old Shelley-Wordsworth lark?
Even now, I prithee,
Hark
Him hammer
On Heaven's harmonious stithy,
Dew-drunken – like my grammar!

And O the trees!
Beneath their shade the hairless coot
Waddles at ease,
Hushing the magic of his gurgling beak;
Or haply in Tree-worship leans his cheek
Against their blind
And hoary rind,
Observing how the sap
Comes humming upwards from the tap –
Root!
Thrice happy, hairless coot!

And O the sun!
See, see, he shakes
His big red hands at me in wanton fun!
A glorious image that! it might be Blake's,
Or even Crackanthorpe's!
For though the latter writes in prose
He actually is a bard;

Yet Heaven knows
I find it passing hard
To think of any rhyme but *corpse*
For 'Crackanthorpe's'.

And O the stars! I cannot say
I see a star just now,
Not at this time of day;
But anyhow
The stars are all my brothers;
(This verse is shorter than the others).

O Constitution Hill!
(This verse is shorter still).

Oh! London, London in the Spring!
You are, you know you are,
So full of curious sights,
Especially by nights.
From gilded bar to gilded bar
Youth goes his giddy whirl,
His heart fulfilled of Music-Hall,
His arm fulfilled of girl!
I frankly call
That last effect a perfect pearl!

I know it's
Not given to many poets
To frame so fair a thing
As this of mine, of Spring.
Indeed, the world grows Lilliput
All but
A precious few, the heirs of utter godlihead,
Who wear the yellow flower of blameless
        bodlihead!

And they, with Laureates dead, look down
On smaller fry unworthy of the crown,
Mere mushroom men, puff-balls that advertise
And bravely think to brush the skies.
Great is advertisement with little men!

Moi, qui vous parle, L-G-ll-nn-.
Have told them so;
I ought to know!

WILLIAM KEAN SEYMOUR

Peter Gink

(*After Sherwood Anderson*)

Peter had spent the day varnishing coffins in the iron shed at the rear of old Ephraim Gink's shop. Venomously hissing *John Brown's Body* he had worked and worked with little dancing shapes of death in his thoughts.

'They are all dead,' he had repeated a thousand times as he smoothed the polish over the pitch pine. 'They are all dead, they are all dead.' Soon his father's friends in Main Street would be dead, in fact, frilled and furbished and brass-plated and mourned – for a day. Only for a day, or a month at most. But if they but knew they were dead now, creeping along Main Street with their dead souls shining like codfish. He sniggered at the thought. So convinced was he that they were dead that, as he worked, he composed little crude epitaphs.

> Bill Whelan lies here,
> Slit from ear to ear.

That was one of them, and when he went along Main Street he stopped by the kerosene-store and looked across the street at Bill Whelan frying his pork under the gas-flares. Their cross-eyes never met, but Bill Whelan shuddered and dropped a hand of pork.

> 'Bill Whelan lies here,
> Slit from ear to ear.'

Peter Gink hissed the rhyme to himself, and then crooning softly, 'Dead, all dead,' passed on. At the cutler's shop he stopped and thought of Reverend Tomkins. He would like to stab him a million times with the glittering nail scissors hanging there on the brass wire. He passed on; a definite determination had come into his mind. No he wouldn't kill Bill Whelan with a razor, or Reverend Tomkins with the scissors; he would lure them separately to Cyrus Bone's disused lean-to in the centre of the beanfields, tie their limbs up with coffin-tape, and gnaw them with his teeth till they were dead and unrecognizable.

Returning home along Main Street, he lingered only to fill his coat-pocket with hot peanuts. He went straight up to his room, sniggering quietly. Inside he was safe with his dream. He gnawed ecstatically at the last remaining knob of the bedstead. 'All dead,' he gasped, 'all dead.'

His mother found him dead there the next morning. He had gnawed the curtains into paper pulp, the legs of the chairs had been nibbled to matchstick proportions, holes gaped in the plaster walls where his sharp teeth had been working frantically, and pinned in the remains of the bolster was the crude rhyme:

> Bill Whelan lies here,
> Gnawed from ear to ear.

W. C. SELLAR & R. J. YEATMAN

1066 And All That

Britain Conquered Again

The withdrawal of the Roman legions to take part in Gibbon's Decline and Fall of the Roman Empire (due to a clamour among the Romans for pompous amusements such as bread and circumstances) left Britain defenceless and subjected Europe to that long succession of Waves of which History is chiefly composed. While the Roman Empire was overrun by waves not only of Ostrogoths, Vizigoths, and even Goths, but also of Vandals (who destroyed works of art) and Huns (who destroyed everything and everybody, including Goths, Ostrogoths, Vizigoths, and even Vandals), Britain was attacked by waves of Picts (and, of course, Scots) who had recently learnt how to climb the wall, and of Angles, Saxons, and Jutes who, landing at Thanet, soon overran the country with fire (and, of course the sword).

Important Note

The Scots (originally Irish, but by now Scotch) were at this time inhabiting Ireland, having driven the Irish (Picts) out of Scotland; while the Picts (originally Scots) were now Irish (living in brackets) and *vice versa*. It is essential to keep these distinctions clearly in mind (and *verce visa*).

Humiliation of the Britons

The brutal Saxon invaders drove the Britons westward into Wales and compelled them to become Welsh; it is now considered doubtful whether this was a Good Thing. Memorable among the Saxon warriors were Hengist and his wife (? or horse), Horsa. Hengist made himself King in the South. Thus Hengist was the first English King and his wife (or horse), Horsa, the first English Queen (or horse). The country was now almost entirely inhabited by Saxons and was therefore renamed England, and thus (naturally) soon became C. of E. This was a Good Thing, because previously the Saxons had worshipped some dreadful gods of their own called Monday, Tuesday, Wednesday, Thursday, Friday, and Saturday.

CHAPTER 3
The Conversion of England

Noticing some fair-haired children in the slave market one morning, Pope Gregory, the memorable Pope, said (in Latin), 'What are those?' and on being told that they were Angels, made the memorable joke – '*Non Angli, sed Angeli*' ('*not* Angels, but *Anglicans*') and commanded one of his Saints called St Augustine to go and convert the rest.

The conversion of England was thus effected by the landing of St Augustine in Thanet and other places, which resulted in the country being overrun by a Wave of

Saints. Among these were St Ive, St Pancra, the great St Bernard (originator of the clerical collar), St Bee, St Ebb, St Neot (who invented whisky), St Kit and St Kin, and the Venomous Bead (author of *The Rosary*).

England was now divided into seven kingdoms and so ready were the English to become C. of E. that on one memorable occasion a whole Kingdom was easily converted by a sparrow.

Wave of Egg-Kings

Soon after this event Egg-Kings were found on the thrones of all these kingdoms, such as Eggberd, Eggbreth, Eggfroth, etc. None of them, however, succeeded in becoming memorable — except in so far as it is difficult to forget such names as Eggbirth, Eggbred, Eggbeard, Eggfish, etc. Nor is it even remembered by what kind of Eggdeath they perished.

CHAPTER 4
Britain Conquered Again

The conversion of Britain was followed by a Wave of Danes, accompanied by their sisters or *Sagas*, and led by such memorable warriors as Harold Falsetooth and Magnus the Great, who, landing correctly in Thanet, overran the country from right to left, with fire.* After this the Danes invented a law called the Danelaw, which easily proved that since there was nobody else left alive there, all the right-hand part of England belonged to them. The Danish Conquest was, however, undoubtedly a *Good Thing*, because although it made the Danes top nation for a time it was the cause of Alfred the Cake (and in any case they were beaten utterly *in the end* by Nelson).

By this time the Saxons had all become very old like the Britons before them and were called *ealdormen*; when they had been defeated in a battle by the Danes they used to sing little songs to themselves such as the memorable fragment discovered in the Bodleian Library at Oxford:

---

* And, according to certain obstinate historians, the Sword.

Old-Saxon Fragment

Syng a song of Saxons
In the Wapentake of Rye
Four and twenty eaoldormen
Too eaold to die. ...

                              Anon

The Danes, on the other hand, wrote a very defiant kind of Epic poetry, e.g. :

Beoleopard
OR
The Witan's Whail

Whan Cnut Cyng the Witan wold enfeoff
Of infangthief and outfangthief
Wonderlich were they enwraged
And wordwar waged
Sware Cnut great scot and lot
Swingë wold ich this illbegotten lot.

Wroth was Cnut and wrothword spake.
Well wold he win at wopantake.
Fain wold he brakë frith and crackë heads
And than they shold worshippe his redes.

Swingéd Cnut Cyng with swung sword
Howléd Witanë hellë but hearkened his word
Murië sang Cnut Cyng
Outfangthief is Damgudthyng.

CHAPTER 5
Alfred the Cake

King Alfred was the first Good King, with the exception of Good King Wenceslas, who, though he looked 4th, really came first (it is not known, however, what King Wenceslas was King of). Alfred ought never to be confused with King Arthur, equally memorable but probably non-existent and therefore perhaps less important historically (unless he did exist).

There is a story that King Arthur once burnt some cakes belonging to Mrs Girth, a great lady of the time, at a place called Atheling. As, however, Alfred could not have been an Incendiary King *and* a Good King, we may dismiss the story as absurd, and in any case the event is supposed to have occurred in a marsh where the cakes would not have burnt properly. Cf. the famous lines of poetry about King Arthur and the cakes:

'Then slowly answered Alfred from the marsh –'

Arthur, Lord Tennyson

CHAPTER 6
Exgalahad and the British Navy

King Arthur invented Conferences because he was secretly a Weak King and liked to know what his memorable thousand and one Knights wanted to do next. As they were all parfitly jealous Knights he had to have the Memorable Round Table made to have the Conferences at, so that it was impossible to say which was top knight. He had a miraculous sword called Exgalahad with which he defeated the Danes in numerous battles. In this he was also much assisted by his marine inventions, including the water-clock and the British Navy. The latter invention occurred as follows.

Alfred noticed that the Danes had very long ships, so he built a great many more much longer ones, thus cleverly founding the British Navy. From that time onwards foreigners, who, unlike the English, do not prefer to fight against long odds, seldom attacked the British Navy. Hence the important International Law called the Rule Britannia, technically known as the Freedom of the Seas.

Humiliation of the Danes

The English resisted the Danes heroically under Alfred, never fighting except against heavy odds, till at the memorable Peace of Wedmore Alfred compelled the Danes, who were now (of course) beaten, to stop being Danes and become English and therefore C. of E. and get properly married.

For this purpose they were made to go back and start again at Thanet, after which they were called in future Thanes instead of Danes and were on our side and in the right and very romantic.

CHAPTER 7
Lady Windermere. Age of Lake Dwellers

Alfred had a very interesting wife called Lady Windermere (The Lady of the Lake), who was always clothed in the same white frock, and used to go bathing with Sir Launcelot (also of the Lake) and was thus a Bad Queen. It was also in King Arthur's time that the *Anglo-Saxon Chronicle* was published; this was the first English newspaper and had all the news about his victories, and Lady Windermere, and the Cakes, etc.

CHAPTER 8
Ethelread the Unready: A Weak King

Ethelread the Unready was the first Weak King of England and was thus the cause of a fresh Wave of Danes.

He was called the Unready because he was never ready when the Danes were. Rather than wait for him the Danes used to fine him large sums called Danegold, for not being ready. But though they were always ready, the Danes had very bad memories and often used to forget that they had been paid the Danegeld and come back for it almost before they had sailed away. By that time Ethelread was always unready again.

Finally, Ethelread was taken completely unawares by his own death and was succeeded by Canute.

CHAPTER 9
Canute, an Experimental King

This memorable monarch, having set out from Norway

to collect some Danegeld, landed by mistake at Thanet, and thus became King.

Canute and the Waves

Canute began by being a Bad King on the advice of his Courtiers, who informed him (owing to a misunderstanding of the Rule Britannia) that the King of England was entitled to sit on the sea without getting wet. But finding that they were wrong he gave up this policy and decided to take his own advice in future – thus originating the memorable proverb, 'Paddle your own Canute' – and became a Good King and C. of E., and ceased to be memorable. After Canute there were no more aquatic kings till William IV (see later, Creation of Piers).

Canute had two sons, Halfacanute and Partacanute, and two other offspring, Rathacanute and Hardlicanute, whom, however, he would never acknowledge, denying to the last that he was their Fathacanute.

CHAPTER 10
Edward the Confessor

On his death Canute's Kingdom was divided between two further sons, who had been previously overlooked, Aftercanute and Harold Harebrush. These were succeeded by Edward the Confessor. It was about this time that the memorable Mac Beth ('Ian Hay') known as the Bane of Fife, murdered a number of his enemies, including Mac-Duff, Lord Dunsinaney, Sleep, etc.

Edward the Confessor was with difficulty prevented from confessing to all these and many other crimes committed in his reign, as he was in the habit of confessing whether he had done it or not, and was thus a Weak King.

With Edward the Confessor perished the last English King (viz. Edward the Confessor), since he was succeeded by Waves of Norman Kings (French), Tudors (Welsh), Stuarts (Scottish), and Hanoverians (German), not to mention the memorable Dutch King – Williamanmary.

TEST PAPER I
Up to the End of 1066

1. Which do you consider were the more alike, Caesar or Pompey, or *vice versa*? (Be brief.)
2. Discuss, in latin or gothic (*but not both*), whether the Northumbrian Bishops were more schismatical than the Cumbrian Abbots. (Be bright.)
3. Which came first, A.D. or B.C.? (Be careful.)
4. Has it never occurred to you that the Romans *counted backwards*? (Be honest.)
5. How angry would you be if it was suggested
   (i) That the XIth Chap. of the *Consolations of Boethius* was an interpolated palimpsest?
   (ii) That an eisteddfod was an agricultural implement?
6. How would you have attempted to deal with
   (a) The Venomous Bead?
   (b) A Mabinogion or Wapentake? (Be quick.)
7. What would have happened if (a) Boadicea had been the daughter of Edward the Confessor? (b) Canute had succeeded in sitting on the waves?
   Does it matter?

CHAPTER 34
James I : A Tidy King

James I slobbered at the mouth and had favourites; he was thus a Bad King. He had, however, a very logical and tidy mind, and one of the first things he did was to have Sir Walter Raleigh executed for being left over from the previous reign. He also tried to straighten out the memorable confusion about the Picts, who, as will be remembered, were originally Irish living in Scotland, and the Scots, originally Picts living in Ireland. James tried to make things tidier by putting the Scots in Ulsters and planting them in Ireland, but the plan failed because the Picts had been lost sight of during the Dark Ages and were now nowhere to be found.

Gunpowder Plot

There were a great many plots and Parliaments in James
I's reign, and one of the Parliaments was called the Addled
Parliament because the plots hatched in it were all such
rotten ones. One plot, however, was by far the best plot
in History, and the day and month of it (although not, of
course, the year) are well known to be *utterly* and even
maddeningly MEMORABLE.

The Gunpowder Plot arose in the following way: the
King had recently invented a new table called *Avoirduroi*,
which said:

1 New Presbyter = 1 OLD PRIEST
0 Bishop   = 0 King.

James was always repeating, 'No Bishop, No King', to
himself, and one day a certain loyal citizen called Sir
Guyfawkes, a very active and conscientious man, over-
heard him, and thought it was the slogan of James's new
policy. So he decided to carry it out at once and made a
very loyal plan to blow up the King and the bishops and
everybody else in Parliament assembled, with gun-
powder.* Although the plan failed, attempts are made
every year on St Guyfawkes' Day to remind the Parliament
that it would have been a Good Thing.

Pilgrims' Progress

It was at this time that some very pious Englishmen, known
as the Early Fathers, who were being persecuted for not
learning *Avoiduroi*, sailed away to America in a ship
called the *Mayfly*; this is generally referred to as the Pilgrims' Progress and was one of the chief causes of America.

CHAPTER 35
Charles I and the Civil War

With the ascension of Charles I to the throne we come at
last to the Central Period of English History (not to be
confused with the Middle Ages, of course), consisting in

---

* Recently invented by Francis Bacon, author of Shakespeare, etc.

the *utterly memorable Struggle between the Cavaliers (Wrong but Wromantic) and the Roundheads (Right and Repulsive)*.

Charles I was a Cavalier King and therefore had a small pointed beard, long flowing curls, a large, flat, flowing hat, and *gay attire*. The Roundheads, on the other hand, were clean-shaven and wore tall conical hats, white ties, and *sombre garments*.

Under these circumstances a Civil War was inevitable.

The Roundheads, of course, were so called because Cromwell had all their heads made perfectly round, in order that they should present a uniform appearance when drawn up in line.

Besides this, if any man lost his head in action, it could be used as a cannon-ball by the artillery (which was done at the Siege of Worcester).

For a long time before the Civil War, however, Charles had been quarrelling with the Roundheads about what was right. Charles explained that there was a doctrine called the Divine Right of Kings, which said that:

(a) He was King, and that was right.
(b) Kings were divine, and that was right.
(c) Kings were right, and that was right.
(d) Everything was all right.

But so determined were the Roundheads that all this was all wrong that they drew up a Petition called the Petition of Right to show in more detail which things were wrong. This Petition said:

(a) That it was wrong for anyone to be put to death more than once for the same offence.
(b) *Habeas Corpus*, which meant that it was wrong if people were put in prison except for some reason, and that people who had been mutilated by the King, such as Prynne, who had often had his ears cut off, should always be allowed to keep their bodies.
(c) That Charles's memorable methods of getting money, such as Rummage and Scroungeage, were wrong.

But the most important cause of the Civil War was

Ship Money

Charles I said that any money which was Ship Money belonged to him; but while the Roundheads declared that Ship Money could be found only in the Cinq Ports, Charles maintained that no one but the King could guess right which was Ship Money and which wasn't. This was, of course, part of his Divine Right. The climax came when a villager called Hampden (memorable for his dauntless breast) advised the King to divine again.

This so upset Charles that he went back to Westminster, and after cinquing several ports burst into the House of Commons and asked in a very royal way for some birds which he said were in there. The Parliament, who were mostly Puritans, were so shocked that they began making solemn Leagues and Countenances. Charles therefore became very angry and complaining that the birds had flown raised his standard at Nottingham and declared war against Hampden and the Roundheads.

The War

At first the King was successful owing to Prince Rupert of Hentzau, his famous cavalry leader, who was very dashing in all directions. After this, many indecisive battles were fought at such places as Newbury, Edgehill, Newbury, Chalgrove Field, Newbury, etc., in all of which the Cavaliers were rather victorious.

The Roundheads therefore made a new plan in order to win the war after all. This was called the Self-Denying Ordnance and said that everyone had to deny everything he had done up to that date, and that nobody was allowed to admit who he was: thus the war could be started again from the beginning. When the Roundheads had done this they were called the New Moral Army and were dressed up as Ironclads and put under the command of Oliver Cromwell, whose Christian name was Oliver and who was therefore affectionately known as 'Old Nick'. Cromwell was not only moral and completely round in the head but had a large (round) wart on the nose. He was consequently victorious in all the remaining battles such as Newbury, Marston Moor, Edgehill (change for Chalgrove), Naseby, Newbury, etc.

Blood and Ironclads

When Charles I had been defeated he was brought to trial by the Rump Parliament – so-called because it had been sitting for such a long time – and was found guilty of being defeated in a war against himself, which was, of course, a form of High Treason. He was therefore ordered by Cromwell to go and have his head cut off (it was, the Roundheads pointed out, the wrong shape, anyway). So romantic was Charles, however, that this made little difference to him and it is very memorable that he walked and talked Half an hour after his Head was cut off.

On seeing this, Cromwell was so angry that he picked up the mace (the new and terrible Instrument of Government which he had invented) and, pointing it at the Head, shouted: 'Take away that Marble,' and announced that his policy in future would be just Blood and Ironclads. In order to carry out this policy he divided the country into twelve districts and set a Serjeant-Major over each of them.

Rule of the Serjeant-Majors

Nothing sickened the people of the rule of the Serjeant-Majors so much as their cruel habit of examining little boys *viva-voce*. For this purpose the unfortunate children were dressed in their most uncomfortable satins and placed on a stool. The Serjeant-Major would then ask such difficult questions as 'How's your Father?' or 'Animal, Vegetable, or Mineral?' and those who could not answer were given a cruel medicine called Pride's Purge. All this was called the Crommonwealth and was right but repulsive.

The Crowning Mercy

The Roundheads at length decided to offer Cromwell the

Crown. Cromwell, however, was unwilling and declared it was a Crowning Mercy when he found that it would not fit, having been designed for a Cavalier King.

Soon after, Cromwell died of a surfeit of Pride, Purges, Warts, and other Baubles.

WILLIAM SHAKESPEARE

Two Gentlemen Of Verona

Act II, Scene III. Verona. A Street
Enter LAUNCE, *leading a dog*

LAUNCE : Nay, 'twill be this hour ere I have done weeping : all the kind of the Launces have this very fault. I have received my proportion, like the prodigious son, and am going with Sir Proteus to the imperial's court. I think Crab my dog be the sourest-natured dog that lives : my mother weeping, my father wailing, my sister crying, our maid howling, our cat wringing her hands, and all our house in a great perplexity, yet did not this cruel-hearted cur shed one tear. He is a stone, a very pebble stone, and has no more pity in him than a dog; a Jew would have wept to have seen our parting : why, my grandam, having no eyes, look you, wept herself blind at my parting. Nay, I'll show you the manner of it. This shoe is my father; no, this left shoe is my father; no, no this left shoe is my mother; nay, that cannot be so neither – yes, it is so; it is so; it hath the worser sole. This shoe, with the hole in, is my mother, and this my father. A vengeance on't! there 'tis : now, sir, this staff is my sister; for, look you, she is as white as a lily and as small as a wand; this hat is Nan, our maid : I am the dog; no, the dog is himself, and I am the dog, – O! the dog is me, and I am myself; ay, so, so. Now come I to my father; 'Father, your blessing;' now should not the shoe speak a word for weeping; now should I kiss my father; well, he weeps on. Now come I to my mother; – O, that she could speak now like a wood woman!

Well, I kiss her; why, there 'tis; here's my mother's breath up and down. Now come I to my sister; mark the moan she makes: Now the dog all this while sheds not a tear nor speaks a word; but see how I lay the dust with my tears.

The Merry Wives Of Windsor

Act IV, Scene I
... Enter SIR HUGH EVANS.

How now, Sir Hugh! No school to-day?

EVANS. No; Master Slender is let the boys leave to play.

QUICK. Blessing of his heart!

MRS. PAGE. Sir Hugh, my husband says my son profits nothing in the world at his book: I pray you, ask him some questions in his accidence.

EVANS. Come hither, William; hold up your head; come.

MRS. PAGE. Come on, sirrah; hold up your head; answer your master, be not afraid.

EVANS. William, how many numbers is in nouns?

WILL. Two.

QUICK. Truly, I thought there had been one number more, because they say 'Od's nouns'.

EVANS. Peace your tattlings! What is *fair*, William?

WILL. *Pulcher.*

QUICK. Polecats! there are fairer things than polecats, sure.

EVANS. You are a very simplicity 'oman; I pray you peace. What is *lapis*, William?

WILL. A stone.

EVANS. And what is a *stone*, William?

WILL. A pebble.

EVANS. No, it is *lapis*: I pray you remember in your prain.

WILL. *Lapis.*

EVANS. That is good William. What is he, William, that does lend articles?

WILL. Articles are borrowed of the pronoun, and be thus
declined, *Singulariter, nominativo, hic, haec, hoc.*

EVANS. *Nominativo, hig, hag, hog;* pray you, mark:
genitivo, hujus. Well, what is your accusative case?

WILL. *Accusativo, hinc.*

EVANS. I pray you, have your remembrance, child;
accusativo, hung, hang, hog.

QUICK. Hang hog is Latin for bacon, I warrant you.

EVANS. Leave your prabbles, 'oman. What is the focative
case, William?

WILL. *O vocativo, O.*

EVANS. Remember, Willam: focative is *caret.*

QUICK. And that's a good root.

EVANS. 'Oman, forbear.

MRS. PAGE. Peace!

EVANS. What is your genitive case plural, William?

WILL. Genitive case?

EVANS. Ay.

WILL. *Genitive, horum, harum, horum.*

QUICK. Vengeance of Jenny's case! fie on her! Never name
her, child, if she be a whore.

Much Ado About Nothing

Act III, Scene III

DOGB. Are you good men and true?

VERG. Yea, or else it were pity but they should suffer
salvation, body and soul.

DOGB. Nay, that were a punishment too good for them, if
they should have any allegiance in them, being chosen
for the prince's watch.

VERG. Well, give them their charge, neighbour Dogberry.

DOGB. First, who think you the most desartless man to be
constable?

FIRST WATCH. Hugh Oatcake, sir, or George Seacoal; for
they can read and write.

DOGB. Come hither, neighbour Seacoal. God hath blessed

you with a good name: to be a well-favoured man is the gift of fortune; but to write and read comes by nature.

SEC. WATCH. Both which, Master constable.

DOGB. You have; I knew it would be your answer. Well, for your favour, sir, why, give God thanks, and make no boast of it; and for your writing and reading, let that appear when there is no need of such vanity. You are thought here to be the most senseless and fit man for the constable of the watch; therefore bear you the lanthorn. This is your charge: you shall comprehend all vagrom men; you are to bid any man stand, in the prince's name.

WATCH. How, if a' will not stand?

DOGB. Why, then, take no note of him, but let him go; and presently call the rest of the watch together, and thank God you are rid of a knave.

VERG. If he will not stand when he is bidden, he is none of the prince's subjects.

DOGB. True, and they are to meddle with none but the prince's subjects. You shall also make no noise in the streets; for, for the watch to babble and to talk is most tolerable and not to be endured.

SEC. WATCH. We will rather sleep than talk: we know what belongs to a watch.

DOGB. Why, you speak like an ancient and most quiet watchman, for I cannot see how sleeping should offend; only have a care that your bills be not stolen. Well, you are to call at all the alehouses, and bid those that are drunk get them to bed.

WATCH. How if they will not?

DOGB. Why then, let them alone till they are sober: if they make you not then the better answer, you may say they are not the men you took them for.

Love's Labour's Lost

Act V, Scene I. Nathaniel & Holofernes
HOL. *Satis quod sufficit.*

NATH. I praise God for you, sir: your reasons at dinner have been sharp and sententious; pleasant without scurrility, witty without affection, audacious without impudency, learned without opinion, and strange without heresy. I did converse this quondam day with a companion of the king's, who is intituled, nominated, or called, Don Adriano de Armado.

HOL. *Novi hominem tanquam te:* his humour is lofty, his discourse peremptory, his tongue filed, his eye ambitious, his gait majestical, and his general behaviour vain, ridiculous, and thrasonical. He is too picked, too spruce, too affected, too odd, as it were, too peregrinate, as I may call it.

NATH. A most singular and choice epithet. (*Draws out his tablebook*)

HOL. He draweth out the thread of his verbosity finer than the staple of his argument. I abhor such fanatical phantasimes, such insociable and point-devise companions; such rackers of orthography, as to speak dout, fine, when he should say, doubt; det, when he should pronounce, debt, –d, e, b, t, not d, e, t; he clepeth a calf, cauf; half, hauf; neighbour *vocatur* nebour, neigh abbreviated ne. This is abhominable, which he would call abominable, it insinuateth me of insanie: *anne intelligis, domine?* To make frantic, lunatic.

NATH. *Laus Deo bone intelligo.*

HOL. *Bone? bone,* for *bene*: Priscian a little scratched; 'twill serve.

Enter ARMADO, MOTH, *and* COSTARD.

NATH. *Videsne quis venit?*

HOL. *Video, et gaudeo.*

ARM. (*To Moth*) Chirrah!

HOL. *Quare* Chirrah, not sirrah?

ARM. Men of peace, well encountered.

HOL. Most military sir, salutation.

MOTH (*Aside to* COSTARD) They have been at a great feast of languages, and stolen the scraps.

COST. O! they have lived long on the alms-basket of words.

I marvel thy master hath not eaten thee for a word; for thou are not so long by the head as *honorificabilitudinitatibus*; thou art easier swallowed than a flap-dragon.

A Midsummer-Night's Dream

Act V, Scene I
PROL. *Gentles, perchance you wonder at this show;*
But wonder on, till truth make all things plain,
This man is Pyramus, if you would know;
This beauteous lady Thisby is, certain.
This man, with lime and rough-cast, doth present
Wall, that vile Wall which did these lovers sunder;
And through Wall's chink, poor souls, they are content
To whisper, at the which let no man wonder.
This man, with lanthorn, dog, and bush of thorn,
Presenteth Moonshine; for, if you will know,
By moonshine did these lovers think no scorn
To meet at Ninus' tomb, there, there to woo.
This grisly beast, which Lion hight by name,
The trusty Thisby, coming first by night,
Did scare away, or rather did affright;
And, as she fled, her mantle she did fall,
Which Lion vile with bloody mouth did stain.
Anon comes Pyramus, sweet youth and tall,
And finds his trusty Thisby's mantle slain;
Whereat, with blade, with bloody blameful blade,
He bravely broach'd his boiling bloody breast;
And Thisby, tarrying in mulberry shade,
His dagger drew, and died. For all the rest,
Let Lion, Moonshine, Wall, and lovers twain,
At large discourse, while here they do remain.
(*Exeunt* PROLOGUE, PYRAMUS, THISBE, LION, *and* MOONSHINE)
THESEUS. I wonder, if the lion be to speak.
DEMETRIUS. No wonder, my lord: one lion may when many asses do.

WALL. *In this same interlude it doth befall*
That I, one Snout by name, present a wall;
And such a wall, as I would have you think,
That had in it a crannied hole or chink,
Through which the lovers, Pyramus and Thisby,
Did whisper often very secretly.
This loam, this rough-cast, and this stone doth show
That I am that same wall; the truth is so;
And this the cranny is, right and sinister,
Through which the fearful lovers are to whisper.

THE. Would you desire lime and hair to speak better?

DEM. It is the wittiest partition that ever I heard discourse, my lord.

THE. Pyramus draws near the wall; silence!

Re-enter PYRAMUS.

PYR. *O grim-look'd night! O night with hue so black!*
O night, which ever art when day is not!
O night! O night! alack, alack, alack!
I fear my Thisby's promise is forgot.
And thou, O wall! O sweet, O lovely wall!
That stand'st between her father's ground and mine;
Thou wall, O wall! O sweet, and lovely wall!
Show me thy chink to blink through with mine eyne
(WALL *holds up his fingers*)
Thanks, courteous wall: Jove shield thee well for this!
But what see I? No Thisby do I see.
O wicked wall! through whom I see no bliss;
Curs'd be thy stones for thus deceiving me!

THE. The wall, methinks, being sensible, should curse again.

PYR. No, in truth, sir, he should not. 'Deceiving me', is Thisby's cue: she is to enter now, and I am to spy her through the wall. You shall see, it will fall pat as I told you. Yonder she comes.

Re-enter THISBE.

THIS. *O wall! full often hast thou heard my moans,*
For parting my fair Pyramus and me:
My cherry lips have often kiss'd thy stones,

Thy stones with lime and hair knit up in thee.
PYR. *I see a voice: now will I to the chink,*
To spy an I can hear my Thisby's face. Thisby!
THIS. *My love! thou art my love, I think.*
PYR. *Think what thou will, I am thy lover's grace;*
And, like Limander, am I trusty still.
THIS. *And I like Helen, till the Fates me kill.*
PYR. *Not Shafalus to Procrus was so true.*
THIS. *As Shafalus to Procrus, I to you.*
PYR. *O! kiss me through the hole of this vile wall.*
THIS. *I kiss the wall's hole, not your lips at all.*
PYR. *Wilt thou at Ninny's tomb meet me straightaway?*
THIS. *'Tide life, 'tide death, I come without delay.*
Exeunt PYRAMUS *and* THISBE.
WALL. *Thus have I, Wall my part discharged so;*
And, being done, thus Wall away doth go. Exit.
THE. Now is the mural down between the two neighbours.
DEM. No remedy, my lord, when walls are so wilful to hear without warning.
HIP. This is the silliest stuff that ever I heard.
THE. The best in this kind are but shadows, and the worst are no worse, if imagination amend them.

'TIMOTHY SHY'
(D. B. WYNDHAM LEWIS)

Highbrows' Lure

Ever striving to keep abreast of the latest developments in the contemporary theatre, I have the honour and pleasure to bring to your notice the work of Lúny Bonéd, a dramatist of the day-after-tomorrow. Bonéd is a Moldavo-Slavonian by birth and writes his plays standing erect, with his forehead resting on the ground; at the same time revolving in a clockwise direction and emitting loud hoots. In this way he is best able to express his *ego*. As yet, I believe, the domed heads of London do not know know Bonéd's work; it will soon be our privilege to raise our eyebrows at them with a slight (but scornful) smile.

The short piece we are about to discuss is *Plonk* (in English Do?), which is considered Lúny Bonéd's most brilliant and characteristic work, combining high intellectual and emotional ecstasy with a lambent and sublimated embolism. Very well, then.

PLONK
By LÚNY BONÉD

THE YOUNG MAN	THE STRANGER
THE OLD WOMAN	THE MILKMAN

SCENE I. — *A cottage in the Forest of Cszchlpóny. Night. The* OLD WOMAN *sits with her head in the empty stove, moaning. The* STRANGER *enters.*

THE STRANGER: Is this the house of Stepán Gombony?

THE YOUNG MAN: No.

THE STRANGER: I beg your pardon. (*Goes out mysteriously. A thunder-bolt falls and demolishes the hut. Scene closes*).

SCENE II. — *A gorge in the Mizzl Mountains. Dawn. The* YOUNG MAN *sits by the road, thinking of the Battle of Smacz* (A.D. 1355). *The* MILKMAN *comes down the pass.*

THE MILKMAN: Holà!

THE YOUNG MAN (*dully*): Holà!

THE MILKMAN: I sell milk.

THE YOUNG MAN: Do you? (*Storm. An avalanche sweeps away the* MILKMAN. *Scene closes*).

SCENE III. — *An inn on the road to Bilj. The* OLD WOMAN *sits under the table, weeping. The* YOUNG MAN *enters.*

THE YOUNG MAN: Under the dark arches of the past there is no Future.

THE OLD WOMAN: Had we done what we had to do we should not have done what we were about to do.

THE YOUNG MAN (*agitatedly*): What do you mean?

THE OLD WOMAN (*sombrely*): I do not know. (*The* STRANGER *enters mysteriously*).

THE STRANGER: Yes! You do. (*Goes out through the window. Scene closes*).

SCENE IV. – *The fair at Bilj. Peasants singing. The* YOUNG MAN *brooding*.

PEASANTS: Ho cszlapány.
                Pn zlompány.
                Oomcz habány.
                Hu!

THE YOUNG MAN: Is that a national song?

AN OLD PEASANT: Yes!

THE YOUNG MAN: Oh. (*Goes out sideways. Scene closes*).

SCENE V. – *The Piffl Pass. The* OLD WOMAN *weaving, with her head in a sack.*
The YOUNG MAN *enters.*

THE YOUNG MAN: Only the Infinite is imponderable.

THE OLD WOMAN: Homogeneous yet impalpable, correlated with introspective determinism, yet static!

THE YOUNG MAN: Have you a cheese?

THE OLD WOMAN (*sadly*): No. (*They weep together. Snowstorm. Scene closes*).

SCENE IV – *A street in Pomplóny. The* YOUNG MAN *walking quickly. The* OLD WOMAN *enters from the opposite direction.*

THE YOUNG MAN: Is that you?

THE OLD WOMAN: Yes.

THE YOUNG MAN: On! On! (*They pass each other, and are soon lost in the darkness*).

SCENE VII. – *A hut in the mountains. Night. The* OLD WOMAN *with her head under a tub, moaning. The Spirit of the* MILKMAN *enters.*

SPIRIT OF THE MILKMAN: I once sold milk.

THE OLD WOMAN (*dully*): Did you? (*The Spirit of the* MILKMAN *drifts out. The* YOUNG MAN *enters, hastily*).

THE YOUNG MAN (*desperately*): Why am I here?

THE OLD WOMAN (*in a muffled voice*): You were led by Fate. (*The* STRANGER *enters*).

THE STRANGER: No! You think you were led by Fate, but you were not led by Fate. Nobody is led by Fate except those whose fate is to be led. Those who feel they are led are not those who feel that they would not have been led; had they felt that, their fate would have remained the same, though it would not have been the same had they never thought that they would not have been led; and *vice versa.*

THE YOUNG MAN: Who are you?

THE STRANGER: I am Fate. (*Disappears up the chimney. A long silence*).

PEASANTS (*singing in the distance*):

> *Czu tompány*
> *Gnu zhábny,*
> *Pn!*

THE OLD WOMAN (*in a stifled voice*): They are singing.

THE YOUNG MAN (*thickly*): Yes. They are singing.

THE OLD WOMAN: It is a national song.

THE YOUNG MAN (*face downwards*): Is it? (*Storm. Thunder. A waterburst sweeps down the gorge and blots out the hut, the* YOUNG MAN, *and the* OLD WOMAN. *Earthquake. The mountain bursts into eruption*).

A VOICE IN THE MOUNTAINS: *Plonk!* (*Scene closes*).

I fancy this will give the Stage Society something to think about.

A Problem of Conduct

Yesterday it rained heavily, persistently, doggedly, stupefyingly, and damnably, like Lord Boreham making a speech on Diocesan Finance in the Upper House. A veil of thick mist hung about my Downs and the soaked fields, and the birds who make my village a Singing Island were silent, or at least reduced to one chirrup an hour. I therefore took down from a shelf and read with great relish, a volume of plays of the Elizabethan Have-at-You School, and by lunch time I was up to the doublet in gore. And that reminds me of a Problem of Conduct which I should like to propound to you. It would probably arise very rarely today, but it must have worried a sixteenth-century Venetian considerably. Here it is:

A, a stranger to Venice, is invited by B, a noble of that place, to a banquet. Owing to unforeseen circumstances A arrives late, and does not meet his host B or his hostess C until he is actually shown into the dining-room. On entering he finds D, a noble with whom he has a slight acquaintance, lying on the floor with a dagger in his breast; E, F, and G, all nobles of whom he has heard B speak slightingly, leaning on the table with every appearance of having been poisoned in their wine; H, the charming daughter of the house, being strangled at the sideboard by a masked stranger; and I and J, the two sons of B, conducting a duel with knives in the window.

As A is announced B rises from the table and says coldly, 'Why are you late? We were looking forward to seeing you at seven.' A's hostess, C, says nothing, but stealthily draws a stiletto from her stocking.

A does not know B or C very well, and he is by nature shy and retiring, though a gentleman.

What should A do?

I think that is a very sound and satisfactory problem, well up to *British Weekly* standard. Among the answers already judged incorrect is that of my friend the Squire, who says that A should kick B smartly in the stomach, at the same time deftly upper-cutting C, and then run like blazes. I think he has missed the essential point that A is a gentleman. Another answer adjudged incorrect is that A should take a bomb from his pocket and, first uttering a courteous word of greeting and apology, throw it into the mob and leg it downstairs for dear life. This, again, fails, because a man of breeding of the Renaissance would not blow his hostess – whom he hardly knows at all – into little bits merely to cover an awkward pause in the conversation. Should A advance, keeping an eye on C's

stiletto, with some laughing phrase as 'What a lot of
bodies!' or 'How the evenings are drawing in'? Should
he ignore the whole business, and take his seat at table,
chatting to his host about San Marco, or the Lido, or the
Doge's new economic policy concerning coastwise trade?
(He would, of course, politely refuse wine, saying that his
doctor had told him that it was death to him; which would
be, in the circumstances, strictly true). And, even if he got
clear out of dinner, what about the bravoes lurking downstairs? Should he cut his way through or join them and go
fifty-fifty in the loot?

Elephants And A Drama

SCENE — *A handsome and well-equipped room is indicated.
In the middle a rosewood table. A* WOMAN *and* TWO MEN
sit around it.

FIRST MAN:
>   I can't explain why,
>   But I don't quite like buying
>   Furniture
>   On credit.

SECOND MAN:
>   I have no objections
>   To cash transactions,
>   Mr Everyman!

FIRST MAN:
>   But I can't —

SECOND MAN:
>   I quite understand.
>   We none of us can. That's why
>   We use credit!
>   Some men,
>   Who build their businesses on credit,
>   Fight shy of it
>   For building their homes!
>   But folks are getting over

This sort of prejudice nowadays, Mr Everyman.

There is a fine passage a little later, as the play warms up:

SECOND MAN:
What can you conveniently manage,
Mr Everyman?

FIRST MAN:
Not more than £10 now
and 45s. a month.

SECOND MAN:
Fine! Now how about
Delivery? If convenient to Mrs Everyman,
Your furniture will be delivered
In plain motors
Two days from now!

After which the First Man has a fine impassioned speech in praise of the Second Man, and the scene closes. In the next scene, which is closely modelled on the Tolloller method, there are semi-choruses by various groups – a Group of Furniture Removers, a Group of Motor-Drivers, a Group of Taxicab-men, and so forth. Here is an extract:

A FOREMAN:
Easy there, with
That pianner!
When I says 'To me! –'

GROUP OF FURNITURE REMOVERS:
Brothers!
Let us work and rejoice!
Tenderly heaving out
This exquisite sideboard, and with loving care
Removing the wrappings which enfold it.

> *A Pause. Three men named* SMITH
> *slowly cross the stage, thinking
> about gas.*

A NAMELESS PLUMBER:
How ennobling is labour!
There is no sight more beautiful.

GROUP OF DISEMBODIED GASFITTERS:

> Brothers! We are with you
> In spirit!
> Longing to share your toil,
> Yearning to help.

>> *A pause. A dead paperhanger, with
>> ghostly, noiseless steps, crosses the
>> stage gibbering.*

Murgle tells me that (like Franz Tolloller) he wrote this elemental, dynamic, throbbing play shivering as with fever. It is certainly a fine piece of work, and the *intelligentsia* will probably eat it when it is produced by a Sunday night society. The piece ends on a note of quiet sorrow:

THE WOMAN:

> George, why did you not choose
> A chiffonier?

>> *Her arms hang into space with an
>> immense helplessness.* THE MAN, *with
>> a gesture of despair, sinks to the
>> floor.*

THE WOMAN (*in a far-off voice*):

> George, why did you not choose
> A chiffonier?

>> THE MAN *breaks down, hiding his
>> face behind the piano.*

THE WOMAN (*as if transfigured*):

> George, why did you not choose
> A chiffonier?

>> THE MAN *moans softly, gnawing
>> the carpet in the intensity of his
>> pain. Three jobbing gardeners cross
>> the stage, with gestures expressive
>> of having an aunt in Balham named
>> Mrs Higgs.*
>> *The stage closes*

If Tolloller's play has any advantage over this, it is that

the explosions in it will keep the critics awake. But you can't have everything.

Variations On A Simple Theme

The question is often asked in the Athenaeum Club 'How would LE QUEUX do?'; 'What would ETHEL do with such and such a situation?' And a mellow episcopal voice may often add 'In what manner would NAT GOULD treat it?' For Literature is justly honoured in that solemn place, where even Cabinet Ministers (Conservative) may be seen on hot summer afternoons swatting flies with the *Times Literary Supplement*. The event of the year, I am informed, was the Bodger Prize Competition for an imaginative work founded on a theme suggested by a member of the Literary Circle. The theme selected was a well-known verse of English lyric poetry.

> Jack and Jill went up the hill
> To get a pail of water;
> Jack fell down and broke his crown
> And Jill came tumbling after.

We may as well reprint characteristic extracts from the winning compositions.

THE STORK'S NEST
A complete short story from the Slavo-Jazcslovak of Bunga Piffzl

On the fourth floor of the old house in the suburbs of Jazzcsyl lived Jýl, a plump young woman with black sparkling eyes, with her aged parents. Jýl was always laughing, and when her old father stamped screaming on her old mother's wrinkled, careworn face she would smile and say, 'How beautiful is the Spring! How lovely the elder-blossom! How white the snow on Hjycszlcsy!' On the floor below lived the young workman Ják, a tall handsome youth whose father had been a convict but was now caretaker of the town museum. When he met Jýl on the stairs Ják would say, 'How I love your little young fat face! It is as lovely as a round new white soft Grnórkscy cheese!'; and Jýl would laugh, and Ják would laugh too and finger his knife under his blouse, for he loved her. In the old house Jýl's mother lay under the bed and never stopped screaming, and the pigs and hens ran about the place grunting and chirping with pleasure, and Jýl would laugh and sing 'How beautiful is the elder-tree!' All was sunshine in the old house; even the lean dark peasant in the basement flogged his thin weak wife with a happy smile, and the married couple from Sznórcz often stopped biting each other to sing about the Spring and the willows. Every time Ják met Jýl on the stairs he would say, 'How perfect is your young white large neck!' and he longed to plunge his knife into the girl. How the sun shone! And the little white clouds sailed over the roof-tops and over the lime-trees! Jýl would laugh at them, and Ják would laugh too, and stab at anyone who happened to be passing, out of pure happiness.

One day Ják, meeting the girl on the stairs, said 'How I love your thin small straight feet! Let us go up the hill! How I hate the nose of my aunt! It is like an old thick red hat. How beautiful the wind is on the hill, and the lilac is out. I must go and draw water for the old women. *Grzcsh!*' And Jýl said with a merry laugh, 'Yes, we will go together! The buds are out on the plane-trees. Hurrah for the Spring!' and hand in hand they wandered out of the suburbs, past the market-gardens of Ksńmsc, out into the wide country, and up the hill to the spring, where Ják drew a bucket of the cold clear water and fell to the ground, bruising his head, with Jýl sliding and falling beside him; but all she said was 'Hark at the birds in the elder-trees! Hurrah!' She tied up Ják's wound with a shawl her aunt Tázsca had brought from the fair of Polcszóvny and they returned home. As they passed the corner of the street where they lived they heard the old house resounding with yells, and Jýl laughed and said to

Ják, 'Hark! They are happy! It is the Spring!' and ran indoors, but Ják took a very large knife from his blouse and stuck it into a very old man who was standing near and screaming, and when Jý came laughing down the stairs he said gaily, 'Look, Jýl! He has an old hairy face like a little piece of mud!' and as the girl stopped to look he raised his knife again.

'How they all bleed,' thought Ják, suddenly despondent, listening to the howls of the old women in the house.

FROM 'THE SECRET HILL'

Note – This manuscript novel bore no signature, and appears to be the joint work of two or three serious analytical novelists. It is a most unhealthy tale, and full of repressions and introspective morbidity. It is not clear whether it is of English or American origin, but is the sort of thing that would get a column in the heavier reviews.

In the first fourteen chapters the heroine is struggling with something which may be either the Medea-complex or an ingrowing toe-nail; it is not quite clear which. Anyway it is very unhealthy. We will quote an extract from the scene where she has a nerve-storm about something on the farm, but it is all curiously muffled and significant, like a neurotic woman with large teeth speaking through five layers of blanket, and of course very brilliant.

XV

He came to her in the afternoon and said abruptly, 'I am going to the hill.'

'The hill?'

'Yes.'

She felt the dark waters rushing over her again, rushing from him to her. She heard him speaking, as it were, from within herself, from an infinite distance, and yet near, and within herself another voice was repeating drearily, 'The hill. The hill. The hill. The hill. The hill.' She felt as though the moment had come at last when her inmost soul shuddered and recoiled, with a dreary knowledge of what was between her and him – and yet not between, but as it were something outside herself, something she could not see, definite and precise yet looming ever nearer and away, so that she felt herself saying. 'No, No,' and then, 'But yes. Yes,' and grappling dimly (so it seemed to her) with the tremendous urging of necessity; and so she straightened herself to receive, as it were, what might be coming, conscious – or unconscious? she could not have said – that from him to her, inevitably, almost, there passed half-felt, half-feared, wholly incomprehensible floods of beingness, great searching tides that washed in and out of her and left her feeling – what? She did not yet know.

He was speaking again, more sharply.

'I am going for water. I shall take the bucket.'

'The bucket?'

'Yes.'

She caught her breath sharply. So this, then, was what she had been half-visualising, half-fleeing from, half catching to her breast in the hope that he would, somehow, have given her of his own will something she could not formulate, even to herself, save that she felt it to be, reaching out and grasping and retiring again, and, as it were, clutching at her consciousness – for so she deemed it – and fading again into a kind of interior dullness of experience which made her ache, though she said to herself, 'No, No'; but then again the reassuring return of that previous half-glimpsed permanence, the half-dim hope, as she realised it, spreading out and broadening from her to him, and narrowing and becoming more implied and constant, and concentrating finally in a crystallised and palpable imminence. . . .

'What is that paper you are tearing up?' he asked sharply.

She looked down. It was a page of *The Delphic*. Strange, she thought dully, that it should be that! It was her favourite magazine. She found in it the vague echo of her own thoughts, and often, when striving to formulate, to impel, some enveloping idea that wrapped her round oozily like warm, wet cotton-wool she had thought of writing it down – if indeed she could tear it from herself and rid herself of its soft, clinging, amorphous embrace – and sending it to the Editor in place of his own leading article.

'Will you come?' he said, more kindly, glimpsing the tremendous forces at war in her, 'I am going to take the old yellow wooden bucket.'

Old? Yellow? Wooden? She tried to quiet her storming nerves, to grasp the significance of what he was saying.

'Why?'

'To get water.'

She shrank back, trying to hold off, as it were, to repel, to push away, to drive out, expel the hidden consciousness that rose like a well between her and the realisation she felt surging beneath her, the purpose of her hidden aspiring, the panting urgency of the current that, so it seemed to her, pulsated and swung out and poured back and flooded her with an unformulated dread of understating – perhaps overemphasing, perhaps sidetracking – the accumulated force of static inhibitions which bound her thought – how loosely, how incoherently, with what secret value she knew not – to his.

'You are going to the hill?' Her voice was quite flat and toneless now.

'Yes.'

'To get water?'

'Yes. In the bucket.'

'Where from?'

She held her breath. The answer came slowly.

'The well.'

She heard herself repeating dully under her breath, 'The well. The well. The well. The well. The well. The well.'

'Will you come?' His voice had a pleading urgent note.

'Where?'

'To the hill.'

'What is there?'

'The well. I am going to get water.' (Water!)

He said very slowly and distinctly, 'I shall take the bucket.' (The bucket!)

'Now?'

'Yes.'

'Why?'

'To get water.'

She checked herself in the very act of saying 'what in?' She did not know what made her stop saying that. But rather wearily, and with a defeated sense that there were hesitancies at work in her soul, trying to encompass, to envelop, to surround, to conquer, to inhabit the fastness of her comprehension, she rose and went upstairs to put on her hat.

PETER SIMPLE

Now Write On

'*Nigerian company wishes to import used clothing, cars, cleaning rags, refrigerators, etc. Can export gum arabic, cow bones, alligator pepper, fruits and onions.*' (advertisement in the Holland Herald.)

'Well, Watson, what do you make of it?'

I stared at the scrap of paper Holmes had tossed over to me, a slight smile playing over his lean features.

'I confess I'm completely bewildered,' I replied, after a pause. 'This Nigerian company – why should it want used cleaning rags? And who in England wants cow bones or alligator pepper – whatever that may be?'

My friend slowly took up his violin, then laid it down again as a thought evidently struck him. His eye gleamed with inductive light. 'Let us assume,' he said, meditatively filling his pipe, 'that the list of imports is simply a blind, an attempt to get certain people interested. What sort of man would own a lot of used cleaning rags?'

'A man with a lot of cars and refrigerators?'

'Precisely. A man of considerable means. A man who has the means to indulge his whims, however fantastic.'

'You mean —'

'I mean this, my dear Watson. Consider: what sort of pastime, hobby or interest would you connect with gum arabic, cow bones and alligator pepper?'

'What is alligator pepper?'

For answer Holmes opened a drawer of his bureau and took out a small, finely carved ebony box, evidently of African provenance. He opened it and I had hardly time to observe the fine yellowish grains inside when I fell back, overcome by a fit of sneezing which lasted for several minutes and left me limp and exhausted.

'First render your victims helpless with a powerful sneezing agent derived from the powdered claws of alligators,' Holmes went on. 'Then fix them to the ground or to a prepared base with gum arabic and glue made from boiled cow bones. It's one of the most powerful adhesives known. The ancient Egyptians used it to secure the foundations of the Great Pyramid.'

'Amazing,' I gasped. 'But what does it all mean?'

'It means, my dear Watson, that the man we have to deal with is a madman with a taste for living statuary, a madman, moreover, of vast wealth and curious knowledge. It means we have not a moment to lose. Come, Watson. To Paddington!'

As I stood irresolute, my friend seized a valise and threw a tartan travelling rug over my head....

What Would You Do?

A man walking in the street sees a fire-engine rushing past. He notices that the fire-engine is itself on fire. Should he run to the nearest telephone and ring for the fire brigade? Should he go to the nearest public reference library, sit down and try to think things over quietly? Or should be ignore the incident, regarding it as part of the Human Predicament?

Haggard's Christmas

Dec. 22, 1771: Fog. Obadiah Horseworthy blown to pieces while trying to turn lead into gold. Sept a.m. evicting Blind Benjamin and enclosg. common land for mine own use. An unusual event occurred in p.m., viz. the appearance of my wife whom I had not seen since I flung a pease pddg. at her last Michaelmas. She informed me that her brother Daniel sends word he is coming tomorrow to spend Christmas with us. This threw me into apoplexy as the man is a canting Dissenter, but I cannot refuse him as I owe him 30,000 sovs. Drank a vat of punch to recover.

Dec. 23: Storms. Spat on elderly Jew in a.m. Evicted Crippled Simon and Deaf Peter, also re-evicted Blind Benjamin who was lodging with Deaf Peter. Brother Daniel arrived in p.m. but I was unable to greet him as I was lying insensible in the fireplace. When I recovered he told me that if I drank anything more he would be compelled to call for his 30,000 sovs. for the good of my soul. ITEM: To physick £0 os 0½d.

Dec. 24: Snow. Shot unusual crippled poacher in a.m. Evicted Halfwitted William. While chasing a fleeing tenant I fell into a snowdrift and to restore myself pulled forth a flask of brandy, only to find Daniel had filled it with barley water. The rage for drink so possessed me I was fain to ask the Rector for something, but the canting dog gave me nettle wine. ITEM: To emetics £0 os 0¾d.

Dec. 25: Today being that feast most sacred to all men, viz. Quarter Day, I was out early evicting Palsied Peter, Granny Turnip and Blind Benjamin, who had moved in with Granny Turnip. Granny Turnip snivelled 'Did I not know what day it was,' to which I replied 'Rent Day,' which caused me much mirth. On returning home was nauseated to see jugs of barley water on table for dinner, whereupon I hit upon an ingenious Device, pouring a pint

of laudanum into Daniel's jug. Halfway through dinner, he collapsed insensible and I then made merry with six botts. of Madeira, a pint of brandy and three maidservants.
ITEM : To gift for wife, one groat.

Haggard's Journal

June 1, 1772 : Rain. An American colonist named Franklin reported to have been blown up whilst flying a kite in a thunderstorm in order to study the effects of the Electric Fluid. Ate a capon for dinner but it was bad, so I gave the remains to my wife who presently turned green and was conveyed to her chamber insensible.

June 2, 1772 : Thunder and lightning. Amos Hornblower put in the stocks for stealg. an egg. Whilst visitg. Soup Hales in a.m. in order to tear down some cottages, a one-legged person bumped into me and upon my horse-whippg. him complained in the French tongue, whereupon I gave him an extra half-dozen blows for being a canting foreigner. Spent p.m. jumping up and down in front of Amos Hornblower in the stocks, puttg. my fingers to my nose and suchlike merry japes.

Ate a pease pddg. for dinner but it was bad, so I sent it to Amos Hornblower. I then called for the cook and dismissed him by the simple expedient of discharging my fowling-piece at him as he entered the room.

June 3, 1772 : Floods. Amos Hornblower removed to the Spital insensible. Grunge, my butler, left to hire a new cook. Drank a bott. of port for breakfast but Grunge informed me he had hired a cook and a sumptuous meal appeared for dinner. As I was eating Grunge informed me that the new cook was a one-legged Frenchman lately arrive in Soup Hales, whereupon, peering closely into the pie, I percvd. small slivers of glass floatg. in the gravy.
ITEM : To emetics, £0 0s 0½d.

N. F. SIMPSON

The Best I Can Do By Way Of A Gate-Leg Table is a Hundredweight of Coal

ANTIQUE SHOP
OWNER and BRO

OWNER: Yes. I know the kind of thing you mean. But I'm not sure what we've got that would quite fill the bill. Unless this sort of thing's of any interest. (*He indicates a stone font with ornate cover*) Old Chippendale font. Chinese carvings underneath.

BRO: No – it's more something to ...

OWNER: ... fill up a corner. What about these? (*He picks up a box and opens it*) Set of Regency style false teeth.

BRO: Ah.

OWNER: In a whalebone case. (*He takes out a pair of hinged false teeth*)

BRO: Yes. (*He takes them*)

OWNER: As used by the Duke of Wellington at the Waterloo Dinners.

BRO: (*Examining them*) Mother-of-pearl molars.

OWNER: I think there should be a hallmark under there.

BRO: Yes. There is. Exquisite, aren't they? (*He puts them down*)

OWNER: Failing that, I can only suggest a pair of four-teenth-century brass rocking-chairs. (*He leads* BRO *towards chairs*)

BRO: Yes. It's not quite, though ...

OWNER: Little cup-shaped object soldered on here, probably for goats' milk.

BRO: Ah.

OWNER: Put the lid on like that, you see, rock back-wards and forwards in the chair for a week or two, and your goats' milk's gone rancid. Which is the way they liked it. Or there's this over here. (*He leads* BRO *to an old mangle*) Thing they used at one time for wringing out clothes.

BRO: A mangle, isn't it?

OWNER: That's right. I don't know whether it's got a date on it. Eighteen ninety-three, I should think or thereabouts. They were mostly put on the market about then. Queen Victoria. Had one specially made and set the trend.

BRO: Vintage model, then.

OWNER: What we call semi-vintage. Be absolutely honest.

BRO: Beauty. Isn't it?

OWNER: Very sought after. That particular model. They only made three.

BRO: Pity they went out.

OWNER: It's the laundries. That's what spelt the doom of those things. Never the same again, once the laundries came in 1923.

BRO: Short lived.

OWNER: Thirty years.

BRO: Not very long.

OWNER: People just had time to get really mangle-conscious, and then ...

BRO: It's the way it is.

OWNER: But I gather what you're looking for is something to fill up an odd corner.

BRO: That's right.

OWNER: Not too big, not too small. How are you placed for bell pulls?

BRO: Ah.

They cross the shop. Doorbell chimes.

HALL

MIDDIE *walking to front door. Opens it. Two men, one short, neat, sharp, other big, bluff, chatty.*

BBC: Space Utilization Council.
MIDDIE: Oh.
BBC: If we could come in and have a look round.
MIDDIE: Yes. Yes, of course. Come in.
BBC: Thank you.

ANTIQUE SHOP
Owner is holding up, for BRO'S *inspection, a six or seven foot length of ornately decorated bell pull material, with a large tassle on the end.*

OWNER: I don't know whether that would take up sufficient room for your purposes, but it's a lovely piece of work.
BRO: It's gold thread, isn't it?
OWNER: Embroidered by the nuns of West Bromwich Albion in 1226. Pudding basin motif down the side, and scenes from Robinson Crusoe in between the little interstices.

BEDROOM
MIDDIE *taking the* TWO MEN *in.*

MIDDIE: This is the main bedroom. If you want to start here.
BBC: Yes. We've got to start somewhere, haven't we? Right.
         They look round, sizing it up.
SNS: Rather more space here than you're effectively using, Mrs ... (*He peers down between chair and chest of drawers*) Good eight or nine cubic feet down there, for a start.
MIDDIE: Yes, well ... we ...
         BBC MAN *peers.*
SNS: Down here, between the ...
BBC: Yes.
SNS: Another one over there. Back of the ...
BBC: Tidy old cubic foot or two going begging up there, as well.

SNS: Yes.

BBC: Above the picture rail.

MIDDIE: We've been meaning to get rid of some of it, but ...

BBC: (*Peering under the bed*) Come and look at this.
SNS MAN *peers under bed and straightens up.*

SNS: Seventy five cubic feet?

BBC: Not far off. (*To* MIDDIE) It's only little bits, but they add up, you see!

SNS: (*Taking out notebook and measure*) We'll have to get down to this.

BBC: (*To* MIDDIE) Have you got a stepladder, Mrs. ...?

MIDDIE: Yes, we have ...

BBC: Downstairs, is it?

MIDDIE: It's in the cupboard under the stairs.

BBC: I'll come down and get them, then. If you'll show me where they are.

MIDDIE: Yes. (*Leading him out*) It's only an old pair, but ...

BBC: (*To* SNS) I'll leave you to it for a minute, Ralph.

SNS: (*To himself*) Getting away with murder here.

ANTIQUE SHOP

Owner handing bell pull, now wrapped in brown paper, to BRO. *It is not rolled or folded in any way, and so has to be held well above head height to avoid trailing on the ground.*

BRO: I shall probably be for it when I get home, but she'll come round to it in time, I think.

OWNER: Oh, yes, they like to make a fuss, don't they? But it's a lovely object to have around.

BRO: It is.

OWNER: And functional. That's the beauty of a thing like that. Hang it from the ceiling in a corner of the room ...

BRO: Yes.

OWNER: (*Seeing* BRO *to the door*) Give beauty and adornment to an otherwise empty space.

BRO: And meaning.

OWNER: And meaning. Can you manage? Let me ...
He helps BRO *through the door with it.*

BRO: Thank you.

OWNER: Right. Well ... any time you've got an odd corner – drop in. May have something new in.

BRO: Yes I'll do that.

OWNER: Careful how you go.
BRO *goes off bearing the bell pull aloft.*

HALL
Men coming down stairs.

SNS: Same thing downstairs I expect. What have we got? So far?

BBC: Cubic feet. Nine hundred and seventy three.

SNS: Best part of a self-service dairy. Where do we go now?
MIDDIE *appears.*

MIDDIE: Oh.

BBC: We've left the stepladder on the landing.

MIDDIE: Oh yes – I'll get Bro to bring those down when he comes in.

SNS: If we could have a look down here as well.

MIDDIE: Yes. (*Leading them in*). This is the living room.

LIVING ROOM
MIDDIE *and* TWO MEN. *They cast their eyes round. Exchange glances.*

SNS: I was wrong. There's about twice as much.
MIDDIE *hovers.*

MIDDIE: Can I get you a cup of tea?

BBC: That would be very welcome, Mrs ... Thank you.

MIDDIE: (*Going*) I'll go and get you some.

SNS: I don't know why we bothered to bring a tape measure. This lot. Just look at it. (*Pointing*) Space, space, space.

BBC: Hoarding it for years.

            DINING ROOM
            The men have wandered through.
SNS: Look at that. (*He points to the space under the table*) Sub Post-Office in there, practically. Small one.
BBC: Making a right old monkey out of the Space Utilization Act.
            SNS opens hatch and looks through into kitchen.
SNS: Come here.
            Both look through.

            KITCHEN
            Men looking through, surveying room, ignoring MIDDIE.
            She sees them.
MIDDIE: It's nearly ready. I'm just waiting for the kettle.

            DINING ROOM
            Men straightening up, SNS closing hatch.
SNS: Go up the wall at head office, when they learn about this.
BBC: It's an eye-opener.
SNS: I wonder how many more there are.
BBC: Up and down the country.
            They go through into living room and to the door.
SNS: It's cheeky, you know. When you come to think of it.

            HALL
            Men coming out as MIDDIE approaches from the kitchen with tea.
MIDDIE: Oh.
BBC: Been having a look at some of your space Mrs ...
MIDDIE: Yes?

BBC: Rather more than you're effectively using.

MIDDIE: Yes – you did say. Before. We'll have to get down to something.
(She offers them the tea.)

MIDDIE: I haven't sugared them, but ...

BBC: I don't think we've really got time, Mrs ... Thank you very much.

BBC: *(Opening front door)* But we'll see that you get proper notification before anything transpires. *(To SNS)* Where do we go now?

SNS: Follow straight down, I should think. Best plan.

BBC: Yes. *(They go out)* Goodbye, Mrs ...

MIDDIE: Goodbye *(She closes door)*

FRONT GARDEN
Men walking to front gate.

SNS: Pressure of space there is in these islands, you'd think people'd have more social conscience.

BBC: Yes.

SNS: Than let it run to waste like that.

BBC: They don't though.
They come out of front gate as BRO arrives at it, hold it open for him, and go off without looking at him.

BBC: Till it hits them.
BRO stands at the gate looking after them. Then he goes in. Two men turn into the gate next door.

BBC: Cubic capacity lying idle, when it's all we can do to find room for a couple of new airfields.

SNS: Yes.

BBC: Not to mention a backlog of about twenty-nine thousand office blocks up and down the country.

SNS: *(Ringing bell)* See what this one brings forth.
The door is opened by the Paradocks' next door neighbour, NORA.

BBC:	Good afternoon. Space Utilization Council.
NORA:	Oh ...
BBC:	If we could step inside.
NORA:	Yes. Yes, of course.

HALL (*in the Paradocks' house*)
BRO, *with bell pull and* MIDDIE.

BRO:	Space what?
MIDDIE:	Space Utilization Council, or something. It's on the card there. That they left. (*Taking bell pull*). Not another thing we've got to hang up?

BRO *looks at card*.

BRO:	Who are they? I've never heard of them.
MIDDIE:	I don't know. They go round. They've been to Doris and Eddie. Where do you want this?
BRO:	What? In there.
MIDDIE:	To do with utilization of space. Whether it's being made proper use of or not.

MIDDIE *goes into living room*. BRO *takes off his coat*.

LIVING ROOM
MIDDIE *entering*.

MIDDIE:	They're going to notify us.

She drapes the wrapped bell pull over the armchair and looks at it.
BRO *enters*.

BRO:	What do they want it for?
MIDDIE:	They didn't say.

Without for the moment unwrapping it, BRO *looks round for a likely place to hang the bell pull*. MIDDIE *watches uneasily*.

BRO:	They're welcome to any space they can find at this address.

PASSAGE FROM HALL IN NORA'S HOUSE
The two men, NORA *hovering*. SNS *looking into cupboard. He withdraws.*

SNS:	Come and have a look in here.

BBC *looks, withdraws. They exchange glances.*

SNS: (*To* NORA) How many more of these have you
          got?

NORA: More?

BBC: Cupboards?

NORA: Oh. Well – that's the only one really. We've
          wardrobes upstairs and that, but ...

BBC: Yes. We'll have a look at them, Mrs ...

NORA: It's this way.

LIVING ROOM

BRO *with bell pull, now unwrapped, looking
for somewhere to hang it. We see* MIDDIE *looking at it with distaste and disapproval.*

MIDDIE: Not where we can knock into it, Bro, every
          time we come into the room.

BRO: Over here, By the ...

MIDDIE: It's not much better there. Either way it's going
          to scream at the wallpaper.

BRO: Just try it over there. In the corner.
          *On one wall in this corner is a glass case with
          a stuffed fish in it.*

MIDDIE: You realize I shall have to get down and re-
          arrange the whole room round it.

BRO: How about that?

MIDDIE: I suppose so.

BRO: As a focal point for the room.

MIDDIE: It's going to be in the way. Wherever you put
          it. Dangling. I don't know why you bring these
          things home.
          BRO *puts it down.*

MIDDIE: What is it, anyway?

BRO: It's a fourteenth century brass rocking chair
          in the form of a set of Regency style false teeth
          made to look like an old Byzantine bell-pull.

MIDDIE: As if we haven't got enough clutter.

BRO: It's the one thing that corner's always wanted,
          I think. To take the bleakness off it. Something
          hanging down.

MIDDIE: What happens if somebody gives it a tug? Accidentally. I suppose the whole lot comes down. Ceiling and all.

BRO: There's no need to give it a tug.

MIDDIE: You get an idea in your head, and instead of stopping to think, you go out and come home with something like that. That's going to be a perpetual eyesore. And a nuisance. When I'm dusting.

BRO: A lot of people would like it. It adds a touch of distinction.

MIDDIE: It's all right if you've got flunkeys in the house. To answer it. What's the good of it to me? And chambermaids.

BRO: A chambermaid wouldn't answer a bell like that, Middie.

MIDDIE: Here, there and everywhere. Getting under your feet.

BRO: What?

MIDDIE: Up to our necks in butlers and pantrymen and I don't know what else. Trooping into the room every time the bell rings.

BRO: But ...

MIDDIE: Holding their hands out for tips every minute of the day and night. When you want to get on.

BRO: This is a *disused* bell pull, Middie!

MIDDIE: Smoking on duty.

BRO: It's past it now. As far as summoning anybody is concerned. It's purely decorative.

MIDDIE: Powdered footmen under your feet.

BRO: Middie.

MIDDIE: Under gardeners. Vying with each other. Drinking after hours.

BRO: Listen ...

MIDDIE: Swinging from the chandeliers on their night off.

BRO: What chandeliers?

MIDDIE: And they've all got to be fed. You realize that, don't you?

BRO: Middie ...

MIDDIE: I've no desire to be up half the night cooking bacon and eggs for them.

BRO: I don't think you understand, Middie. This isn't that kind of bell pull.

MIDDIE: Then what's the good of it?

BRO: Well, it's ...

MIDDIE: I know. It's five thousand years old. And very valuable.

BRO: It's priceless, Middie. A thing like that. You don't seem to realize.

MIDDIE: Yes.

BRO: It's an antique. The kind of thing people spend years of their lives scouring about in the depths of the South American jungle for.

MIDDIE: So you keep saying.

BRO: We're lucky to have a specimen like this. In the house.

MIDDIE: All right then. Put it up.

BRO: Very lucky.

MIDDIE: Put it up. But don't blame me if we have trouble with it.

GATES AND DRIVEWAY TO LARGE, PALATIAL COUNTRY SEAT
The two men going in through gates.

BBC: Tidy old run for their money, I shouldn't be surprised. Looks as if it's been here since the year dot.

SNS: See how they shape up to the new pattern of things.
They walk up driveway towards house.

LIVING ROOM
The bell pull in position. It hangs from the ceiling, a little way out from the wall, in the corner where the stuffed fish is. BRO *standing back to*

look at it. He goes up, adjusts it, surveys it again.

HALL

BRO *coming out of living room with glass case containing stuffed fish.*

MIDDIE: What's that?

BRO: I've decided to take it down.

MIDDIE: But that's the one Aunt Meg and Miss Prentiss gave us.

BRO: There just isn't room for it, Middie. Anymore.

MIDDIE: There's been room for it all this time. Since three Christmases ago. When they gave it to us. Where are you taking it to?

BRO: It can go in the cupboard.

MIDDIE: You mean you've taken that down to make room for ...?

           (*She goes into the living room*)

LIVING ROOM

MIDDIE *enters. Looks at bell pull.*

MIDDIE: Really!

HALL

BRO *leaning folded camp bed against wall beside cupboard.*

MIDDIE: And what's that?

BRO: It's the camp bed.

MIDDIE: You're not leaving it there.

BRO: It can go back up with the other stuff. In the loft.

MIDDIE: And what am I supposed to say to Aunt Meg? When she comes. And wants to know what we're doing with the Mongolian river trout they gave us.

BRO: You can tell her we've had a bit of a move round.

MIDDIE: I'm going to put it back.

BRO: (*Getting glass case*) There isn't room for it, Middie. If we're going to have the bell pull we can't have that. There isn't room for both. They don't harmonize. They represent two totally different ways of life.
Phone rings.
That'll be Nora. (*He picks up the 'phone*) Yes ... Speaking ... Hallo, Nora. We thought it might be you ... Oh? ... When was this? ... Without telling you? ... But they can't do that, Nora. They're supposed to notify you ... Oh, yes. They're supposed to by law. They can't just move a betting shop into your spare bedroom without consulting you. Yes, I will. Just a moment, Nora. (*To* MIDDIE) It's Nora. She wants to talk to you. She's let herself get landed.

MIDDIE: (*Into 'phone*) Nora? Bro tells me you've had trouble ... I should get on to someone, Nora. Get some sort of redress ... No. We haven't, as yet. Touch wood. We've been lucky ... No. Where? ... Well, there's nothing in ours. I've just this minute come from it. (*To* BRO) Somebody celebrating midnight mass in the cupboard under the stairs next door to Nora. (*into 'phone*) I'm quite sure they're supposed to notify you ... Yes ... Well, listen Nora ... Yes ... Yes ... Yes ... Yes ... Well, look, I must go Nora. I've got something in the oven. I've just remembered ... Yes ... Yes ... I must go, Nora. It'll be spoiled ... Yes. I will ... Not at all. Goodbye, Nora.

BRO: There's always some tale of woe. Whenever Nora rings. If it's not one thing, it's something else.

MIDDIE: I blame her, as much as anything.
MIDDIE *sits down.*
She invites them in, falls over herself to be

pleasant, gives them cups of tea, lets them go prying into everything. I'm not surprised she's been landed with something.

BRO: She certainly lays herself open.

MIDDIE: It's asking for trouble.

BRO: Yes. I think perhaps I'll go and put this up in the loft, Middie. (*Going*) Is there anything you want while I'm up there?

MIDDIE: You can bring down that bit of old sacking. It'll do to put over the potatoes.

BRO: Right. I'll get it down.

MIDDIE: Which reminds me. Jelly.

MIDDIE *goes to kitchen, as* BRO *disappears upstairs.*

LANDING

BRO *arriving on landing, with camp bed. Puts stepladder in position under loft, steps on to it.*

CELLAR

MIDDIE *comes briskly down cellar steps.*

LANDING. STEPLADDER UNDER LOFT

BRO *stepping on top of stepladder, and putting his head into loft.*

LOFT

BRO'S *head appearing. He looks round. He sees a man in a bowler hat, sitting in a hip bath, and looking towards him, affronted.*

BRO: I beg your pardon.

BRO'S *head quickly withdraws.*

LANDING

BRO, *stunned, stands on steps. Then begins descending, bemused.*

CELLAR

MIDDIE *with jelly on plate, returning to foot of steps. She sees a gipsy fortune-teller, with client, gazing into crystal ball. She checks in*

momentary disbelief, then continues thought-
fully up the steps.

LANDING
BRO *at foot of steps, looking up to loft and then*
slowly walking towards top of stairs.

KITCHEN
MIDDIE *enters through door from cellar, gives*
a baleful glance down, closes door, continues
across kitchen, and out into passage.

HALL
BRO *coming down stairs.* MIDDIE *approaching*
from kitchen. They stop, look at each other.
Fade.

BANQUETING HALL IN PALATIAL COUNTRY SEAT
The two men surveying it for space.

SNS : Question is, do we take the total cubic capacity
in bits and pieces as it stands. What is it?

BBC : Four million, two hundred and ninety three
thousand five hundred and eighteen cubic feet.

SNS : ... or do we shift them around a bit, and get
it all together in one area? Say, the central
block here and the whole of the west wing as
one clear space.

BBC : I'd say leave it as it is, and fill up with whatever we've got in any odd corner that's going.
Where's the list?

SNS : Here.

BBC : Turkish Baths. That could go easily under the
minstrels gallery. In the long Hall there.

SNS : Or beside the chest of drawers on the landing
up there by the window.

BBC : What else have we got to find room for?
Broadcasting House. Smithfield Meat Market.
Bank of England.

SNS : Over here. There's an alcove. On the stairs.

BBC: Let's make a note of this. Before we lose track.

LIVING ROOM
BRO, MIDDIE, *with their neighbours*, NORA, ALBERT, *are chatting over tea and biscuits.*

NORA: Not so much as a whisper of May I? Or anything like that.

ALBERT: It's where they have you, you see.

MIDDIE: More tea in that cup, Nora?

NORA: Thank you, Middie.

ALBERT: They come round, while you're out, wife lets them in ...

BRO: And hey presto.

ALBERT: Chap up the road. They came in. Same story. He was out down the darts club. Friday, wasn't it?

NORA: Friday or Saturday.

ALBERT: Wife lets them in, yes, sir, no, sir, three bags full sir – Next thing he knows they've moved this lumbering great old Victorian soup kitchen in on them.

NORA: Supposed to be for down and outs.

MIDDIE: Let me fill your cup, Albert.

ALBERT: Oh, thank you, Middie.

BRO: It's like us. One up in the loft, one down in the cellar.

ALBERT: Yes.

NORA: You feel hemmed in.

MIDDIE: Well, you do.

ALBERT: But as far as the soup kitchen was concerned, this was in their best bedroom. It's officialdom run riot.

NORA: Somebody knocks on the door, six or seven huge great buckets on the doorstep. What's this? she says. He says, tomato soup.

MIDDIE: No.

NORA: She says, we know they've got to eat.

ALBERT: But not in somebody else's best bedroom.

MIDDIE: Well, quite.

NORA: And they don't mind where they slop it to, on the way upstairs.

BRO: I shouldn't think having people in and out at all hours of the day and night to drink it can be all that congenial either.

ALBERT: Caterwauling.

NORA: Quite.

MIDDIE: In the small hours.

ALBERT: And carrying on.

NORA: The neighbours are complaining of course.

MIDDIE: It's not surprising.

NORA: And they're all down and outs that come.

BRO: They would be.

NORA: They never get anybody decent coming for it. (*To* ALBERT) Do they? Once in the blue moon.

ALBERT: Old Mr. Sayers sometimes.

NORA: Only when it's oxtail or mulligatawny.

ALBERT: And then it's as much for old time's sake.

NORA: But with most of them, it's only the free soup they come for.

MIDDIE: And because they're getting that, they think it gives them carte blanche.

ALBERT: Quite.

BRO: To come trailing in and out over somebody else's carpet.

NORA: She's had to take it up. Hasn't she? On the landing.

MIDDIE: It's no joke is it?

NORA: What with the crumbs. And the rings where they put the buckets down.

ALBERT: The one I really feel for is little old Mrs. Cobley-Willett. Down the road.

MIDDIE: Yes. Bro was saying.

ALBERT: Just because she had a little bit of space she wasn't using under the draining board.

NORA: What's this, then? I hadn't heard this.

ALBERT: Little old Mrs. Cobley-Willett. What is she? Ninety-three?

BRO: Getting on.

ALBERT: Gave her the fright of her life. (*To* NORA) Cupboard under the sink. Opened the door – found she'd had Beaverbrook House wished on to her during the night.

MIDDIE: Printing presses. Everything. Reporters.

NORA: No!

ALBERT: Yes – she wondered what had hit her.

BRO: I think she thought she was going to be asked to get in there and bring out the Daily Express single handed.

NORA: What? Every day?

BRO: I think that's what she had in the back of her mind.

NORA: Enough to give her a stroke, poor old soul.

BRO: I don't think she even knows how to use a typewriter, does she?

MIDDIE: Probably not.

BRO: Which is the first requirement.

ALBERT: They say the chap who brings it out now can only type with one finger but he's got all day.

NORA: Of course he has.

BRO: I wouldn't like to do it myself part time.

ALBERT: Tall order.

NORA: I should think it was. I wouldn't dream of letting you.

ALBERT: Get home after a hard day's work, all ready for a quiet evening in front of the telly, and find that job staring you in the face the moment you open a cupboard door.

BRO: Your life's not your own.

NORA: It isn't.

MIDDIE: The thing, of course, that's getting Mrs. Cobley-Willett down is having a lot of men in green eyeshields under her feet the whole time.

NORA: In and out, I suppose.

ALBERT: It's not only that. It's the language.

BRO: And the cigarette ends.

MIDDIE: I think it's the eyeshields.

BRO: The eyeshields are part of it, but it's as much the language when they're off duty.

ALBERT: The eyeshields can get you down, of course.

NORA: I'm sure.

ALBERT: It's not as if they ever take them off.

MIDDIE: Oh no. They wear them all the time.

BRO: Go out in them.

NORA: No. Do they?

MIDDIE: Oh yes.

BRO: So Mrs. Cobley-Willett was saying.

NORA: Heavens above.

MIDDIE: Think nothing of walking out through the front door as large as life with their eyeshields on. If they're not watched. For everybody to see. Who happens to be passing. In fact, she was talking about putting a notice up. Just inside the front door. For them to see. As they're going out.

ALBERT: Please do not go beyond this door with your eyeshields on, and oblige. A. Cobley-Willett.

MIDDIE: Oh – she's put it up, has she?

ALBERT: Yesterday. Helped her tack it up.

NORA: I never knew she was A. Cobley-Willett, before.

ALBERT: Yes. She always signs herself A. Cobley-Willett.

NORA: I never knew that.

BRO: What is it? Alice?

ALBERT: Adelaide. Isn't it? Adelaide or Alice.

BRO: I always thought it was Alice. But I may be wrong.

MIDDIE: It's Alice.

ALBERT: Yes. You may be right.

NORA: Agnes, perhaps.

BRO: No. I think you'll find it's Alice, Nora.

MIDDIE: It is. It's Alice.

ALBERT: I know she never signs herself anything but A. Whatever that signifies.

NORA: Fancy. All these years, and I never knew that.

ALBERT:	It's got to stand for something. Adelaide, Alice. One of them.
NORA:	Who was it, come to think of it, in the self-service was saying something about Mrs. Cobley-Willett and her Christian name beginning with A? Mrs. Fisher, was it?
MIDDIE:	Mrs. Fisher's a friend of hers.
NORA:	That's who it'll have been, then.
ALBERT:	We must be going, Nora.
NORA:	We must. Yes. Is that the time? Good heavens. We certainly must. (*Getting up*) Yes. What did she say the A stood for? She did say. Antonia? I don't know.
BRO:	I think you'll find it's Alice, Nora.
NORA:	Very likely. Although I thought it was something longer.
ALBERT:	Well. Thank you, Middie. For the tea.
NORA:	Yes. It was a nice cup of tea.
MIDDIE:	You must come again.
	NORA *notices bell pull.*
NORA:	I like your ...
MIDDIE:	It's a bell pull.
NORA:	Very novel. (*To* ALBERT) Isn't it? Their bell pull.
ALBERT:	It is. It's novel.
MIDDIE:	Bro managed to get hold of it.
NORA:	It's nice.
ALBERT:	It's a novel thing.
NORA:	(*Going out*) We'll have to try and get one, Albert.
MIDDIE:	(*Going out*) They're not very easy to come by, Nora, as a matter of fact. Bro was lucky.
ALBERT:	Tidy old price.
BRO:	They're not cheap. But it gives a touch of ... to the room.
ALBERT:	Certain rarity value.

HALL

MIDDIE:	And it gives a focal point to the room.

NORA: Where did I put my ... oh yes, here it is.

MIDDIE: Unless they decide to move something else in on us.

NORA: Well, that's the problem, isn't it?

LIVING ROOM

ALBERT: I mean, there's no doubt about it we're over-crowded. As an island. No doubt at all about that. And there's no doubt it's got to come. In time.

BRO: It's the *way* they do it.

HALL

MIDDIE: (*Opening front door*) Have you got your tomatoes, Nora?

NORA: Yes, I've picked those up.

MIDDIE: Goodbye then, Nora.

ALBERT: Goodbye, Middie.

BRO: (*To* ALBERT) See you on Tuesday, Albert. Goodbye, Nora.

NORA: Goodbye, Bro. Goodbye, Middie.
They go. MIDDIE *closes door.*

MIDDIE: Goodness. They do go on.

LIVING ROOM
BRO *and* MIDDIE *enter*

BRO: They've always been the same.

MIDDIE: Now I've got to clear this lot up. See if they've finished in the kitchen, will you?
BRO *goes into dining room, and slides the hatch gingerly open.*

PARTIAL VIEW OF KITCHEN THROUGH HATCH
We see part of an oak-panelled, book-lined thickly carpeted Harley Street consulting-room. Consultant sitting behind elegant and imposing desk. Client sitting opposite.

CONS: And the trousers you got back from the cleaners the day before yesterday.

CLIENT: That's right.
BRO *closes hatch.*

DINING ROOM

BRO: No.

MIDDIE: They're not still on, surely. I've got a cake in the oven.

BRO: Once they get the bit between their teeth.

BRO *looks out through front windows into the garden*

BRO: It's looking a bit brighter out there. I think I might get out into the garden.

LIVING ROOM

MIDDIE *is standing by the bureau. Through the open doors we see a vast, empty, hangar-like exhibition building. The caretaker is chatting with* MIDDIE.

CARE: Big exhibitions. Mass meetings. All means extra work.

MIDDIE: Are you on your own?

CARE: I've got Fred over there. Fred!

FRED *doesn't hear. He's too busy.*

CARE: Last week but one. Dairy show in here. Mess! You never saw anything like it. Cows, pigs, Stilton cheese – it was like a circus.

BRO *has come up.*

MIDDIE: (*To* BRO) Mr. Willbelow here's just telling me about the Dairy Show they had in here the other week.

CARE: Oh yes. Ideal Home Exhibition. Eton and Harrow Match. They're all held in here.

BRO: Go on?

CARE: Every week practically. Some function or other.

BRO: Makes a lot of work.

MIDDIE: It must do.

CARE: Billy Graham. He's another one comes here a lot.

BRO: Oh yes?

CARE: Revivalists.

MIDDIE :   (*To* BRO) Surely they're not still at it out there.
BRO :   You can go and see.
CARE :   In and out a lot, they are. Revivalists.
BRO :   Go out there. Knock on the door.
MIDDIE :   I'll go and look through. (*Goes to hatch*)
BRO :   They won't have finished. Not by a long chalk.

KITCHEN (AS CONSULTING ROOM)
CONSULTANT *and* CLIENT *as before.*

CONS :   And the jacket, of course. That's a different proposition.
CLIENT :   Well – in a way.
CONS :   Yes.
CLIENT :   In a way, not.
CONS :   Have you been through the lining?
CLIENT :   No, I can't say I have.
CONS :   I should go through the lining.
CLIENT :   Yes. I'll do that.
CONS :   Go through the lining and see where it brings you out.
CLIENT :   Yes.
CONS :   You can do it in ten minutes on a bike.

DINING ROOM
MIDDIE *at hatch, straightening up and closing it.*

MIDDIE :   They go on and on. There's no stopping them.

LIVING ROOM
BRO *at bureau with caretaker.*

CARE :   Sheepdog trials. That's the bane of my life.
BRO :   Yes.
CARE :   Every Friday. Dogs all over the place. Shepherds. It's murder, I can tell you.
            MIDDIE *enters.*
BRO :   Yes. It would be.
CARE :   Nice size, though. All in all.
MIDDIE :   They're still on.
BRO :   I'll go out there.

MIDDIE:	It's his private practice, Bro. You can't do that.
BRO:	I'll tell him you've got a cake in the oven.
MIDDIE:	It's unprofessional. While he's got a client with him.
BRO:	I'll just look through the door. (*He goes*)
MIDDIE:	(*To* BRO) Be careful. We don't want him suing us.

MIDDIE *goes through to dining room to look through hatch.*

KITCHEN (AS CONSULTING ROOM)
CLIENT *and* CONSULTANT *getting up.*

CONS:	That's my advice to you, Mr. Greenchild.
CLIENT:	Well, thank you.
CONS:	Not at all. It's what I'm here for.

Hatch slowly opens. MIDDIE *looks through.*

CONS:	Is there anything I can get you before I go?
CLIENT:	Oh. That's very kind of you.
CONS:	Cigarette? Cigar? Sherry?

Door in view. BRO *looking in.*

CLIENT:	A small bottle of mayonnaise would be very welcome if you have one.
CONS:	Ah ...
CLIENT:	Or an old Swiss cuckoo clock. But it doesn't matter.
	Anything at all that you happen to have.

BRO *withdrawing and gently closing door.*

CLIENT:	I don't want to trespass on your hospitality.

MIDDIE *withdrawing from hatch and closing it.*

CONS:	I'm afraid the best I can do by way of a gate-leg table is a hundredweight of coal.

LIVING ROOM
BRO *enters from passage.*

BRO:	Just the formalities.
MIDDIE:	About time.

KITCHEN (AS CONSULTING ROOM)
CONSULTANT *showing* CLIENT *out by back door.*

CONS :   You can find your way down, I expect.

CLIENT :   Yes. Yes, I think I'm all right. It's like the Black
Hole of Calcutta, but ...
Sound of crashing ironmongery.

CONS :   Goodbye, Mr. Greenchild.

LIVING ROOM
BRO *and* MIDDIE. BRO *switching on TV.*

MIDDIE :   That sounds like it.

BRO :   Yes.

MIDDIE :   (*Going*) Let's hope they've left it as they found
it.
BRO *sits to watch TV. Notices bureau, gets up
hastily to close it as he sees* CARETAKER *approaching.*

KITCHEN
MIDDIE *enters, goes to the oven, and takes out
cake. It is burnt to a cinder.*

LIVING ROOM
BRO *is watching the television. On the screen
we see Fyfe Robertson. A coalmine in the background.*

ROB :   ... or for that matter how many times have
you stood behind frosted glass at seventeen or
eighteen degrees below zero in the hope of
being mistaken for Alexander the Great at the
North Pole? This is a question ...

PASSAGE
MIDDIE *coming from kitchen. She passes cupboard door. Its contents of brooms, bucket,
mop, steps, etc., are stacked neatly against the
wall beside the door.* MIDDIE *looks at them.*

LIVING ROOM
BRO *watching TV. Fyfe Robertson speaking.*

ROB :   And yet only a stone's throw away from the
spot where George the Third is said to have

been stung by a swarm of bees, people are still engaged in quarrying slate from one of the largest flour mills in the country.

PASSAGE
MIDDIE *tries the door. It is locked. She looks nonplussed.*

LIVING ROOM
BRO *still at TV. Fyfe Robertson speaking.*

ROB: ... How do they do it? Or is it all the most gigantic fraud ever to have been perpetrated on a gullible public? The controversy rages.

PASSAGE
MIDDIE *with her ear against cupboard door. On track we hear sounds of boat race. Voice shouting: in, out, in out: water splashing. Rhythmic sliding of seats and swivelling of rowlocks. Crowds cheering.* MIDDIE *straightens up. Sounds cease.* MIDDIE *goes into living room.*

LIVING ROOM
BRO *goes to switch off TV as* MIDDIE *comes in.*

ROB: ... one of the oldest butcher's shops in the Pennine Chain.
BRO *switches off.*

MIDDIE: What was that?

BRO: Panorama.
BRO *takes up paper and sits with it.*
MIDDIE *sits down to her rug.*
BRO *does crossword.*

BRO: Turned into a pillar of salt. Wasn't that the Wife of Bath?

MIDDIE: Yes.

BRO: It doesn't fit.
MIDDIE'S *attention is attracted towards the corner behind* BRO *where the bell pull is. She is watching something going on.*

MIDDIE: I told you that was a ridiculous place to put it.

BRO: What?

MIDDIE: The bell pull.

            BRO *looks round.*

            We see corner of room. Surgical operation in progress. Each time surgeon bends to make an incision, the tassel on the end of the bell pull bobs in front of his face and obstructs his vision. Eventually he lifts it up between gloved finger and thumb, and hands it to his assistant who gravely holds it up out of the way, and the operation continues.

            We cut back to BRO *and* MIDDIE. BRO *turns back to his crossword.*

MIDDIE: Getting in everyone's way.

BRO: Queen of Sheba.

            MIDDIE *goes back to her rug. She glances in the direction of the french windows.*

MIDDIE: (*Getting up*) I thought it was draughty. Who opened those? (*She crosses to windows*)

VOICE: Quiet please.

            Through dining room windows we see rocket on launching pad. Along one wall of the room we see for the first time a rocket launching control panel with white-coated technicians at it.

            MIDDIE *has frozen, and dutifully waits.*

VOICE: Ten, nine, eight, seven, six, five, four, three, two, one, zero.

            Rocket rises from launching pad. It is away. Jubilation amongst technicians.

            MIDDIE *continues across to windows.*

            BRO *returns to crossword.*

            MIDDIE *closes windows, and comes back into living room.* MIDDIE *sits down with rug.* BRO *continues with crossword. Neither speaks for a time.*

MIDDIE: What shall we have to drink? For a change?

BRO: Drink?

MIDDIE: Instead of cocoa.
BRO: Oh.
          Silence.
BRO: What's wrong with hot milk?
MIDDIE: Just finish this, and then I'll get it.
          MIDDIE *finishes the rug, and places it on the floor by the fireplace. They both stand looking down at it.*
          Fade.

J. C. SQUIRE

Ballade of Soporific Absorption

Ho! Ho! Yes! Yes! It's very all well,
  You may drunk I am think, but I tell you I'm not,
I'm as sound as a fiddle and fit as a bell,
  And stable quite ill to see what's what.
  I under *do* stand you surprise a got
When I headed my smear with gooseberry jam;
  And I've swallowed, I grant, a beer of lot —
But I'm not so think as you drunk I am.

Can I liquor my stand; Why, yes, like hell!
  I care not how many a tossed I've pot,
I shall stralk quite weight and not yutter an ell,
  My feech will not spalter the least little jot:
  If you knownly had one! — well, I gave him a dot,
And I said to him, 'Sergeant, I'll come like a lamb —
  The floor it seems like a storm in a yacht,
But I'm not so think as you drunk I am.'

For example, to prove it I'll tale you a tell —
  I once knew a fellow named Apricot —
I'm sorry, I just chair over a fell —
  A trifle — this chap, on a very day hot —
  If I hadn't consumed that last whisky of tot! —

As I said now, this fellow, called Abraham —
Ah? One more? Since it's you! Just a do me will spot —
But I'm not so think as you drunk I am.

Envoi
So, Prince, you suggest I've bolted my shot?
Well, like what you say, and soul your damn!
I'm an upple litset by the talk you rot —
But I'm not so think as you drunk I am.

JONATHAN SWIFT

Gulliver's Travels

The first man I saw was of a meagre aspect, with sooty
hands and face, his hair and beard long, ragged and singed
in several places. His cloaths, shirt, and skin, were all of
the same colour. He had been eight years upon a project
for extracting sun-beams out of cucumbers, which were
to be put into vials hermetically sealed, and let out to
warm the air in raw inclement summers. He told me, he
did not doubt, that in eight years more he should be able
to supply the governor's gardens with sunshine at a reasonable rate; but he complained that his stock was low, and
intreated me to give him something as an encouragement
to ingenuity, especially since this had been a very dear
season for cucumbers. I made him a small present, for my
lord had furnished me with money on purpose, because
he knew their practice of begging from all who go to see
them.

I went into another chamber, but was ready to hasten
back, being almost overcome with a horrible stink. My
conductor pressed me forward, conjuring me in a whisper
to give no offence, which would be highly resented, and
therefore I durst not so much as stop my nose. The pro-
jector of this cell was the most ancient student of the
academy; his face and beard were of a pale yellow: his
hands and cloaths dawbed over with filth. When I was

presented to him he gave me a close embrace (a compliment I could well have excused). His employment from his first coming into the academy was an operation to reduce human excrement to its original food by separating the several parts, removing the tincture which it receives from the gall, making the odour exhale, and scumming off the saliva. He had a weekly allowance from the society of a vessel filled with human ordure about the bigness of a Bristol barrel.

I saw another at work to calcine ice into gun-powder, who likewise shewed me a treatise he had written concerning the malleability of fire, which he intended to publish.

There was a most ingenious architect, who had contrived a new method for building houses by beginning at the roof, and working downwards to the foundation, which he justified to me by the like practice of those two prudent insects the bee and the spider.

... The humble PETITION of the Colliers, Cooks, Cookmaids, blacksmiths, Jack-makers, Brasiers, and others, SHEWETH

That whereas certain *virtuosi*, disaffected to the government, and to the trade and prosperity of this kingdoms, taking upon them the name and title of the CATOPTRICAL VICTUALLERS, have presumed by gathering, breaking, folding, and bundling up the *sun-beams*, by the help of certain *glasses*, to make, produce, and kindle up several new *focus's*, or fires, within these his Majesty's dominions, and thereby to boil, bake, stew, fry and dress all sorts of victuals and provisions, to brew, distil spirits, smelt oar, and in general to perform all the offices of culinary fires; and are endeavouring to procure themselves the monopoly of this their said invention : We beg leave humbly to represent to your honours,

That such grant or patent will utterly ruin and reduce to beggary your petitioners, their wives, children, servants, and trades on them depending; there being nothing left to them, after the said invention, but warming of cellars, and dressing of suppers in the winter-time. That the abolishing so considerable a branch of the coasting trade, as that of the colliers, will destroy the *navigation* of this kingdom. That whereas the said *catoptrical victuallers* talk of making use of the *moon* by night, as of the *sun* by day, they will utterly ruin the numerous body of *tallow chandlers*, and impair a very considerable branch of the *revenue*, which arises from the *tax* upon tallow and candles.

That the said *catoptrical victuallers* do profane the emanations of that glorious luminary the *sun*, which is appointed to *rule the day*, and not to *roast mutton*. And we humbly conceive, it will be found contrary to the known laws of this kingdom, to confine, forestall, and monopolize the beams of the sun. And whereas the said *catoptrical victuallers* have undertaken, by burning glasses made of ice, to roast an ox upon the Thames next winter : we conceive all such practices to be an incroachment upon the rights and privileges of the *company of watermen*.

That the diversity of exposition of the several kitchens in this great city, whereby some receive the rays of the sun sooner, and others later, will occasion great irregularity as to the *time of dining* of the several inhabitants, and consequently great uncertainty and confusion in the dispatch of business : and to those, who, by reason of their northern exposition, will be still forced to be at the expences of culinary fires, it will reduce the price of their manufacture to such inequality, as is inconsistent with common justice : and the same inconveniency will affect *landlords* in the *value* of their *rents*.

That the use of the said glasses will oblige cooks, and cook-maids to study optics and astronomy, in order to know the due distances of the said focus's, or fires, and to adjust the position of their glasses to the several altitudes of the sun, varying according to the hours of the day, and the seasons of the year; which studies, at these years, will be highly troublesome to the said cooks and cookmaids, not to say any thing of the utter incapacity of some of them to go through with such difficult arts; or (which is still a greater inconvenience) it will throw the whole art of *cookery* into the hands of astronomers and glassgrinders, persons utterly unskilled in other parts of that profession, to the great detriment of the *health* of his Majesty's good subjects.

That it is known by experience, that meat roasted with sun-beams is extremely unwholesome; witness several that have died suddenly after eating the provision of the said *catoptrical victuallers*; forasmuch as the sun-beams taken inwardly render the humours too hot and a-dust, occasion great sweatings, and dry up the rectual moisture.

The sun-beams taken *inwardly* shed a malignant influence upon the *brain*, by their natural tendency towards the *moon*; and produce madness and distraction at the time of the full moon. That the constant use of so great quantities of this *inward light* will occasion the growth of *quakerism*, to the danger of the *church*, and of poetry, to the danger of the state.

That the influences of the constellations, through which the sun passes, will, with his beams, be conveyed into the *blood*; and when the sun is among the horned signs, may produce such a spirit of *unchastity*, as is dangerous to the honour of your worships families.

That mankind living much upon the seeds and other parts of plants, these being impregnated with the sun-beams, may *vegetate* and *grow* in the bowels, a thing of more dangerous consequence to human bodies than breeding of worms; and this will fall heaviest upon the poor, who live upon roots; and the weak and sickly, who live upon barley and rice-gruel, *etc.*, for which we are ready to produce to your honours the opinions of eminent physicians, that the taste and property of the victuals is much altered to the worse by the said *solar cookery*, fricassies being deprived of the *haut goût* they acquired by being dressed over charcoal.

Lastly, should it happen by an eclipse of an extraordinary length, that this city should be deprived of the sun-beams for several months: how will his Majesty's subjects subsist in the interim, when common cookery, with the arts depending upon it, is totally lost?

In consideration of these, and many other inconveniences, your petitioners humbly pray, that your honours would either totally prohibite the confining and manufacturing the *sun-beams* for any of the useful purposes of life, or, in the ensuing parliament, procure a *tax to be laid* upon them, which may answer both the duty and price of *coals*, and which we humbly conceive cannot be less than thirty shillings *per yard square*, reserving the sole right and privilege of the *catoptrical cookery* to the *royal society*, and to the commanders and crew of the bomb-vessels, under the direction of Mr. Whiston for finding out the longitude, who, by reason of the remoteness of their stations, may be reduced to straits for want of firing.

And we likewise beg, that your honours, as to the forementioned points, would hear the Reverend Mr. Flamstead, who is the legal officer appointed by the government to *look after the heavenly luminaries*, whom we have constituted our trusty and learned solicitor.

T

JAMES THURBER

If Grant Had Been Drinking at Appomattox

The morning of the ninth of April, 1865, dawned beautifully. General Meade was up with the first streaks of crimson in the eastern sky. General Hooker and General Burnside were up, and had breakfasted, by a quarter after eight. The day continued beautiful. It drew on toward eleven o'clock. General Ulysses S. Grant was still not up. He was asleep in his famous old navy hammock, swung high above the floor of his headquarters' bedroom. Headquarters was distressingly disarranged: papers were strewn on the floor; confidential notes from spies scurried here and there in the breeze from an open window; the dregs of an overturned bottle of wine flowed pinkly across an important military map.

Corporal Shultz, of the Sixty-fifth Ohio Volunteer Infantry, aide to General Grant, came into the outer room, looked around him, and sighed. He entered the bedroom and shook the General's hammock roughly. General Ulysses S. Grant opened one eye.

'Pardon, sir,' said Corporal Shultz, 'but this is the day of surrender. You ought to be up, sir.'

'Don't swing me,' said Grant, sharply, for his aide was making the hammock sway gently. 'I feel terrible,' he added, and he turned over and closed his eye again.

'General Lee will be here any minute now,' said the Corporal firmly, swinging the hammock again.

'Will you cut that out?' roared Grant. 'D'ya want to

make me sick, or what?' Shultz clicked his heels and saluted. 'What's he coming here for?' asked the General.

'This is the day of surrender, sir,' said Shultz. Grant grunted bitterly.

'Three hundred and fifty generals in the Northern armies,' said Grant, 'and he has to come to *me* about this. What time is it?'

'You're the Commander-in-Chief, that's why,' said Corporal Shultz. 'It's eleven twenty-five, sir.'

'Don't be crazy,' said Grant. 'Lincoln is the Commander-in-Chief. Nobody in the history of the world ever surrendered before lunch. Doesn't he know that an army surrenders on its stomach?' He pulled a blanket up over his head and settled himself again.

'The generals of the Confederacy will be here any minute now,' said the Corporal. 'You really ought to be up, sir.'

Grant stretched his arms above his head and yawned.

'All right, all right,' he said. He rose to a sitting position and stared about the room. 'This place looks awful,' he growled.

'You must have had quite a time of it last night, sir,' ventured Shultz.

'Yeh,' said General Grant, looking around for his clothes. 'I was wrassling some general. Some general with a beard.'

Shultz helped the commander of the Northern armies in the field to find his clothes.

'Where's my other sock?' demanded Grant. Shultz began to look around for it. The General walked uncertainly to a table and poured a drink from a bottle.

'I don't think it wise to drink, sir,' said Shultz.

'Nev' mind about me,' said Grant, helping himself to a second, 'I can take it or let it alone. Didn'ya ever hear the story about the fella went to Lincoln to complain about me drinking too much? "So-and-so says Grant drinks too much," this fella said. "So-and-So is a fool," said Lincoln. So this fella went to What's-His-Name and told him what Lincoln said and he came roarin' to Lincoln about it. "Did you tell So-and-So I was a fool?" he said, "No," said Lincoln, "I thought he knew it." ' The General smiled reminiscently, and had another drink. 'That's how I stand with Lincoln,' he said, proudly.

The soft thudding sound of horses' hooves came through the open window. Shultz hurriedly walked over and looked out.

'Hoof steps,' said Grant, with a curious chortle.

'It is General Lee and his staff,' said Shultz.

'Show him in,' said the General, taking another drink. 'And see what the boys in the back room will have.'

Shultz walked smartly over to the door, opened it, saluted, and stood aside. General Lee, dignified against the blue of the April sky, magnificent in his dress uniform, stood for a moment framed in the doorway. He walked in, followed by his staff. They bowed, and stood silent. General Grant stared at them. He only had one boot on and his jacket was unbuttoned.

'I know who you are,' said Grant. 'You're Robert Browning, the poet.'

'This is General Robert E. Lee,' said one of his staff, coldly.

'Oh,' said Grant. 'I thought he was Robert Browning. He certainly looks like Robert Browning. There was a poet for you, Lee: Browning. Did ja ever read "How They Brought the Good News from Ghent to Aix"? "Up Derek, to saddle, up Derek, away, up Dunder, up Blitzen, up Prancer, up Dander, up Bouncer, up Vixen, up —'

'Shall we proceed at once to the matter in hand?' asked General Lee, his eyes disdainfully taking in the disordered room.

'Some of the boys was wrassling here last night,' explained Grant. 'I threw Sherman, or some general a whole lot like Sherman. It was pretty dark.' He handed a bottle of Scotch to the commanding officer of the Southern armies, who stood holding it, in amazement and discomfiture. 'Get a glass, somebody,' said Grant, looking straight at General Longstreet. 'Didn't I meet you at Cold Harbor?' he asked. General Longstreet did not answer.

'I should like to have this over with as soon as possible,' said Lee. Grant looked vaguely at Shultz, who walked up close to him, frowning.

'The surrender, sir, the surrender,' said Corporal Shultz in a whisper.

'Oh sure, sure,' said Grant. He took another drink. 'All right,' he said. 'Here we go.' Slowly, sadly, he unbuckled his sword. Then he handed it to the astonished Lee. 'There you are, General,' said Grant. 'We dam' near licked you. If I'd been feeling better we *would* of licked you.'

There's An Owl In My Room

I saw Gertrude Stein on the screen of a newsreel theater one afternoon and I heard her read that famous passage of hers about pigeons on the grass, alas (the sorrow is, as you know, Miss Stein's). After reading about the pigeons on the grass alas, Miss Stein said, 'This is a simple description of a landscape I have seen many times.' I don't really believe that that is true. Pigeons on the grass alas may be a simple description of Miss Stein's own consciousness, but it is not a simple description of a plot of grass on which pigeons have alighted, are alighting, or are going to alight. A truly simple description of the pigeons alighting on the grass of the Luxembourg Gardens (which, I believe, is where the pigeons alighted) would say of the pigeons alighting there only that they were pigeons alighting. Pigeons that alight anywhere are neither sad pigeons nor gay pigeons, they are simply pigeons.

It is neither just nor accurate to connect the word alas with pigeons. Pigeons are definitely not alas. They have nothing to do with alas and they have nothing to do with hooray (not even when you tie red, white and blue ribbons on them and let them loose at band concerts); they have nothing to do with mercy me or isn't that fine, either.

White rabbits, yes, and Scotch terriers, and blue-jays, and even hippopotamuses, but not pigeons. I happen to have studied pigeons very closely and carefully, and I have studied the effect or rather the lack of effect, of pigeons very carefully. A number of pigeons alight from time to time on the sill of my hotel window when I am eating breakfast and staring out the window. They never alas me, they never make me feel alas; they never make me feel anything.

Nobody and no animal and no other bird can play a scene so far down as a pigeon can. For instance, when a pigeon on my window ledge becomes aware of me sitting there in a chair in my blue polka-dot dressing-gown, worrying, he pokes his head far out from his shoulders and peers sideways at me, for all the world (Miss Stein might surmise) like a timid man peering around the corner of a building trying to ascertain whether he is being followed by some hoofed fiend or only by the echo of his own footsteps. And yet it is *not* for all the world like a timid men peering around the corner of a building trying to ascertain whether he is being followed by a hoofed fiend or only by the echo of his own footsteps, at all. And that is because there is no emotion in the pigeon and no power to arouse emotion. A pigeon looking is just a pigeon looking. When it comes to emotion, a fish, compared to a pigeon, is practically beside himself.

A pigeon peering at me doesn't make me sad or glad or apprehensive or hopeful. With a horse or a cow or a dog it would be different. It would be especially different with a dog. Some dogs peer at me as if I had just gone completely crazy or as if they had just gone completely crazy. I can go so far as to say that most dogs peer at me in that way. This creates in the consciousness of both me and the dog a feeling of alarm or downright terror and legitimately permits me to work into a description of the landscape, in which the dog and myself are figures, a note of emotion. Thus I should not have minded if Miss Stein had written : dogs on the grass, look out, dogs on the grass, look out, look out, dogs on the grass, look out Alice. That would be a simple description of dogs on the grass. But when any writer pretends that a pigeon makes him sad, or makes him anything else, I must instantly protest that this is a highly specialized fantastic impression created in an individual consciousness and that therefore it cannot fairly be presented as a simple description of what actually was to be seen.

People who do not understand pigeons – and pigeons can be understood only when you understand that there is nothing to understand about them – should not go around describing pigeons or the effect of pigeons. Pigeons come closer to a zero of impingement than any other birds. Hens embarrass me the way my old Aunt Hattie used to when I was twelve and she still insisted I wasn't big enough to bathe myself; owls disturb me; if I am with an eagle I always pretend that I am not with an eagle; and so on down to swallows at twilight who scare the hell out of me. But pigeons have absolutely no effect on me. They have absolutely no effect on anybody. They couldn't even startle a child. That is why they are selected from among all birds to be let loose, with colored ribbons attached to them, at band concerts, library dedications, and christenings of new dirigibles. If anybody let loose a lot of owls on such an occasion there would be rioting and catcalls and whistling and fainting spells and throwing of chairs and the Lord only knows what else.

From where I am sitting now I can look out the window and see a pigeon being a pigeon on the roof of the Harvard Club. No other thing can be less what it is not than a pigeon can, and Miss Stein, of all people, should understand that simple fact. Behind the pigeon I am looking at, a blank wall of tired gray bricks is stolidly trying to sleep off oblivion; underneath the pigeon the cloistered windows of the Harvard Club are staring in horrified bewilderment at something they have seen across the street. The pigeon is just there on the roof being a pigeon, having been, and being, a pigeon and, what is more, always going to be, too.

Nothing could be simpler than that. If you read that sentence aloud you will instantly see what I mean. It is a simple description of a pigeon on a roof. It is only with an effort that I am conscious of the pigeon, but I am acutely aware of a great sulky red iron pipe that is creeping up the side of the building intent on sneaking up on a slightly tipsy chimney which is shouting its head off.

There is nothing a pigeon can do or be that would make me feel sorry for it or for myself or for the people in the world, just as there is nothing I could do or be that would make a pigeon feel sorry for itself. Even if I plucked his feathers out it would not make him feel sorry for himself and it would not make me feel sorry for myself or for him. But try plucking the quills out of a porcupine or even plucking the fur out of a jackrabbit. There is nothing a pigeon could be, or can be, rather, which could get into my consciousness like a fumbling hand in a bureau drawer and disarrange my mind or pull anything out of it. I bar nothing at all. You could dress up a pigeon in a tiny suit of evening clothes and put a tiny silk hat on his head and a tiny gold-headed cane under his wing and send him walking into my room at night. It would make no impression on me.

I would not shout, 'Good god almighty, the birds are in charge!' But you could send an owl into my room, dressed only in the feathers it was born with, and no monkey business, and I would pull the covers over my head and scream.

No other thing in the world falls so far short of being able to do what it cannot do as a pigeon does. Of being *unable* to do what it *can* do, too, as far as that goes.

The Wonderful O

There still were those who spoke with O's, and one of these was a boatwright, a man of force and gusto. 'You are still my spouse and not my spuse,' he told his fearful wife, 'and this is my house and not my huse, and I make boats, not bats, and I wear coats, not cats. What,' he asked his youngest son, 'did you learn today in school?'

'It's schl,' his son replied.

'Never hiss at me,' his father cried. 'When I want aloes, I don't want ales, I hate such names. And cameos are cameos, not cames. Yesterday I met a man who wanted four canoes –'

'Fur canes,' his son put in.

'Silence!' his father shouted. 'What did you learn today in school?'

'That mist is always mist, but what is mist isn't always mist,' his son recited.

At this his father rose up like a storm, put on his hat and cat, and stalked to where the door had been, and reached for where the knob once was.

'Where are yu ging?' whispered his anxious wife.

'Ut!' the boatwright cried, and ut he went.

'What did yu say t yur father that made him leave the huse?' the mother asked her son.

'Mist is always moist,' the boy replied in whispers, 'but what is moist isn't always mist.'

And other odd occurrences occurred. A swain who praised his sweetheart's thrat, and said she sang like a chir of riles or a chrus of vires, was slapped. And so it went, and some lads lost their lasses, and most men lost their tempers, and all men lost their patience, and a few men lost their minds.

Then Black called Hyde one day in consultation. 'Some of the people salute me as I pass,' he growled. 'Do you know why?'

'O-lessness is now a kind of cult in certain quarters,' Hyde observed, 'a messy lessness, whose meaninglessness nonetheless attracts the few, first onc or two, then three or four, then more and more. People often have respect for what they cannot comprehend, since some men cannot always tell their crosses from their blessings, their laurels from their thorns. It shows up in the games they still can play. Charades are far more work than fun, and so are Blind Man's Buff and Hide-and-Seek, and Run, Sheep, Run. O lessism may become the ism of the future, and men from far and wide, pilgrims on a pilgrimage, may lay their tributes on your grave.'

Black showed his teeth and made a restless gesture. 'Taking a single letter from the alphabet,' he said, 'should make life simpler.'

'I don't see why. Take the F from life and you have lie. It's adding a letter to simple that makes it simpler. Taking a letter from hoarder makes it harder.' With a small shrug and a little leer, Hyde turned on his heel and walked away.

Black watched him go and scowled. 'He's much too smart,' he said aloud, 'for his own good and for mine.'

... Working with valor and love and hope, the islanders put the O back in everything that had lost it. The name of Goldilocks regained its laughter, and there were locks for keys, and shoes were no longer shes. A certain couple once more played their fond duets on mandolin and glock-enspeil. Ophelia Oliver, who had vanished from the haunts of men, returned, wearing both her O's again. Otto Ott could say his name without a stammer, and dignity returned to human speech and English grammar. Once more a man could say boo to a goose, and tell the difference between to lose and too loose. Every family had again a roof and floor, and the head of the house could say in English, as before: 'Someone open (or close) the door.' Towers rose up again and fountains sparkled. In the spring the robin and the oriole returned. The crows were loud in caucus, and the whippoorwill sang once again at night. The wounds that Black and Littlejack had made were healed by morning-glories, columbine, and clover, and a spreading comforter of crocuses. One April morning, Andreus and Andrea were wed.

The Topaz Cufflinks Mystery

When the motorcycle cop came roaring up, unexpectedly, out of Never-Never Land (the way motorcycle cops do), the man was on his hands and knees in the long grass beside the road, barking like a dog. The woman was driving slowly along in a car that stopped about eighty feet away; its headlights shone on the man: middle-aged, bewildered, sedentary. He got to his feet.

'What's goin' on here?' asked the cop. The woman giggled. 'Cock-eyed,' thought the cop. He did not glance at her.

'I guess it's gone,' said the man. 'I – ah – could not find it.'

'What was it?'

'What I lost?' The man squinted, unhappily. 'Some – some cufflinks; topazes set in gold.' He hesitated; the cop didn't seem to believe him. 'They were the color of a fine Moselle,' said the man. He put on a pair of spectacles which he had been holding in his hand. The woman giggled.

'Hunt things better with ya glasses off?' asked the cop. He pulled his motorcycle to the side of the road to let a car pass. 'Better pull over off the concrete, lady,' he said. She drove the car off the roadway.

'I'm nearsighted,' said the man. 'I can hunt things at a distance with my glasses on, but I do better with them off if I am close to something.' The cop kicked his heavy boots through the grass where the man had been crouching.

'He was barking,' ventured the lady in the car, 'so that I could see where he was.' The cop pulled his machine up on its standard; he and the man walked over to the automobile.

'What I don't get,' said the officer, 'is how you lose ya cufflinks a hundred feet in front of where ya car is, a person usually stops his car *past* the place he loses somethin', not a hundred feet before he gits *to* the place.'

The lady laughed again; her husband got slowly into his car, as if he were afraid the officer would stop him any moment. The officer studied them.

'Been to a party?' he asked. It was after midnight.

'We're not drunk, if that's what you mean,' said the woman, smiling. The cop tapped his fingers on the door of the car.

'You people didn't lose no topazes,' he said.

'Is it against the law for a man to be down on all fours beside a road, barking in a perfectly civil manner?' demanded the lady.

'No, ma'am,' said the cop. He made no move to get on his motorcycle, however, and go on about his business. There was just the quiet chugging of the cycle engine and the auto engine, for a time.

'I'll tell you how it was, Officer,' said the man, in a crisp new tone. 'We were settling a bet. O.K.?'

'O.K.' said the cop. 'Who won?' There was another pulsing silence.

'The lady bet,' said her husband, with dignity, as though he were explaining some important phase of industry to a newly hired clerk, 'the lady bet that my eyes would shine like a cat's do at night, if she came upon me suddenly close to the ground alongside the road. We had passed a cat, whose eyes gleamed. We had passed several persons, whose eyes did *not* gleam —'

'Simply because they were above the light and not under it,' said the lady. 'A man's eyes would gleam like a cat's if people were ordinarily caught by headlights at the same angle as cats are.' The cop walked over to where he had left his motorcycle, picked it up, kicked the standard out, and wheeled it back.

'A cat's eyes,' he said, 'are different than yours and mine. Dogs, cats, skunks, it's all the same. They can see in a dark room.'

'Not in a *totally* dark room,' said the lady.

'Yes, they can,' said the cop.

'No, they can't; not if there is no light at all in the room, not if it's absolutely *black*,' said the lady. 'The question came up the other night; there was a professor there and he said there must be at least a ray of light, no matter how faint.'

'That may be,' said the cop, after a solemn pause, pulling at his gloves. 'But people's eyes don't shine – I go along these roads every night an' pass hundreds of cats and hundreds of people.'

'The people are never close to the ground,' said the lady.

'I was close to the ground,' said her husband.

'Look at it this way,' said the cop. 'I've seen wildcats in *trees* at night and *their* eyes shine.'

'There you are!' said the lady's husband. 'That proves it.'

'I don't see how,' said the lady. There was another silence.

'Because a wildcat in a tree's eyes are higher than the level of a man's,' said her husband. The cop may possibly have followed this, the lady obviously did not; neither one said anything. The cop got on his machine, raced his engine, seemed to be thinking about something, and throttled down. He turned to the man.

'Took ya glasses off so the headlights wouldn't make ya eyes shine, huh?' he asked.

'That's right,' said the man. The cop waved his hand triumphantly, and roared away. 'Smart guy,' said the man to his wife, irritably.

'I still don't see where the wildcat proves anything,' said his wife. He drove off slowly.

'Look,' he said, 'You claim that the whole thing depends on how *low* a *cat's* eyes are; I –'

'I didn't say that; I said it all depends on how *high* a *man's* eyes ...'

Do You Want To Make Something Out Of It?

I'm probably not the oldest word-game player in the country, and I know I'm not the ablest, but my friends will all testify that I'm the doggedest. (We'll come back to the word 'doggedest' later on.) I sometimes keep on playing the game, all by myself, after it is over and I have gone to bed. On a recent night, tossing and spelling, I spent two hours hunting for another word besides 'phlox' that has 'hlo' in it. I finally found seven : 'matchlock', 'decathlon', 'pentathlon', 'hydrochloric', 'chlorine', 'chloroform', and 'monthlong'. There are more than a dozen others, beginning with 'phlo', but I had to look them up in the dictionary the next morning, and that doesn't count.

By 'the game', I mean Superghosts, as some of us call it, a difficult variation of the familiar parlor game known as Ghosts. In Ghosts, as everybody knows, one of a group of sedentary players starts with a letter, and the spelling proceeds clockwise around the group until a player spells a word of more than three letters, thus becoming 'a third of a ghost,' or two-thirds, or a whole ghost. The game goes on until everyone but the winner has been eliminated. Superghosts differs from the old game in one small, tricky, and often exacerbating respect. The rules allow a player to *prefix* a letter to the word in progress, thus increasing the flexibility of the indoor sport. If 'business' comes to a player, he does not have to add the final 's'; he can put an 'n' in front and the player who has to add the 'e' to 'unbusinesslik' becomes part of a ghost. In a recent game in my league, a devious gentleman boldly stuck an 'n' in front of 'sobsiste', stoutly maintaining the validity of 'unsob-sisterlike', but he was shouted down. There is a lot of shouting in the game, especially when it is played late at night.

Starting words in the middle and spelling them in both directions lifts the pallid pastime of Ghosts out of the realm of children's parties and ladies' sewing circles and makes it a game to test the mettle of the mature adult mind. As long ago as 1930, aficionados began to appear in New York parlors, and then the game waned, to be revived, in my circle, last year. The Superghost aficionado is a moody fellow, given to spelling to himself at table, not listening to his wife, and staring dully at his frightened children, wondering why he didn't detect, in yesterday's game, that 'cklu' is the guts of 'lacklustre', and priding himself on having stumped everybody with 'nehe', the middle of 'swineherd'. In this last case, 'bonehead' would have done, since we allow slang if it is in the dictionary, but 'Stonehenge' is out, because we don't allow proper nouns. All compound and hyphenated words are priviliged, even 'jack-o'-lantern' and 'love-in-a-mist', but the speller must indicate where a hyphen occurs.

Many people, who don't like word games and just want to sit around and drink and talk, hate Superghosts and wish it were in hell with Knock, Knock, Who's There? The game is also tough on bad spellers, poor visualizers, mediocre concentrators, ladies and gentlemen of small vocabulary, and those who are, to use a word presently popular with the younger drinking set, clobbered. I remember the night a bad speller, female, put an 'm' on 'ale', thinking, as she later confessed, that 'salamander' is spelled with two 'e's. The next player could have gone to 'alemb' – the word 'alembic' turns up a lot – but he made it 'alema' and was promptly challenged. (You can challenge a player if you think he is bluffing.) What the challenged player had in mind was 'stalemate'. The man who challenged him got sore, because he hadn't thought of 'stalemate', and went home. More than one game has ended in hard feelings, but I have never seen players come to blows, or friendships actually broken.

I said we would get back to 'doggedest', and here we are. This word, if it is a word, caused a lot of trouble during one game, when a lady found 'ogged' in her lap, refused to be bogged, dogged, fogged, jogged, or logged, and added an 'e'. She was challenged and lost, since Webster's unabridged dictionary is accepted as the final judge and authority, and while it gives 'doggedly' and 'doggedness', it doesn't give 'doggedest'. She could also have got out of 'ogged' with an 'r' in front, for 'frogged' is a good word, and also what might be called a lady's word. but she stuck doggedly to 'doggedest'. Then there was the evening a dangerous and exasperating player named Bert Mitchell challenged somebody's 'dogger'. The challenged man had 'doggerel' in mind, of course, but Mitchell said, in his irritating voice, 'You have spelled a word. "Dogger" is a word', and he flipped through the unabridged dictionary, which he reads for pleasure and always has on his lap during a game. 'Dogger' is indeed a word, and quite a word. Look it up yourself.

When I looked up 'dogger' the other day, I decided to have a look at 'dog', a word practically nobody ever looks up, because everybody is smugly confident that he knows what a dog is. Here, for your amazement, are some dogs other than the carnivorous mammal: The hammer in a gunlock. Any of various devices, usually of simple design, for holding, gripping, or fastening something; as (a) any of various devices consisting essentially of a spike, rod, or bar of metal, as of iron, with a ring, hook or claws, lug, or the like, at the end, used for gripping, clutching, or holding something, as by driving, or embedding it in the object, hooking it to the object, etc. See RAFT DOG, TOE DOG. (b) Specif., either of the hooks or claws of a pair of sling dogs. See CRAMPON. (c) An iron for holding wood in a fireplace; a firedog; an andiron. (d) In a lathe, a clamp for gripping the piece of wood and for communicating motion to it from the faceplate. A *clamp dog* consists of two parts drawn together by screws. A *bent-tail dog* has an L-shaped projection that enters a slot in the faceplate for communicating motion. A *straight-tail dog* has a projecting part that engages with a stud fastened to or forming part of the faceplate. A *safety dog* is one equipped with safety setscrews. (e) Any of the jaws in a lathe chuck. (f) A pair of nippers or forceps. (g) A wheeled gripping device for drawing the fillet from which coin blanks are stamped through the opening at the head of the drawbench. (h) Any of a set of adjusting screws for the bed tool of a punching machine. (i) A grapple for clutching and raising a pile-driver monkey or a well-boring tool. (j) A stop or detent; a click or ratchet. (k) A drag for the wheel of a vehicle. (l) A steel block attached to a locking bar or tappet of an interlocking machine, by which locking between bars is accomplished. (m) A short, heavy, sharp-pointed, steel hook with a ring at one end. (n) A steel toothlike projection on a log carriage or on the endless chain that conveys logs into the sawmill.

And now, unless you have had enough, we will get back to Superghosts, through the clanging and clatter of all those dogs. The game has a major handicap, or perhaps I should call it blockage. A player rarely gets the chance to stick the others with a truly tough word, because someone is pretty sure to simplify the word under construction. Mitchell tells me that he always hopes he can get around to 'ug-ug' or 'ach-ach' on his way to 'plug-ugly' and 'stomach-ache'. These words are hyphenated in my Webster's, for the old boy was a great hyphenator. (I like his definition of 'plug-ugly': 'A kind of city rowdy, ruffian, or disorderly tough; a term said to have been originated by a gang of such in Baltimore.') In the case of 'ug', the simplifiers usually go to 'bug', trying to catch someone with 'buggies', or they add an 'l' and the word ends in 'ugliness'. And 'ach' often turns into 'machinery', although it could go in half a dozen directions. Since the simplifiers dull the game by getting into easy words, the experts are fond of a variant that goes like this: Mitchell, for example, will call up a friend and say, 'Get out of "ightf" twenty ways.' Well, I tossed in bed one night and got ten: 'rightful', 'frightful', 'delightful', 'nightfall', 'lightfoot', 'straightforward', 'eightfold', 'light-fingered', 'tight-fisted', and 'tight-fitting'. The next day, I thought of 'light-face', 'rightfooted', and 'night-flowering', and came to a stop. 'Right fielder' is neither compounded nor hyphenated by Webster, and I began to wonder about Mitchell's twenty 'ightf's. I finally figured it out. The old devil was familiar with the ten or more fish and fowl and miscellaneous things that begin with 'nightf'.

It must have been about 1932 that an old player I know

figured that nothing could be got out of 'dke' except 'hand-kerchief', and then, in a noisy game one night this year, he passed that combination on to the player at his left. This rascal immediately made it 'dkee'. He was challenged by the lady on *his* left and triumphantly announced that his word was 'groundkeeper'. It looked an ingenious escape from 'handkerchief', but old Webster let the fellow down. Webster accepts only 'groundman' and 'groundsman', thus implying that there is no such word as 'groundkeeper'.

Mitchell threw 'abc' at me one night, and I couldn't get anything out of it and challenged him. 'Dabchick', he said patronizingly, and added blandly, 'It is the little grebe.' Needless to say, it *is* the little grebe.

I went through a hundred permutations in bed that night without getting anything else out of 'abc' except a word I made up, which is 'grabcheck', one who quickly picks up a tab, a big spender, a generous fellow. I have invented quite a few other words, too, which I modestly bring to the attention of modern lexicographers, if there are any. I think of dictionary-makers as being rigidly conventional gentlemen who are the first to put the new aside. They probably won't even read my list of what I shall call bedwords, but I am going to set it down anyway. A young matron in Bermuda last spring told me to see what I could do with 'sgra', and what I did with it occupied a whole weekend. Outside of 'disgrace' and 'grosgrain', all I could find were 'cross-grained' and 'misgraff', which means to misgraft (obsolete). I found this last word while looking, in vain, for 'misgrade' in the dictionary. Maybe you can think of something else, and I wish you luck. Here, then, in no special order, are my bedwords based on 'sgra'.

PUSSGRAPPLE. A bickering, or minor disturbance; an argument or dispute among effeminate men. Also, less frequently, a physical struggle between, or among, women.

KISSGRANNY. 1. A man who seeks the company of older women, especially older women with money; a designing fellow, a fortune hunter. 2. An overaffectionate old woman, a hugmoppet, a bunny-talker.

GLASSGRABBER. 1. A woman who disapproves of, or interferes with, her husband's drinking; a kill-joy, a shushlaugh, a douselight. 2. A man who asks for another drink at a friend's house, or goes out and gets one in the kitchen.

BLESSGRAVY. A minister or cleric; the head of a family; one who says grace. Not to be confused with praisegravy, one who extols a woman's cooking, especially the cooking of a friend's wife; a gay fellow, a flirt, a seducer. *Colloq.*, a breakvow, a shrugholy.

CUSSGRAVY. A husband who complains of his wife's cooking, more especially a husband who complains of his wife's cooking in the presence of guests; an ill-tempered fellow, a curmudgeon. Also, sometimes, a peptic-ulcer case.

MESSGRANTER. An untidy housekeeper, a careless housewife. Said of a woman who admits, often proudly, that she has let herself go; a bragdowdy, a frumpess.

HISSGRAMMAR. An illiterate fellow, a user of slovenly rhetoric, a father who disapproves of booklearning. Also, more rarely, one who lisps, a twisttongue.

CHORUSGRABLE. *Orig.* a young actress, overconfident of her ability and her future; a snippet, a flappertigibbet. *Deriv.* Betty Grable, an American movie actress.

PRESSGRAPE. One who presses grapes, a grape presser. Less commonly, a crunchberry.

PRESSGRAIN. 1. A man who tries to make whiskey in his own cellar; hence, a secret drinker, a hidebottle, a sneakslug. 2. One who presses grain in a grain presser. *Arch.*

DRESSGRADER. A woman who stares another woman up and down, a starefrock; hence, a rude female, a hobbledehoyden.

FUSSGRAPE. 1. One who diets or toys with his food, a light eater, a person without appetite, a scornmuffin, a shuncabbage. 2. A man, usually American, who boasts of his knowledge of wines, a smugbottle.

BASSGRAVE. 1. Cold-eyed, unemotional, stolid, troutsolemn. 2. The grave of a bass. *Obs.*

LASSGRAPHIC. Of, or pertaining to, the vivid description of

females; as, the guest was so lassgraphic his host asked him to change the subject or get out. Also said of fathers of daughters, more rarely of mothers.

BLISSGRAVE. Aged by marriage. Also, sometimes, discouraged by wedlock, or by the institution of marriage.

GLASSGRAIL. A large nocturnal moth. Not to be confused with smackwindow, the common June bug, or bangsash.

HOSSGRACE. Innate or native dignity, similar to that of the thoroughbred hoss. *Southern U.S.*

BUSSGRANITE. Literally, a stone kisser; a man who persists in trying to win the favor or attention of cold, indifferent, or capricious women. Not to be confused with snatchkiss, a kitchen lover.

TOSSGRAVEL. 1. A male human being who tosses gravel, usually at night, at the window of a female human being's bedroom, usually that of a young virgin; hence, a lover, a male sweetheart, and an eloper. 2. One who is suspected by the father of a daughter of planning an elopement with her, a grablass.

If you should ever get into a game of Superghosts with Mitchell, by the way, don't pass 'bugl' on to him, hoping to send him into 'bugling'. He will simply add an 'o', making the group 'buglo', which is five-sevenths of 'bugloss'. The word means 'hawkweed', and you can see what Mitchell would do if you handed him 'awkw', expecting to make him continue the spelling of 'awkward'. Tough guy, Mitchell. Tough game, Superghosts. You take it from here. I'm tired.

The Shrike And The Chipmunks

Once upon a time there were two chipmunks, a male and a female. The male chipmunk thought that arranging nuts in artistic patterns was more fun than just piling them up to see how many you could pile up. The female was all for piling up as many as you could. She told her husband that if he gave up making designs with the nuts there would be room in their large cave for a great many more and he would soon become the wealthiest chipmunk in the woods. But he would not let her interfere with his designs, so she flew into a rage and left him. 'The shrike will get you,' she said, 'because you are helpless and cannot look after yourself.' To be sure, the female chipmunk had not been gone three nights before the male had to dress for a banquet and could not find his studs or shirt or suspenders. So he couldn't go to the banquet, but that was just as well, because all the chipmunks who did go were attacked and killed by a weasel.

The next day the shrike began hanging around outside the chipmunk's cave, waiting to catch him. The shrike couldn't get in because the doorway was clogged up with soiled laundry and dirty dishes. 'He will come out for a walk after breakfast and I will get him then,' thought the shrike. But the chipmunk slept all day and did not get up and have breakfast until after dark. Then he came out for a breath of air before beginning work on a new design. The shrike swooped down to snatch up the chipmunk, but could not see very well on account of the dark, so he batted his head against an alder branch and was killed.

A few days later the female chipmunk returned and saw the awful mess the house was in. She went to the bed and shook her husband. 'What would you do without me?' she demanded. 'Just go on living, I guess,' he said. 'You wouldn't last five days,' she told him. She swept the house and did the dishes and sent out the laundry, and then she made the chipmunk get up and wash and dress. 'You can't be healthy if you lie in bed all day and never get any exercise,' she told him. So she took him for a walk in the bright sunlight and they were both caught and killed by the shrike's brother, a shrike named Stoop.

Moral: Early to rise and early to bed makes a male healthy and wealthy and dead.

18

JOHN UPDIKE

Pooem

I, too, once hoped to have a hoopoe
Wing its way within my scoopoe,
Crested, quick, and heliotroopoe,
Proud *Upupa epops.*
For what seemed an eternity,
I sat upon a grassy sloopoe,
Gazing through a telescoopoe,
Weaving snares of finest roopoe,
Fit for *Upupa epops.*
At last, one day, there came to me,
Inside a crusty enveloopoe,
This note : 'Abandon hope, you doopoe;
The hoopoe is a misanthroopoe.
(Sighed) Your far-off friend, *U. e.*'

Planting A Mailbox

Prepare the ground when maple buds have burst
And when the daytime moon is sliced so thin
His fibers drink blue sky with litmus thirst.
This moment come, begin.

The site should be within an easy walk,
Beside a road, in stony earth. Your strength
Dictates how deep you delve. The seedling's stalk
Should show three feet of length.

Don't harrow, weed, or water; just apply
A little gravel. Sun, and motor fumes
Perform the miracle; in late July,
A young post office blooms.

GEORGE VILLIERS,
DUKE OF BUCKINGHAM

The Rehearsal

Scene V

Enter four men at one door, and four at another, with their Swords drawn.

1 Soldier	Stand. Who goes there?
2 Sol.	A friend.
1 Sol.	What Friend?
2 Sol.	A Friend to the House.
1 Sol.	Fall on. (*They all kill one another. Music strikes.*
Bayes	Hold, hold (*To the Music. It ceaseth.*

Now here's an odd surprise: all these dead men you shall see rise up presently, at a certain Note that I have made, in *Effaut flat*, and fall a Dancing. Do you hear, dead men? Remember your note in *Effaut flat*. Play on.

(*To the Music* Now, now, now, O Lord, O Lord! (*The music plays his Note, and the dead men rise, but cannot get in order*

Out, out, out! Did ever men spoil a good thing so? no figure, no ear, no time, nothing? Udzookers, you dance worse than the Angels in *Harry the Eighth*, or the fat Spirits in *The Tempest*, I gad.

1 Sol.	Why, Sir, 'tis impossible to do any thing in time, to this Tune.

Bayes   O Lord, O Lord! impossible? why, Gentlemen, if there be any faith in a person that's a Christian, I sate up two whole nights in composing this Air, and apting it for the business: for, if you observe, there are two several Designs in this Tune; it begins swift, and ends slow. You talk of time, and time; you shall see me do't. Look you now.

Here I am dead. (*Lies down flat on his face.*

Now mark my Note *Effaut* flat. Strike up Music.

Now. (*As he rises up hastily, he falls down again.*

Ah, gadsookers, I have broke my Nose.*

Johns   By my troth, Mr. *Bayes*, this is a very unfortunate Note of yours, in *Effaut*.

Bayes   A plague of this damn'd Stage, with your nails, and your tenterhooks,† that a Gentleman cannot come to teach you to Act, but he must break his nose, and his face, and the devil and all. Pray, Sir, can you help me to a wet piece of brown paper?

Smi.   No indeed, Sir; I don't usually carry any about me.

2 Sol.   Sir, I'll go get you some within presently.

Bayes   Go, go then; I follow you. Pray dance out the dance and I'll be with you in a moment. Remember you dance like Horsemen. *Exit* Bayes.

Smi.   Like Horsemen! what, a plague, can that be? (*They dance the Dance, but can make nothing of it.*

1 Sol.   A Devil! let's try this no longer: play my Dance that Mr. *Bayes* found fault with so. (*Dance and exeunt*

---

* A personal hit at Sir William Davenant, whose nose was so snub as to appear deformed.

† tenter-hooks. Hooks for securing cloths stretched over a wooden framework.

Smi.   What can this fool be doing all this while about
          his Nose?

Johns   Pr'ythe lets go see. *Exeunt*
              Finis Actus secundi

the ground, feed slowly bushes, as an animal, leaving
my eye, as flash turns up on the bush. The rose appeared

CHARLES DUDLEY WARNER

How I Killed A Bear

I was in the midst of this tale, when I happened to look some rods away to the other edge of the clearing, and there was a bear! He was standing on his hind legs, and doing just what I was doing – picking blackberries. With one paw he bent down the bush, while with the other he clawed the berries into his mouth – green ones and all. To say that I was astonished is inside the mark. I suddenly discovered that I didn't want to see a bear after all. At about the same moment the bear saw me, stopped eating berries, and regarded me with a glad surprise. It is all very well to imagine what you would do under such circumstances. Probably you wouldn't do it; I didn't. The bear dropped down on his fore-feet, and came slowly towards me. Climbing a tree was of no use with so good a climber in the rear. If I started to run, I had no doubt the bear would give chase; and although a bear cannot run downhill as fast as he can run uphill, yet I felt that he could get over this rough, brush-tangled ground faster than I could.

The bear was approaching. It suddenly occurred to me how I could divert his mind until I could fall back upon my military base. My pail was nearly full of excellent berries much better than the bear could pick himself. I put the pail on the ground, and slowly backed away from it, keeping my eye, as beast tamers do, on the bear. The ruse succeeded.

The bear came up to the berries, and stopped. Not accustomed to eat out of a pail, he tipped it over, and nosed about in the fruit, 'gorming' (if there is such a word) it down, mixed with leaves and dirt, like a pig. The bear is a worse feeder than the pig. Whenever he disturbs a maple-sugar camp in the spring, he always upsets the buckets of syrup, and tramples round in the sticky sweets, wasting more than he eats. The bear's manners are thoroughly disagreeable.

As soon as my enemy's head was down I started and ran. Somewhat out of breath, and shaky, I reached my faithful rifle. It was not a moment too soon. I heard the bear crashing through the brush after me. Enraged at my duplicity, he was now coming on with blood in his eye. I felt that the time of one of us was probably short. The rapidity of thought at such moments of peril is well known. I thought an octavo volume, had it illustrated and published, sold fifty thousand copies, and went to Europe on the proceeds, while the bear was loping across the clearing. As I was cocking the gun I made a hasty and unsatisfactory review of my whole life. I noted that, even in such a compulsory review, it is almost impossible to think of any good thing you have done. The sins come out uncommonly strong. I recollected a newspaper subscription I had delayed paying years and years ago, until both editor and newspaper were dead, and which now never could be paid to all eternity.

The bear was coming on.

I tried to remember what I had read about encounters with bears. I couldn't recall an instance in which a man had run away from a bear in the woods and escaped, although I recalled plenty where the bear had run from the man and got off. I tried to think what is the best way to kill a bear with a gun when you are not near enough to club him with the stock. My first thought was to fire at his head; to plant the ball between his eyes: but this is a dangerous experiment. The bear's brain is very small : and, unless you hit that, the bear does not mind a bullet in his head; that is, not at the time. I remembered that the instant death of the bear would follow a bullet planted just back of his fore-leg, and sent into his heart. This spot is also difficult to reach unless the bear stands off, side towards you, like a target. I finally determined to fire at him generally.

The bear was coming on.

The contest seemed to me very different from anything at Creedmoor. I had carefully read the reports of the shooting there; but it was not easy to apply the experience I had thus acquired. I hesitated whether I had better fire lying on my stomach, or lying on my back and resting the gun on my toes. But in neither position, I reflected, could I see the bear until he was upon me. The range was too short; and the bear wouldn't wait for me to examine the thermometer, and note the direction of the wind. Trial of the Creedmoor method, therefore, had to be abandoned; and I bitterly regretted that I had not read more accounts of off-hand shooting.

For the bear was coming on.

I tried to fix my last thoughts upon my family. As my family is small, this was not difficult. Dread of displeasing my wife, or hurting her feelings, was uppermost in my mind. What would be her anxiety as hour after hour passed on, and I did not return! What would the rest of the household think as the afternoon passed and no blackberries came! What would be my wife's mortification when the news was brought that her husband had been eaten by a bear! I cannot imagine anything more ignominious than to have a husband eaten by a bear. And this was not my only anxiety. The mind at such times is not under control. With the gravest fears the most whimsical ideas will occur. I looked beyond the mourning friends, and thought what kind of an epitaph they would be compelled to put upon the stone. Something like this:

HERE LIE THE REMAINS

OF

**** ****

EATEN BY A BEAR
Aug. 20, 1877.

It is a very unheroic and even disagreeable epitaph. That 'eaten by a bear' is intolerable! It is grotesque. And then I thought what an inadequate language the English is for compact expression. It would not answer to put upon the stone simply 'eaten', for that is indefinite, and requires explanation: it might mean eaten by a cannibal. This difficulty could not occur in the German, where *essen* signifies the act of feeding by a man, and *fressen* by a beast. How simple the thing would be in German:

HEIR LIEGT

HOCHWOHLGEBOREN

HERR——— ———

GEFRESSEN

Aug. 20, 1877.

That explains itself. The well-born one was eaten by a beast, and presumably by a bear – an animal that has a bad reputation since the days of Elisha.

The bear was coming on; he had, in fact, come on. I judged that he could see the whites of my eyes. All my subsequent reflections were confused. I raised the gun, covered the bear's breast with the sight, and let drive. Then I turned, and ran like a deer. I did not hear the bear pursuing. I looked back. The bear had stopped. He was lying down. I then remembered that the best thing to do after having fired your gun is to reload it. I slipped in my charge, keeping my eyes on the bear. He never stirred. I walked back suspiciously. There was a quiver in the hind legs, but no other motion. Still, he might be shamming; bears often sham. To make sure, I approached and put a ball into his head. He didn't mind it now; he minded nothing. Death had come to him with a merciful suddenness. He was calm in death. In order that he might remain so I blew his brains out, and then started for home. I had killed a bear.

Notwithstanding my excitement, I managed to saunter into the house with an unconcerned air. There was a chorus of voices:

'Where are your blackberries?'

'Why were you gone so long?'

'Where's your pail?'

'I left the pail.'

'Left the pail? What for?'

'A bear wanted it.'

'Oh, nonsense!'

'Well, the last I saw of it a bear had it.'

'Oh, come! You didn't really see a bear?'

'Yes, but I did really see a real bear.'

'Did he run?'

'Yes; he ran after me.'

'I don't believe a word of it. What did you do?'

'Oh! nothing particular – except kill the bear.'

Cries of 'Gammon!' 'Don't believe it!' 'Where's the bear?'

'If you want to see the bear, you must go up into the woods. I couldn't bring it down alone.'

Having satisfied the household that something extraordinary had occurred, and excited the posthumous fear of some of them for my own safety, I went down into the valley to get help. The great bear-hunter, who keeps one of the summer boarding-houses, received my story with a smile of incredulity; and the incredulity spread to the other inhabitants and to the boarders as soon as the story was known. However, as I insisted in all soberness, and offered to lead them to the bear, a party of forty or fifty people at last started off with me to bring the bear in. Nobody believed there was any bear in the case, but everybody who could get a gun carried one; and we went into the woods, armed with guns, pistols, pitchforks, and sticks, against all contingencies or surprises – a crowd made up mostly of scoffers and peerers.

But when I led the way to the fatal spot, and pointed out the bear, lying peacefully wrapped in his own skin, something like terror seized the boarders, and genuine excitement the natives. It was a no-mistake bear, by George! and the hero of the fight – well, I will not insist upon that. But what a procession that was carrying the bear home! and what a congregation was speedily gathered in the valley to see the bear! Our best preacher up there never drew anything like it on Sunday.

And I must say that my particular friends, who were sportsmen, behaved very well on the whole. They didn't deny that it was a bear, although they said it was small for a bear. Mr. Deane, who is equally good with a rifle and a rod, admitted that it was a very fair shot. He is probably the best salmon-fisher in the United States, and he is an equally good hunter. I suppose there is no person in America who is more desirous to kill a moose than he. But he needlessly remarked, after he had examined the wound in the bear, that he had seen that kind of a shot made by a cow's horn.

This sort of talk affected me not. When I went to sleep that night, my last delicious thought was, 'I've killed a bear!'

SANDYS WASON

Town

I met a clergymanly man
   Prostrated in the Strand
He sucked a brace of oranges;
   One orange in each hand.

He had a gentle racial air,
   He wore the clothes one wears;
The parting of his ample hair
   Had been there thirty years.

He held his cheek up to the sun;
   He let the sunlight fall
Half in contempt and half in fun
   And bitterly withal.

His words were few and special words;
  They calmed the throbs that rose,
Like crumbs one offers to the birds
  Or biscuits to the does.

Before he spoke, I realised
  How false conventions are:
I sized him up like one who sized
  A cocktail at a bar.

He spoke in minuet of sound.
  I listened all the while
'Life's little ironies' went round
  The Gentlewomen's Mile.

It was not that his words were rare
  Or few and far between
They had the crisp conclusive air
  Of some stray pleiocene.

Of some vague far-off dim trombone,
  Held lengthwise to the breast,
The rapt reverberate monotone
  Of working-men at rest.

He said: 'I round in scarlet kilts
  The Mulberry-bush of Life;
And carve the nightingales of Hope
  With Memory's carving-knife.

'I keep my matches in a box,
  I strike them on the lid,
I climb above the tidal rocks
  Ahasuerus did.

'I take away the strain of Life,
  I walk away its throes;
O I keep couched within my heart
  The Romaunt of the Rose!

'I am a man as men are made;
    I have the feelings men
Deny or gratify in trade
    Or chaffer with a pen.

'I kept a shop in Araby,
    The world was clean and young;
My typist was a Caribee;
    Obese but over-strung.

'I paid him for the work he did
    By piece-time or the hour.
The doorway of the shop was hid
    With pomegranates in flower.

'My customers were Turkish nuns,
    The novices, Chocktaws;
They lived on septic Sally Lunns,
    Devoted to the cause.'

And still at every Christmas time
    I see the old man sit
And suck on at his oranges
    And sit and sit and sit.

A Meditation

There is a window in my soul
    Which opens on the world of art,
Circumference as well as gold
    Of Spirit and its counterpart.

I watched the urgent strife of form,
    Where vistas of a realm unmade
Impinge on the essential norm
    Wherewith posterities have played.

The intuitions of an age
    Too sibilant to be out-won
Too care-free to redeem the rage
    Of services that shrink the sun,

Are windowed in the Absolute
    And over-leap the spume of things,
Unjettisoned upon the mute
    Curtailment of the poet's wings.

And ouphens from an under-world
    Of sentences still-born, and soon
How indeterminately furled
    The promise of a hunter's moon.

*   *   *

There was a young person who grew
A gourd in the shape of a Q —
'If you'll only wait half a bit
All the rest of the alphabet
Shall very soon burst into view.'

Glycerine and Cucumber

Whenas in some high mood of duteousness,
Poised on the uncontaminate confine
Of some caged pool, profound and crystalline,
I there do off the tissue is thy dress
And hold thee in my hand, O Sorceress,
With what proud epithet shall I combine
Thy perfumes of the Ivy or the Vine,
Thy foams more bounteous than the sea's largesse?

Nay, though I should achieve a fortunate round
Might glass thy form, portray thy origin,
And each thy varied loveliness emphrase,
The secret of thy substance to profound,
Let him adventure whose high harp may win
A praise to praise thee, synonym of Praise.

Alphabet

A was the Author, who wrote a romance
And B was the Book itself, 'Percival Prance'.
C were the Characters, all of high birth,
A and D were the Dresses (Lucile and Worth).
E was the End, at page nine-eighty-four,
A and F were the Freckles the heroine wore.
G was the Grip of the scene at the Docks
A and H was the Hero in openwork socks.
I was the critic who noticed the grammar,
A and J were the Jokes, hammered in with a hammer.
K were the Kisses (chaps. 3, 5, 16),
A and L were the Lips of the fair heroine.
M was the Marriage at Hanover Square,
And N the Nobility mustering there.
O was the Opening, Star-shine and dew,
A and P were the Passages, some of them blue,
Q was the Quest of the wandering hero,
And R his Return, in the guise of pierrot.
S was the Skeleton, found in the closet
And T was the Talk, done as everyone does it.
U was the Upper-Crust, loafing at Monte,
And V the Viscountesses in the Viscounty.
W was the Wood where the fiances ranged,
And X was the number of kisses exchanged.
Y was the 'yes,' Bride and Bridegroom employed,
A and Z was the Zenith of bliss unalloyed.

Ecstasy

The wintry moon like a jellyfish hung
In a circle of clouds that swirled and swung,
A mother-of-pearly rosary flung
From the hand of a Titan, deeply stung
By a bumble-bee of a star that clung
The cowls of his tortured limbs among.

And the boy came out in the moony heat;
He was mild as mutton, and pink as peat,
Or a girl who at Bridge has tried to cheat,
Or a monk who has made a good retreat,
Or a *filet-de-boeuf*, supremely beat,
Or anything else that is new to eat.

He was only a bounding boy, and free
Of the earth and the sky and the apple-tree
And it would have lightened your heart to see
The orange flame of his muffettee,
And he sate with his hand on the stony knee
Of a Bye-and-Bye and Never-to-be.

He had had a really remarkable day,
He had frightened the owls and bats away
From his uncle's elaborate ricks of hay,
He had been to a problem matinee;
It was really time that he came to lay
His head on the infinite mound of May.

BIOGRAPHICAL NOTES ON THE AUTHORS

ARISTOPHANES: *c.* 450–385 B.C. The supreme writer of Greek comedies, rich in burlesque, satire and parody.

MAX ADELER: 1841–1915. American comic writer, to whom Thurber has acknowledged indebtedness. His best-known book is called *Out of the Hurly-burly*.

BEACHCOMBER: b. 1893. The pen-name of John Cameron Andrieu Bingham Michael Morton. He took over the famous *By the Way* column (created by D. B. Wyndham Lewis, q.v) in 1924, peopling it with a host of characters from Dr. Strabismus to the poet Roland Milk, and observing modern lunacy with such precision that 'it's pure Beachcomber' is many people's instinctive way of describing an absurd situation.

MAX BEERBOHM: 1872–1956. Caricaturist, drama critic, essayist and especially in *Zuleika Dobson*, quintessential wit of an Oxford now vanished. Said by Oscar Wilde (probably) to write only in evening dress.

HILAIRE BELLOC: b. 1870 St. Cloud, France, of Anglo-French stock, nationalised English 1902. After brilliant Oxford career, enormous output of historical writings, essays, novels, verse, political satire, and apologetics for Roman Catholicism in which he was associated with his friend G. K. Chesterton (they were corporately dubbed by Shaw as 'the Chesterbelloc'). d. 1953.

ROBERT BENCHLEY: 1889–1945. A giant even among American humorists. He once, improbably, did industrial personnel work (1914–15). In addition to writing for many papers including the New York Tribune Sunday and the New Yorker he made some imperishable short comic films with Fox.

EDMUND CLERIHEW BENTLEY: 1875–1956. Member of Inner Temple (barrister), journalist (Daily News) and author (*Trent's Last Case* etc.), he is also immortalised by the unique verse-form which he created and which bears his middle name.

CYRANO DE BERGERAC: 1620–1655. The eponymous hero of Rostand's play *did* serve in the French royal guard. Said to have admired philosophers such as Gassendi and Leibniz, he mixed burgeoning science with romance in a way that influenced Swift and Poe.

BASIL BOOTHROYD: b. 1910. Punch writer (and its Assistant Editor 1952–70), also writer of authorised biography of Prince Philip.

ERNEST BRAMAH: d. 1942 after a long writing career which began with *English Farming* in 1894. Best known for the ornate joke mandarin prose of the Kai Lung stories, which were much admired by Belloc.

ROBERT JONES BURDETTE: b. 1844 in Pennsylvania. Editor of a paper with the kind of title papers don't have any more; the *Burlington Hawkeye*.

GELETT BURGESS: b. Boston 1866, d. 1951. Author of many humorous books including *Gooks and How to be Them*, and works for children (*The Lively City o' Ligg* etc.) and inventor of the word *blurb* as well as many others not so universally accepted.

PATRICK CAMPBELL: 3rd Baron Glenavy, b. 1913. Anglo-Irish humorist, he graduated via Lilliput and the Sunday Dispatch to a column in the Sunday Times.

CANNING, FRERE, AND ELLIS: *The Rovers* was the result of collaboration between John Hookham Frere (1769–1846), diplomatist, George Canning (1770–1877) who became Prime Minister in 1827, and George Ellis (1753–1815), another contributor to the *Anti-Jacobin*.

HENRY CAREY: d. 1743. He was a musician as well as author,

LEWIS CARROLL: 1832–1898. The undisputed father of 'modern' nonsense, Charles Lutwidge Dodgson an Oxford don, wrote such works as *A Syllabus of Plane Algebraical Geometry* and *Elementary Treatise on Determinants* before finding his true length with the immortal Alice.

ALAN COREN: b. 1938. Educated at Oxford *and* Yale, a prolific humorous writer (and talker, not always the same thing). Deputy Editor of Punch.

IVOR CUTLER: b. 1932 Ibrox (Glasgow). Actor and monologuist with a deadpan surrealism all his own, he once taught at A. S. Neill's famous Summerhill School, now does the same in London. Also writes children's books.

PAUL DEHN: 1912–1976. Drama critic, poet and essayist, he also wrote many revue sketches, having grown up under the tutelage of James Agate. Also the author of many film scripts, such as that of *The Spy Who Came in from the Cold.*

CHARLES DICKENS: 1812–1870. Charles Dickens.

H. F. ELLIS: b. 1907. Creator of the schoolmaster character A. J. Wentworth, rugby expert, prolific contributor to the New Yorker and Punch, of which he was Deputy Editor from 1949 to 1953.

HERBERT FARJEON: 1887–1945. Drama critic, author and theatre manager.

GUSTAVE FLAUBERT: 1821–1880. The author of *Madame Bovary* and *A Sentimental Education* believed so passionately in purity of style that the choice of the exact word could cause him days of agony. His rigorous avoidance of clichés, paradoxically, enabled him to compile the marvellous list of them quoted here.

MARJORY FLEMING: b. 1803 and d., alas, in 1811.

PETER FLEMING: 1909–1971. Took a first in English at Oxford, was an adventurous explorer: *Brazilian Adventure* was a best-seller account of a journey in search of the lost Colonel Fawcett. Dramatic war in Greece. Essayist (pen-name Strix) and drama critic of the Spectator. Wrote Times Fourth Leaders, in the good old days when they *had* Fourth Leaders.

SAMUEL FOOTE: 1720–1777. Actor, famous mimic in his day, and dramatist.

HARRY GRAHAM: 1874–1936: Captain, Coldstream Guards. Although he is best known for his Ruthless Rhymes, his varied writing career also included part-authorship of such very unruthless, or ruthful, shows as *White Horse Inn* and *Land of Smiles*.

JOEL CHANDLER HARRIS: 1848–1908 American journalist who, when he collected negro legends, among them the famous *Uncle Remus* stories, aroused the usual controversy, some saying they were *Indian* legends. *He* said he just listened and wrote them down, which is all that matters really, since they went through the transformation of his style.

A. P. HERBERT (Sir): 1890–1971. Trained as a barrister, 'APH' was not only M.P. for Oxford University (and a survivor of Gallipoli) and a campaigner against legal anomalies (*Misleading Cases* etc.) but a passionate lover of and sailor on the Thames, as well as being perhaps the best known name in English humorous writing between the wars, pouring out verse, Punch articles, novels, and libretti for musicals such as *Bless the Bride*.

SAMUEL HOFFENSTEIN: b. 1890 in Lithuania, d. 1947, educated at public schools in New York, made his name with *Poems in Praise of Practically Nothing*, later lived in Hollywood as script-writer where he 'spoke with sardonic raillery, larded with astonishing word combinations'.

OLIVER WENDELL HOLMES: 1809–1894. Not to be confused with his son, assistant Justice of the U.S. Supreme Court, whose name was Oliver Wendell Holmes. Earning his M.D. at Cambridge, Mass., he later charmed everyone with *The Autocrat of the Breakfast Table* and several urbane sequels.

RICHARD HUGHES: b. 1900 at Fairford, Glos., but really very Welsh. His most famous book was *High Wind in Jamaica*, but his children's stories as such have an even more wild inventiveness. d. 1976.

LEIGH HUNT: 1784–1859. Essayist, journalist, poet, imprisoned for two years for an attack on the Prince Regent, friend of Shelley, Keats and Byron.

NORMAN HUNTER: b. 1899. He says 'Beckenham County School tried to educate me but failed.' Member of Magic Circle, 200 appearances at Maskelyne and Devant as conjuror before the war.

EUGENE IONESCO: b. 1912 in Rumania, now lives in Paris. A Founding Father of the theatre of the absurd.

PAUL JENNINGS: b. 1918. First resident humorist of the Observer 1949–66 with *Oddly Enough* column, subsequently freelance journalist.

JOHN KEATS: 1795–1821. The romantic poet above all who introduced adolescents to the glories of English verse in the days before English was taught as a cross between crypto-graphy and sociology.

RING LARDNER: 1885–1933. If he had done nothing else, would deserve to be remembered by the immortal dialogue ' "Are we lost, Daddy?" "Shut up!" I explained.'; a major figure in America's supply (inexhaustible till the 60s, then drying up as everywhere else) of comic writers, with such titles as *Gullible's Travels, Own your Own Home* and *My 4 Weeks in France* (1918).

STEPHEN LEACOCK: 1869–1944. Another giant, this time Canadian. He was Head of Economics and Political Science at McGill University, and some people, therefore, must have read his words in these subjects; they are happily outnum-bered by the readers of *Sunshine Sketches of a Little Town, Nonsense Novels*, and the rest of his large humour output.

EDWARD LEAR : 1812–1888. Perhaps the use of the phrase 'another giant' was premature. For many Lear is *the* giant; the long vowels in his nonsense poems (*The Great Gromboolian Plain*, *The Dong with the Luminous Nose*) have a Tennysonian magic. He also, of course, pioneered the limerick. His nonsense reflects his profession of artist (many paintings of places like Greece and Albania), as Carroll's reflects his of mathematician.

JOHN LENNON : b. 1940. Player of guitar, organ, piano and harmonica. Lyricist, responsible with Paul McCartney for many of the songs of the Beatles.

RICHARD MALLETT : 1910–1972. A frequent Punch contributor, still remembered by many for a series called *The Table Talk of Amos Intolerable*; he was also the Punch film critic.

ARCHIBALD MARSHALL (The Hon.) : 1866–1934. English novelist, who also wrote *Boswell's Johnson* in 1927.

JAMES MICHIE : b. 1927. A classical scholar, he published a book of poems called *Possible Laughter* and translations of Horace and Martial.

SPIKE MILLIGAN : b. 1918. Britain's most famous licensed eccentric, he was the main inspiration of the *Goon Show* which, with Peter Sellers and Harry Secombe, and because of the limitless imaginative possibilities of radio, pushed pure, abstract humour to a peak that seems unattainable now. Even his throwaway lines have genius, e.g. ending a fairly normal poetry recital with 'remember folks, any man can be 62, but it takes a bus to be 62A.'

OGDEN NASH : 1902–1971. America's pioneer of far fetched rhymes ('And look at the days, how autumn has shortened 'em/some people like autumn. Well, autumn or autn'tumn?). Started in Doubleday's advertising department, later was on New Yorker staff.

DENIS NORDEN : b. 1922. Made his name as co-writer, with Frank Muir, of the BBC's long-running radio comedy show, *Take It From Here*. Now a film and TV script-writer and panel game expert (the fantasy here reproduced is from the longest-running of all, radio's *My Word!*).

BARRY PAIN: 1864–1928. After leaving Cambridge he devoted his whole life to humorous fiction and essays, among them the *Eliza* books, popular in their time.

S. J. PERELMAN: b. 1904. America's unchallenged high priest of verbal slapstick, script-writer on the immortal early Marx Brothers films such as *Horse Feathers* and *Monkey Business* and (with Ogden Nash) *One Touch of Venus*. A long-serving New Yorker contributor.

MONTY PYTHON: *M. P.'s Flying Circus* represents the nearest that TV has come to the wild, freewheeling humour of radio's *Goon Show* (see *Spike Milligan*); although it is more literary some think its anarchy includes moral anarchy too. It is the corporate work of John Cleese, Graham Chapman, Terry Gilliam, Eric Idle, Terry Jones and Michael Palin, all in their twenties or thirties.

ARTHUR QUILLER-COUCH (Sir): 1863–1944. Best known as the editor of the *Oxford Book of English Verse* (1900), he was Professor of English Literature at Cambridge. Besides much editorial work he wrote criticism and journalistic pieces under the pseudonym 'Q'.

RUDOLPH ERICH RASPE: 1737–1793. German-born scientist and antiquarian, commentator on Ossian, pioneer of the Gothic revival (if it ever *needed* reviving) in Germany; chiefly known, of course, as the creator of Baron Munchausen, the classic teller of all tales.

JAMES REEVES: b. 1909. Poet, editor and children's writer.

E. V. RIEU: 1887–1972. Editor of Penguin Classics 1944–64, he translated the Odyssey, the Iliad, the Gospels, and much Virgil as well as writing enchanting verses for children.

ANTHONY ROBERTSON: Nothing is known, even by Punch, except that in the thirties he wrote *How to Do and Say in England* (a trim kompaktikum of Englisch Talk and Society Behaviourism). If any reader knows anything it will be gratefully received and put in the second edition of this work, if there is one.

OWEN SEAMAN (Sir): 1861–1936. Barrister, Professor of Literature at Durham College of Science, Newcastle. Successively staff member (1897), assistant editor (1902) and editor (1906) of Punch.

W. ST. LEDGER: *Floruit*, he flourished, it says in this book's only predecessor, the *Nonsensibus* of D. B. Wyndham Lewis (q.v.), whence this well-known verse is taken, 1885–1894. Well, lots of people don't even flourish for *one* year. Nine is good.

W. C. SELLAR & R. J. YEATMAN: d. 1951 and 1968 respectively. They met at Oxford in 1920. There were other books, with inevitable sequel-titles like *And Now All This*; but it was their immortal collaboration on *1066 And All That* which raised the howler to a classic art-form.

WILLIAM SHAKESPEARE: William Shakespeare, 1564–1616. The world's most famous grammar-school boy, to the intense rage of people who think you need a more exotic background for a mind like that.

PETER SIMPLE: the satirical column appearing four times a week in the Daily Telegraph over this name is edited and for the most part written by Michael Wharton, b. 1913; Oxford, wartime army service, 10 years in BBC features, and the column ever since. By far the best satire from the right, and better than most of it from *anywhere*.

N. F. SIMPSON: b. 1919. England's answer to Ionesco. Won 3rd prize in the Observer play competition 1957 with *A Resounding Tinkle*. Subsequent successes were *The Hole* (1958) and *One-way Pendulum* (1959), followed by several TV plays.

J. C. SQUIRE (Sir): 1884–1958. A familiar figure in the literary scene now disposed of by some with the words 'Georgian' and/or 'middlebrow'. Editor, journalist, poet, cricketer, President of the Stonehenge Preservation Society and the Architectural Association.

JONATHAN SWIFT: 1667–1745. Dean of St. Patrick's, Dublin, supreme master of satire and irony. Best known for *Gulliver's Travels*, followed at some distance by *Tales of a Tub*.

JAMES THURBER: 1894–1961. The inventor and founding father of modern humour. His cartoons of puzzled, invertebrate men and women, his baffled pieces about modern industrial life, have an exactitude which if anything increased as blindness made words almost tangible *things* to him. His most famous tale, *Walter Mitty*, in about 2,000 elegant words pre-dates by about thirty years countless novels and plays about modern man searching for his identity (and is much funnier).

JOHN UPDIKE: b. 1932 near New York, educated Harvard and Ruskin School of Drawing, Oxford. A contributor to the New Yorker, but now known primarily as novelist: *The Poorhouse Fair, Couples, Rabbit Redux* etc. (fairly sexplicit works).

GEORGE VILLIERS, Second Duke of Buckingham: 1627–1688. On the Royalist side in the Civil War, he was a pretty wild man even for the Restoration court. *The Rehearsal is* a parody of Dryden.

CHARLES DUDLEY WARNER: b. at Plainsfield, Mass., 1829. Surveyor in the West, then a lawyer, finally a humour and travel writer, especially with the *Hartford Courant*.

SANDYS WASON (The Rev.): The incumbent of Cury-cum-Gunwalloe, Cornwall. A friend, among others, of Compton Mackenzie.

D. B. WYNDHAM LEWIS: 1894–1957. Started the Beachcomber column on the Daily Express, then wrote under the name of Timothy Shy for the Daily Mail. Like J. B. Morton, his successor as Beachcomber, he was a Catholic, and well versed in the culture of France and Spain, to which country he retired. Edited classic anthology of bad verse, *The Stuffed Owl* (with Charles Lee).

ACKNOWLEDGEMENTS

The editor and publisher would like to thank the following for permission to include copyright material:

The university of Michigan Press for extracts from *The Birds* translated by William Arrowsmith; A. D. Peters & Co. for extracts from Beachcomber; William Heinemann Ltd for *Savonarola Brown* by Max Beerbohm; Duckworth Ltd for the poems by Hilaire Belloc; Routledge & Kegan Paul Ltd for *Voyage to the Moon* from *Voyage to the Moon and Voyage to the Sun* by Cyrano de Bergerac, translated by Richard Aldington; Punch Publications Ltd for *Can you Read Music?* and *Why Dogs Bite Gardeners* by Basil Boothroyd, *Once I Put it Down, I Could not Pick it Up Again* by Alan Coren, *How to Do and Say in England* by Anthony Robertson, and *A Fair Gallop of Analogies* by W. St. Ledger; Cassell, Collier Macmillan for extracts from Robert Benchley; A. P. Watt & Son and the Estate of Ernest Bramah for *Kai Lung Unrolls His Mat* by Ernest Bramah, A. P. Watt & Son and the Estate of Harry Graham for *Political Economy* by Harry Graham, A. P. Watt & Son and Lady Herbert for *A Criminal Type* and *Love Lies Bleeding* by A. P. Herbert, and A. P. Watt & Son, the Estate of Ogden Nash and J. M. Dent & Sons for *The Wild Jackass*, *The Wendigo*, and *The Private Dining Room* by Ogden Nash: Blond & Briggs Ltd for *Noulded into a Shake* by Patrick Campbell; Oxford University Press Ltd for *The Rovers* by Canning, Frere and Ellis, *Chrononhotonthologos* by Henry Carey, and *The Rehearsal* by George Villiers, from *Burlesque Plays of the Eighteenth Century* edited by Simon Trussler; the author for *How to Make Friends* and *The False God* by Ivor Cutler; Dehn Enterprises Ltd for *Schotto Bottled* by Paul Dehn; the author for *Helicopters* by H. F. Ellis; Laurence Pollinger Ltd and The Bodley Head for *Dictionary of Accepted Ideas* by Gustav Flaubert translated by Jacques Barzun; Nicho-

Hamilton Ltd and the Estate of James Thurber for extracts from *Vintage Thurber* by James Thurber; and Victor Gollancz Ltd and the author for *Hoping for a Hoopoe* and *Planting a Mailbox* from *Hoping for a Hoopoe* by John Updike.

While every effort has been made to trace copyright holders, in some cases this has proved impossible and the publishers would be very happy to hear from anyone not here acknowledged.